YOUNG ADULT

DETROIT PUBLIC LIBRARY

3 5674 04631644 5

GN

LINCOLN BRANCH LIBRARY
1221 E. SEVEN MILE
DETROIT, MI 48203

D1399417

JUL L T 2007

NARRATION OF LOVE at 17

Vol. 1

Kyungok Kang

NETCOMICS

Narration of Love at 17 Vol. 1

Story and Art by Kyungok Kang

English translation rights in USA,
Canada, UK, NZ, Australia arranged by
Ecomix Media Company
395-21 Seogyo-dong, Mapo-gu, Seoul, Korea 121-840
info@ecomixmedia.com

- Produced by **Ecomix Media Company**
- Translator **Jennifer Park**
- Editors **Zhanna Veyts, Rob Rosenberger**
- Managing Editor **Soyoung Jung**
- Graphic Design **Soohyun Park, Yeongsook Yi**
- President & Publisher **Heewoon Chung**

P.O.Box 16484, Jersey City, NJ 07306
info@netcomics.com
www.NETCOMICS.com

© 1991 Kyungok Kang. All rights reserved.
English Text © 2006 NETCOMICS. All rights reserved.
No portion of this book may be reproduced or transmitted in any form
or by any means without written permission from the copyright holders.
This is a fictional work. Any resemblance to actual events
or locales or persons, living or dead, is entirely coincidental.

ISBN: 1-60009-120-2

First printing: June 2006
10 9 8 7 6 5 4 3 2 1
Printed in Korea

NARRATION OF LOVE at 17

Vol. 1

Kyungok Kang

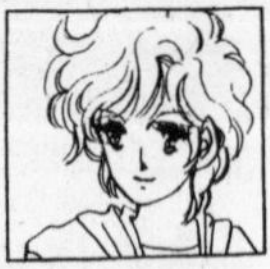

CONTENTS

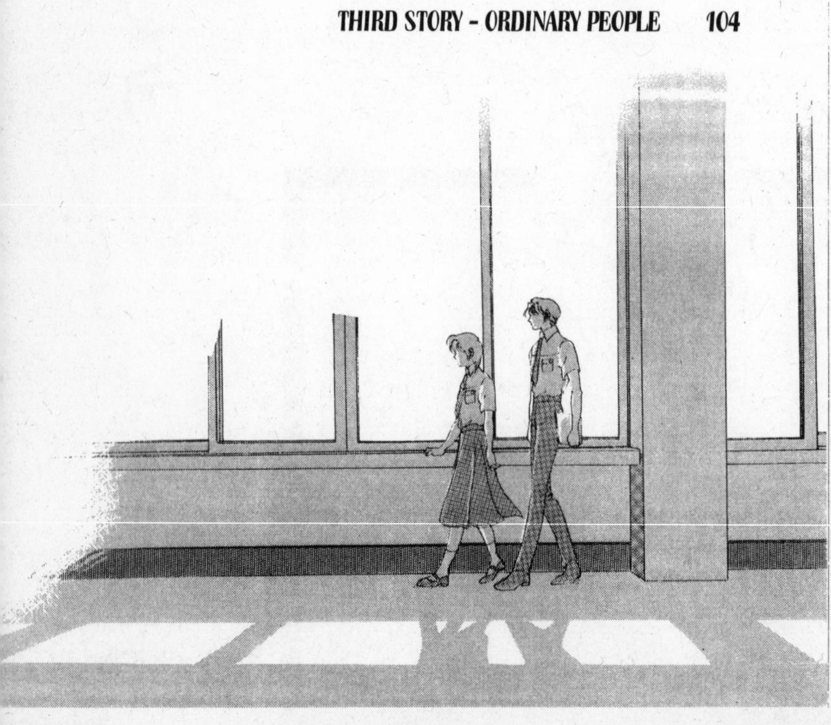

FIRST STORY

I LIKE YOU

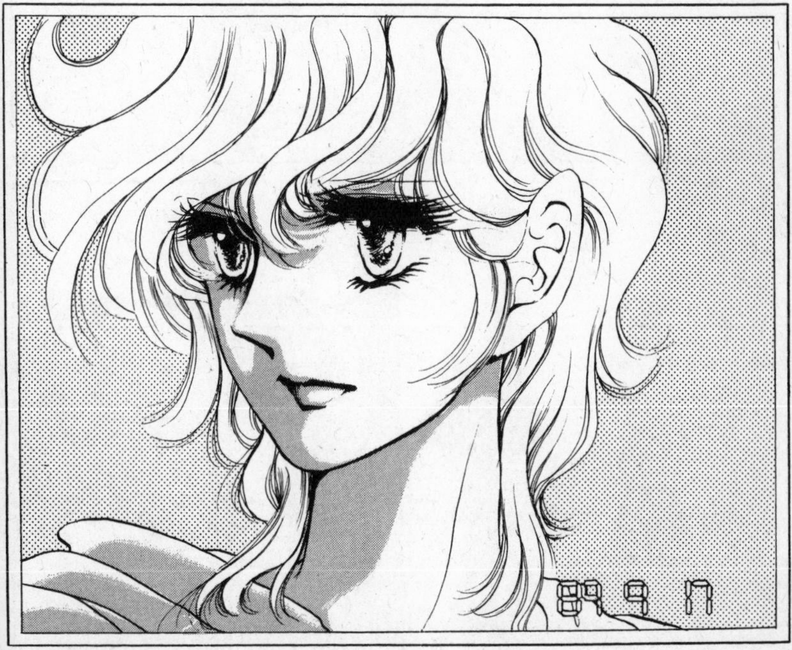

89.9.17

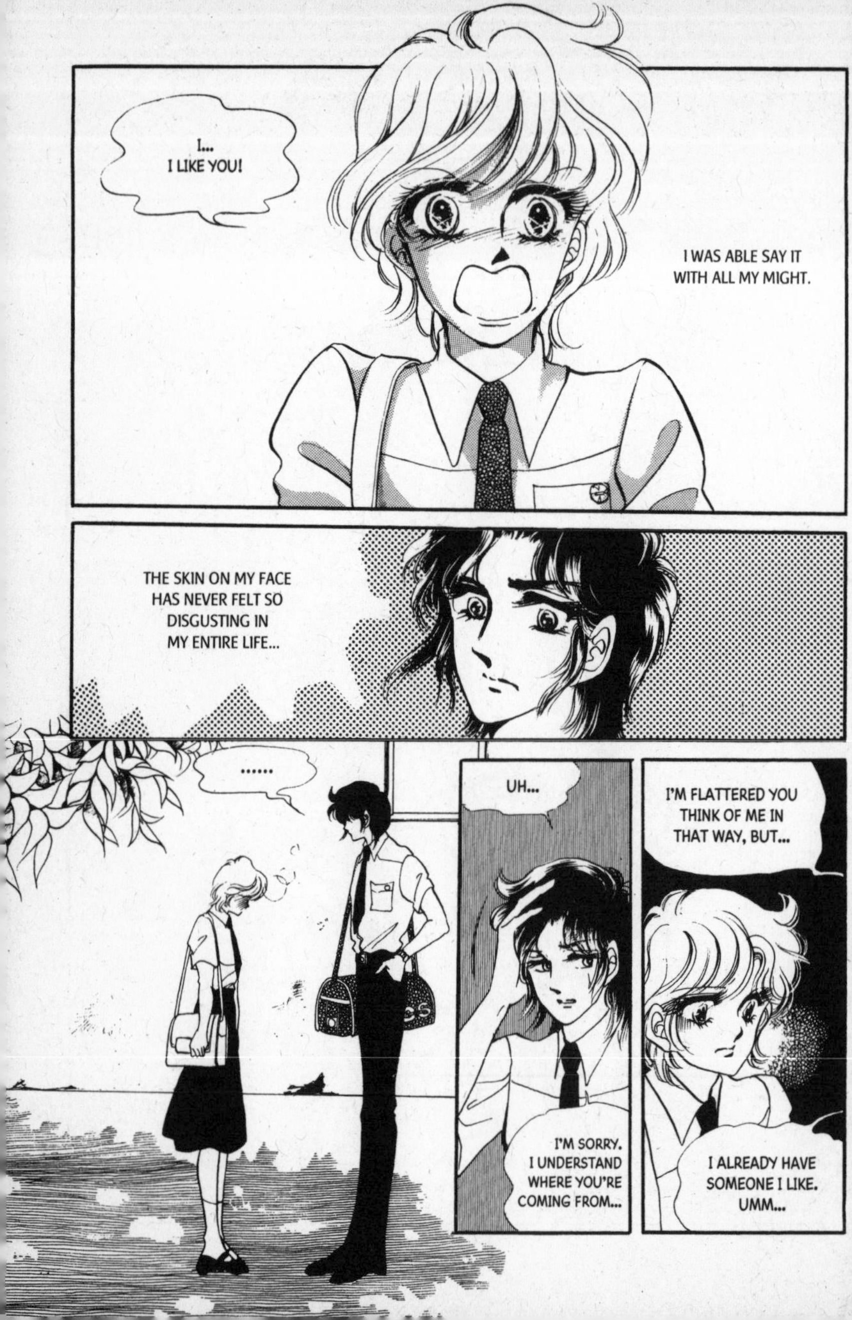
I...
I LIKE YOU!
I WAS ABLE SAY IT
WITH ALL MY MIGHT.
THE SKIN ON MY FACE
HAS NEVER FELT SO
DISGUSTING IN
MY ENTIRE LIFE...
......
UH...
I'M SORRY.
I UNDERSTAND
WHERE YOU'RE
COMING FROM...
I'M FLATTERED YOU
THINK OF ME IN
THAT WAY, BUT...
I ALREADY HAVE
SOMEONE I LIKE.
UMM...

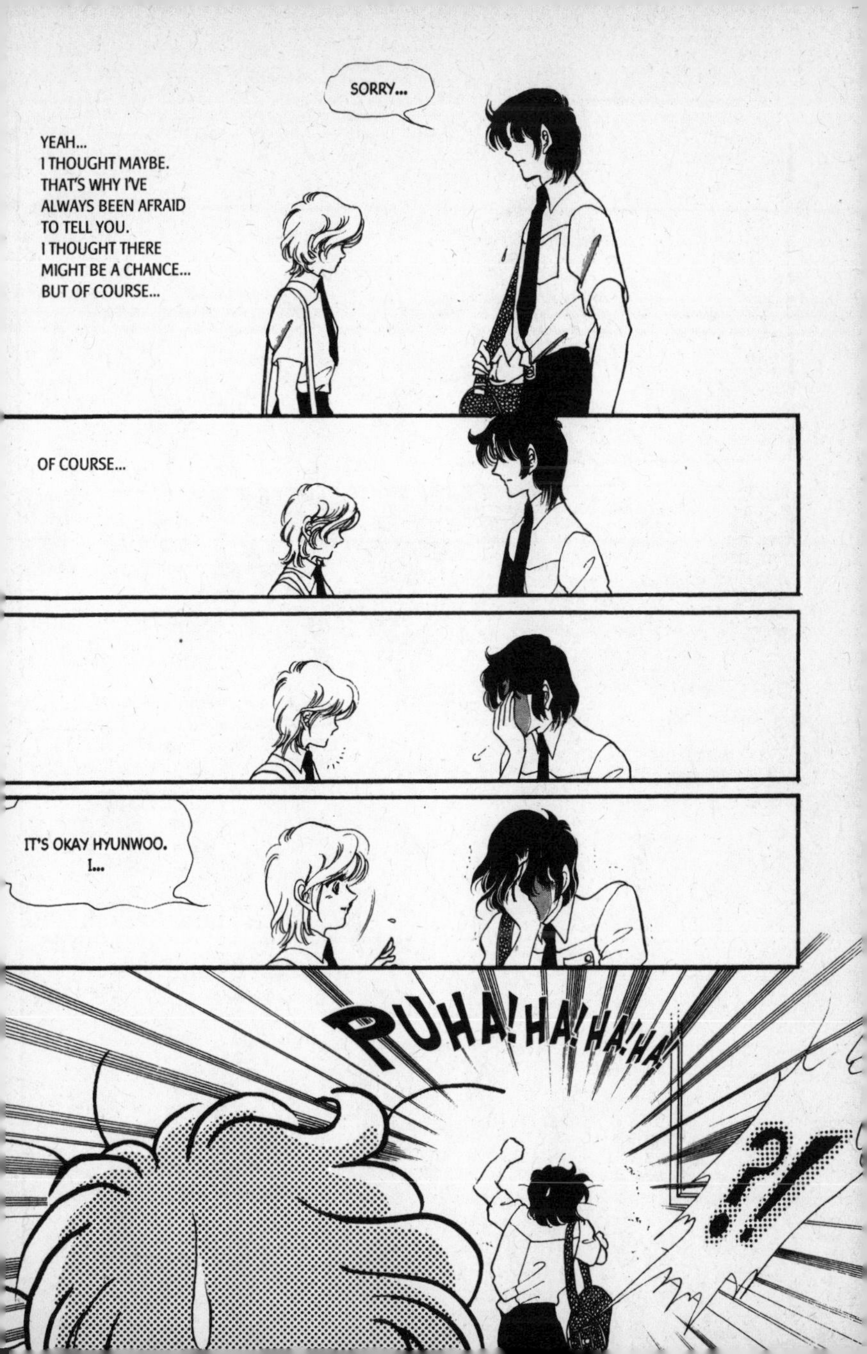
SORRY...
YEAH...
I THOUGHT MAYBE.
THAT'S WHY I'VE
ALWAYS BEEN AFRAID
TO TELL YOU.
I THOUGHT THERE
MIGHT BE A CHANCE...
BUT OF COURSE...
OF COURSE...
IT'S OKAY HYUNWOO.
I...
PUHA! HA! HA! HA!
?!

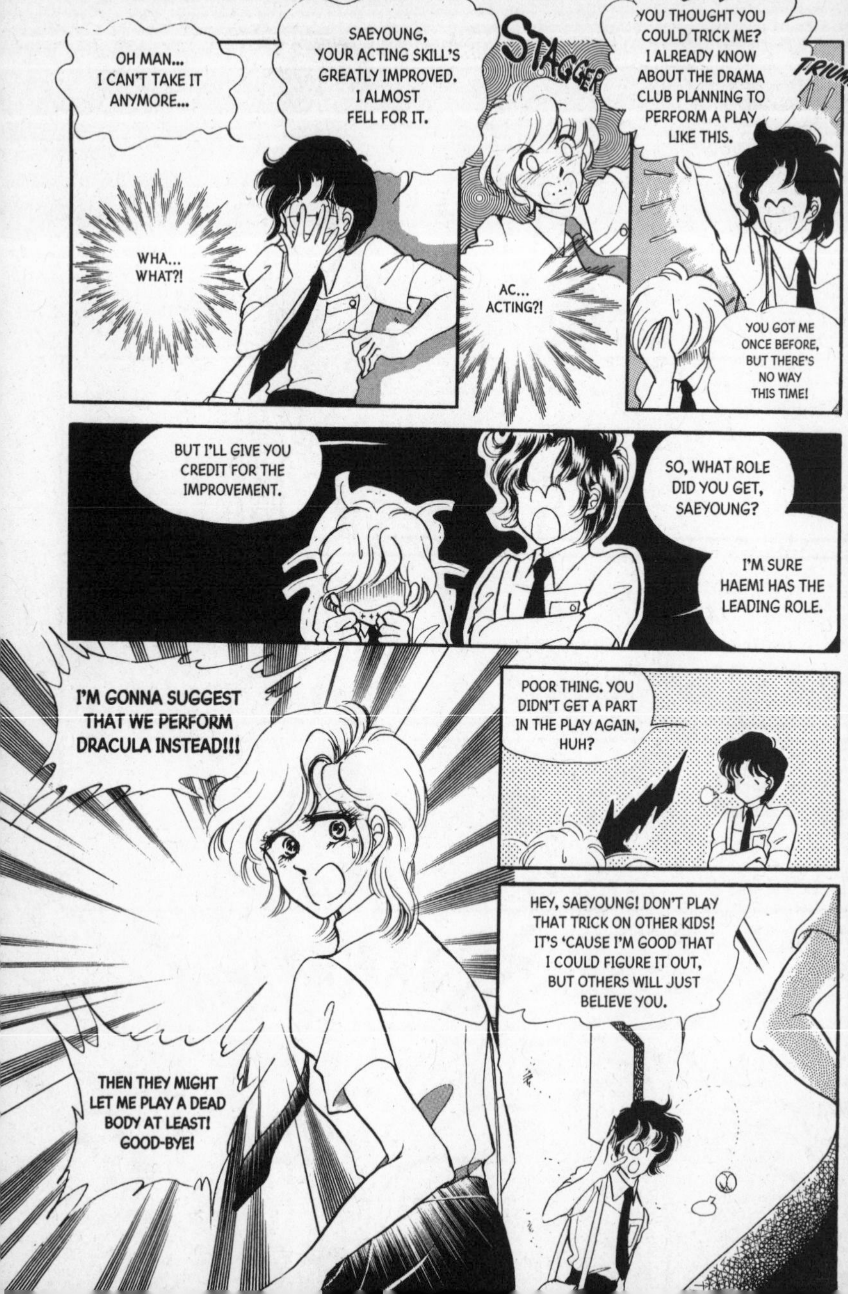
OH MAN... I CAN'T TAKE IT ANYMORE...
SAEYOUNG, YOUR ACTING SKILL'S GREATLY IMPROVED. I ALMOST FELL FOR IT.
WHA... WHAT?!
STAGGER
AC... ACTING?!
YOU THOUGHT YOU COULD TRICK ME? I ALREADY KNOW ABOUT THE DRAMA CLUB PLANNING TO PERFORM A PLAY LIKE THIS.
TRIUM
YOU GOT ME ONCE BEFORE, BUT THERE'S NO WAY THIS TIME!
BUT I'LL GIVE YOU CREDIT FOR THE IMPROVEMENT.
SO, WHAT ROLE DID YOU GET, SAEYOUNG?
I'M SURE HAEMI HAS THE LEADING ROLE.
I'M GONNA SUGGEST THAT WE PERFORM DRACULA INSTEAD!!!
THEN THEY MIGHT LET ME PLAY A DEAD BODY AT LEAST! GOOD-BYE!
POOR THING. YOU DIDN'T GET A PART IN THE PLAY AGAIN, HUH?
HEY, SAEYOUNG! DON'T PLAY THAT TRICK ON OTHER KIDS! IT'S 'CAUSE I'M GOOD THAT I COULD FIGURE IT OUT, BUT OTHERS WILL JUST BELIEVE YOU.

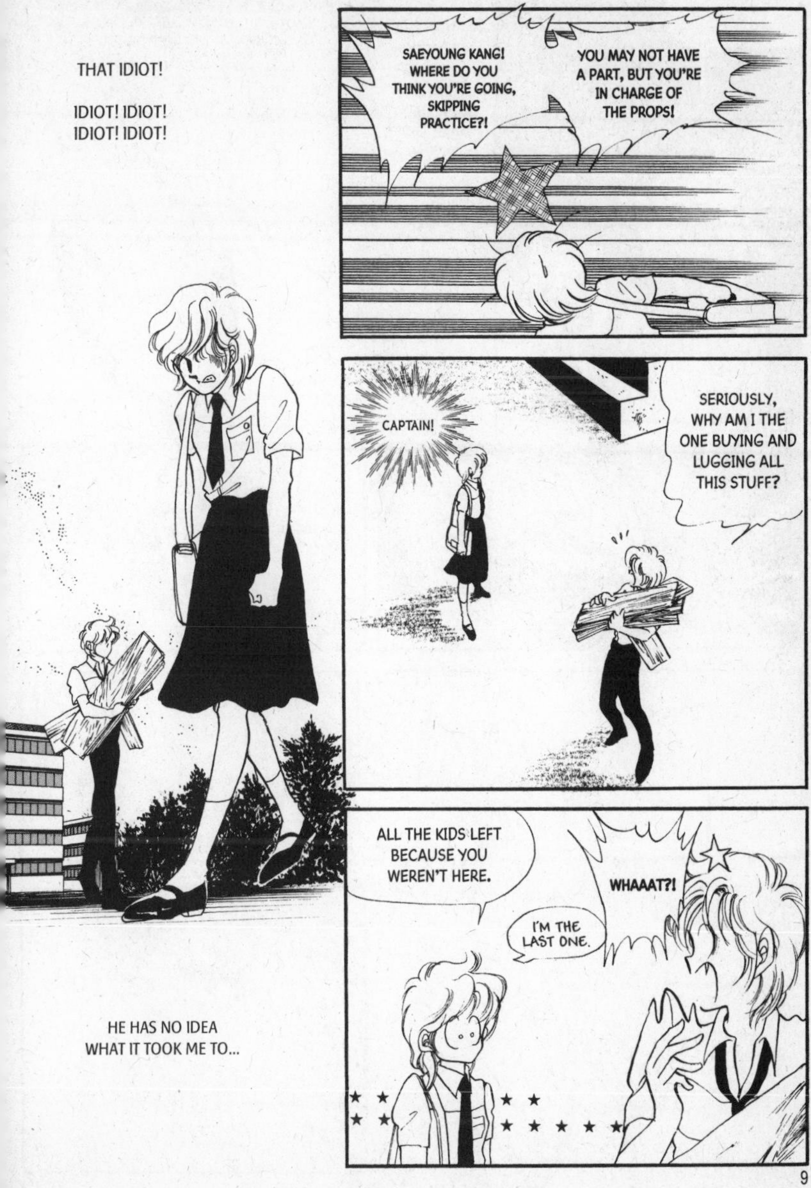
THAT IDIOT!
IDIOT! IDIOT! IDIOT! IDIOT!
HE HAS NO IDEA WHAT IT TOOK ME TO...
SAEYOUNG KANG! WHERE DO YOU THINK YOU'RE GOING, SKIPPING PRACTICE?!
YOU MAY NOT HAVE A PART, BUT YOU'RE IN CHARGE OF THE PROPS!
CAPTAIN!
SERIOUSLY, WHY AM I THE ONE BUYING AND LUGGING ALL THIS STUFF?
ALL THE KIDS LEFT BECAUSE YOU WEREN'T HERE.
I'M THE LAST ONE.
WHAAAT?!

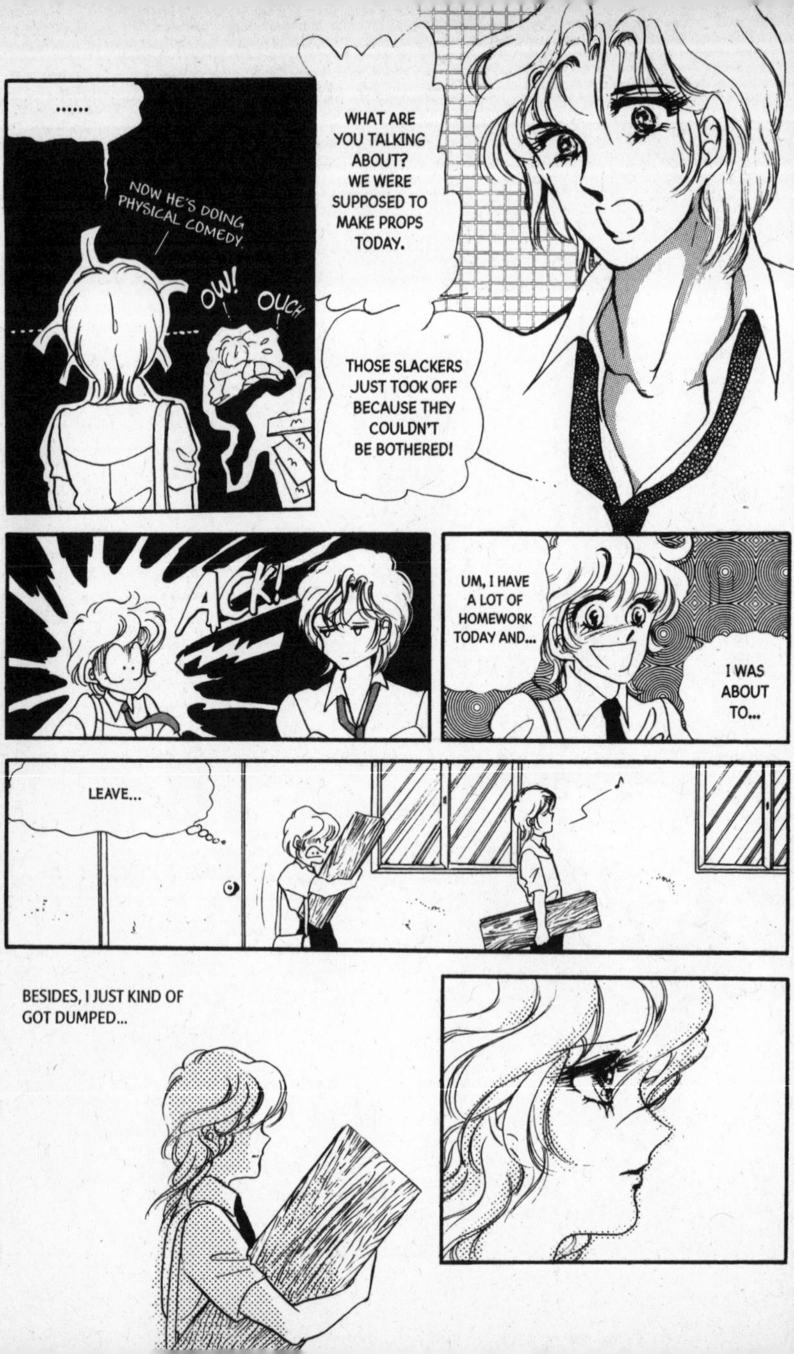
......
NOW HE'S DOING PHYSICAL COMEDY.
OW!
OUCH
WHAT ARE YOU TALKING ABOUT? WE WERE SUPPOSED TO MAKE PROPS TODAY.
THOSE SLACKERS JUST TOOK OFF BECAUSE THEY COULDN'T BE BOTHERED!
ACK!
UM, I HAVE A LOT OF HOMEWORK TODAY AND...
I WAS ABOUT TO...
LEAVE...
BESIDES, I JUST KIND OF GOT DUMPED...

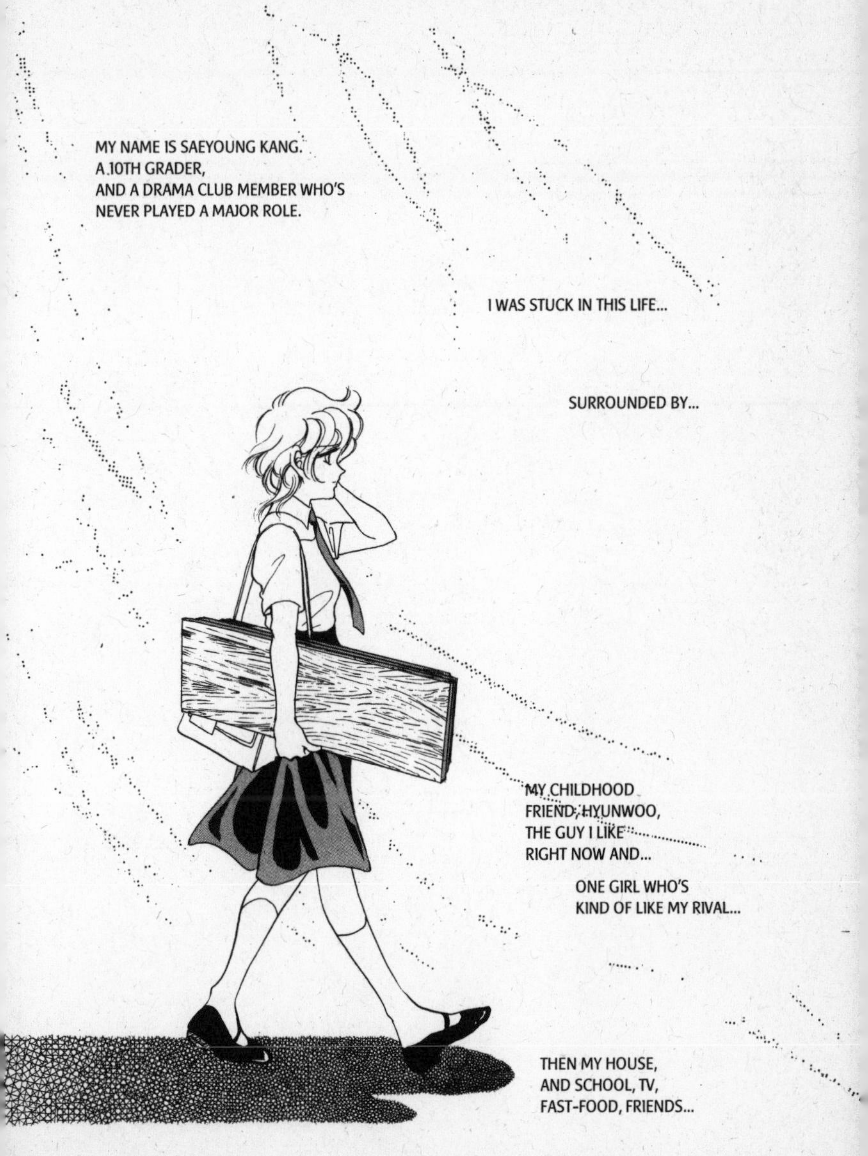
MY NAME IS SAEYOUNG KANG.
A 10TH GRADER,
AND A DRAMA CLUB MEMBER WHO'S
NEVER PLAYED A MAJOR ROLE.
I WAS STUCK IN THIS LIFE...
SURROUNDED BY...
MY CHILDHOOD
FRIEND, HYUNWOO,
THE GUY I LIKE
RIGHT NOW AND...
ONE GIRL WHO'S
KIND OF LIKE MY RIVAL...
THEN MY HOUSE,
AND SCHOOL, TV,
FAST-FOOD, FRIENDS...

SURROUNDED BY
SUCH DISGUSTINGLY
ORDINARY THINGS.

WITHOUT BEGINNING OR END,

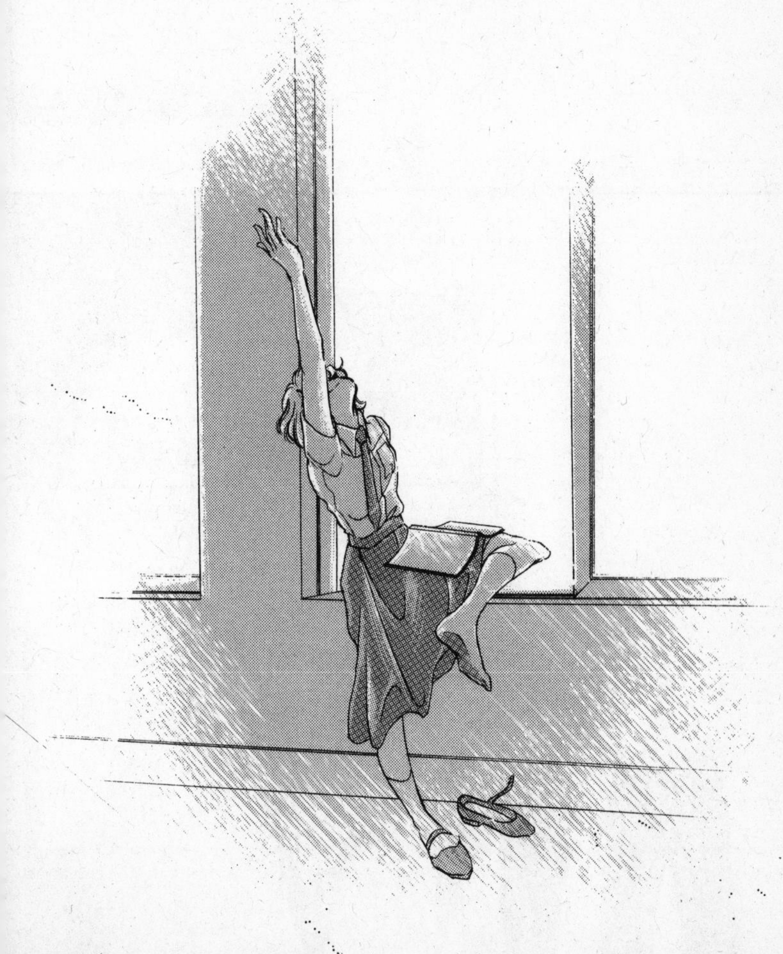

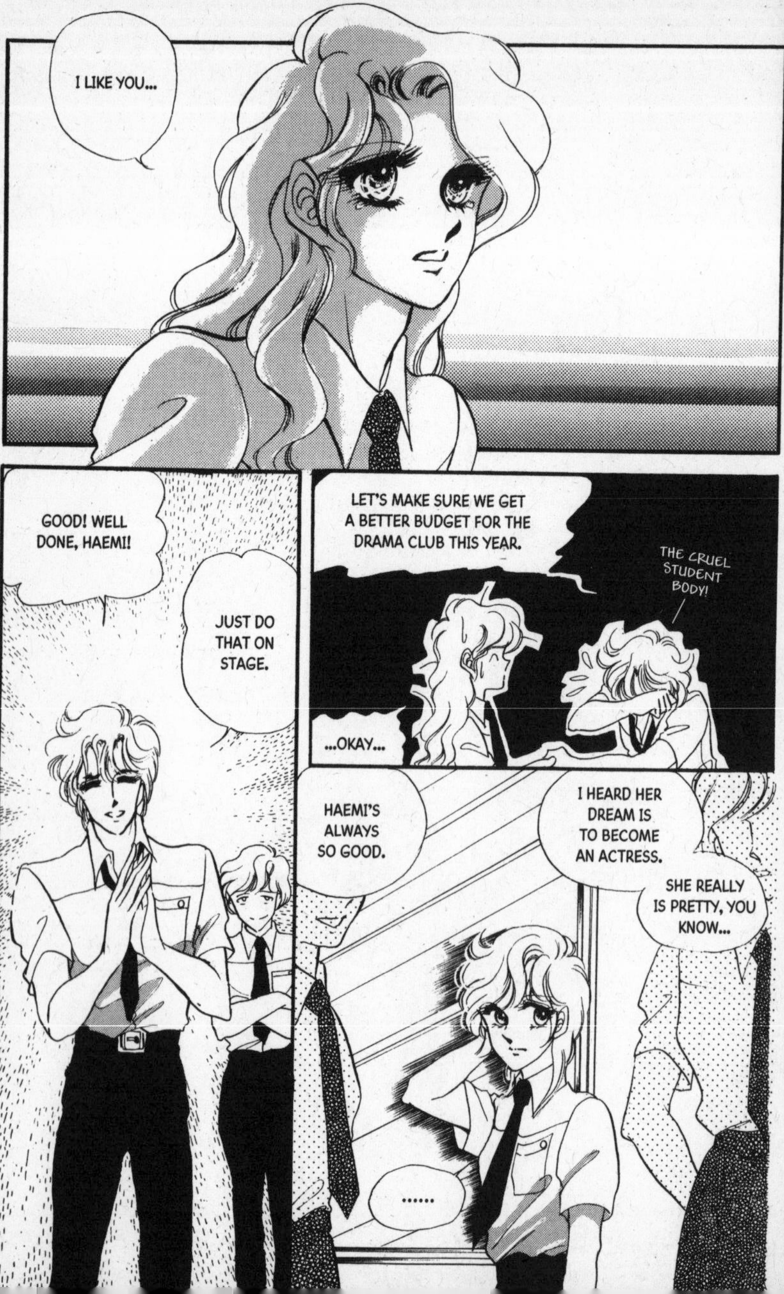
I LIKE YOU...
GOOD! WELL DONE, HAEMI!
JUST DO THAT ON STAGE.
LET'S MAKE SURE WE GET A BETTER BUDGET FOR THE DRAMA CLUB THIS YEAR.
THE CRUEL STUDENT BODY!
...OKAY...
HAEMI'S ALWAYS SO GOOD.
I HEARD HER DREAM IS TO BECOME AN ACTRESS.
SHE REALLY IS PRETTY, YOU KNOW...
......

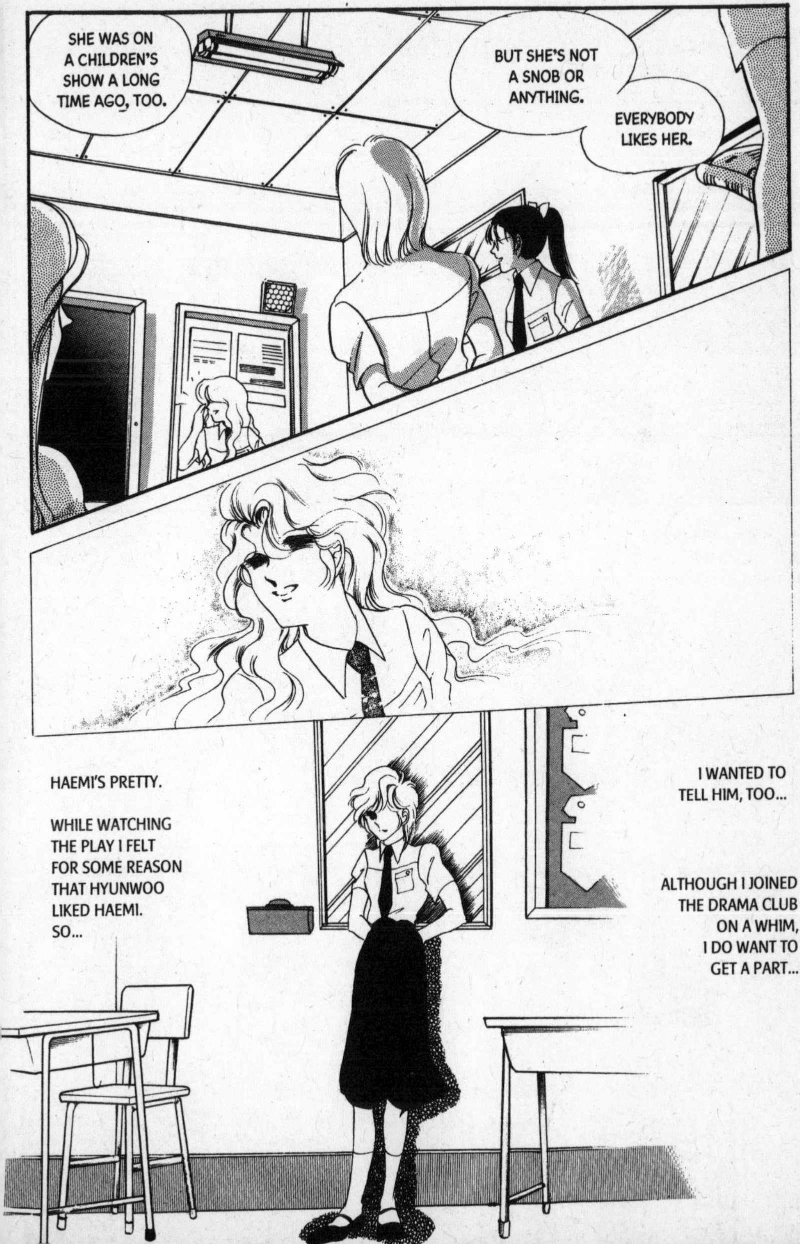
SHE WAS ON A CHILDREN'S SHOW A LONG TIME AGO, TOO.
BUT SHE'S NOT A SNOB OR ANYTHING.
EVERYBODY LIKES HER.
HAEMI'S PRETTY.
WHILE WATCHING THE PLAY I FELT FOR SOME REASON THAT HYUNWOO LIKED HAEMI. SO...
I WANTED TO TELL HIM, TOO...
ALTHOUGH I JOINED THE DRAMA CLUB ON A WHIM, I DO WANT TO GET A PART...

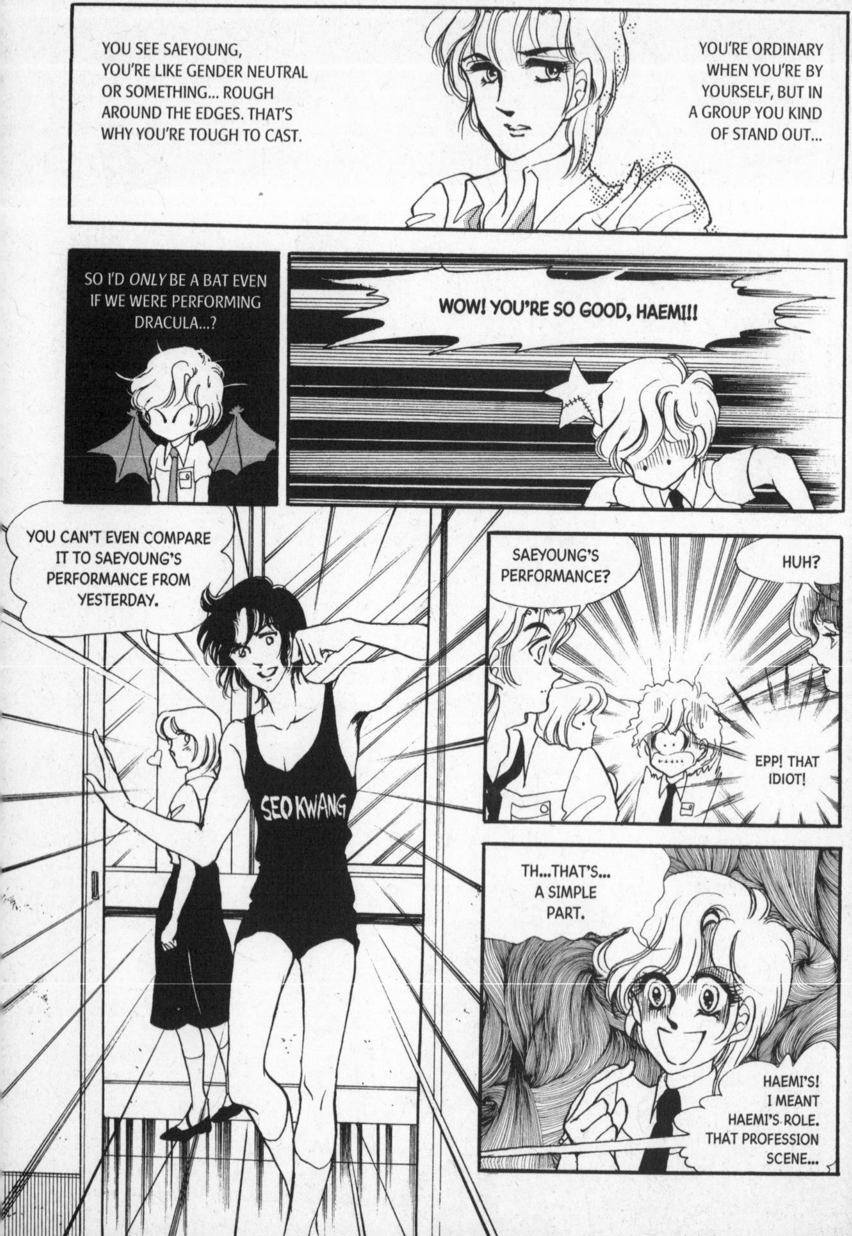
YOU SEE SAEYOUNG, YOU'RE LIKE GENDER NEUTRAL OR SOMETHING... ROUGH AROUND THE EDGES. THAT'S WHY YOU'RE TOUGH TO CAST.
YOU'RE ORDINARY WHEN YOU'RE BY YOURSELF, BUT IN A GROUP YOU KIND OF STAND OUT...
SO I'D *ONLY* BE A BAT EVEN IF WE WERE PERFORMING DRACULA...?
WOW! YOU'RE SO GOOD, HAEMI!!
YOU CAN'T EVEN COMPARE IT TO SAEYOUNG'S PERFORMANCE FROM YESTERDAY.
SEO KWANG
SAEYOUNG'S PERFORMANCE?
HUH?
EPP! THAT IDIOT!
TH...THAT'S... A SIMPLE PART.
HAEMI'S! I MEANT HAEMI'S ROLE. THAT PROFESSION SCENE...

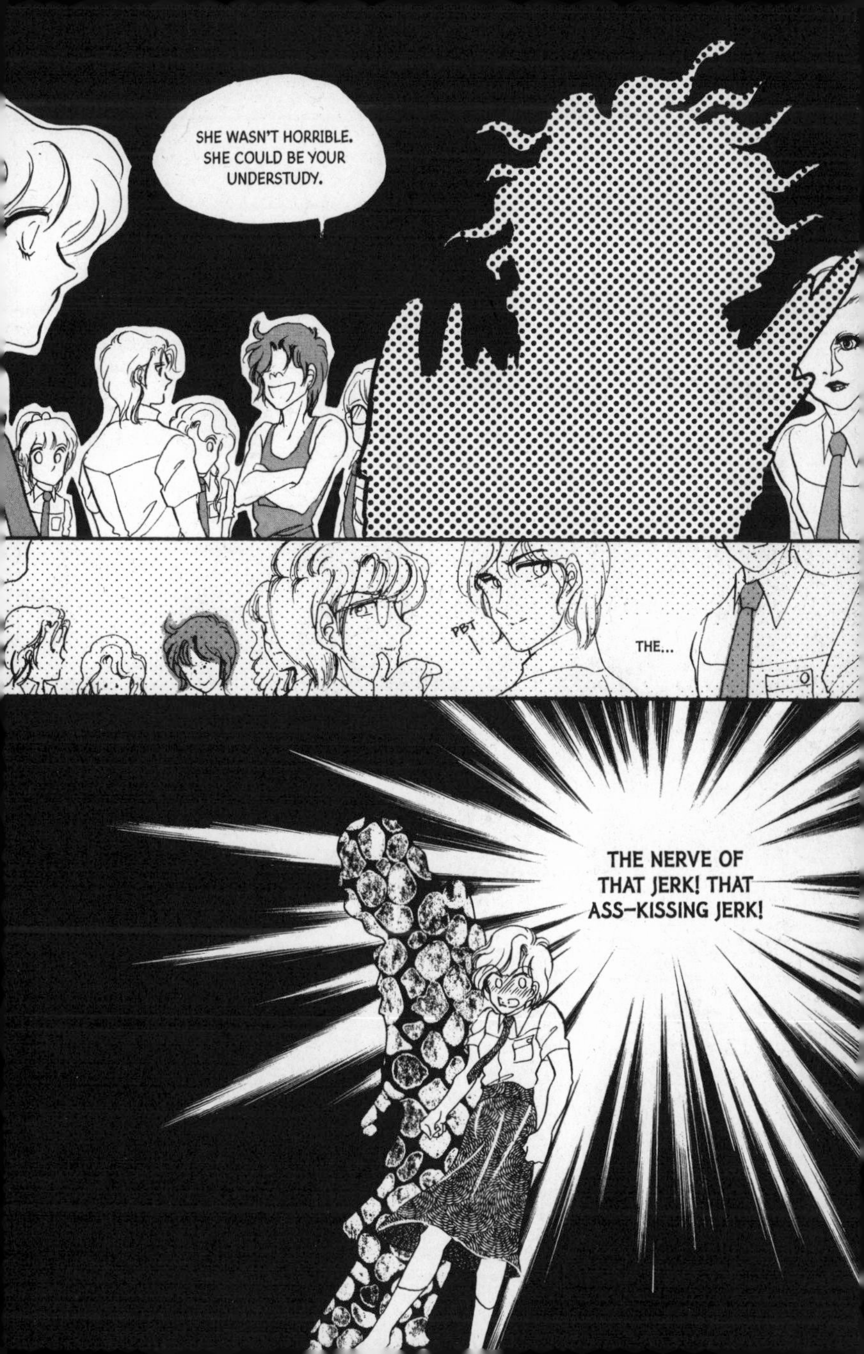
SHE WASN'T HORRIBLE. SHE COULD BE YOUR UNDERSTUDY.
PBT
THE...
THE NERVE OF THAT JERK! THAT ASS-KISSING JERK!

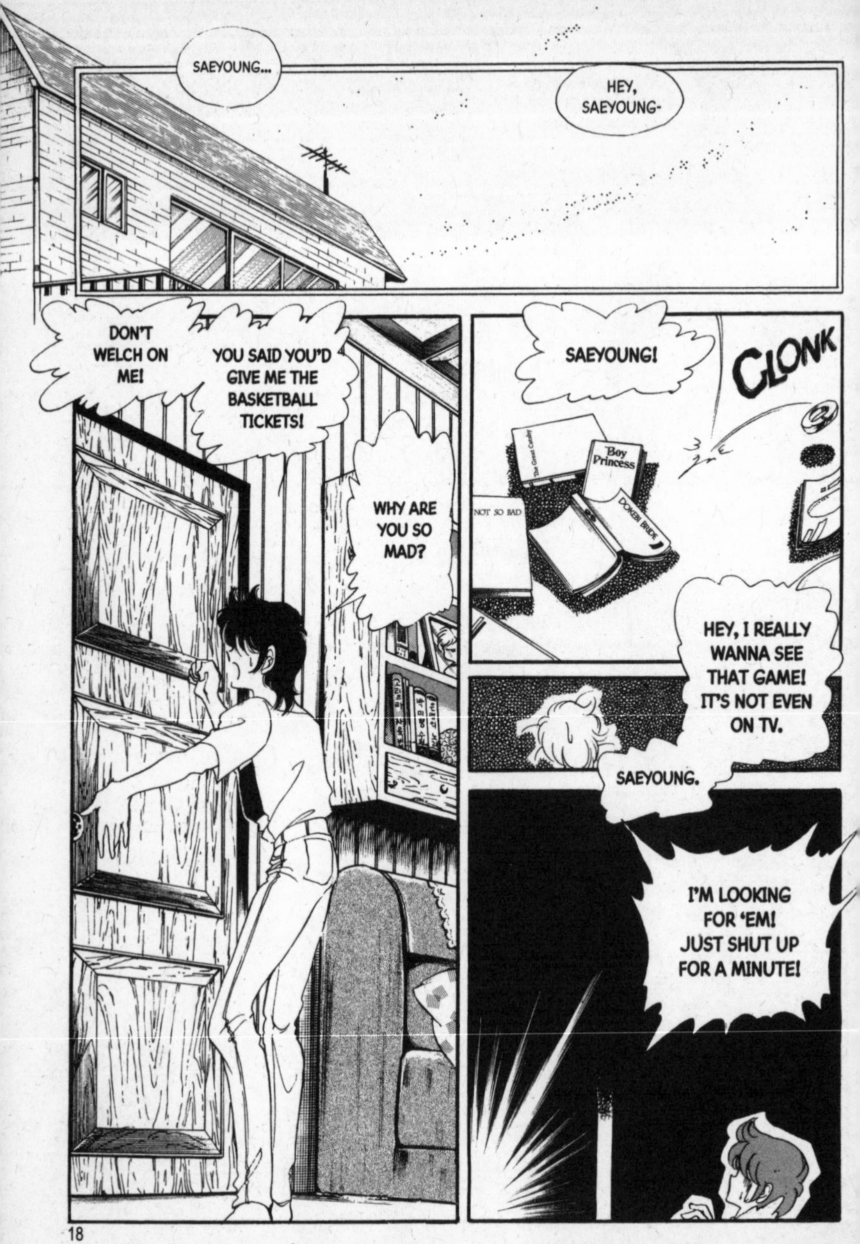
SAEYOUNG...
HEY, SAEYOUNG-
DON'T WELCH ON ME!
YOU SAID YOU'D GIVE ME THE BASKETBALL TICKETS!
WHY ARE YOU SO MAD?
SAEYOUNG!
CLONK
The Great Gatsby
Boy Princess
NOT SO BAD
DOKEBI BRIDE
HEY, I REALLY WANNA SEE THAT GAME! IT'S NOT EVEN ON TV.
SAEYOUNG.
I'M LOOKING FOR 'EM! JUST SHUT UP FOR A MINUTE!

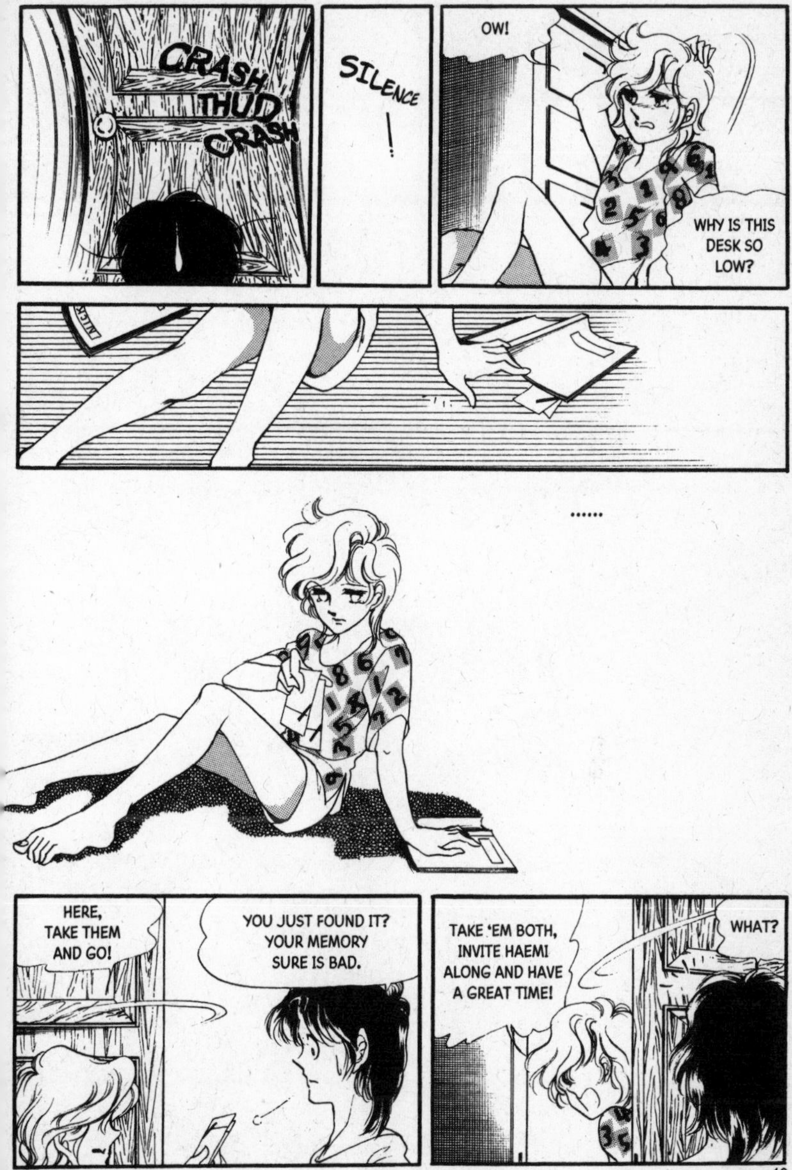
CRASH THUD CRASH
SILENCE
!
OW!
WHY IS THIS DESK SO LOW?
......
HERE, TAKE THEM AND GO!
YOU JUST FOUND IT? YOUR MEMORY SURE IS BAD.
TAKE 'EM BOTH, INVITE HAEMI ALONG AND HAVE A GREAT TIME!
WHAT?

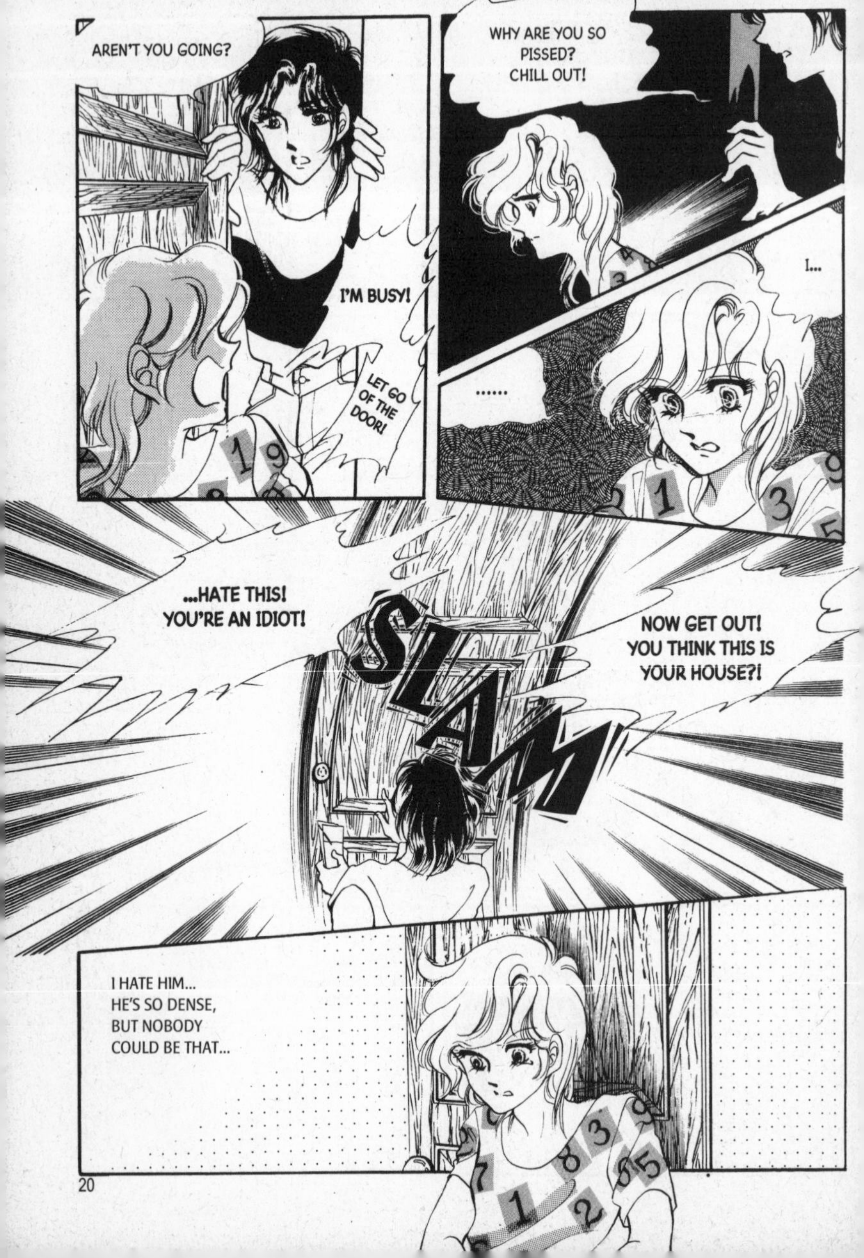
AREN'T YOU GOING?
I'M BUSY!
LET GO OF THE DOOR!
WHY ARE YOU SO PISSED? CHILL OUT!
I...
......
...HATE THIS! YOU'RE AN IDIOT!
SLAM
NOW GET OUT! YOU THINK THIS IS YOUR HOUSE?!
I HATE HIM... HE'S SO DENSE, BUT NOBODY COULD BE THAT...

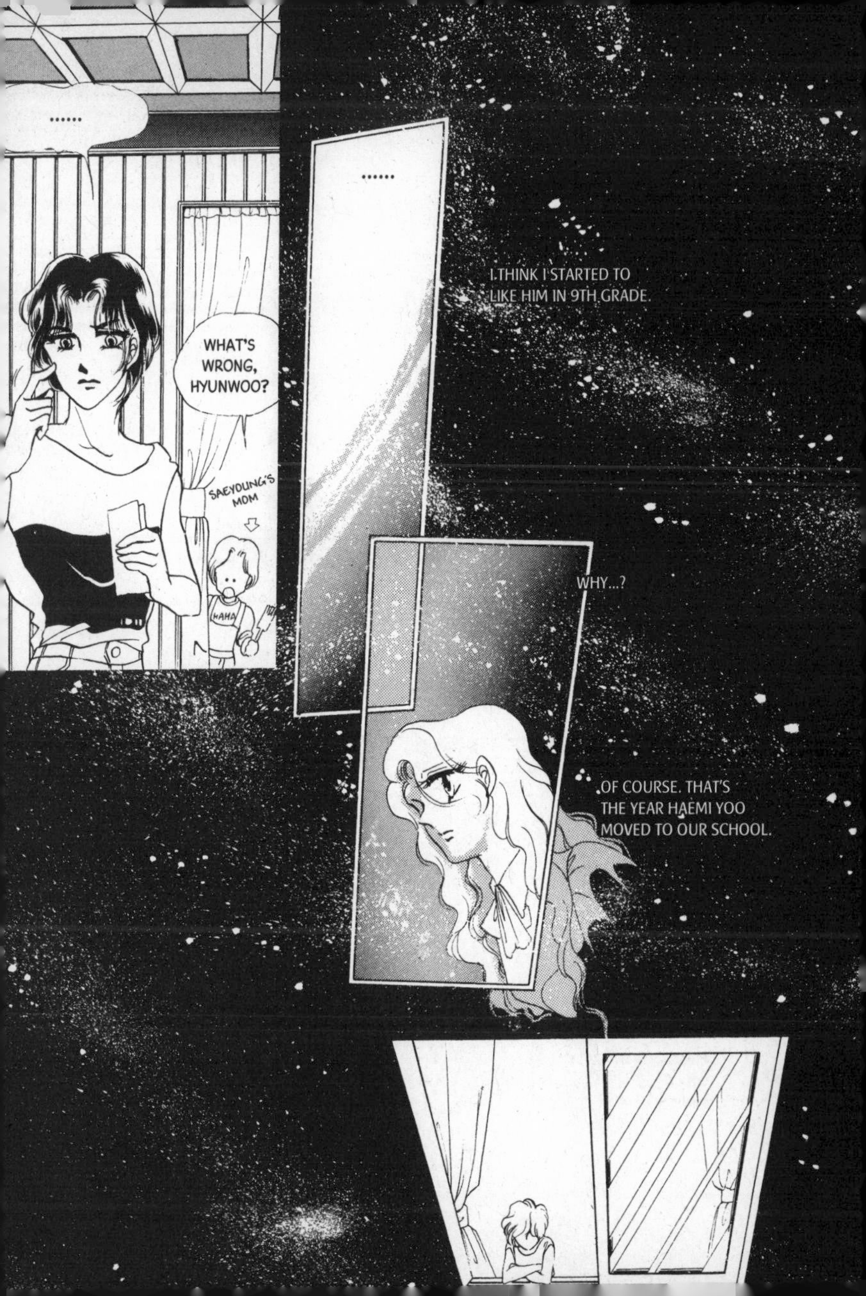

......
WHAT'S WRONG, HYUNWOO?
SAEYOUNG'S MOM
HAHA
......
I THINK I STARTED TO LIKE HIM IN 9TH GRADE.
WHY...?
OF COURSE. THAT'S THE YEAR HAEMI YOO MOVED TO OUR SCHOOL.

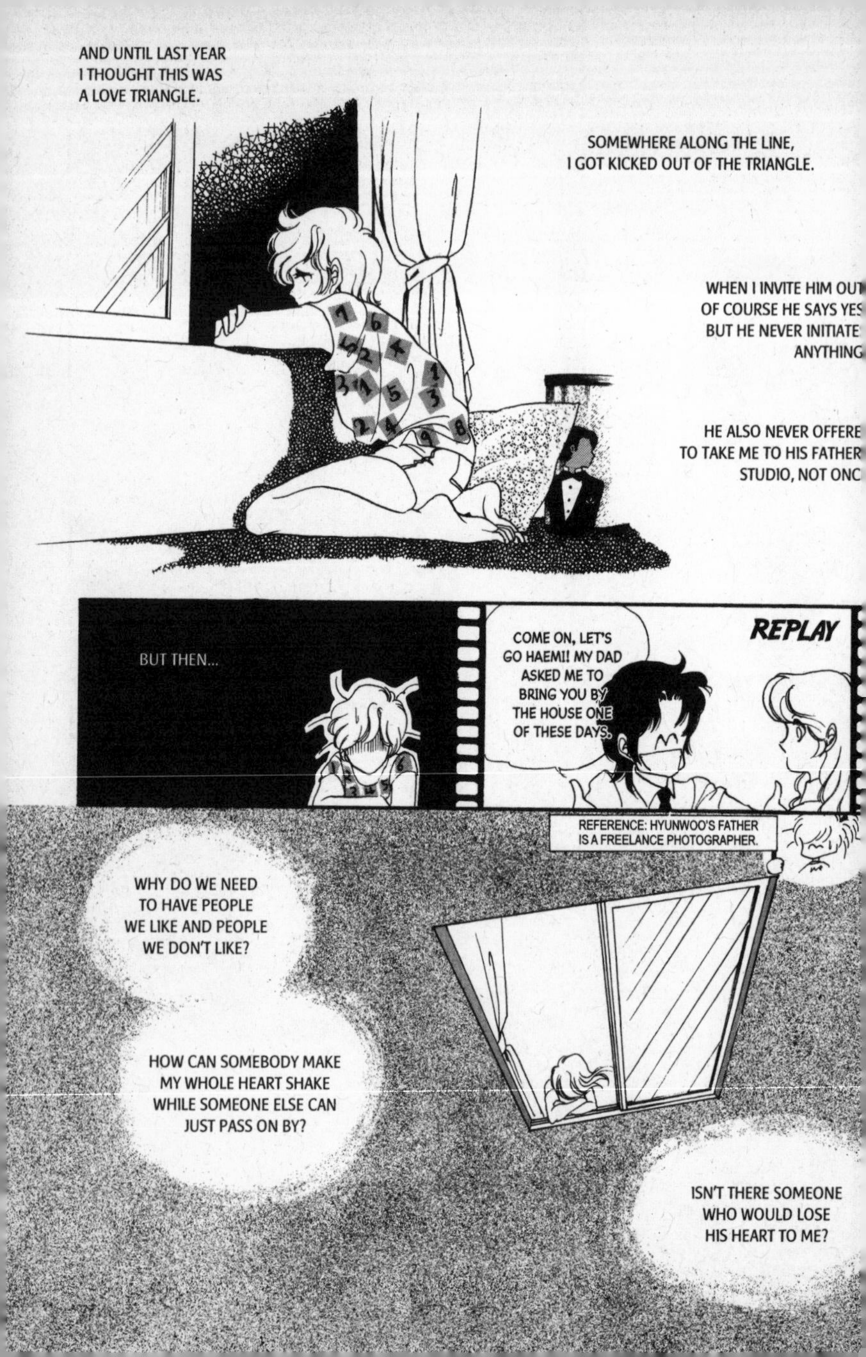
AND UNTIL LAST YEAR I THOUGHT THIS WAS A LOVE TRIANGLE.
SOMEWHERE ALONG THE LINE, I GOT KICKED OUT OF THE TRIANGLE.
WHEN I INVITE HIM OUT OF COURSE HE SAYS YES BUT HE NEVER INITIATE ANYTHING
HE ALSO NEVER OFFERE TO TAKE ME TO HIS FATHER STUDIO, NOT ONC
BUT THEN...
REPLAY
COME ON, LET'S GO HAEMI! MY DAD ASKED ME TO BRING YOU BY THE HOUSE ONE OF THESE DAYS.
REFERENCE: HYUNWOO'S FATHER IS A FREELANCE PHOTOGRAPHER.
WHY DO WE NEED TO HAVE PEOPLE WE LIKE AND PEOPLE WE DON'T LIKE?
HOW CAN SOMEBODY MAKE MY WHOLE HEART SHAKE WHILE SOMEONE ELSE CAN JUST PASS ON BY?
ISN'T THERE SOMEONE WHO WOULD LOSE HIS HEART TO ME?

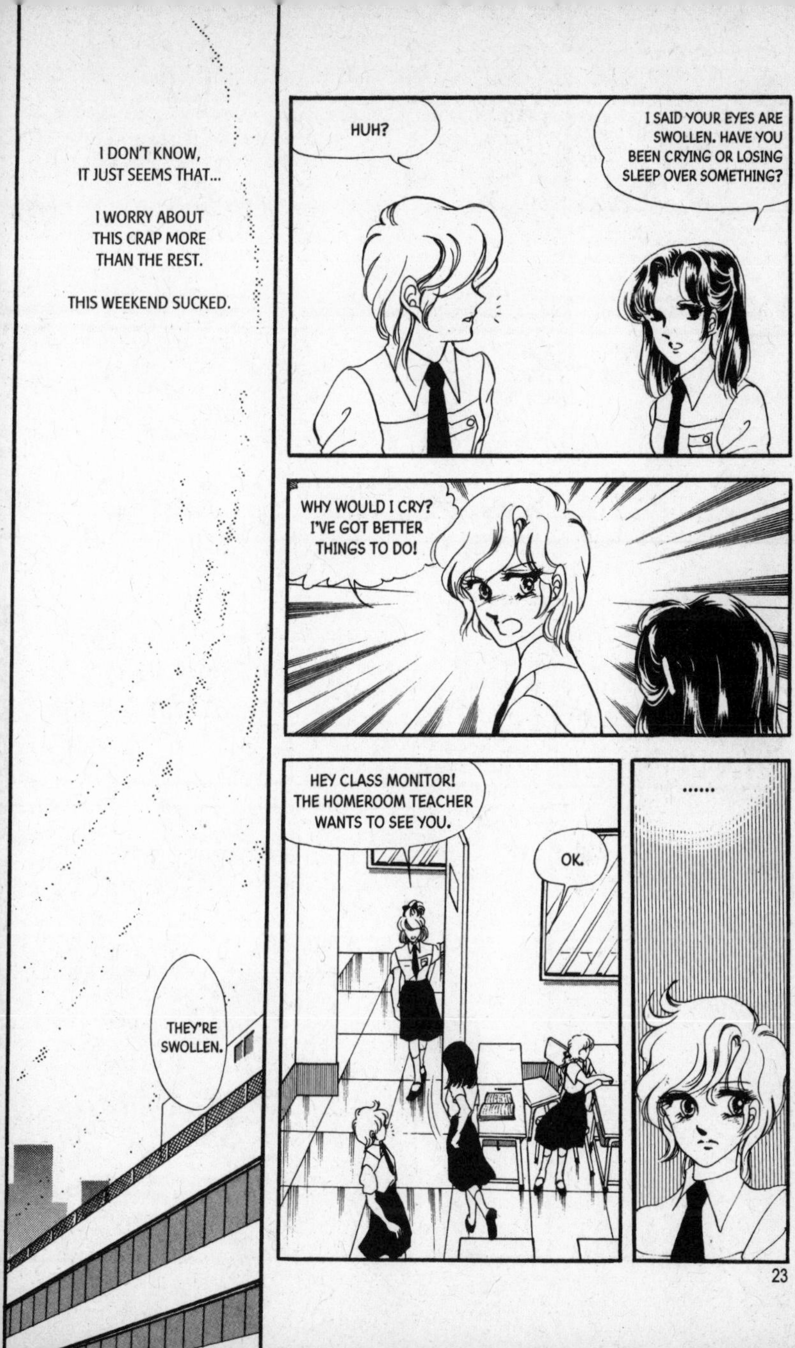
I DON'T KNOW, IT JUST SEEMS THAT...
I WORRY ABOUT THIS CRAP MORE THAN THE REST.
THIS WEEKEND SUCKED.
THEY'RE SWOLLEN.
HUH?
I SAID YOUR EYES ARE SWOLLEN. HAVE YOU BEEN CRYING OR LOSING SLEEP OVER SOMETHING?
WHY WOULD I CRY? I'VE GOT BETTER THINGS TO DO!
HEY CLASS MONITOR! THE HOMEROOM TEACHER WANTS TO SEE YOU.
OK.
......

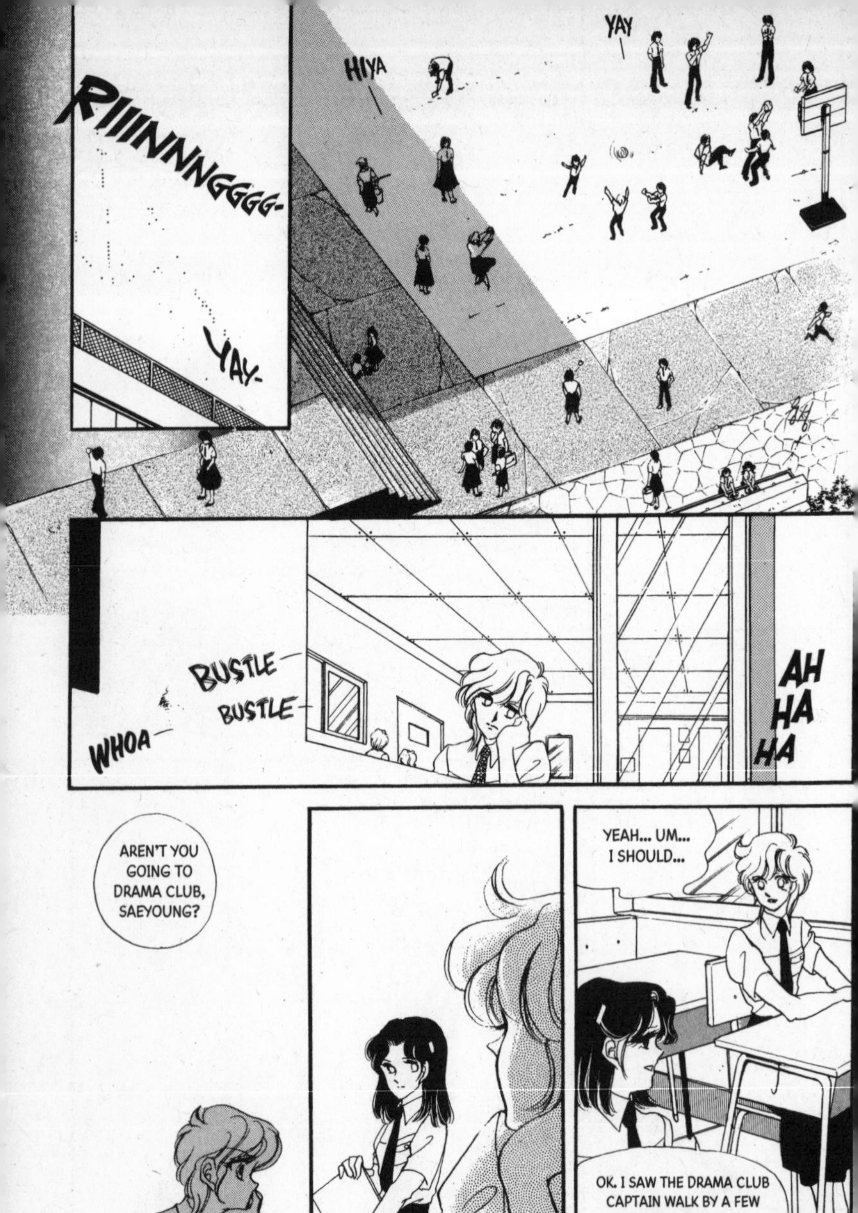
RIIIINNNGGGG-
YAY-
HIYA
YAY
BUSTLE
BUSTLE
WHOA
AH HA HA
AREN'T YOU GOING TO DRAMA CLUB, SAEYOUNG?
YEAH... UM... I SHOULD...
OK. I SAW THE DRAMA CLUB CAPTAIN WALK BY A FEW MINUTES AGO. GO ON BEFORE YOU'RE LATE.

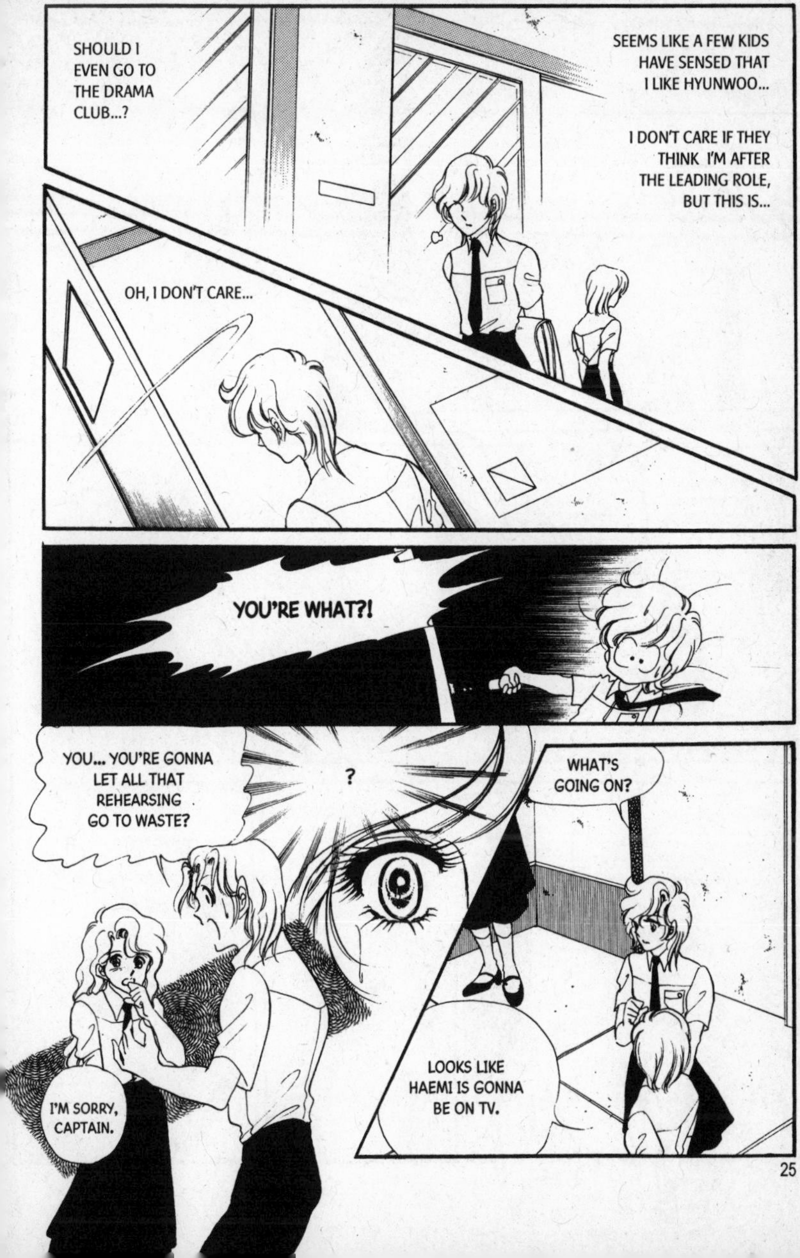
SHOULD I EVEN GO TO THE DRAMA CLUB...?
SEEMS LIKE A FEW KIDS HAVE SENSED THAT I LIKE HYUNWOO...
I DON'T CARE IF THEY THINK I'M AFTER THE LEADING ROLE, BUT THIS IS...
OH, I DON'T CARE...
YOU'RE WHAT?!
YOU... YOU'RE GONNA LET ALL THAT REHEARSING GO TO WASTE?
?
I'M SORRY, CAPTAIN.
WHAT'S GOING ON?
LOOKS LIKE HAEMI IS GONNA BE ON TV.

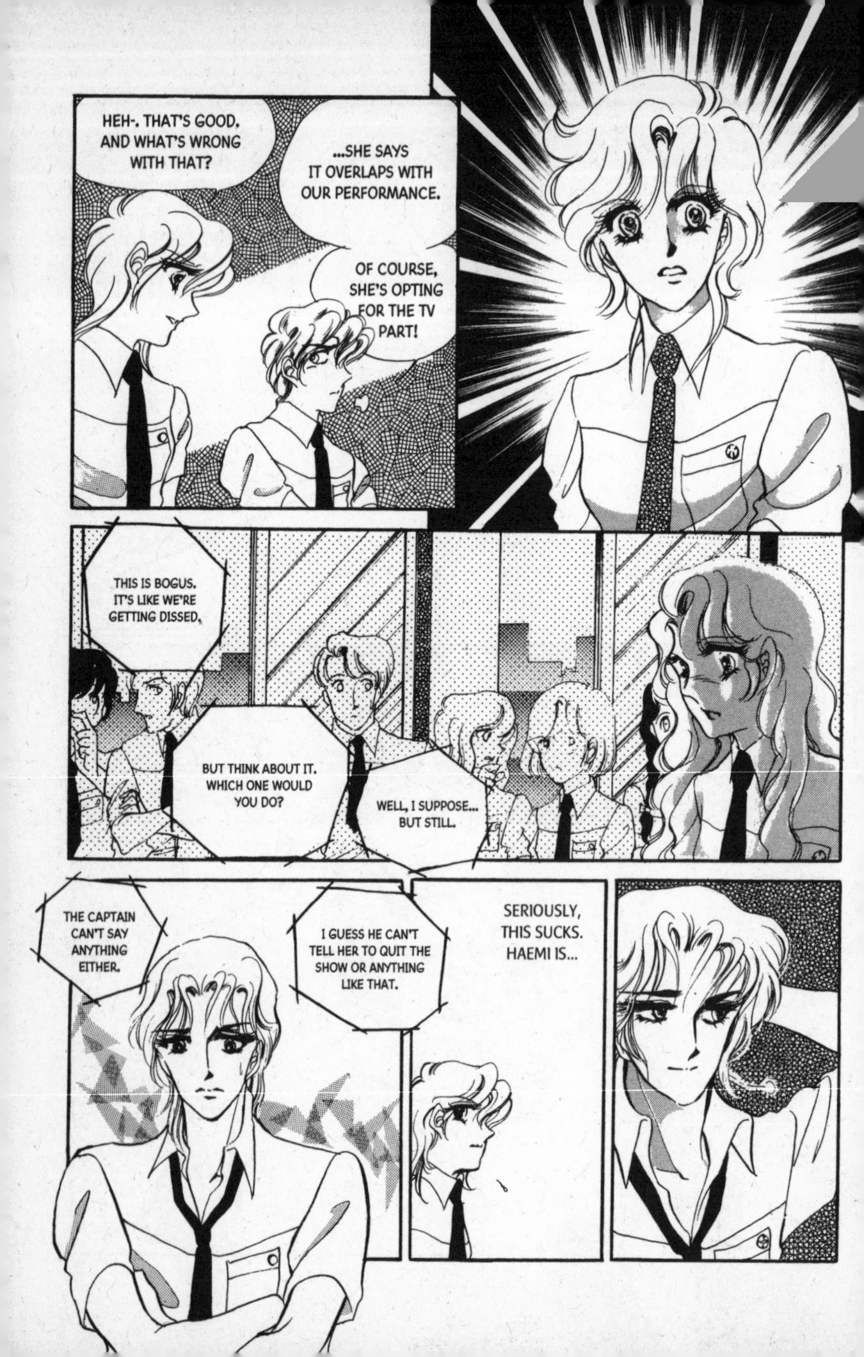
HEH-. THAT'S GOOD. AND WHAT'S WRONG WITH THAT?
...SHE SAYS IT OVERLAPS WITH OUR PERFORMANCE.
OF COURSE, SHE'S OPTING FOR THE TV PART!
THIS IS BOGUS. IT'S LIKE WE'RE GETTING DISSED.
BUT THINK ABOUT IT. WHICH ONE WOULD YOU DO?
WELL, I SUPPOSE... BUT STILL.
THE CAPTAIN CAN'T SAY ANYTHING EITHER.
I GUESS HE CAN'T TELL HER TO QUIT THE SHOW OR ANYTHING LIKE THAT.
SERIOUSLY, THIS SUCKS. HAEMI IS...

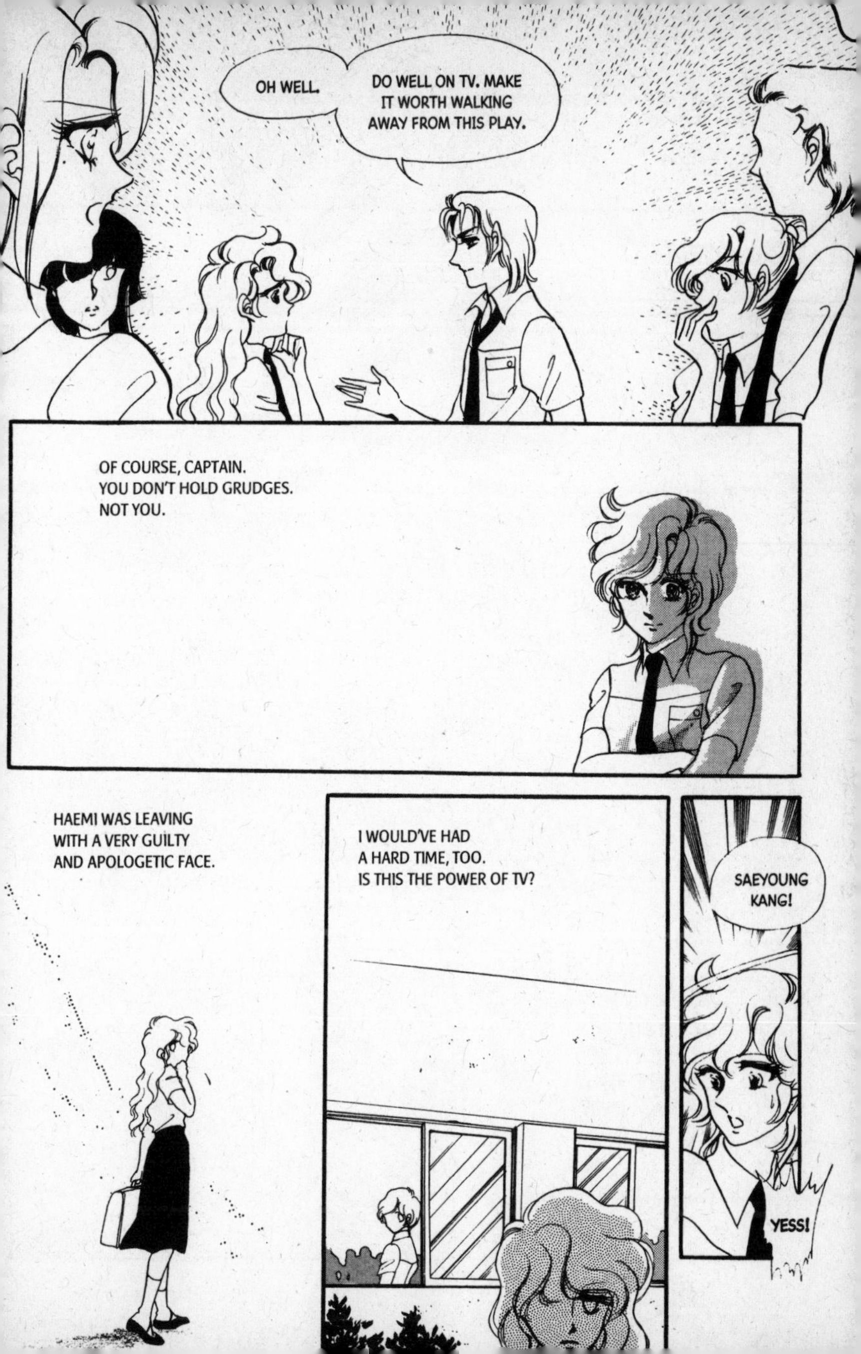
OH WELL.
DO WELL ON TV. MAKE IT WORTH WALKING AWAY FROM THIS PLAY.
OF COURSE, CAPTAIN. YOU DON'T HOLD GRUDGES. NOT YOU.
HAEMI WAS LEAVING WITH A VERY GUILTY AND APOLOGETIC FACE.
I WOULD'VE HAD A HARD TIME, TOO. IS THIS THE POWER OF TV?
SAEYOUNG KANG!
YESS!

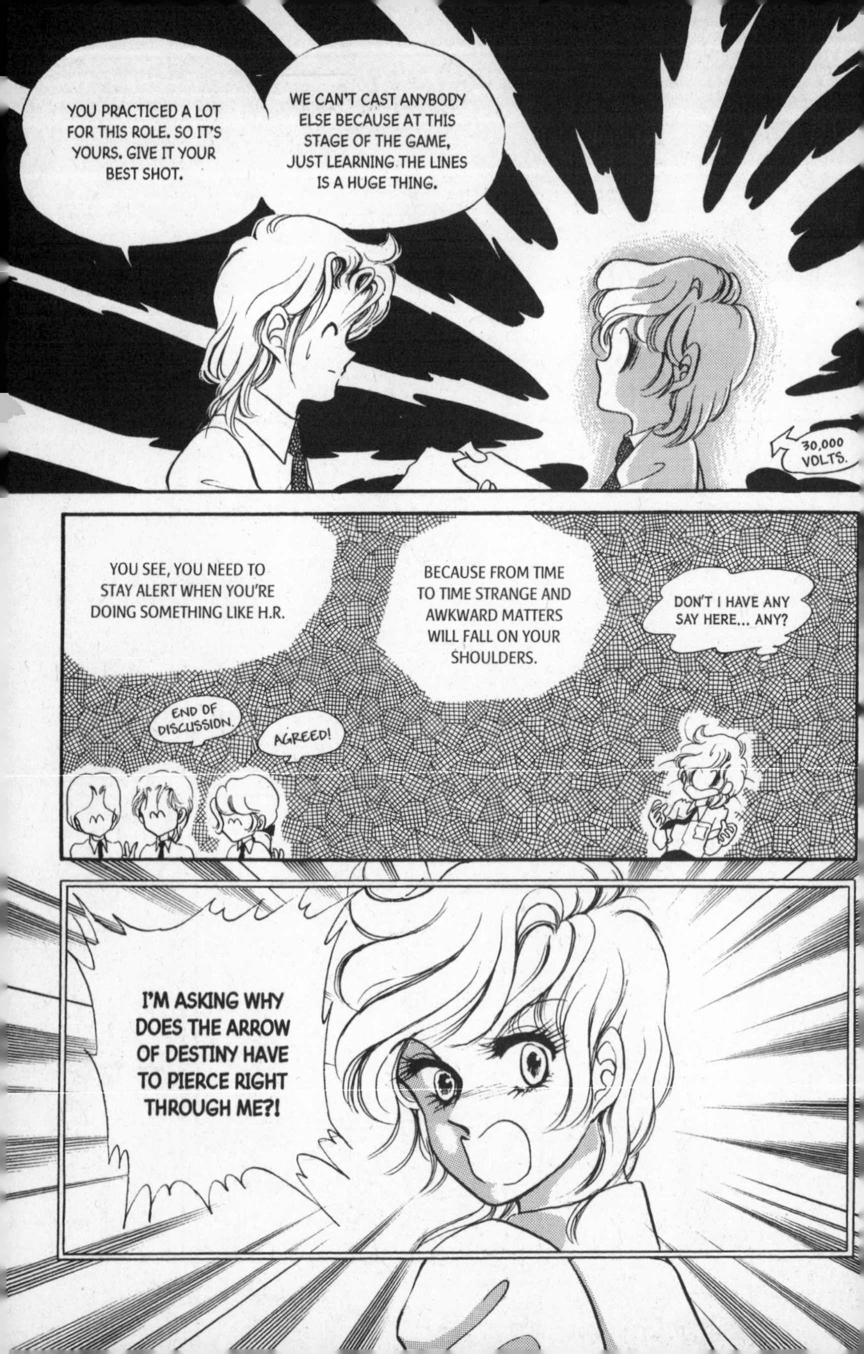
YOU PRACTICED A LOT FOR THIS ROLE. SO IT'S YOURS. GIVE IT YOUR BEST SHOT.
WE CAN'T CAST ANYBODY ELSE BECAUSE AT THIS STAGE OF THE GAME, JUST LEARNING THE LINES IS A HUGE THING.
30,000 VOLTS.
YOU SEE, YOU NEED TO STAY ALERT WHEN YOU'RE DOING SOMETHING LIKE H.R.
BECAUSE FROM TIME TO TIME STRANGE AND AWKWARD MATTERS WILL FALL ON YOUR SHOULDERS.
DON'T I HAVE ANY SAY HERE... ANY?
END OF DISCUSSION.
AGREED!
I'M ASKING WHY DOES THE ARROW OF DESTINY HAVE TO PIERCE RIGHT THROUGH ME?!

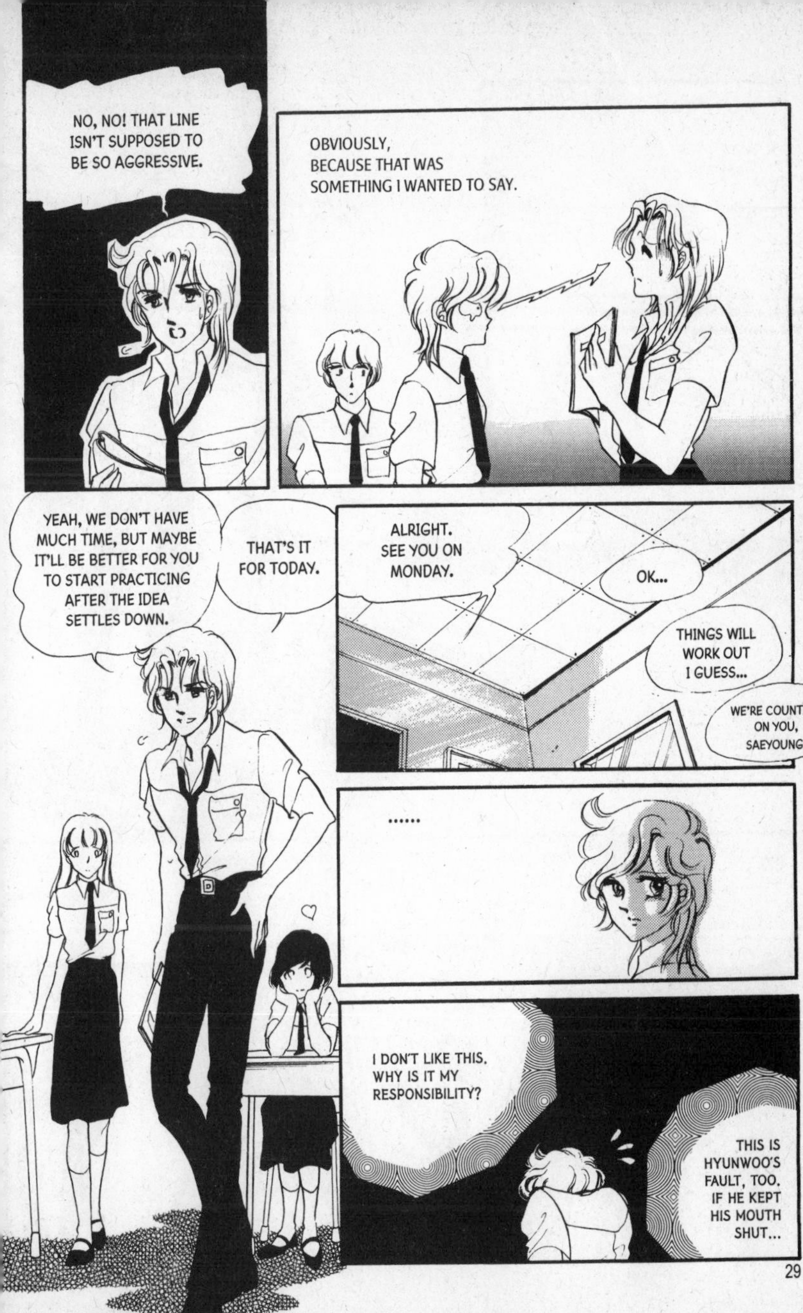
NO, NO! THAT LINE ISN'T SUPPOSED TO BE SO AGGRESSIVE.
OBVIOUSLY, BECAUSE THAT WAS SOMETHING I WANTED TO SAY.
YEAH, WE DON'T HAVE MUCH TIME, BUT MAYBE IT'LL BE BETTER FOR YOU TO START PRACTICING AFTER THE IDEA SETTLES DOWN.
THAT'S IT FOR TODAY.
ALRIGHT. SEE YOU ON MONDAY.
OK...
THINGS WILL WORK OUT I GUESS...
WE'RE COUNTING ON YOU, SAEYOUNG.
......
I DON'T LIKE THIS. WHY IS IT MY RESPONSIBILITY?
THIS IS HYUNWOO'S FAULT, TOO. IF HE KEPT HIS MOUTH SHUT...

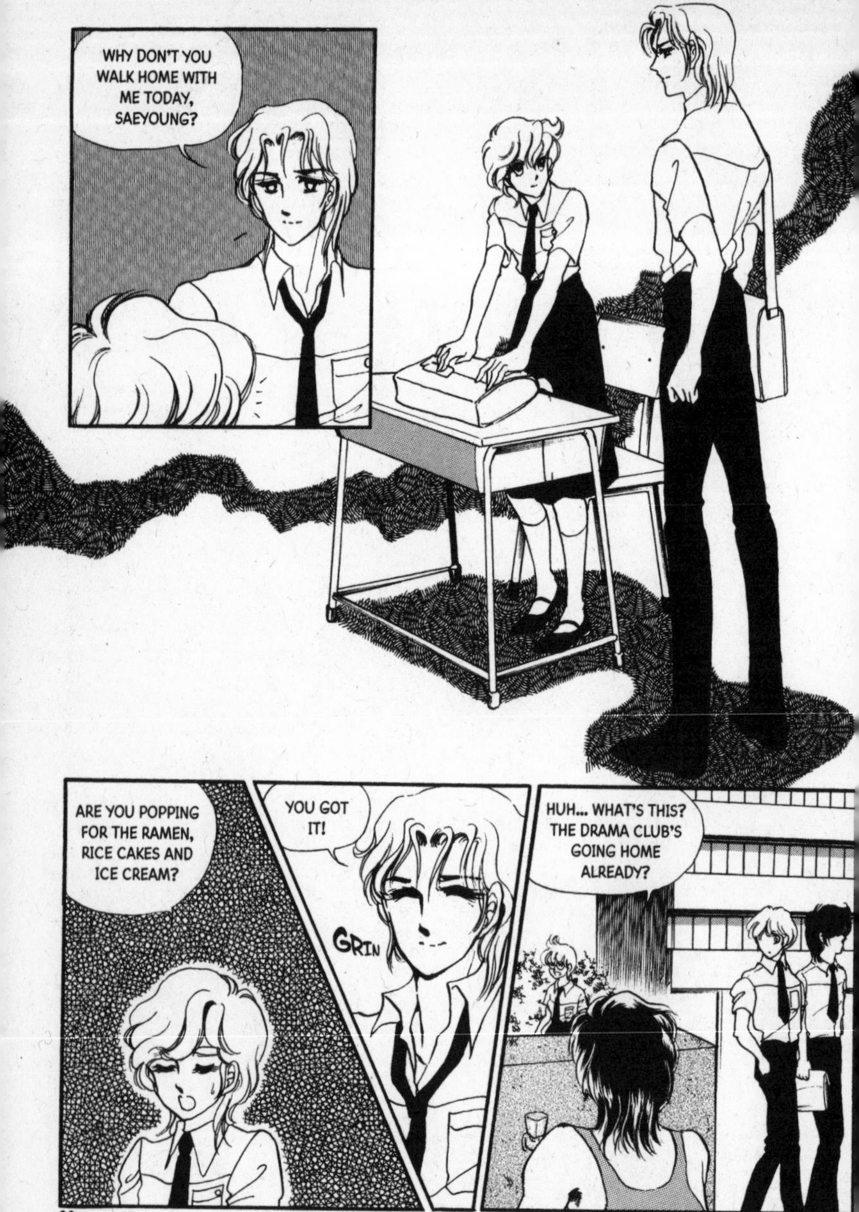
WHY DON'T YOU WALK HOME WITH ME TODAY, SAEYOUNG?
ARE YOU POPPING FOR THE RAMEN, RICE CAKES AND ICE CREAM?
YOU GOT IT!
GRIN
HUH... WHAT'S THIS? THE DRAMA CLUB'S GOING HOME ALREADY?

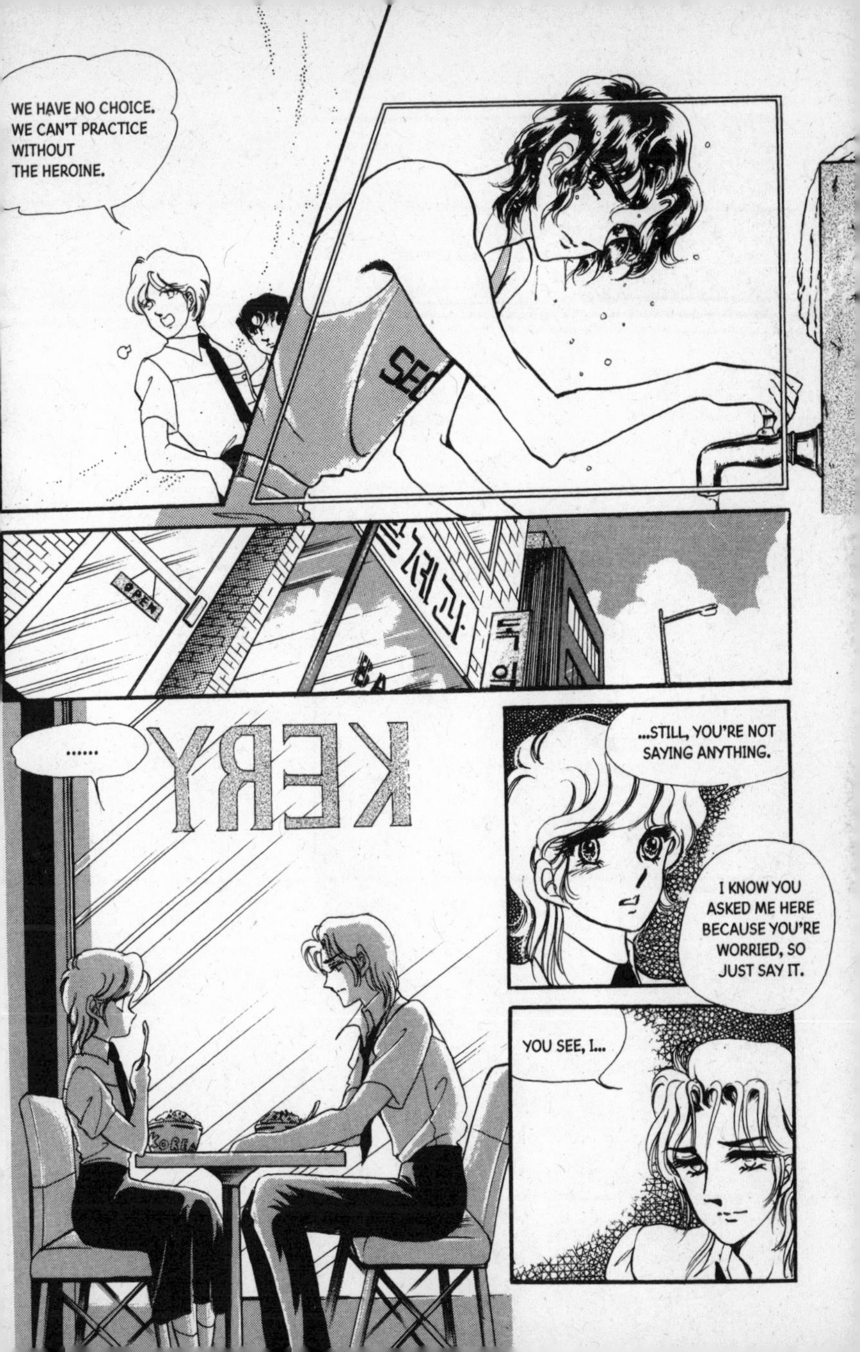
WE HAVE NO CHOICE. WE CAN'T PRACTICE WITHOUT THE HEROINE.
OPEN
......
...STILL, YOU'RE NOT SAYING ANYTHING.
I KNOW YOU ASKED ME HERE BECAUSE YOU'RE WORRIED, SO JUST SAY IT.
YOU SEE, I...

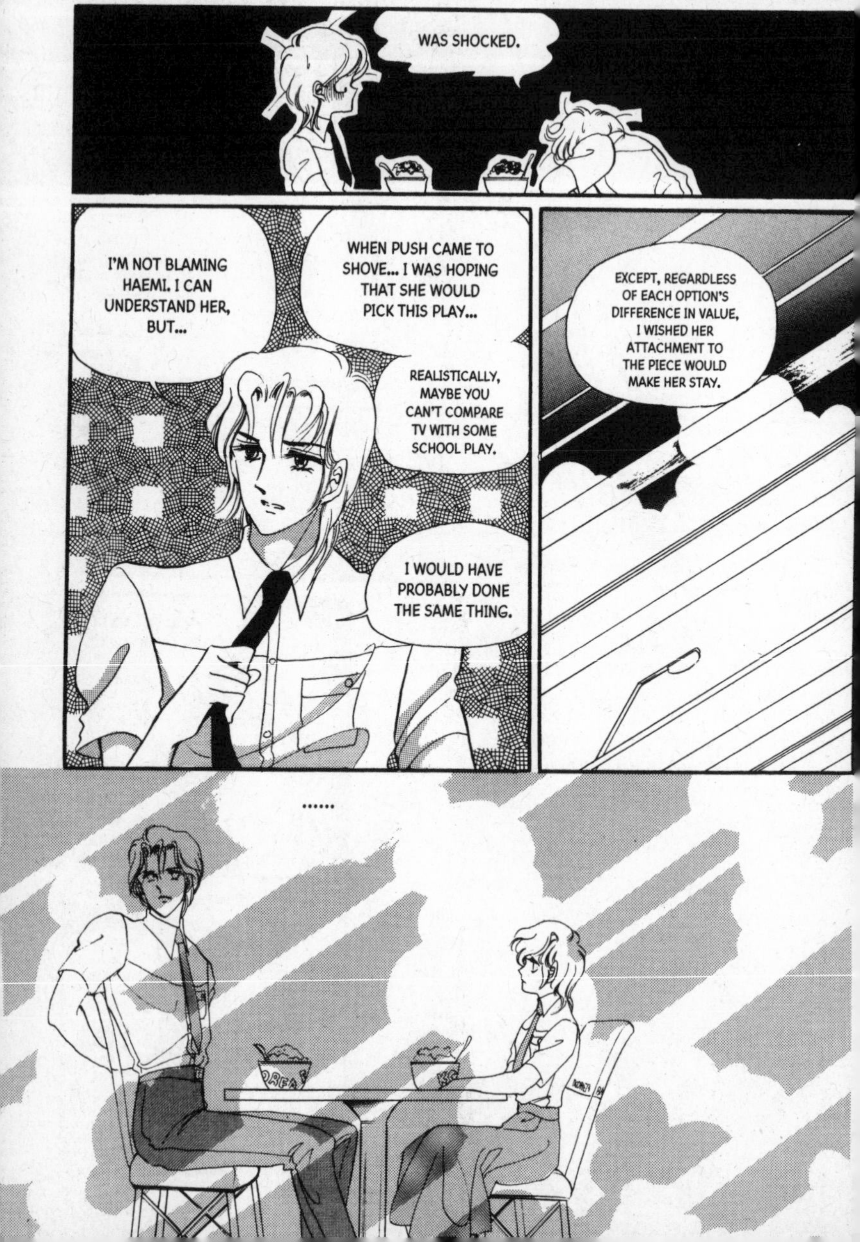
WAS SHOCKED.
I'M NOT BLAMING HAEMI. I CAN UNDERSTAND HER, BUT...
WHEN PUSH CAME TO SHOVE... I WAS HOPING THAT SHE WOULD PICK THIS PLAY...
REALISTICALLY, MAYBE YOU CAN'T COMPARE TV WITH SOME SCHOOL PLAY.
I WOULD HAVE PROBABLY DONE THE SAME THING.
EXCEPT, REGARDLESS OF EACH OPTION'S DIFFERENCE IN VALUE, I WISHED HER ATTACHMENT TO THE PIECE WOULD MAKE HER STAY.
......

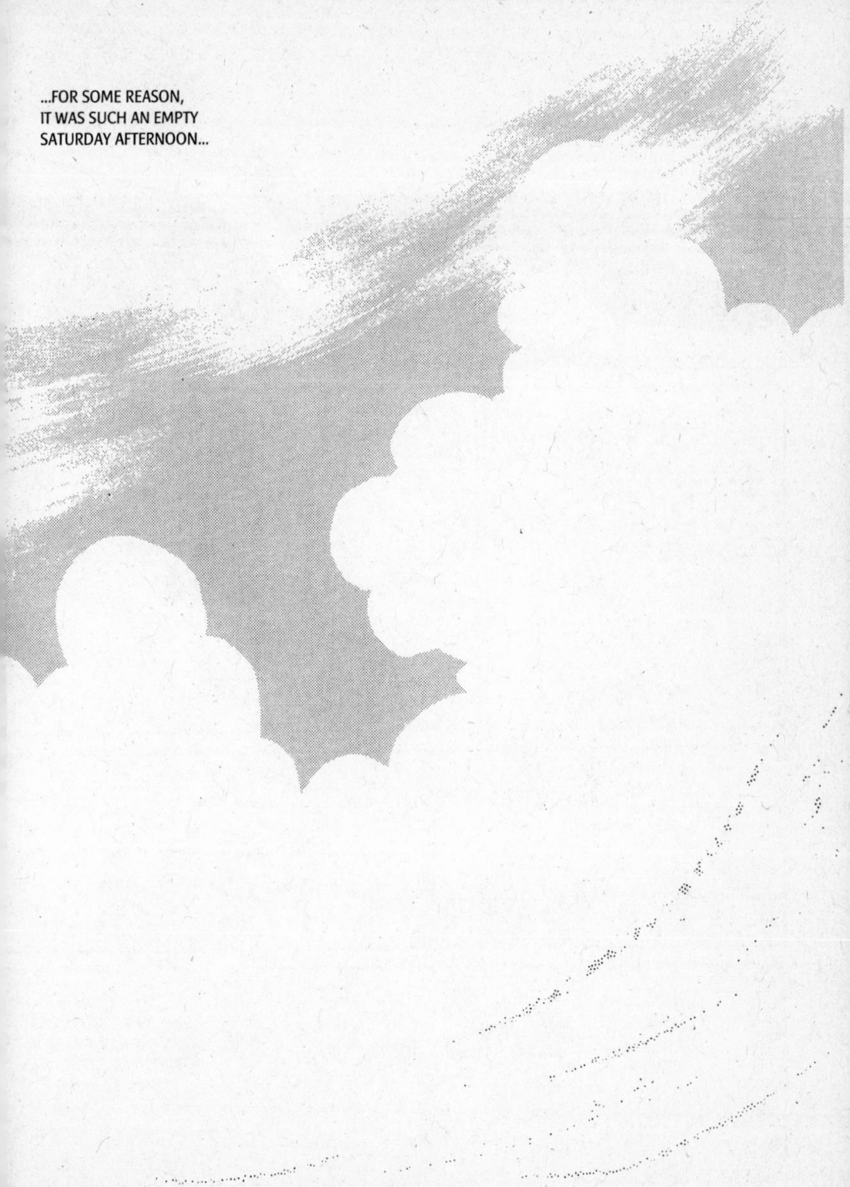
...FOR SOME REASON, IT WAS SUCH AN EMPTY SATURDAY AFTERNOON...

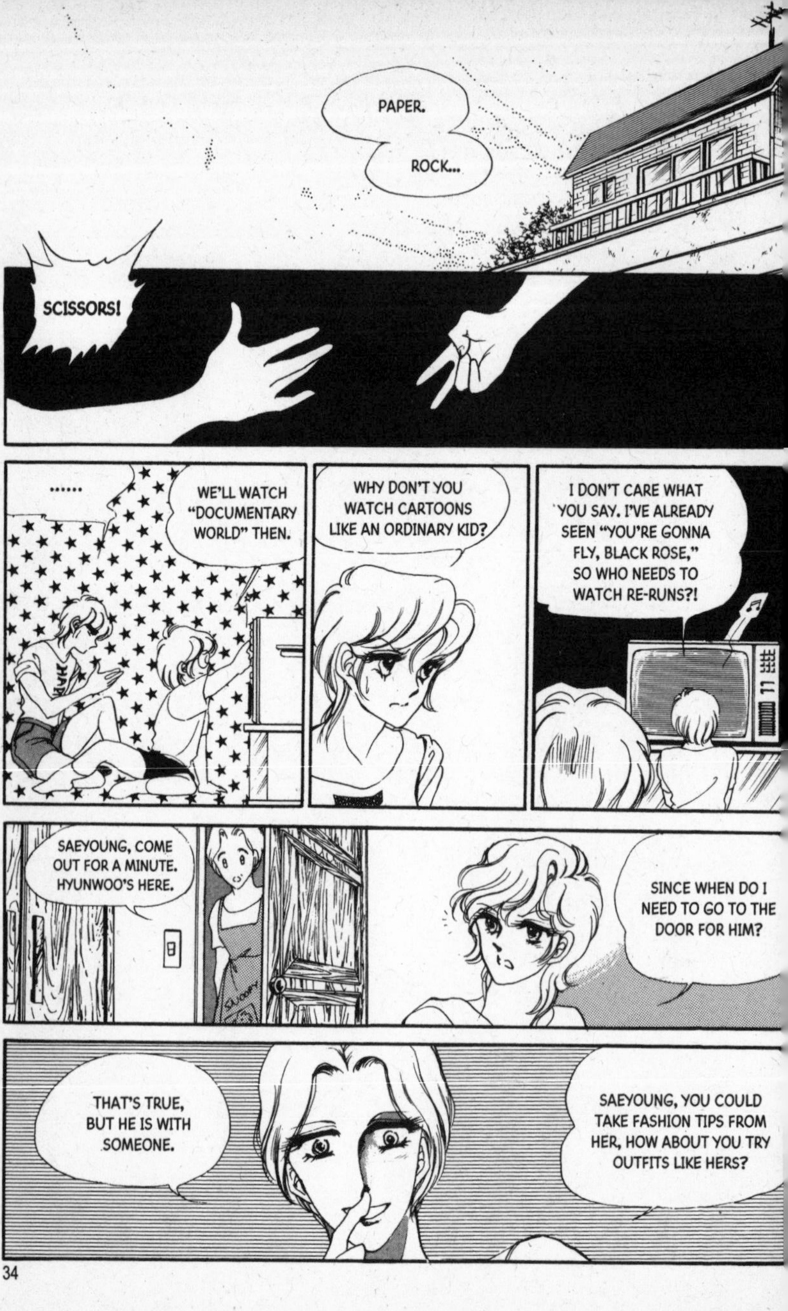
PAPER.
ROCK...
SCISSORS!
......
WE'LL WATCH "DOCUMENTARY WORLD" THEN.
WHY DON'T YOU WATCH CARTOONS LIKE AN ORDINARY KID?
I DON'T CARE WHAT YOU SAY. I'VE ALREADY SEEN "YOU'RE GONNA FLY, BLACK ROSE," SO WHO NEEDS TO WATCH RE-RUNS?!
SAEYOUNG, COME OUT FOR A MINUTE. HYUNWOO'S HERE.
SINCE WHEN DO I NEED TO GO TO THE DOOR FOR HIM?
THAT'S TRUE, BUT HE IS WITH SOMEONE.
SAEYOUNG, YOU COULD TAKE FASHION TIPS FROM HER, HOW ABOUT YOU TRY OUTFITS LIKE HERS?

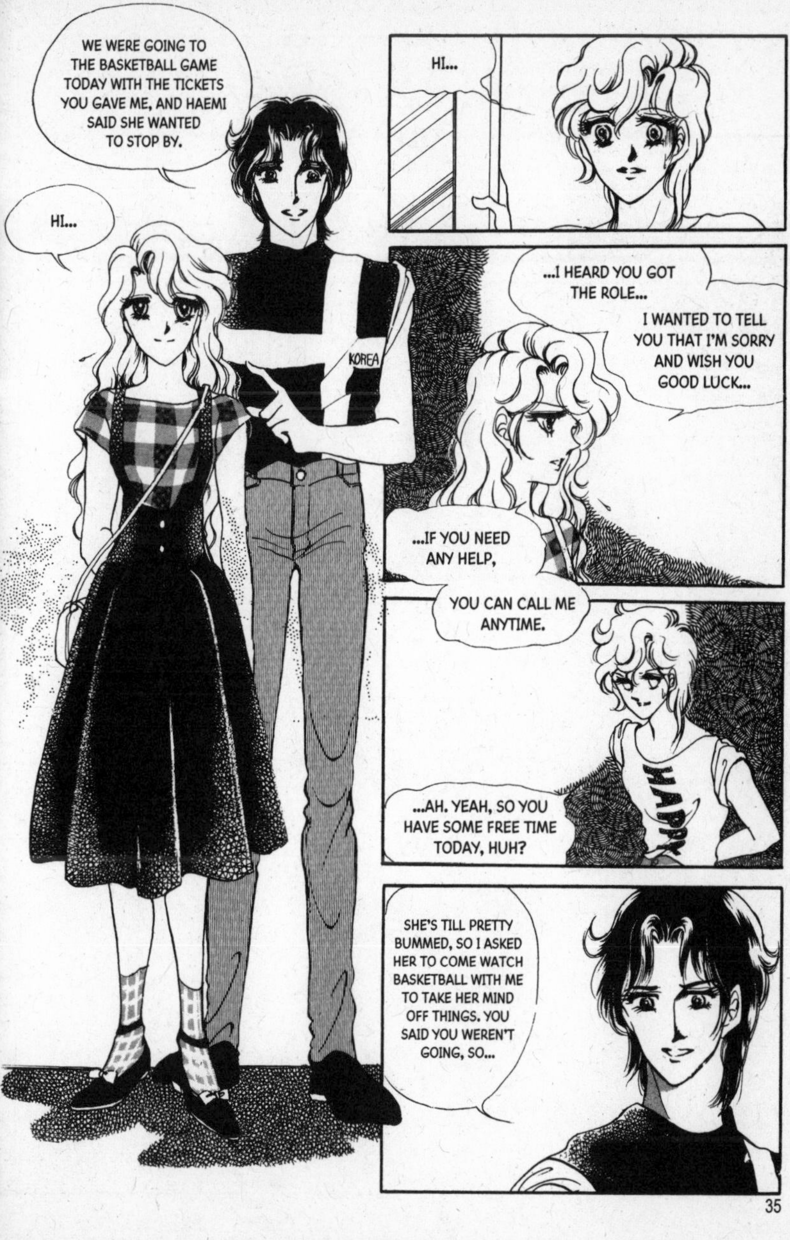

WE WERE GOING TO THE BASKETBALL GAME TODAY WITH THE TICKETS YOU GAVE ME, AND HAEMI SAID SHE WANTED TO STOP BY.
HI...
KOREA
HI...
...I HEARD YOU GOT THE ROLE...
I WANTED TO TELL YOU THAT I'M SORRY AND WISH YOU GOOD LUCK...
...IF YOU NEED ANY HELP,
YOU CAN CALL ME ANYTIME.
...AH. YEAH, SO YOU HAVE SOME FREE TIME TODAY, HUH?
SHE'S TILL PRETTY BUMMED, SO I ASKED HER TO COME WATCH BASKETBALL WITH ME TO TAKE HER MIND OFF THINGS. YOU SAID YOU WEREN'T GOING, SO...

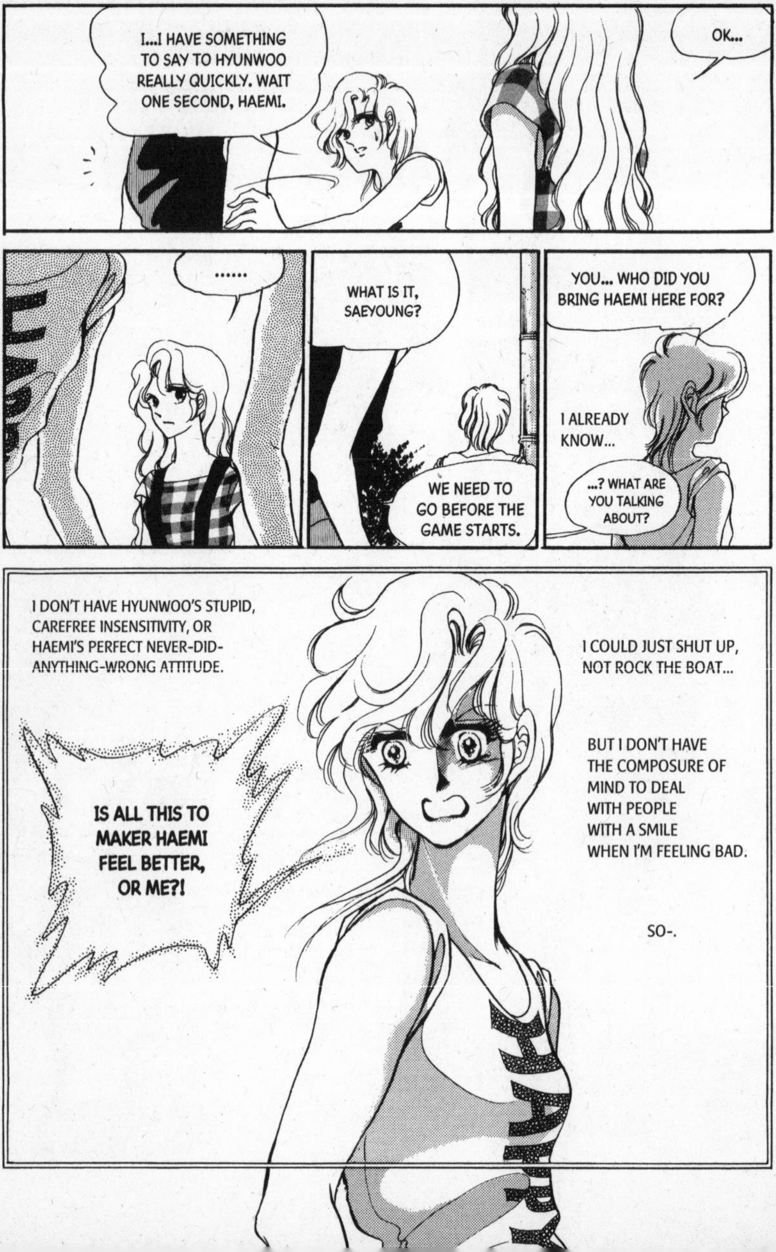
I...I HAVE SOMETHING TO SAY TO HYUNWOO REALLY QUICKLY. WAIT ONE SECOND, HAEMI.
OK...
......
WHAT IS IT, SAEYOUNG?
WE NEED TO GO BEFORE THE GAME STARTS.
YOU... WHO DID YOU BRING HAEMI HERE FOR?
I ALREADY KNOW...
...? WHAT ARE YOU TALKING ABOUT?
I DON'T HAVE HYUNWOO'S STUPID, CAREFREE INSENSITIVITY, OR HAEMI'S PERFECT NEVER-DID-ANYTHING-WRONG ATTITUDE.
I COULD JUST SHUT UP, NOT ROCK THE BOAT...
BUT I DON'T HAVE THE COMPOSURE OF MIND TO DEAL WITH PEOPLE WITH A SMILE WHEN I'M FEELING BAD.
SO-.
IS ALL THIS TO MAKER HAEMI FEEL BETTER, OR ME?!

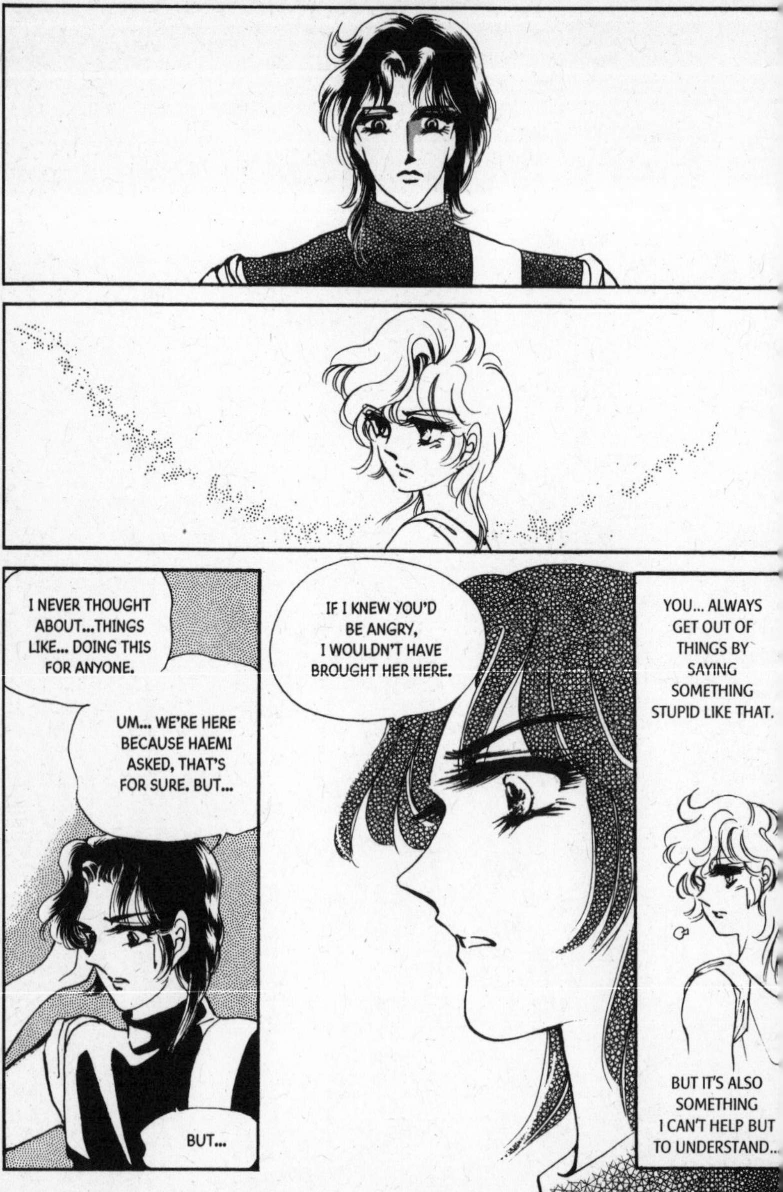
I NEVER THOUGHT ABOUT...THINGS LIKE... DOING THIS FOR ANYONE.
UM... WE'RE HERE BECAUSE HAEMI ASKED, THAT'S FOR SURE. BUT...
BUT...
IF I KNEW YOU'D BE ANGRY, I WOULDN'T HAVE BROUGHT HER HERE.
YOU... ALWAYS GET OUT OF THINGS BY SAYING SOMETHING STUPID LIKE THAT.
BUT IT'S ALSO SOMETHING I CAN'T HELP BUT TO UNDERSTAND...

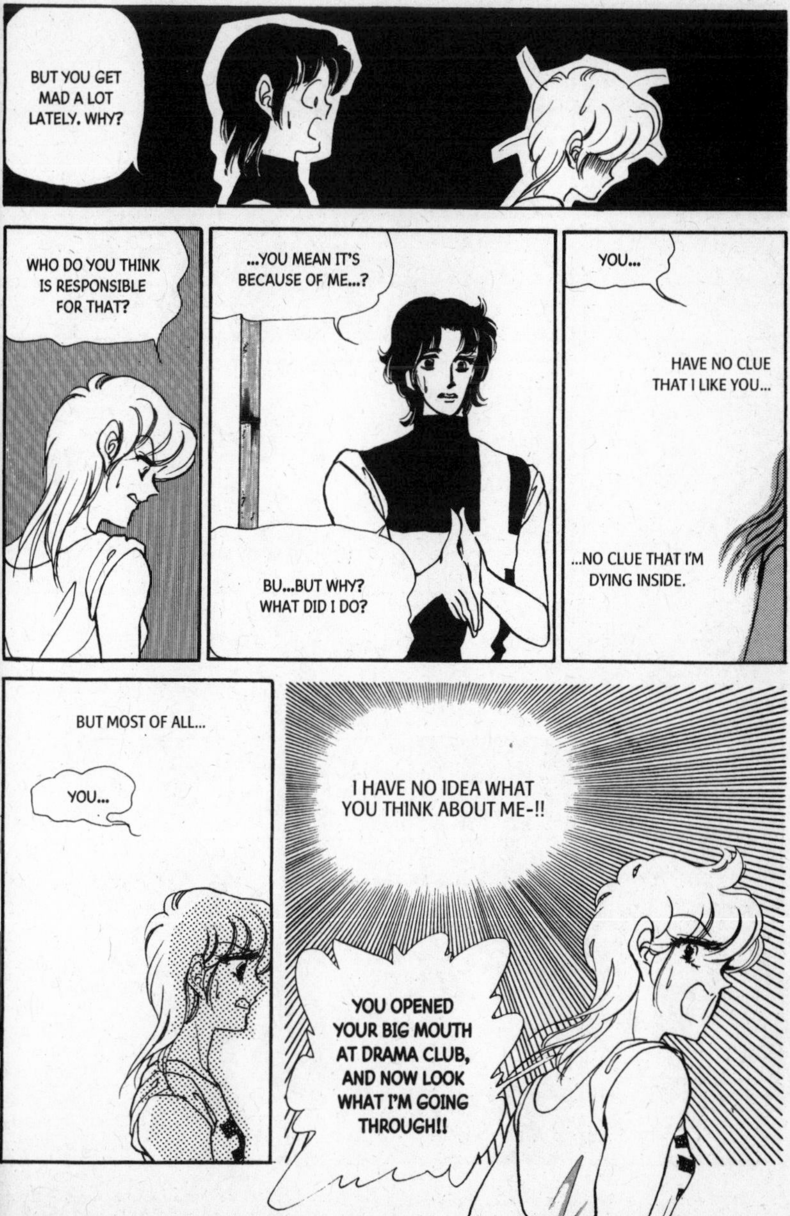

BUT YOU GET MAD A LOT LATELY. WHY?
WHO DO YOU THINK IS RESPONSIBLE FOR THAT?
...YOU MEAN IT'S BECAUSE OF ME...?
BU...BUT WHY? WHAT DID I DO?
YOU...
HAVE NO CLUE THAT I LIKE YOU...
...NO CLUE THAT I'M DYING INSIDE.
BUT MOST OF ALL...
YOU...
I HAVE NO IDEA WHAT YOU THINK ABOUT ME-!!
YOU OPENED YOUR BIG MOUTH AT DRAMA CLUB, AND NOW LOOK WHAT I'M GOING THROUGH!!

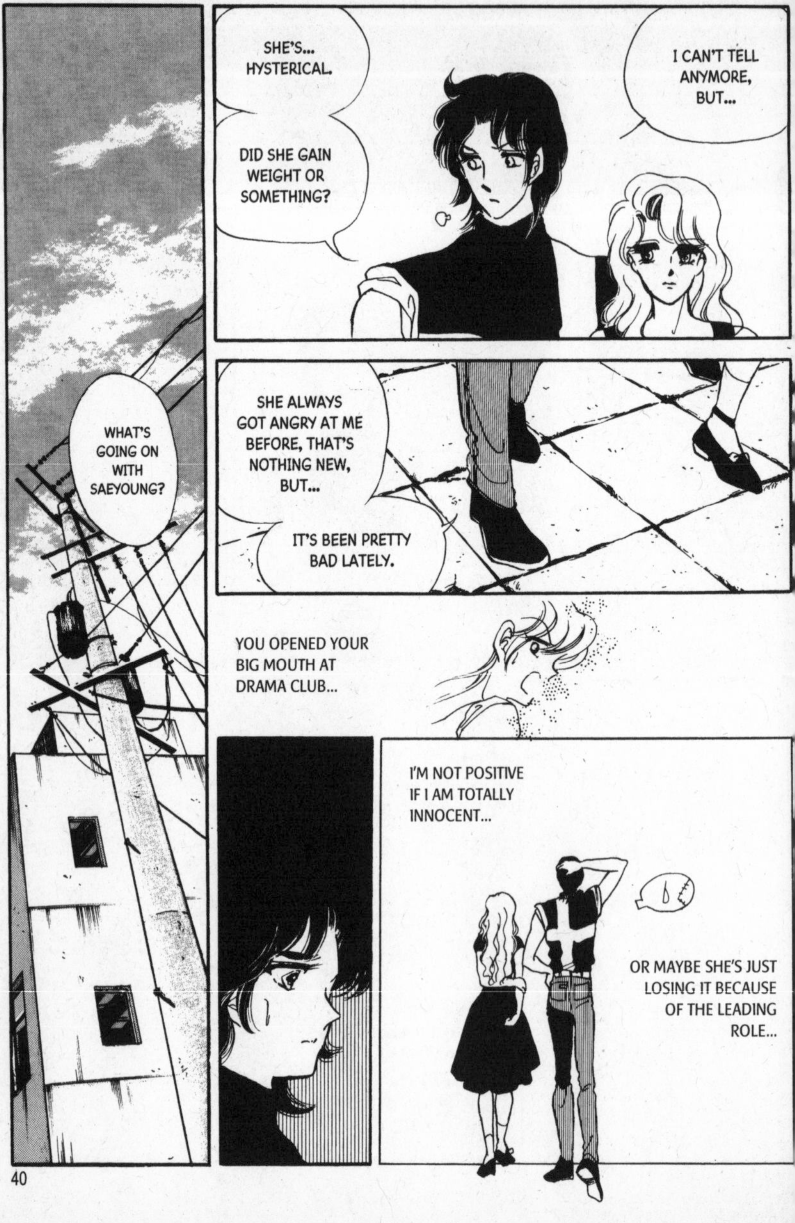
WHAT'S GOING ON WITH SAEYOUNG?
SHE'S... HYSTERICAL.
DID SHE GAIN WEIGHT OR SOMETHING?
I CAN'T TELL ANYMORE, BUT...
SHE ALWAYS GOT ANGRY AT ME BEFORE, THAT'S NOTHING NEW, BUT...
IT'S BEEN PRETTY BAD LATELY.
YOU OPENED YOUR BIG MOUTH AT DRAMA CLUB...
I'M NOT POSITIVE IF I AM TOTALLY INNOCENT...
OR MAYBE SHE'S JUST LOSING IT BECAUSE OF THE LEADING ROLE...

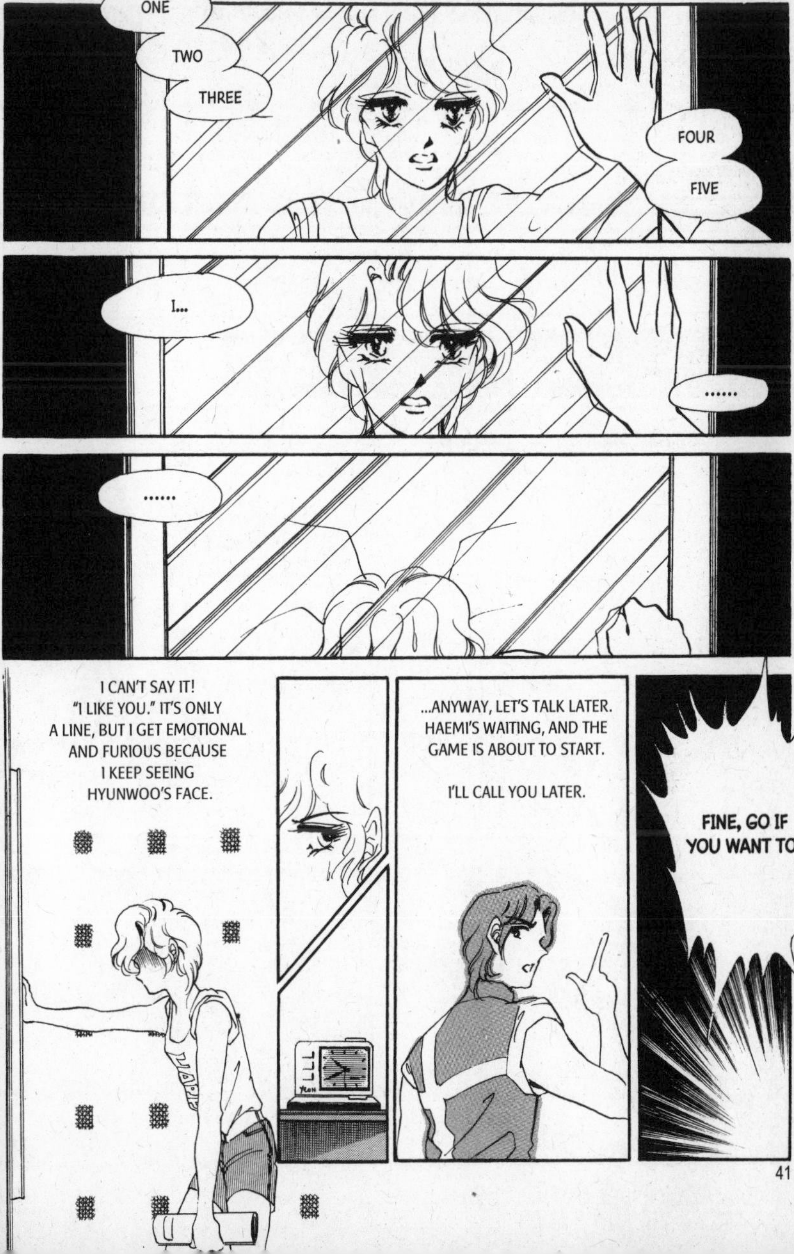
ONE
TWO
THREE
FOUR
FIVE
I...
......
......
I CAN'T SAY IT! "I LIKE YOU." IT'S ONLY A LINE, BUT I GET EMOTIONAL AND FURIOUS BECAUSE I KEEP SEEING HYUNWOO'S FACE.
...ANYWAY, LET'S TALK LATER. HAEMI'S WAITING, AND THE GAME IS ABOUT TO START.
I'LL CALL YOU LATER.
FINE, GO IF YOU WANT TO!

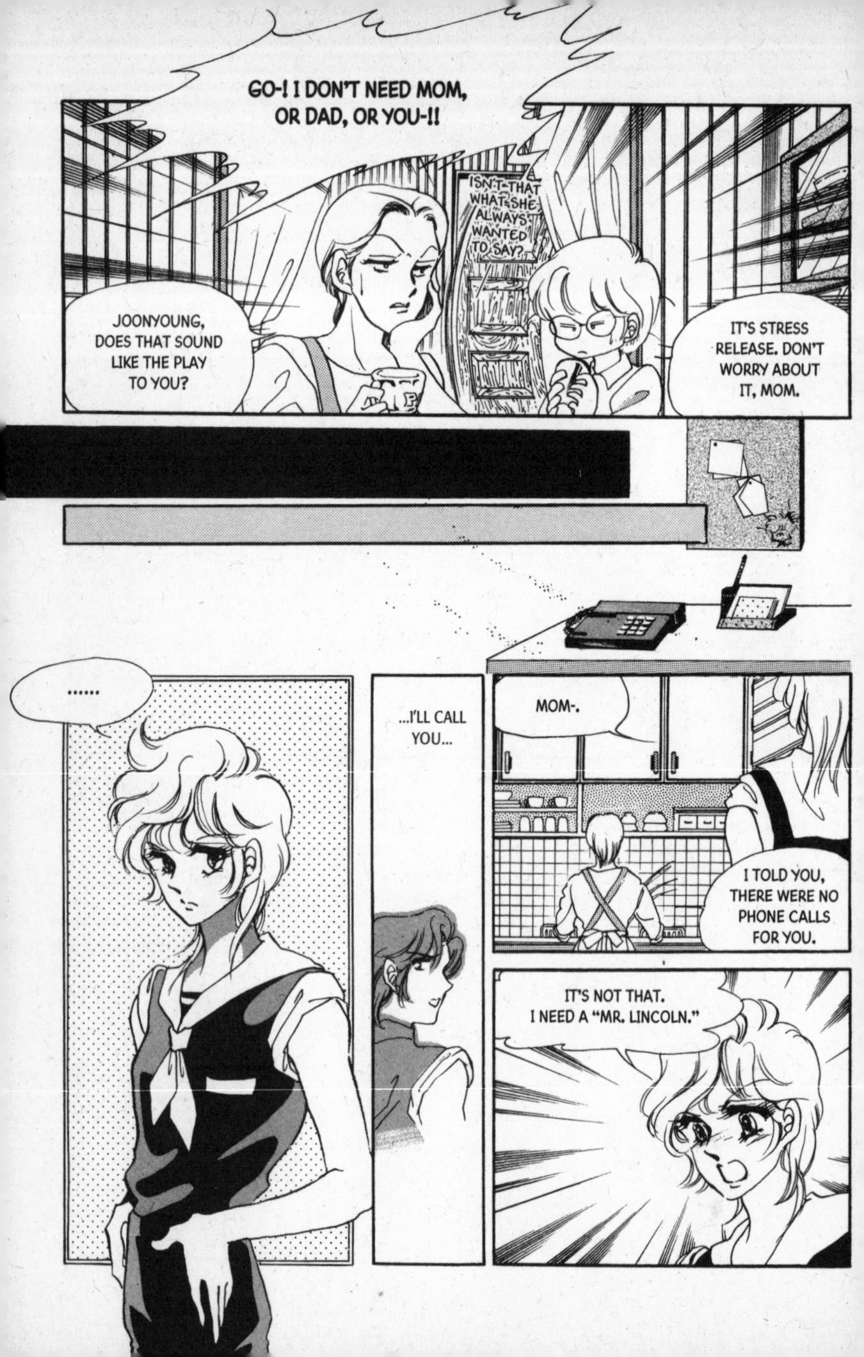
GO-! I DON'T NEED MOM, OR DAD, OR YOU-!!
JOONYOUNG, DOES THAT SOUND LIKE THE PLAY TO YOU?
ISN'T THAT WHAT SHE ALWAYS WANTED TO SAY?
IT'S STRESS RELEASE. DON'T WORRY ABOUT IT, MOM.
......
...I'LL CALL YOU...
MOM-.
I TOLD YOU, THERE WERE NO PHONE CALLS FOR YOU.
IT'S NOT THAT. I NEED A "MR. LINCOLN."

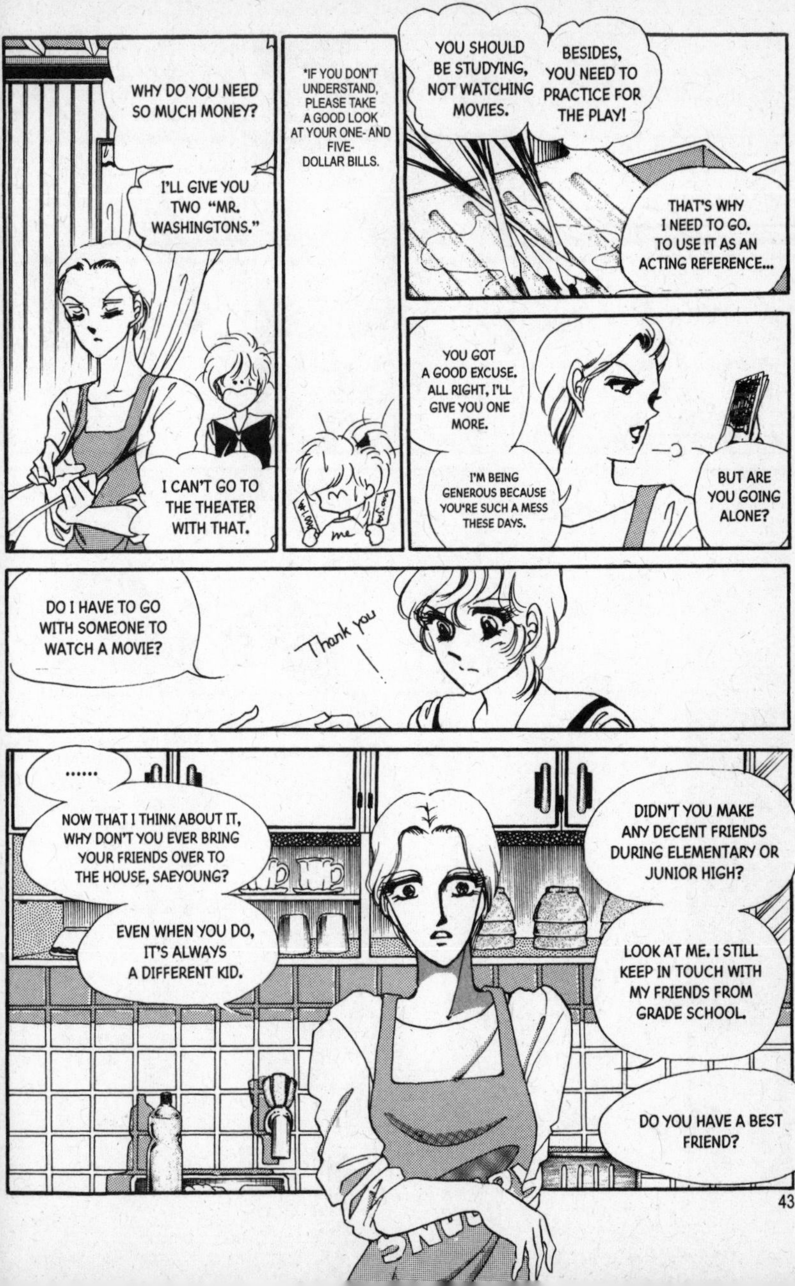
WHY DO YOU NEED SO MUCH MONEY?
I'LL GIVE YOU TWO "MR. WASHINGTONS."
I CAN'T GO TO THE THEATER WITH THAT.
*IF YOU DON'T UNDERSTAND, PLEASE TAKE A GOOD LOOK AT YOUR ONE- AND FIVE-DOLLAR BILLS.
me
YOU SHOULD BE STUDYING, NOT WATCHING MOVIES.
BESIDES, YOU NEED TO PRACTICE FOR THE PLAY!
THAT'S WHY I NEED TO GO. TO USE IT AS AN ACTING REFERENCE...
YOU GOT A GOOD EXCUSE. ALL RIGHT, I'LL GIVE YOU ONE MORE.
I'M BEING GENEROUS BECAUSE YOU'RE SUCH A MESS THESE DAYS.
BUT ARE YOU GOING ALONE?
DO I HAVE TO GO WITH SOMEONE TO WATCH A MOVIE?
Thank you
......
NOW THAT I THINK ABOUT IT, WHY DON'T YOU EVER BRING YOUR FRIENDS OVER TO THE HOUSE, SAEYOUNG?
EVEN WHEN YOU DO, IT'S ALWAYS A DIFFERENT KID.
DIDN'T YOU MAKE ANY DECENT FRIENDS DURING ELEMENTARY OR JUNIOR HIGH?
LOOK AT ME. I STILL KEEP IN TOUCH WITH MY FRIENDS FROM GRADE SCHOOL.
DO YOU HAVE A BEST FRIEND?

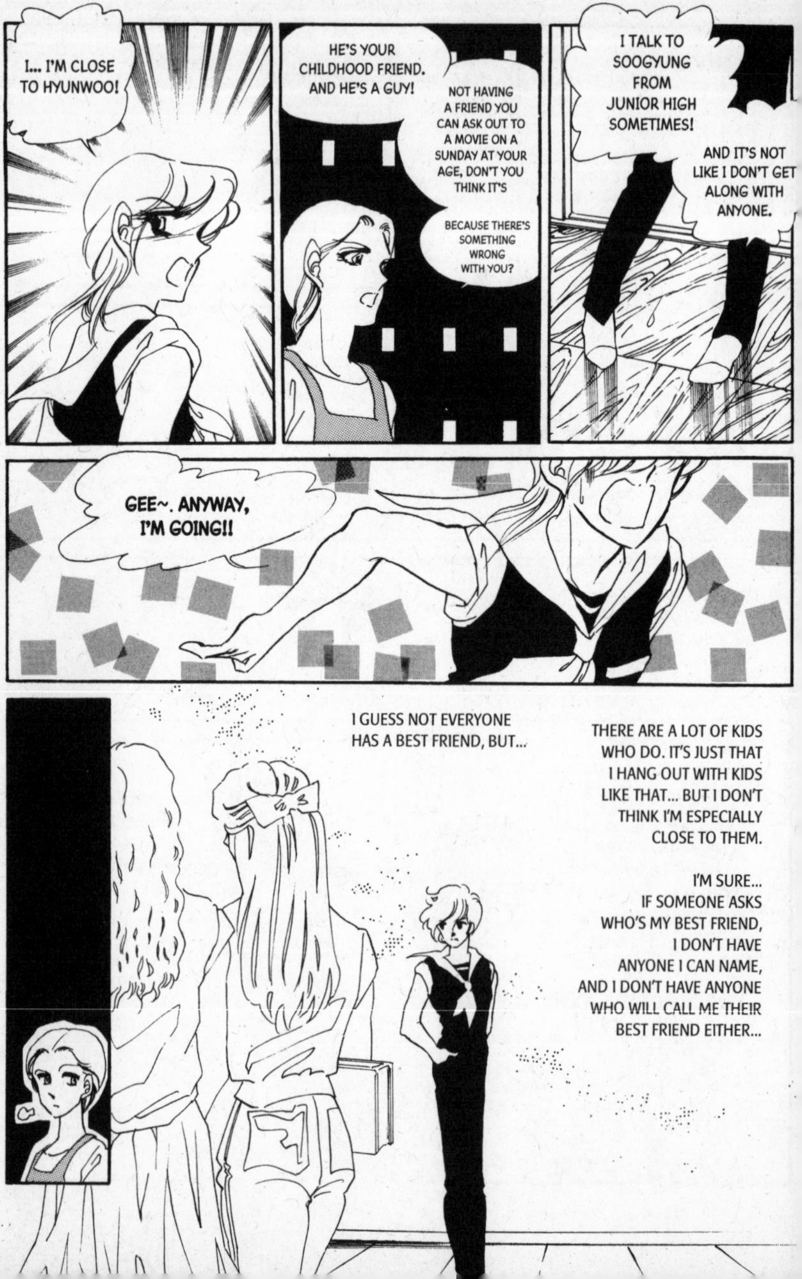
I... I'M CLOSE TO HYUNWOO!
HE'S YOUR CHILDHOOD FRIEND. AND HE'S A GUY!
NOT HAVING A FRIEND YOU CAN ASK OUT TO A MOVIE ON A SUNDAY AT YOUR AGE, DON'T YOU THINK IT'S
BECAUSE THERE'S SOMETHING WRONG WITH YOU?
I TALK TO SOOGYUNG FROM JUNIOR HIGH SOMETIMES!
AND IT'S NOT LIKE I DON'T GET ALONG WITH ANYONE.
GEE~. ANYWAY, I'M GOING!!
I GUESS NOT EVERYONE HAS A BEST FRIEND, BUT...
THERE ARE A LOT OF KIDS WHO DO. IT'S JUST THAT I HANG OUT WITH KIDS LIKE THAT... BUT I DON'T THINK I'M ESPECIALLY CLOSE TO THEM.
I'M SURE... IF SOMEONE ASKS WHO'S MY BEST FRIEND, I DON'T HAVE ANYONE I CAN NAME, AND I DON'T HAVE ANYONE WHO WILL CALL ME THEIR BEST FRIEND EITHER...

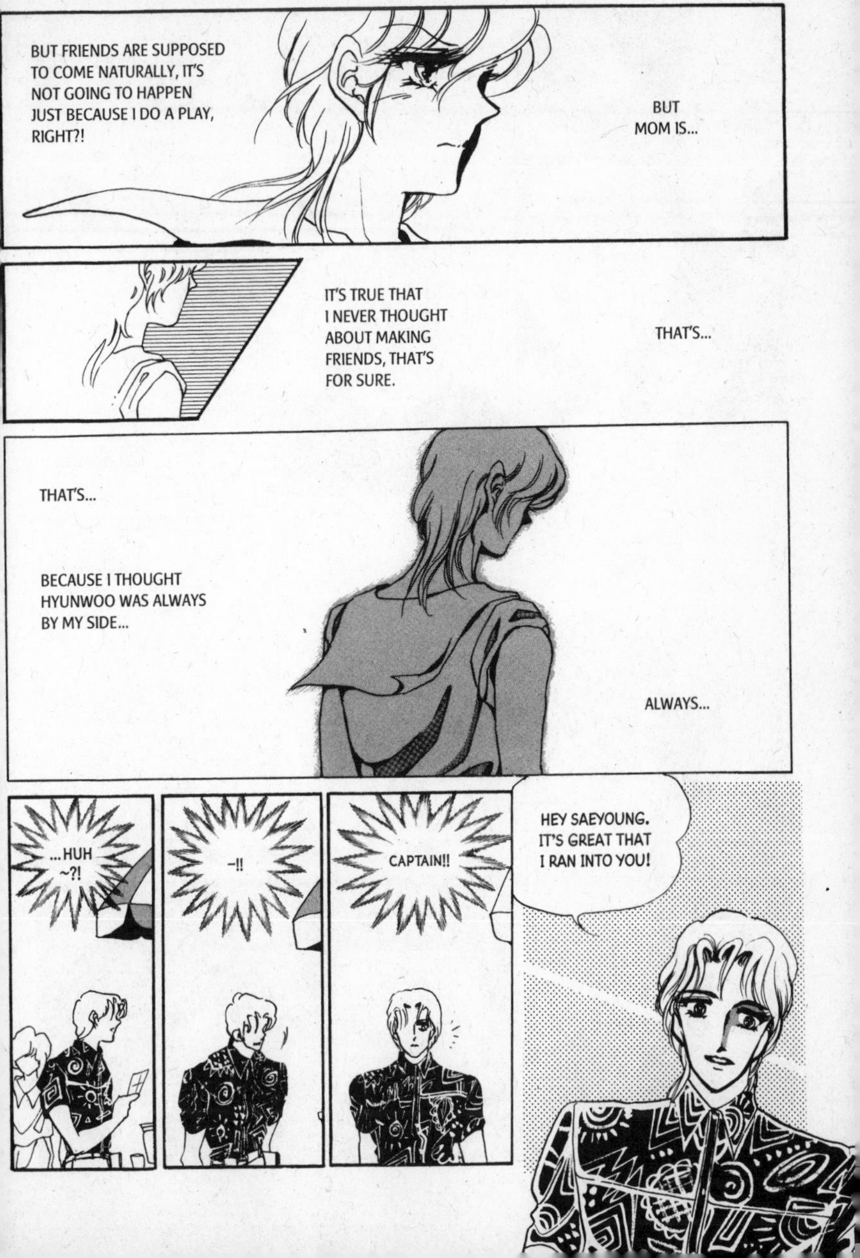
BUT FRIENDS ARE SUPPOSED TO COME NATURALLY, IT'S NOT GOING TO HAPPEN JUST BECAUSE I DO A PLAY, RIGHT?!
BUT MOM IS...
IT'S TRUE THAT I NEVER THOUGHT ABOUT MAKING FRIENDS, THAT'S FOR SURE.
THAT'S...
THAT'S...
BECAUSE I THOUGHT HYUNWOO WAS ALWAYS BY MY SIDE...
ALWAYS...
...HUH ~?!
-!!
CAPTAIN!!
HEY SAEYOUNG. IT'S GREAT THAT I RAN INTO YOU!

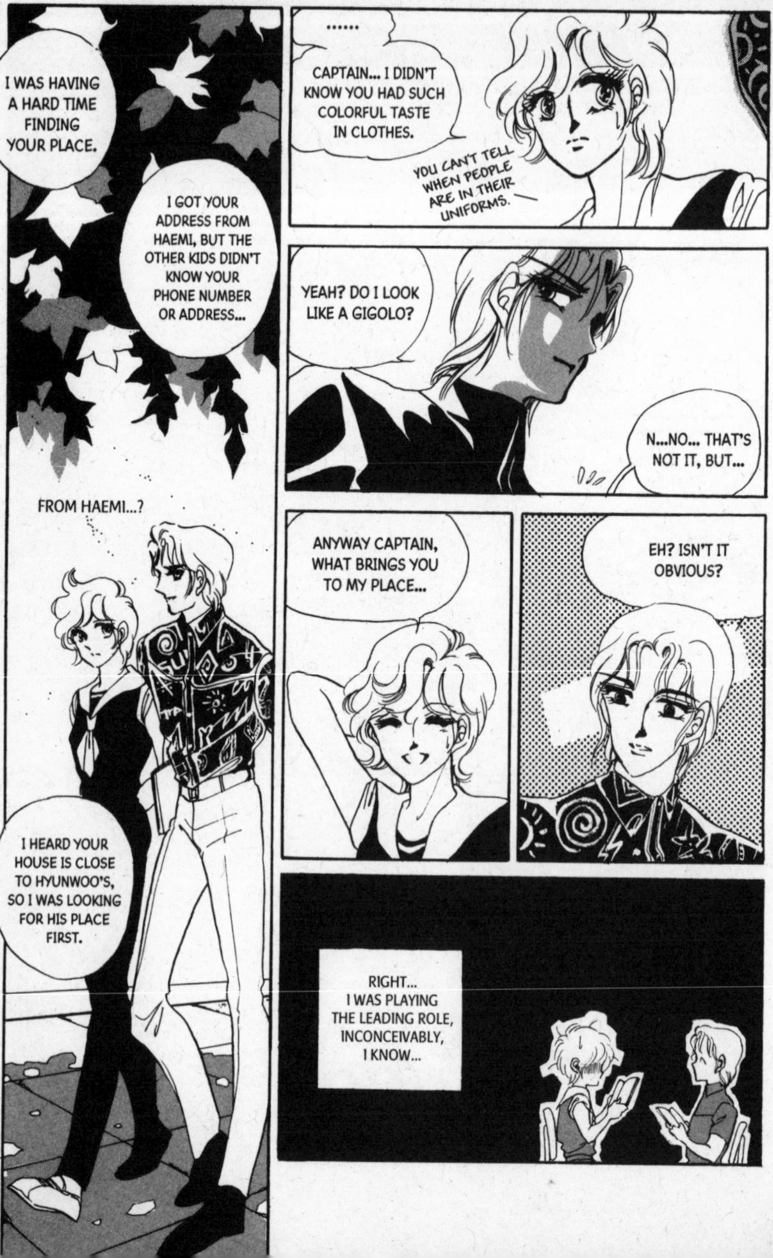
I WAS HAVING A HARD TIME FINDING YOUR PLACE.
I GOT YOUR ADDRESS FROM HAEMI, BUT THE OTHER KIDS DIDN'T KNOW YOUR PHONE NUMBER OR ADDRESS...
FROM HAEMI...?
I HEARD YOUR HOUSE IS CLOSE TO HYUNWOO'S, SO I WAS LOOKING FOR HIS PLACE FIRST.
......
CAPTAIN... I DIDN'T KNOW YOU HAD SUCH COLORFUL TASTE IN CLOTHES.
YOU CAN'T TELL WHEN PEOPLE ARE IN THEIR UNIFORMS.
YEAH? DO I LOOK LIKE A GIGOLO?
N...NO... THAT'S NOT IT, BUT...
ANYWAY CAPTAIN, WHAT BRINGS YOU TO MY PLACE...
EH? ISN'T IT OBVIOUS?
RIGHT... I WAS PLAYING THE LEADING ROLE, INCONCEIVABLY, I KNOW...

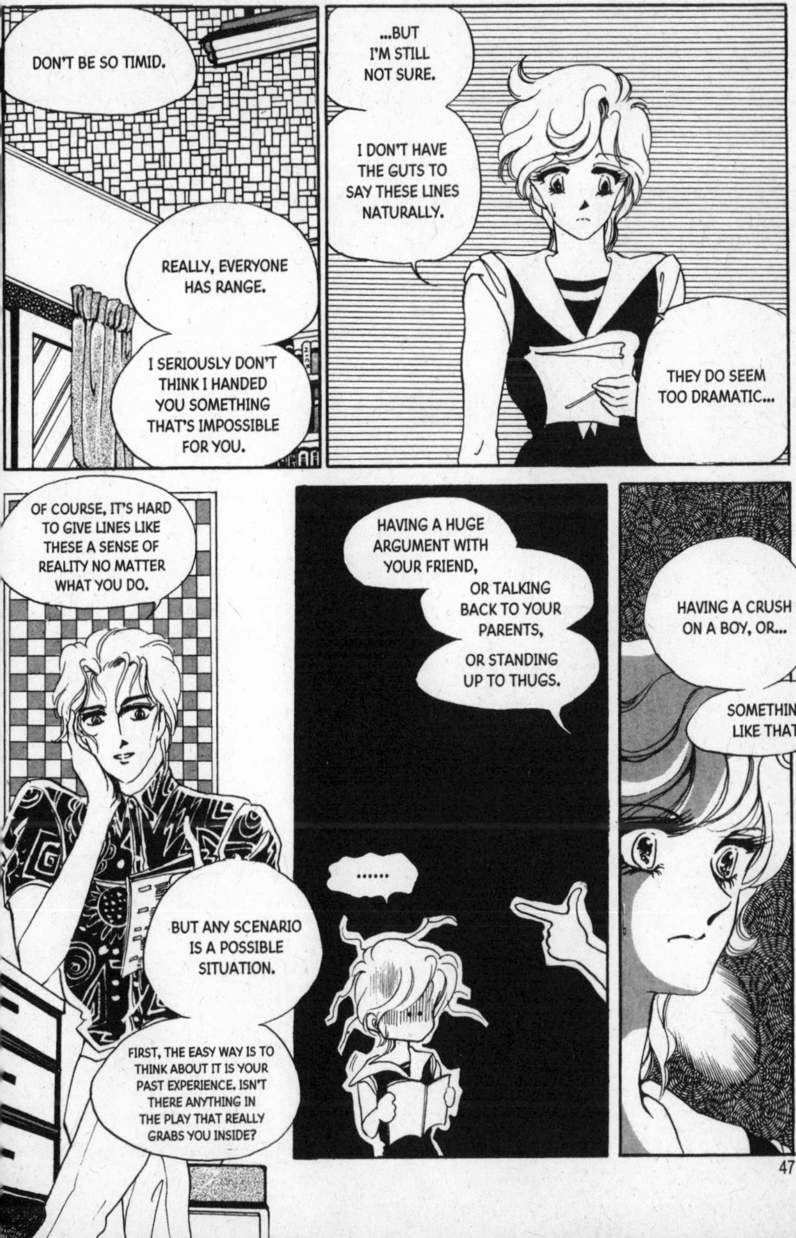
DON'T BE SO TIMID.
REALLY, EVERYONE HAS RANGE.
I SERIOUSLY DON'T THINK I HANDED YOU SOMETHING THAT'S IMPOSSIBLE FOR YOU.
...BUT I'M STILL NOT SURE.
I DON'T HAVE THE GUTS TO SAY THESE LINES NATURALLY.
THEY DO SEEM TOO DRAMATIC...
OF COURSE, IT'S HARD TO GIVE LINES LIKE THESE A SENSE OF REALITY NO MATTER WHAT YOU DO.
BUT ANY SCENARIO IS A POSSIBLE SITUATION.
FIRST, THE EASY WAY IS TO THINK ABOUT IT IS YOUR PAST EXPERIENCE. ISN'T THERE ANYTHING IN THE PLAY THAT REALLY GRABS YOU INSIDE?
HAVING A HUGE ARGUMENT WITH YOUR FRIEND,
OR TALKING BACK TO YOUR PARENTS,
OR STANDING UP TO THUGS.
......
HAVING A CRUSH ON A BOY, OR...
SOMETHING LIKE THAT.

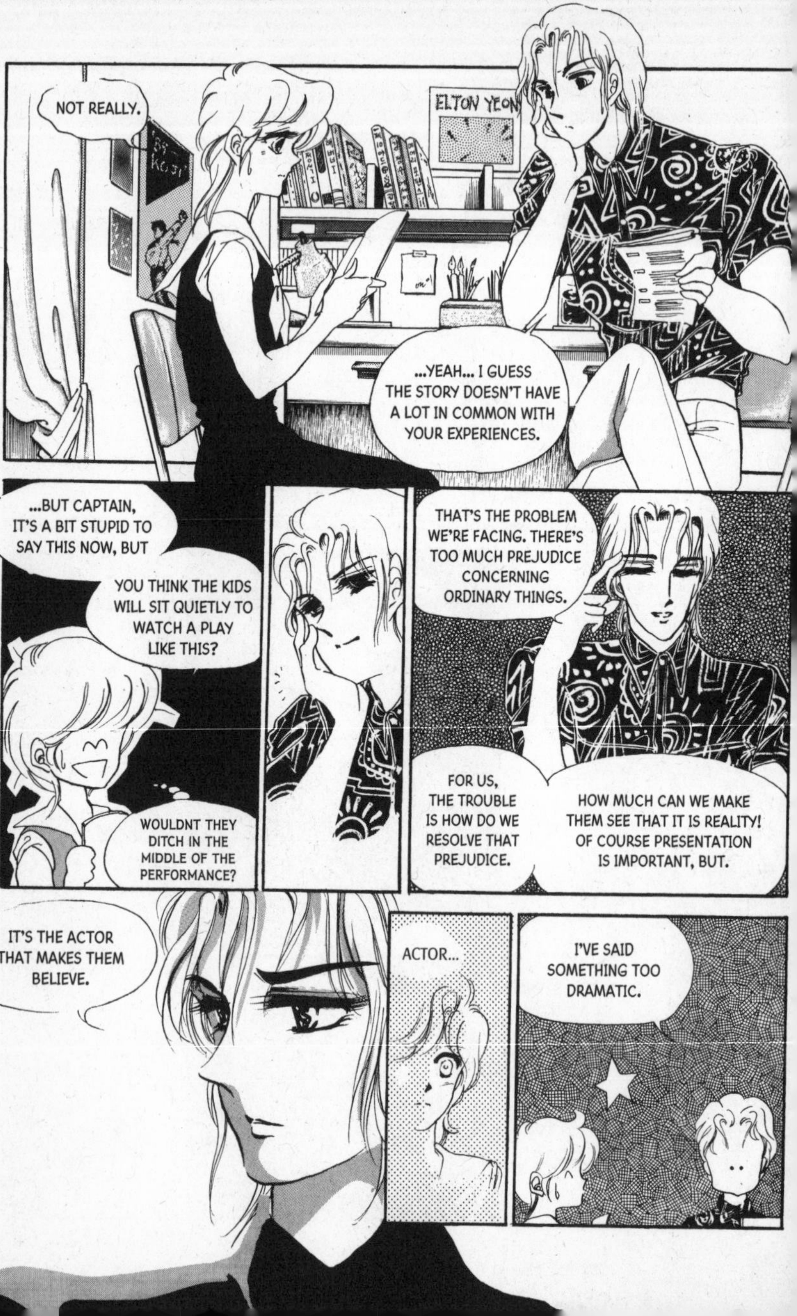
NOT REALLY.
ELTON YEON
...YEAH... I GUESS THE STORY DOESN'T HAVE A LOT IN COMMON WITH YOUR EXPERIENCES.
...BUT CAPTAIN, IT'S A BIT STUPID TO SAY THIS NOW, BUT
YOU THINK THE KIDS WILL SIT QUIETLY TO WATCH A PLAY LIKE THIS?
WOULDNT THEY DITCH IN THE MIDDLE OF THE PERFORMANCE?
THAT'S THE PROBLEM WE'RE FACING. THERE'S TOO MUCH PREJUDICE CONCERNING ORDINARY THINGS.
FOR US, THE TROUBLE IS HOW DO WE RESOLVE THAT PREJUDICE.
HOW MUCH CAN WE MAKE THEM SEE THAT IT IS REALITY! OF COURSE PRESENTATION IS IMPORTANT, BUT.
IT'S THE ACTOR THAT MAKES THEM BELIEVE.
ACTOR...
I'VE SAID SOMETHING TOO DRAMATIC.

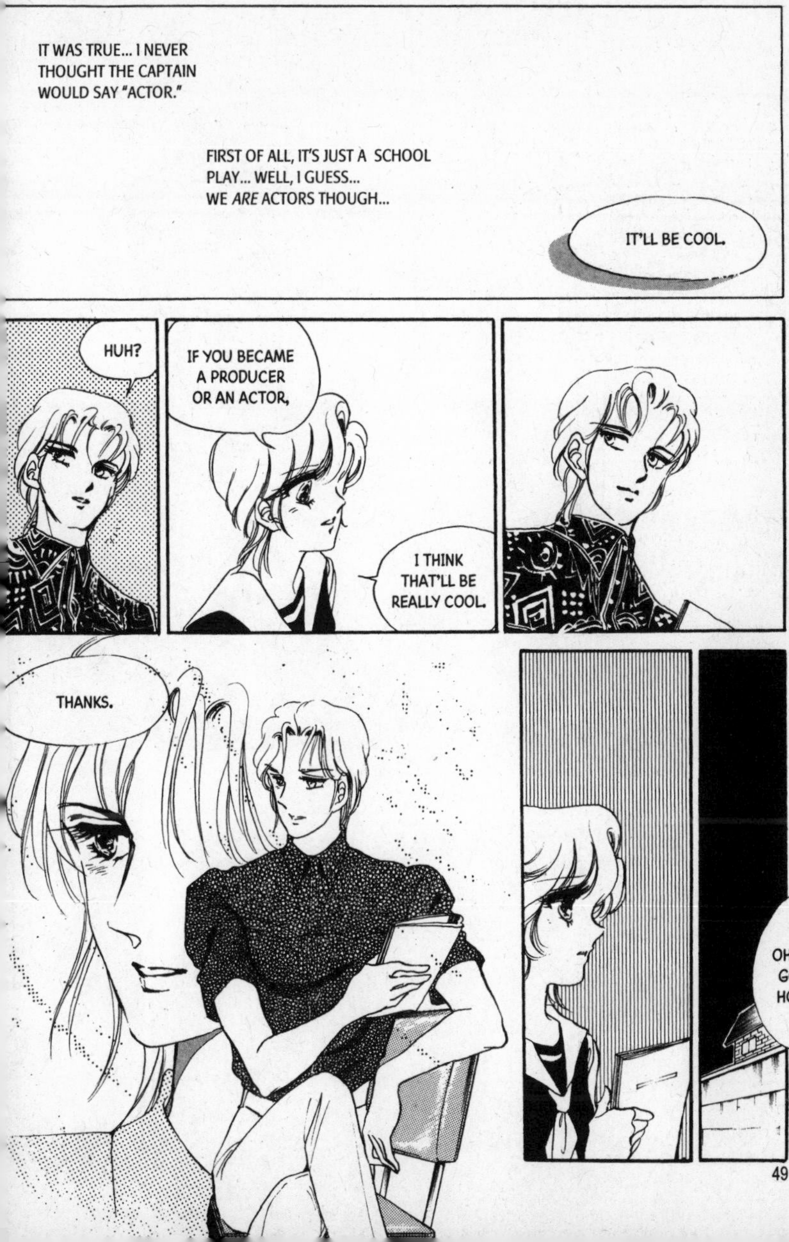

IT WAS TRUE... I NEVER THOUGHT THE CAPTAIN WOULD SAY "ACTOR."
FIRST OF ALL, IT'S JUST A SCHOOL PLAY... WELL, I GUESS... WE *ARE* ACTORS THOUGH...
IT'LL BE COOL.
HUH?
IF YOU BECAME A PRODUCER OR AN ACTOR,
I THINK THAT'LL BE REALLY COOL.
THANKS.
OH, YOU GOING HOME?

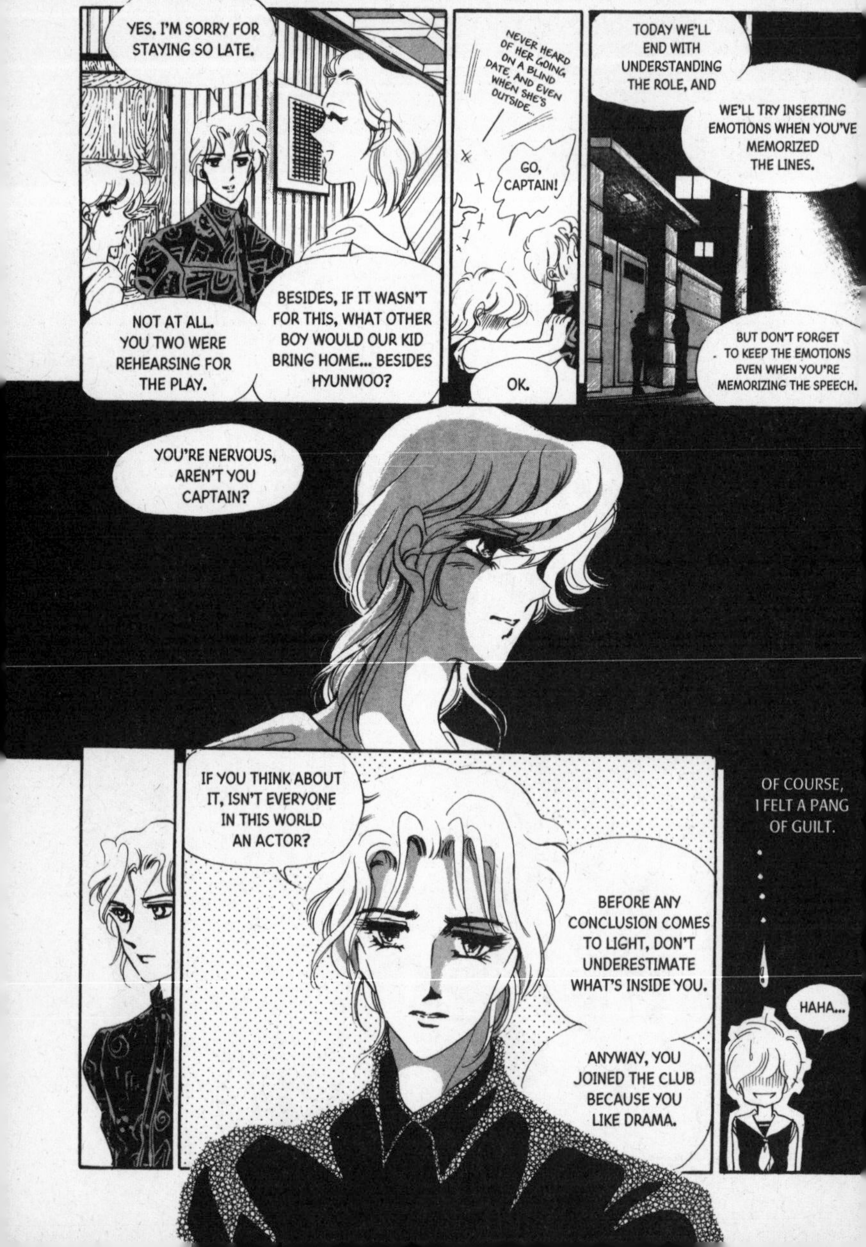
YES. I'M SORRY FOR STAYING SO LATE.
NOT AT ALL. YOU TWO WERE REHEARSING FOR THE PLAY.
BESIDES, IF IT WASN'T FOR THIS, WHAT OTHER BOY WOULD OUR KID BRING HOME... BESIDES HYUNWOO?
NEVER HEARD OF HER GOING ON A BLIND DATE, AND EVEN WHEN SHE'S OUTSIDE...
GO, CAPTAIN!
OK.
TODAY WE'LL END WITH UNDERSTANDING THE ROLE, AND
WE'LL TRY INSERTING EMOTIONS WHEN YOU'VE MEMORIZED THE LINES.
BUT DON'T FORGET TO KEEP THE EMOTIONS EVEN WHEN YOU'RE MEMORIZING THE SPEECH.
YOU'RE NERVOUS, AREN'T YOU CAPTAIN?
IF YOU THINK ABOUT IT, ISN'T EVERYONE IN THIS WORLD AN ACTOR?
BEFORE ANY CONCLUSION COMES TO LIGHT, DON'T UNDERESTIMATE WHAT'S INSIDE YOU.
ANYWAY, YOU JOINED THE CLUB BECAUSE YOU LIKE DRAMA.
OF COURSE, I FELT A PANG OF GUILT.
HAHA...

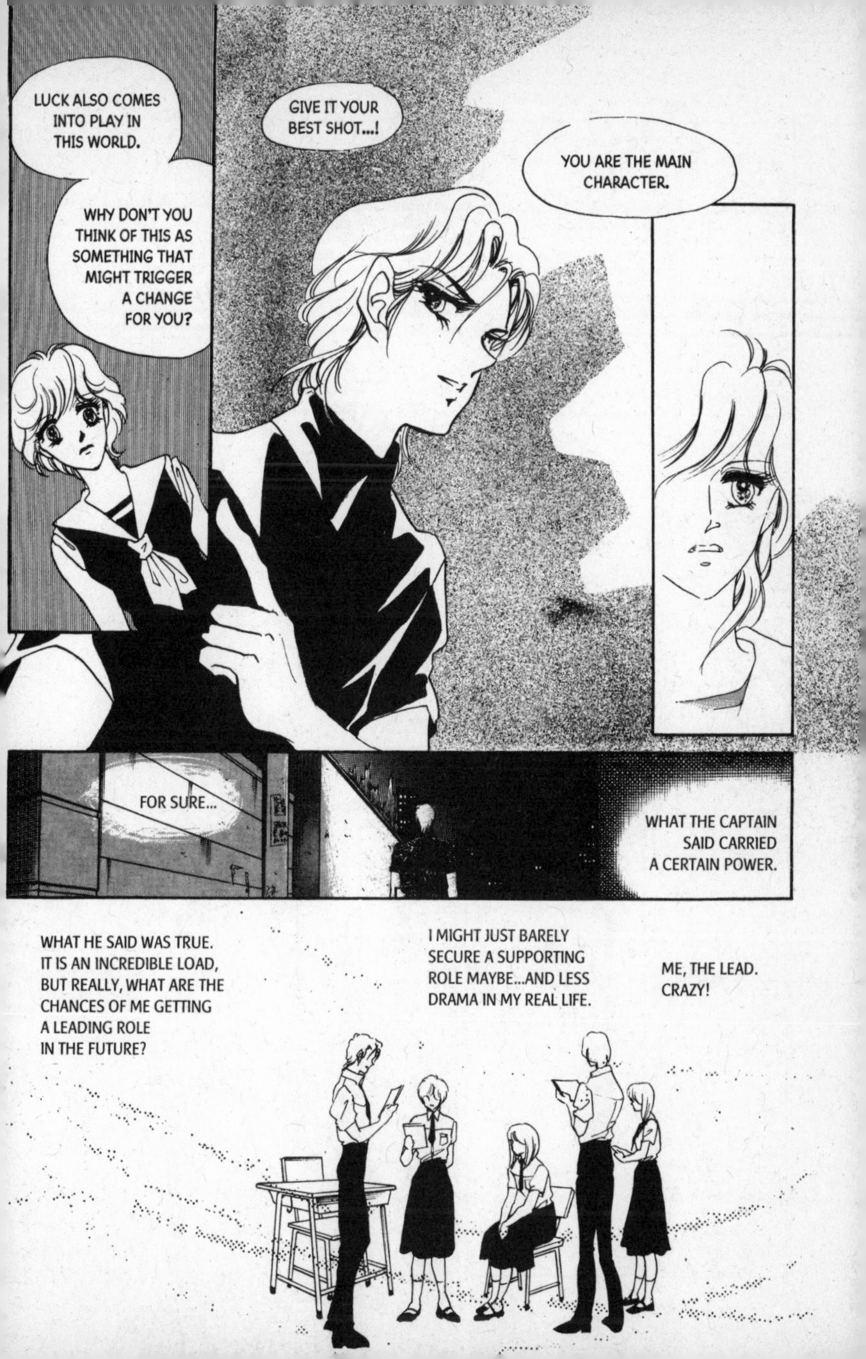
LUCK ALSO COMES INTO PLAY IN THIS WORLD.
WHY DON'T YOU THINK OF THIS AS SOMETHING THAT MIGHT TRIGGER A CHANGE FOR YOU?
GIVE IT YOUR BEST SHOT...!
YOU ARE THE MAIN CHARACTER.
FOR SURE...
WHAT THE CAPTAIN SAID CARRIED A CERTAIN POWER.
WHAT HE SAID WAS TRUE. IT IS AN INCREDIBLE LOAD, BUT REALLY, WHAT ARE THE CHANCES OF ME GETTING A LEADING ROLE IN THE FUTURE?
I MIGHT JUST BARELY SECURE A SUPPORTING ROLE MAYBE...AND LESS DRAMA IN MY REAL LIFE.
ME, THE LEAD. CRAZY!

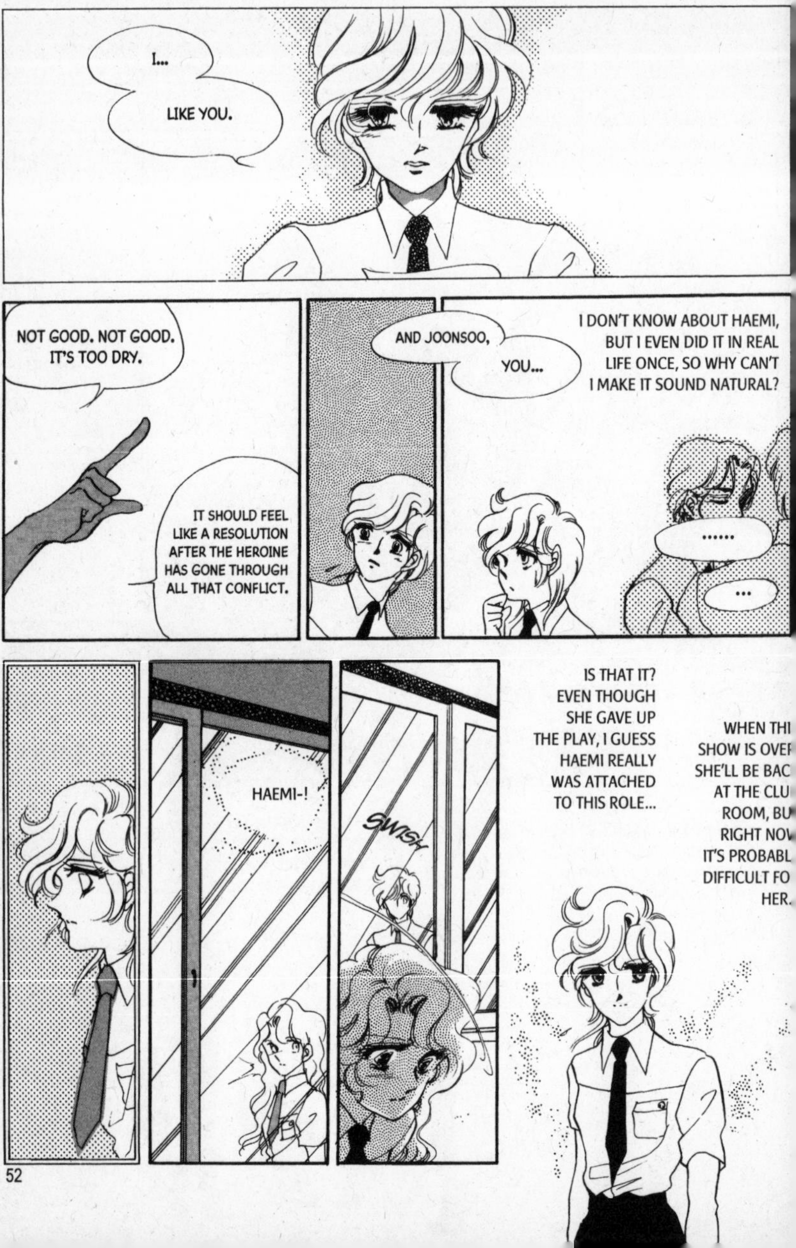
I...
LIKE YOU.
NOT GOOD. NOT GOOD. IT'S TOO DRY.
IT SHOULD FEEL LIKE A RESOLUTION AFTER THE HEROINE HAS GONE THROUGH ALL THAT CONFLICT.
AND JOONSOO,
YOU...
I DON'T KNOW ABOUT HAEMI, BUT I EVEN DID IT IN REAL LIFE ONCE, SO WHY CAN'T I MAKE IT SOUND NATURAL?
......
...
HAEMI-!
SWISH
IS THAT IT? EVEN THOUGH SHE GAVE UP THE PLAY, I GUESS HAEMI REALLY WAS ATTACHED TO THIS ROLE...
WHEN THI SHOW IS OVEI SHE'LL BE BAC AT THE CLU ROOM, BU RIGHT NOV IT'S PROBABL DIFFICULT FO HER.

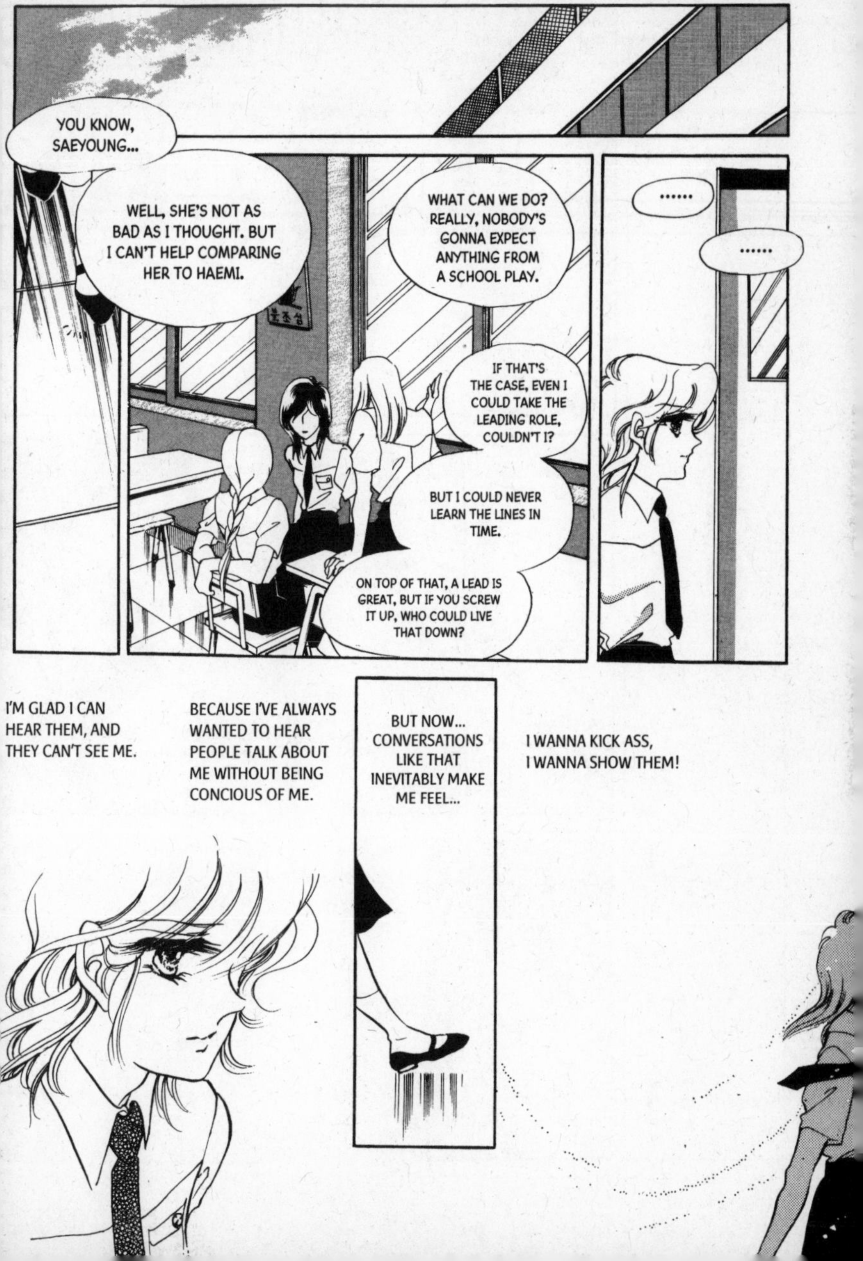

YOU KNOW, SAEYOUNG...
WELL, SHE'S NOT AS BAD AS I THOUGHT. BUT I CAN'T HELP COMPARING HER TO HAEMI.
WHAT CAN WE DO? REALLY, NOBODY'S GONNA EXPECT ANYTHING FROM A SCHOOL PLAY.
IF THAT'S THE CASE, EVEN I COULD TAKE THE LEADING ROLE, COULDN'T I?
BUT I COULD NEVER LEARN THE LINES IN TIME.
ON TOP OF THAT, A LEAD IS GREAT, BUT IF YOU SCREW IT UP, WHO COULD LIVE THAT DOWN?
......
......
I'M GLAD I CAN HEAR THEM, AND THEY CAN'T SEE ME.
BECAUSE I'VE ALWAYS WANTED TO HEAR PEOPLE TALK ABOUT ME WITHOUT BEING CONCIOUS OF ME.
BUT NOW... CONVERSATIONS LIKE THAT INEVITABLY MAKE ME FEEL...
I WANNA KICK ASS, I WANNA SHOW THEM!

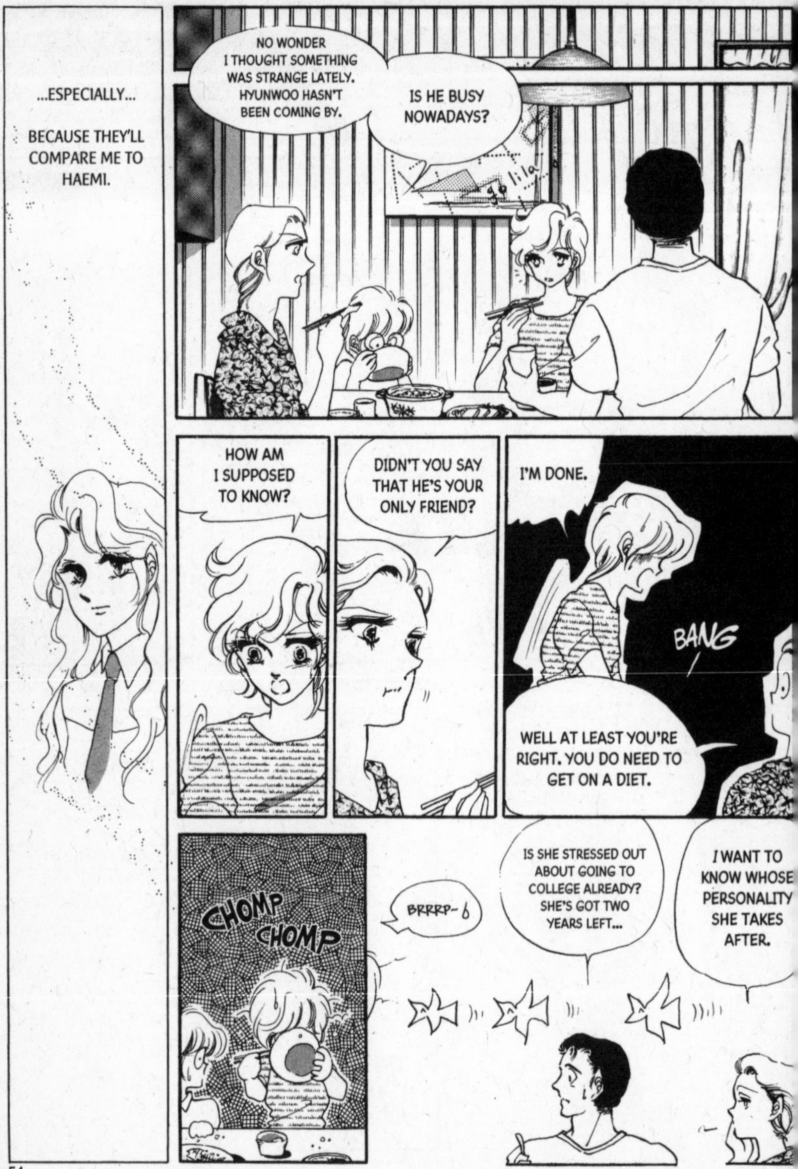
...ESPECIALLY...
BECAUSE THEY'LL COMPARE ME TO HAEMI.
NO WONDER I THOUGHT SOMETHING WAS STRANGE LATELY. HYUNWOO HASN'T BEEN COMING BY.
IS HE BUSY NOWADAYS?
HOW AM I SUPPOSED TO KNOW?
DIDN'T YOU SAY THAT HE'S YOUR ONLY FRIEND?
I'M DONE.
BANG
WELL AT LEAST YOU'RE RIGHT. YOU DO NEED TO GET ON A DIET.
CHOMP CHOMP
BRRRP-
IS SHE STRESSED OUT ABOUT GOING TO COLLEGE ALREADY? SHE'S GOT TWO YEARS LEFT...
I WANT TO KNOW WHOSE PERSONALITY SHE TAKES AFTER.

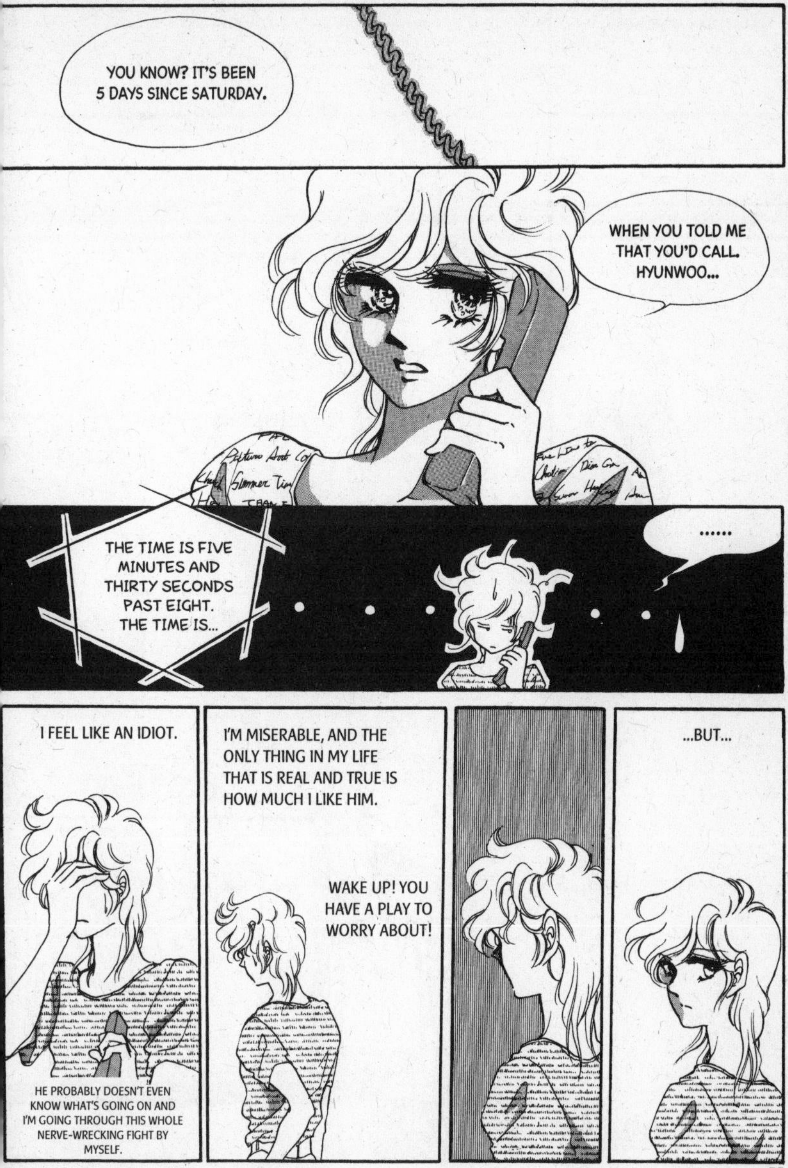
YOU KNOW? IT'S BEEN 5 DAYS SINCE SATURDAY.
WHEN YOU TOLD ME THAT YOU'D CALL. HYUNWOO...
THE TIME IS FIVE MINUTES AND THIRTY SECONDS PAST EIGHT. THE TIME IS...
......
I FEEL LIKE AN IDIOT.
HE PROBABLY DOESN'T EVEN KNOW WHAT'S GOING ON AND I'M GOING THROUGH THIS WHOLE NERVE-WRECKING FIGHT BY MYSELF.
I'M MISERABLE, AND THE ONLY THING IN MY LIFE THAT IS REAL AND TRUE IS HOW MUCH I LIKE HIM.
WAKE UP! YOU HAVE A PLAY TO WORRY ABOUT!
...BUT...

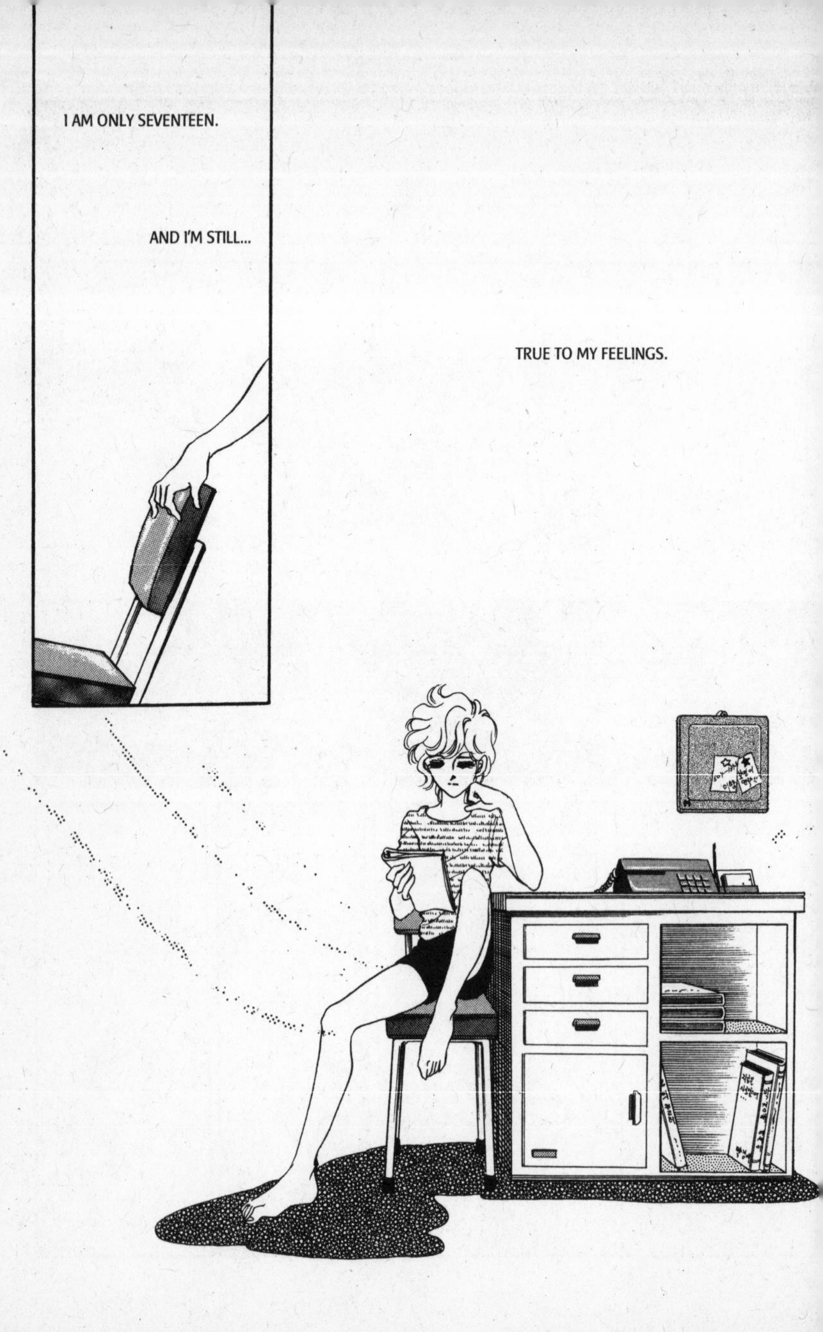
I AM ONLY SEVENTEEN.
AND I'M STILL...
TRUE TO MY FEELINGS.

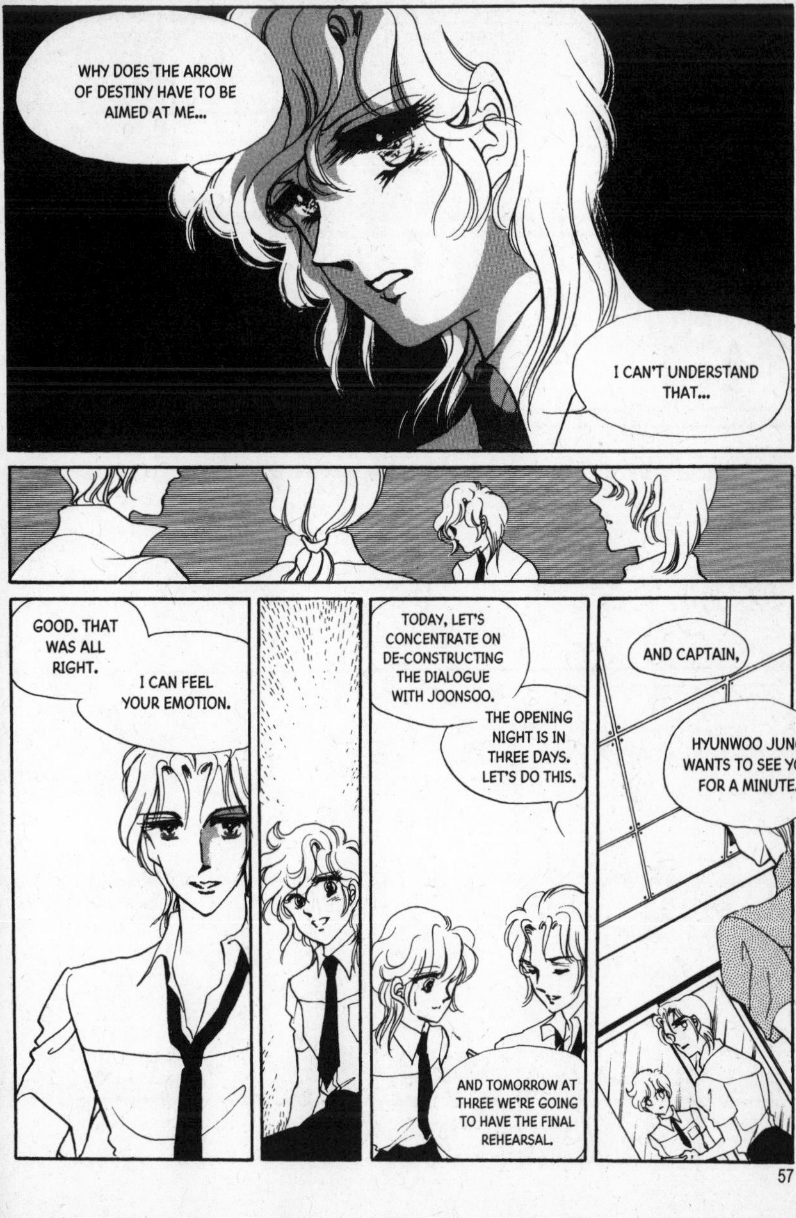
WHY DOES THE ARROW OF DESTINY HAVE TO BE AIMED AT ME...
I CAN'T UNDERSTAND THAT...
GOOD. THAT WAS ALL RIGHT.
I CAN FEEL YOUR EMOTION.
TODAY, LET'S CONCENTRATE ON DE-CONSTRUCTING THE DIALOGUE WITH JOONSOO.
THE OPENING NIGHT IS IN THREE DAYS. LET'S DO THIS.
AND TOMORROW AT THREE WE'RE GOING TO HAVE THE FINAL REHEARSAL.
AND CAPTAIN,
HYUNWOO JUNG WANTS TO SEE YOU FOR A MINUTE.

HEY SAEYOUNG.

I HAVEN'T BEEN TO YOUR PLACE LATELY.

THAT MORON, HE MUST HAVE COMPLETELY FORGOTTEN ABOUT CALLING ME.

......

IS SHE MAD AGAIN?

WHAT'S GOING ON, HYUNWOO?

YEAH, CAPTAIN.

BUT WHY DOES HYUNWOO NEED TO SEE THE CAPTAIN?

ANYWAY, THE PLAY'S GOING BETTER.

I'VE MANAGED TO MEMORIZE THE LINES THANKS TO MY NOT-SO-BAD MEMORY (THOUGH IT ALSO MAKES ME REMEMBER THINGS THAT I DON'T LIKE). AND I THINK THIS WILL ALL BE A SUCCESS IF I JUST AVOID MAKING A FOOL OF MYSELF ON STAGE.

IN THE END, MAYBE HYUNWOO'S STUPID BIG MOUTH ACTUALLY DID ME SOME GOOD.

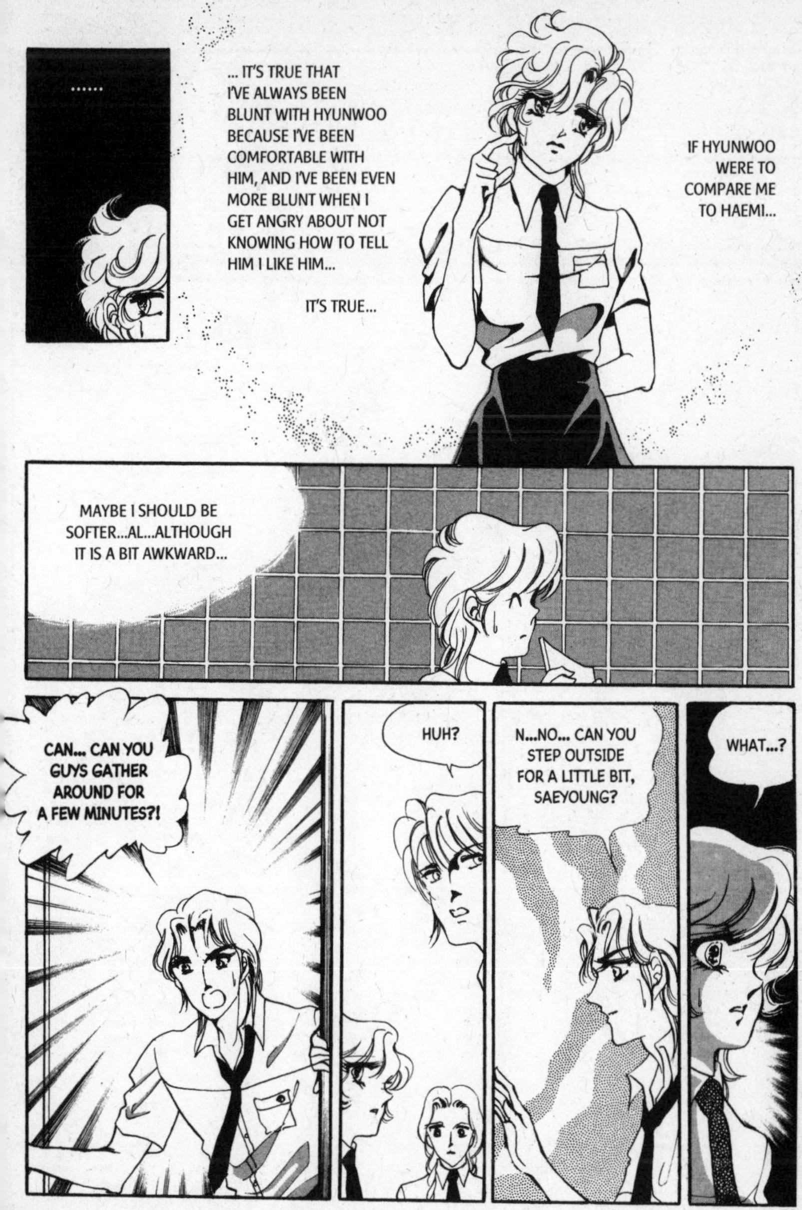
......
... IT'S TRUE THAT I'VE ALWAYS BEEN BLUNT WITH HYUNWOO BECAUSE I'VE BEEN COMFORTABLE WITH HIM, AND I'VE BEEN EVEN MORE BLUNT WHEN I GET ANGRY ABOUT NOT KNOWING HOW TO TELL HIM I LIKE HIM...
IT'S TRUE...
IF HYUNWOO WERE TO COMPARE ME TO HAEMI...
MAYBE I SHOULD BE SOFTER...AL...ALTHOUGH IT IS A BIT AWKWARD...
CAN... CAN YOU GUYS GATHER AROUND FOR A FEW MINUTES?!
HUH?
N...NO... CAN YOU STEP OUTSIDE FOR A LITTLE BIT, SAEYOUNG?
WHAT...?

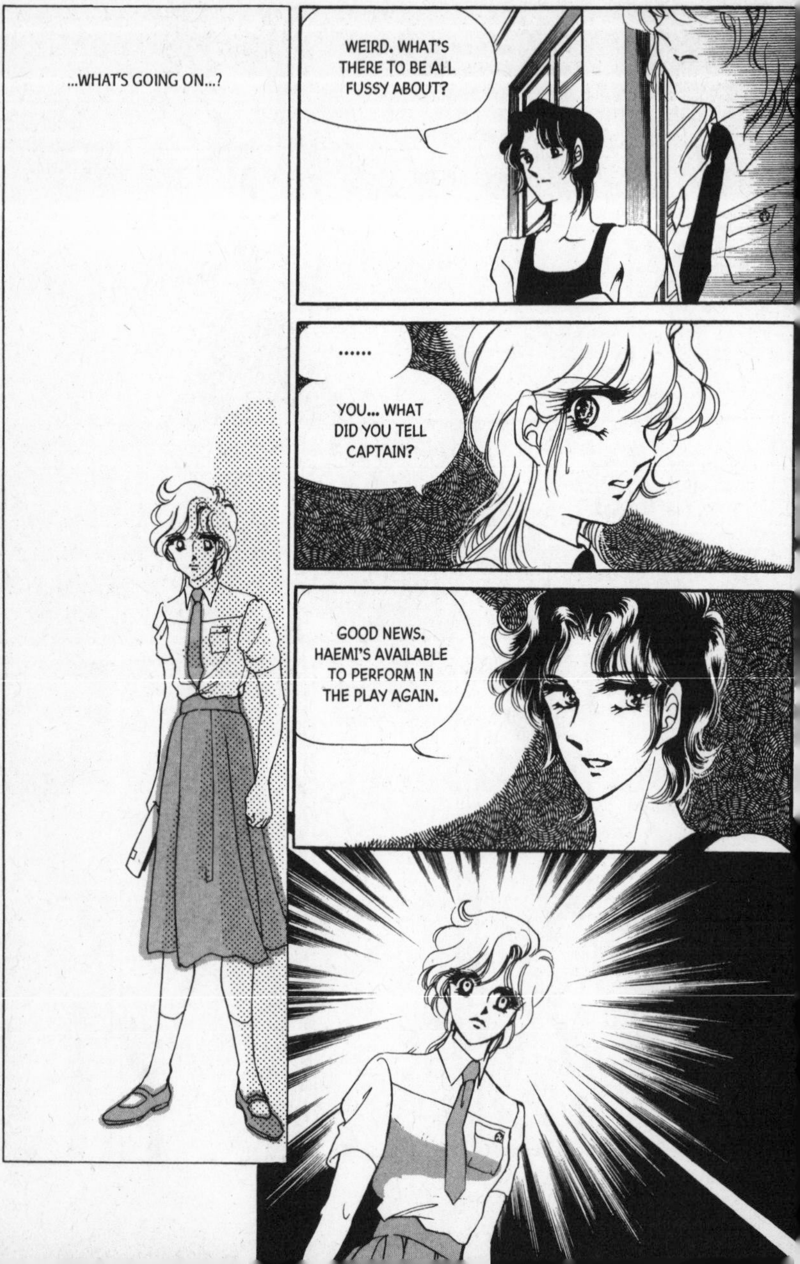
...WHAT'S GOING ON...?
WEIRD. WHAT'S THERE TO BE ALL FUSSY ABOUT?
......
YOU... WHAT DID YOU TELL CAPTAIN?
GOOD NEWS. HAEMI'S AVAILABLE TO PERFORM IN THE PLAY AGAIN.

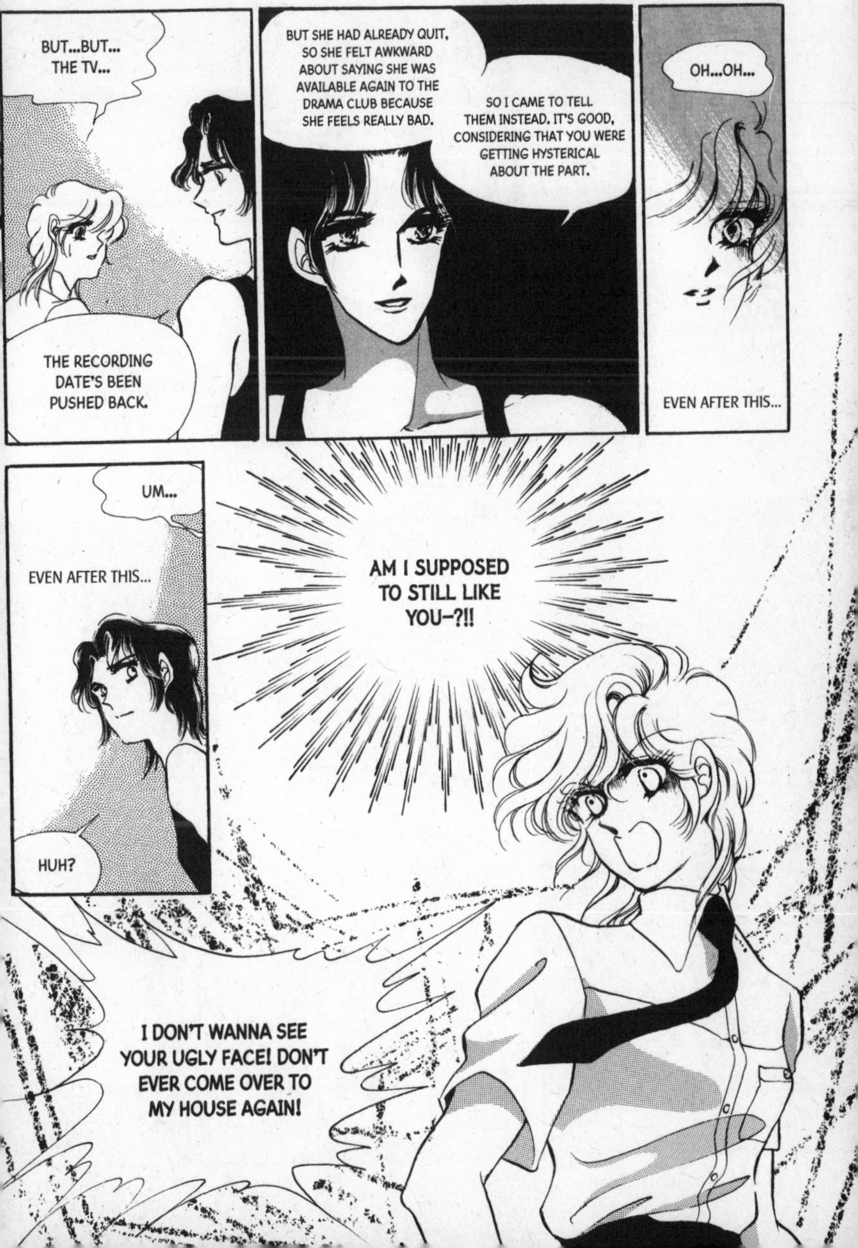
BUT...BUT... THE TV...
THE RECORDING DATE'S BEEN PUSHED BACK.
BUT SHE HAD ALREADY QUIT, SO SHE FELT AWKWARD ABOUT SAYING SHE WAS AVAILABLE AGAIN TO THE DRAMA CLUB BECAUSE SHE FEELS REALLY BAD.
SO I CAME TO TELL THEM INSTEAD. IT'S GOOD, CONSIDERING THAT YOU WERE GETTING HYSTERICAL ABOUT THE PART.
OH...OH...
EVEN AFTER THIS...
UM...
EVEN AFTER THIS...
HUH?
AM I SUPPOSED TO STILL LIKE YOU–?!!
I DON'T WANNA SEE YOUR UGLY FACE! DON'T EVER COME OVER TO MY HOUSE AGAIN!

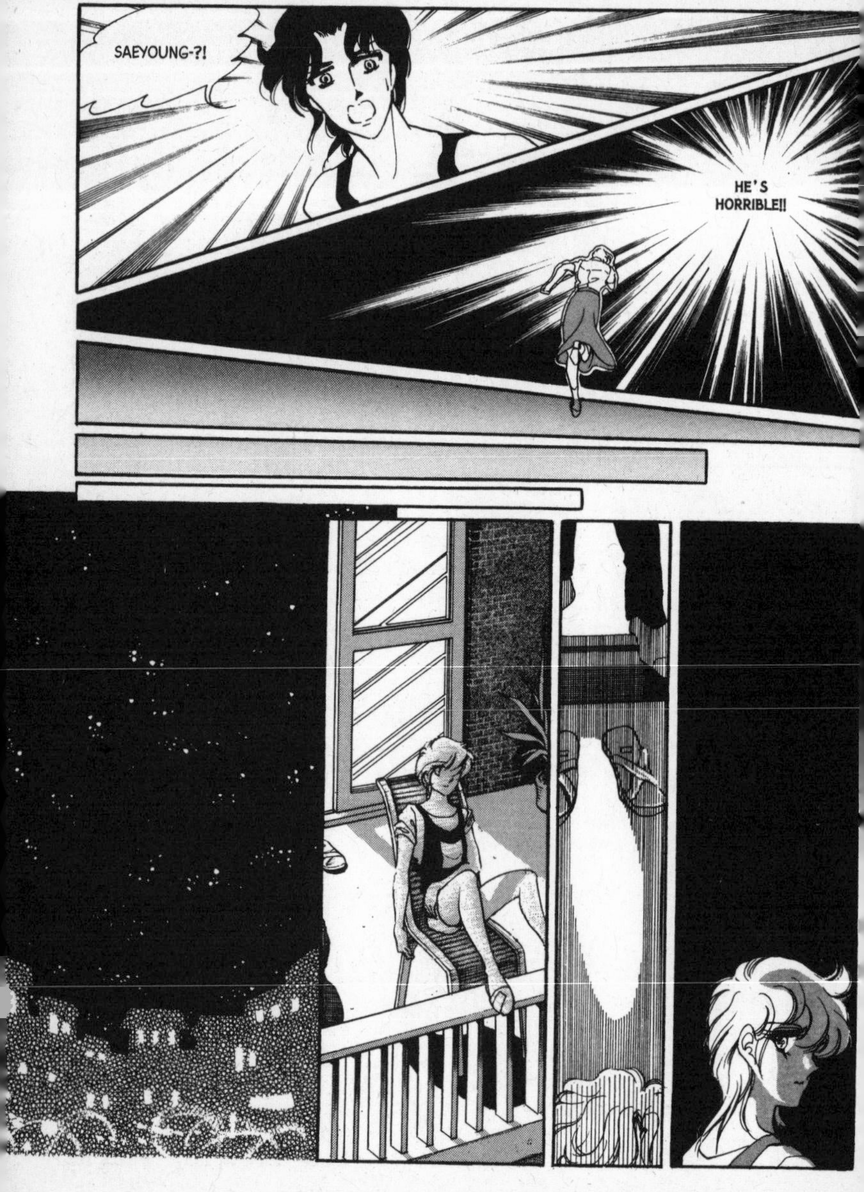
SAEYOUNG-?!
HE'S HORRIBLE!!

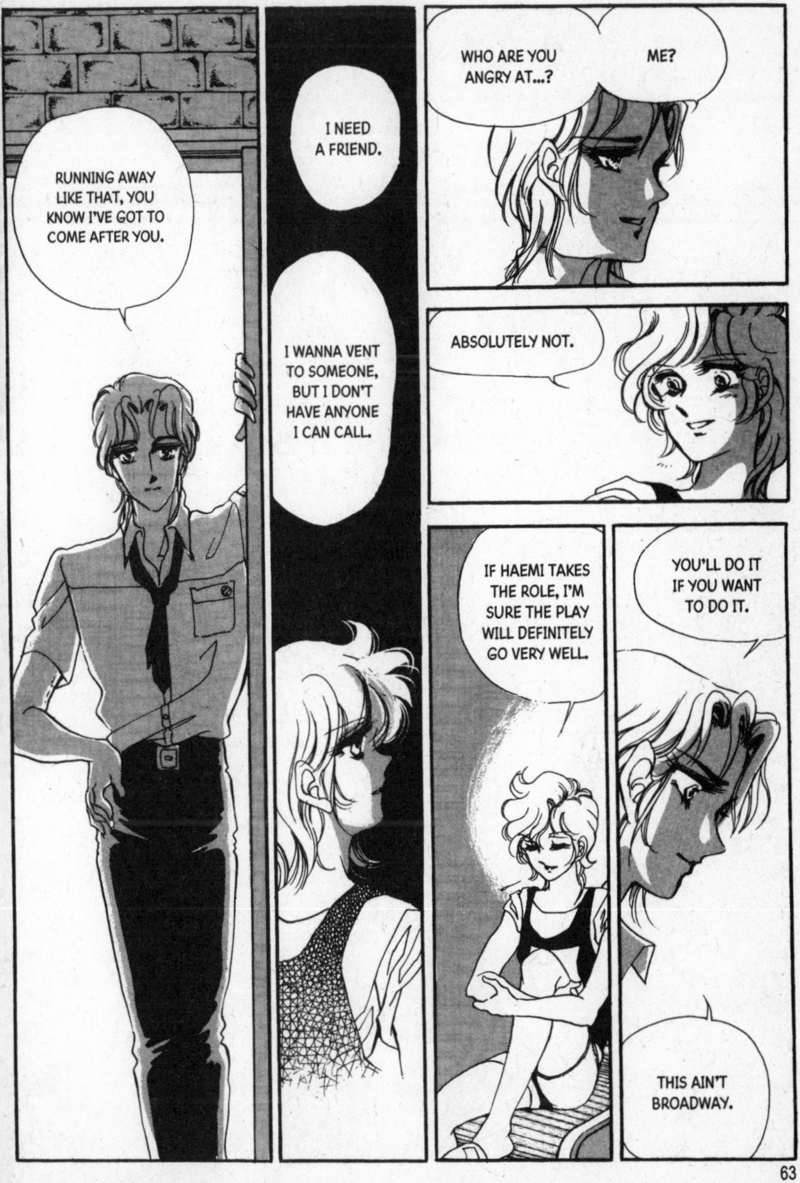
RUNNING AWAY LIKE THAT, YOU KNOW I'VE GOT TO COME AFTER YOU.
I NEED A FRIEND.
I WANNA VENT TO SOMEONE, BUT I DON'T HAVE ANYONE I CAN CALL.
WHO ARE YOU ANGRY AT...?
ME?
ABSOLUTELY NOT.
IF HAEMI TAKES THE ROLE, I'M SURE THE PLAY WILL DEFINITELY GO VERY WELL.
YOU'LL DO IT IF YOU WANT TO DO IT.
THIS AIN'T BROADWAY.

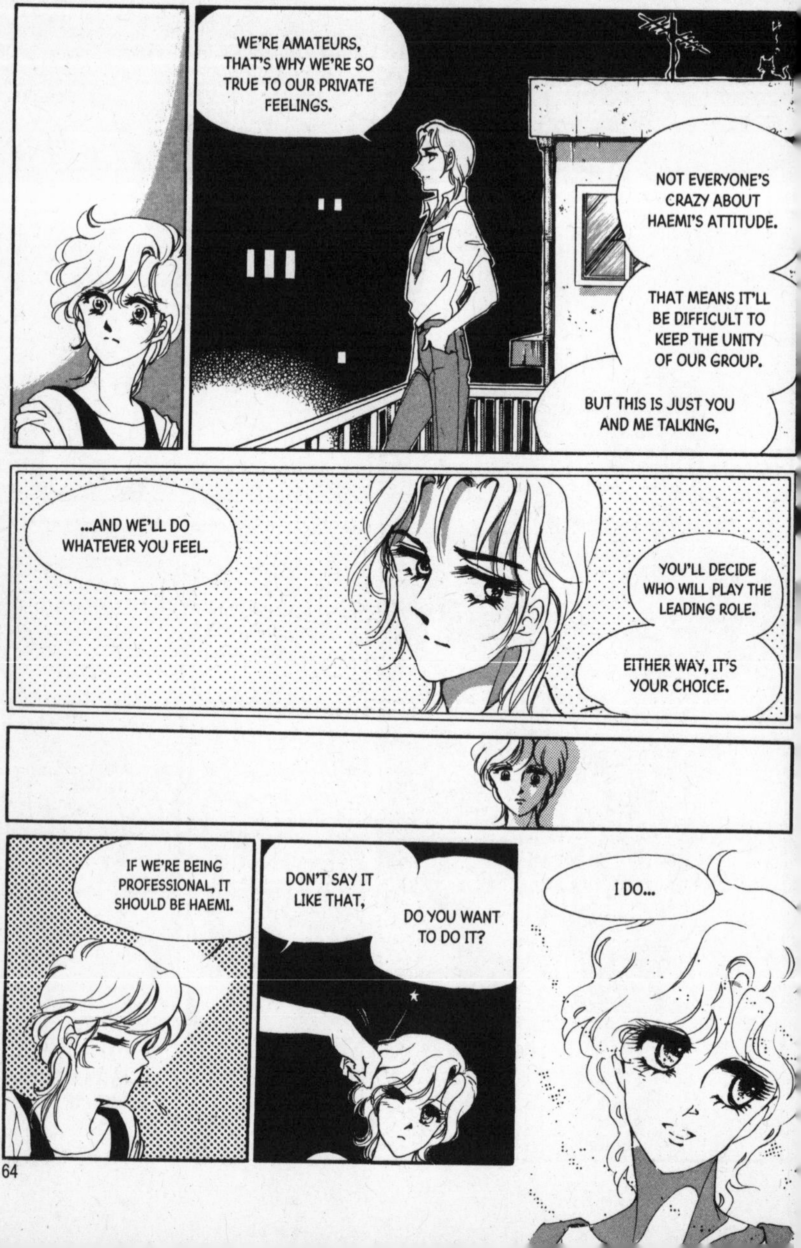
WE'RE AMATEURS, THAT'S WHY WE'RE SO TRUE TO OUR PRIVATE FEELINGS.
NOT EVERYONE'S CRAZY ABOUT HAEMI'S ATTITUDE.
THAT MEANS IT'LL BE DIFFICULT TO KEEP THE UNITY OF OUR GROUP.
BUT THIS IS JUST YOU AND ME TALKING,
...AND WE'LL DO WHATEVER YOU FEEL.
YOU'LL DECIDE WHO WILL PLAY THE LEADING ROLE.
EITHER WAY, IT'S YOUR CHOICE.
IF WE'RE BEING PROFESSIONAL, IT SHOULD BE HAEMI.
DON'T SAY IT LIKE THAT,
DO YOU WANT TO DO IT?
I DO...

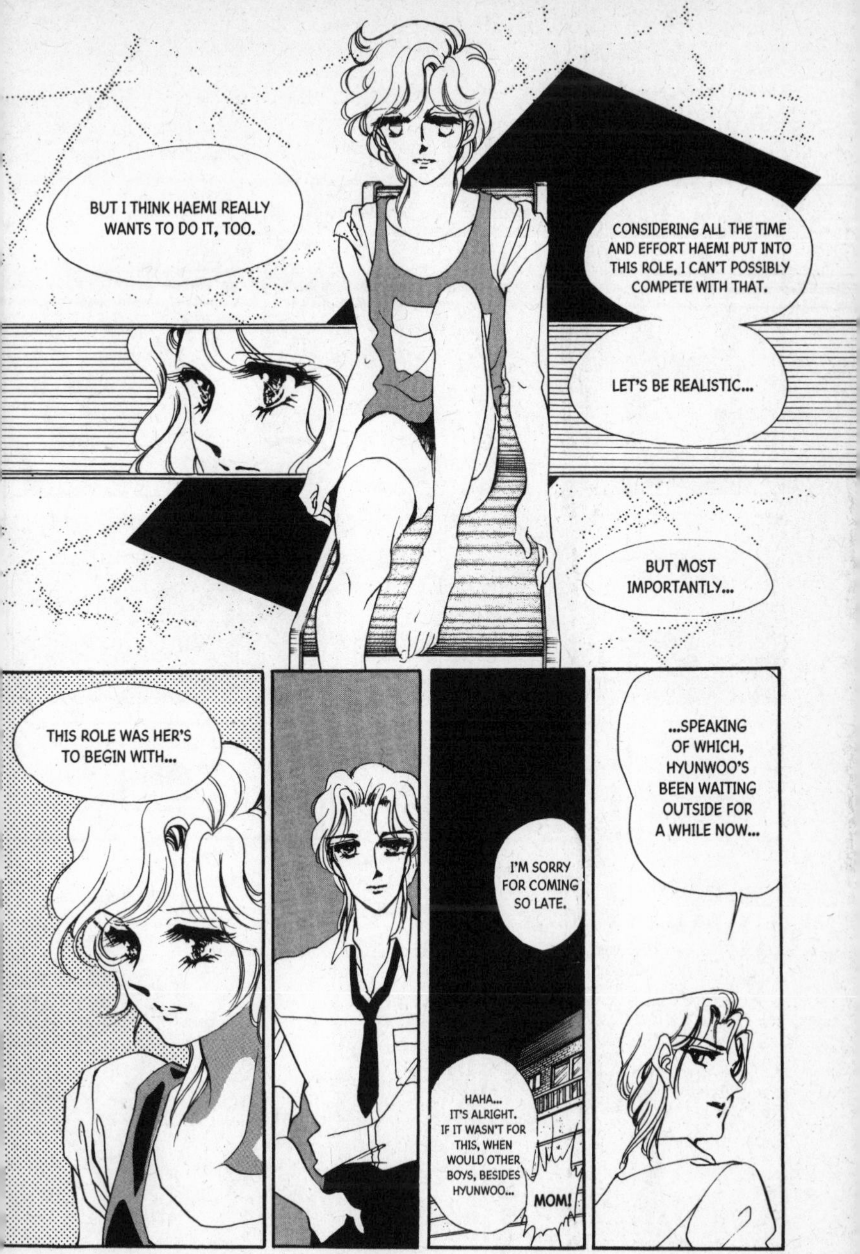
BUT I THINK HAEMI REALLY WANTS TO DO IT, TOO.
CONSIDERING ALL THE TIME AND EFFORT HAEMI PUT INTO THIS ROLE, I CAN'T POSSIBLY COMPETE WITH THAT.
LET'S BE REALISTIC...
BUT MOST IMPORTANTLY...
THIS ROLE WAS HER'S TO BEGIN WITH...
I'M SORRY FOR COMING SO LATE.
HAHA... IT'S ALRIGHT. IF IT WASN'T FOR THIS, WHEN WOULD OTHER BOYS, BESIDES HYUNWOO...
MOM!
...SPEAKING OF WHICH, HYUNWOO'S BEEN WAITING OUTSIDE FOR A WHILE NOW...

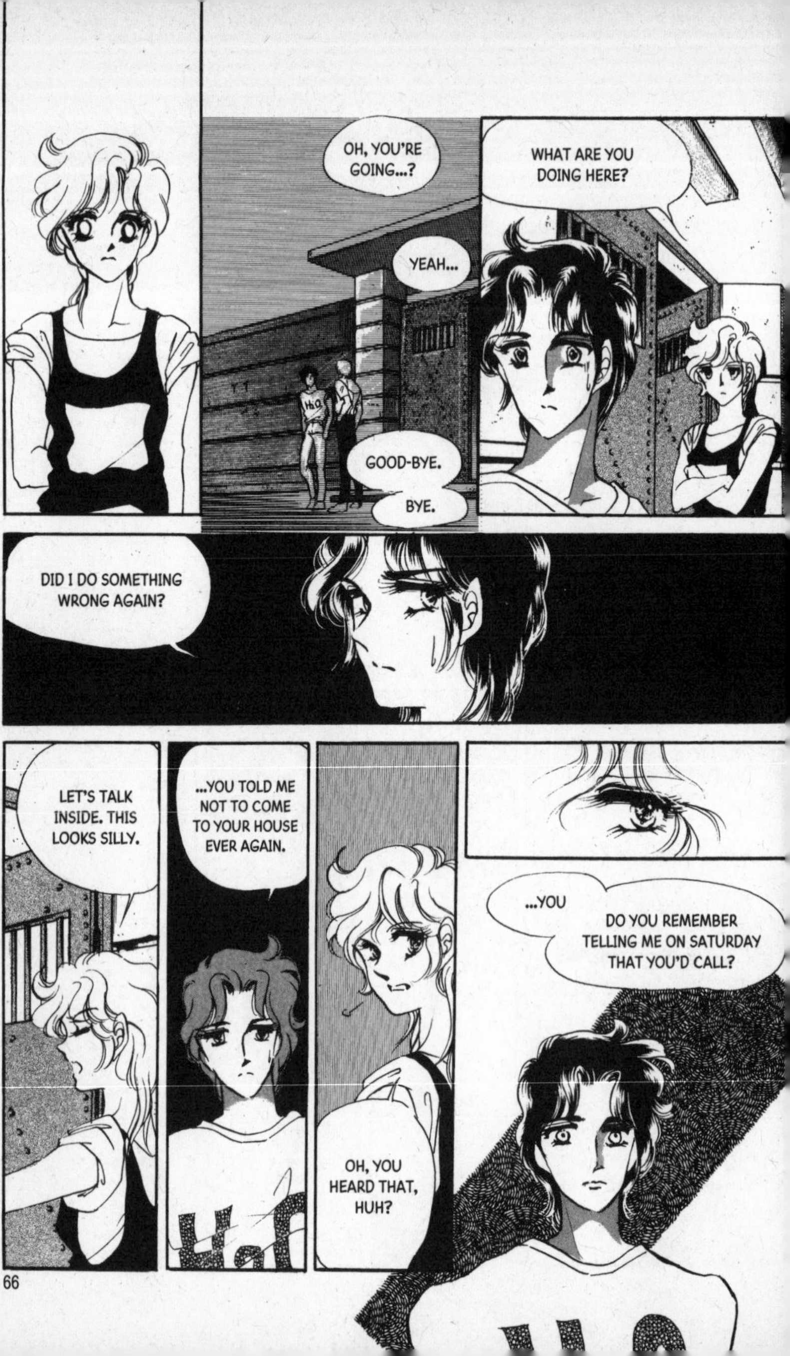

OH, YOU'RE GOING...?
YEAH...
GOOD-BYE.
BYE.
WHAT ARE YOU DOING HERE?
DID I DO SOMETHING WRONG AGAIN?
LET'S TALK INSIDE. THIS LOOKS SILLY.
...YOU TOLD ME NOT TO COME TO YOUR HOUSE EVER AGAIN.
OH, YOU HEARD THAT, HUH?
...YOU
DO YOU REMEMBER TELLING ME ON SATURDAY THAT YOU'D CALL?

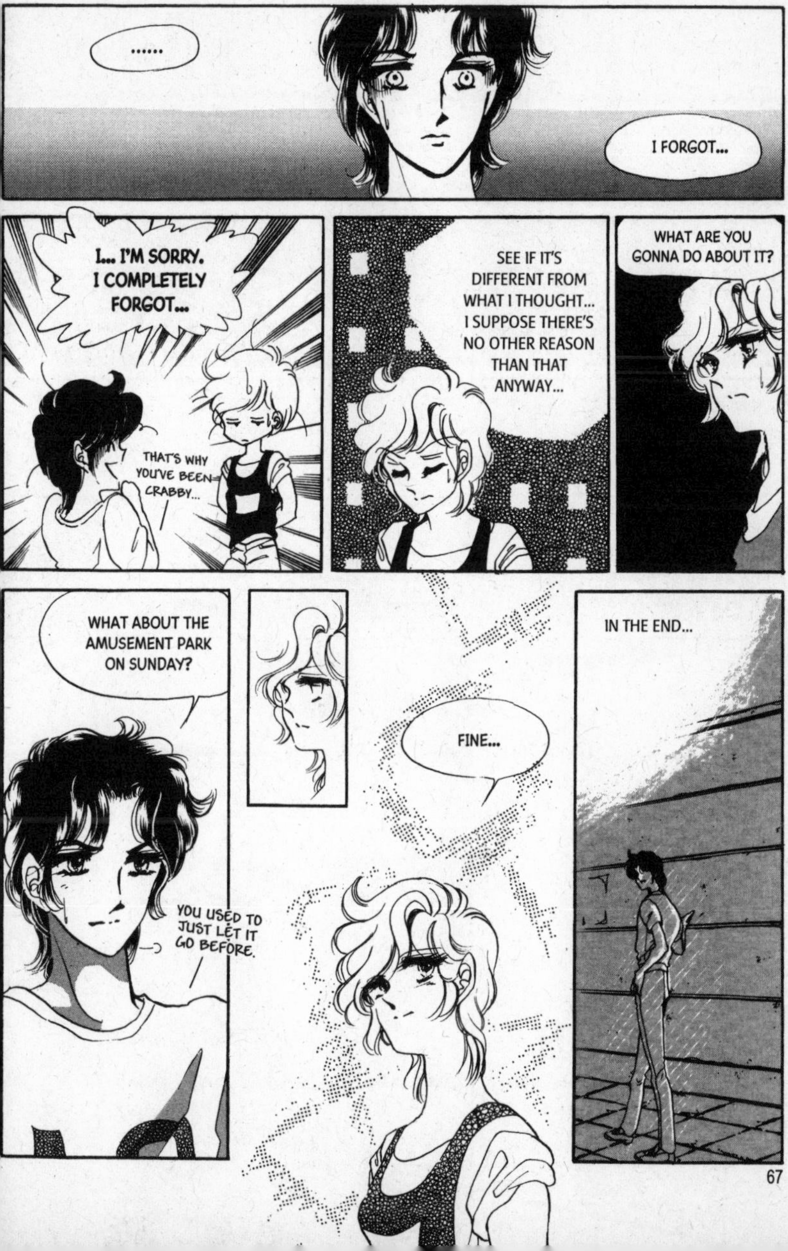
......
I FORGOT...
I... I'M SORRY. I COMPLETELY FORGOT...
THAT'S WHY YOU'VE BEEN CRABBY...
SEE IF IT'S DIFFERENT FROM WHAT I THOUGHT... I SUPPOSE THERE'S NO OTHER REASON THAN THAT ANYWAY...
WHAT ARE YOU GONNA DO ABOUT IT?
WHAT ABOUT THE AMUSEMENT PARK ON SUNDAY?
YOU USED TO JUST LET IT GO BEFORE.
FINE...
IN THE END...

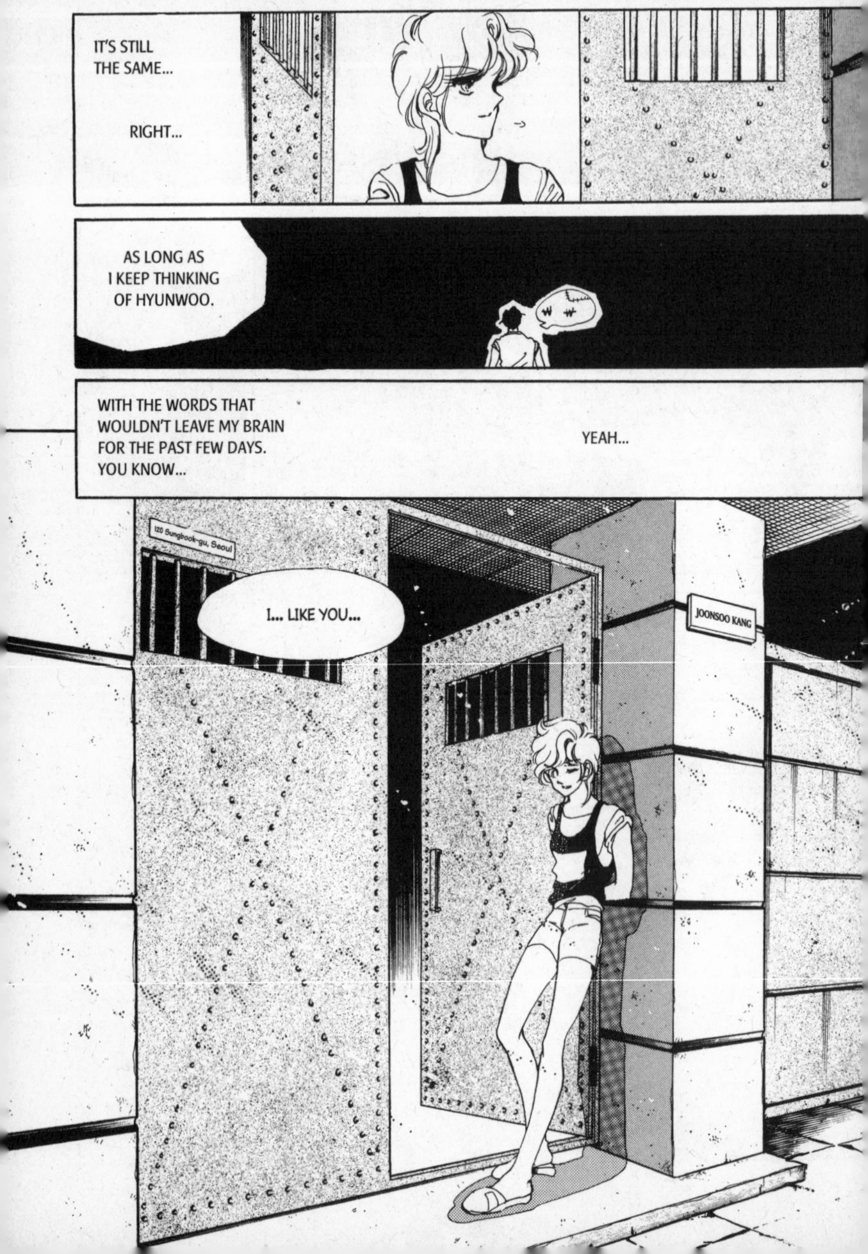
IT'S STILL THE SAME...
RIGHT...
AS LONG AS I KEEP THINKING OF HYUNWOO.
WITH THE WORDS THAT WOULDN'T LEAVE MY BRAIN FOR THE PAST FEW DAYS. YOU KNOW...
YEAH...
120 Sungbook-gu, Seoul
I... LIKE YOU...
JOONSOO KANG

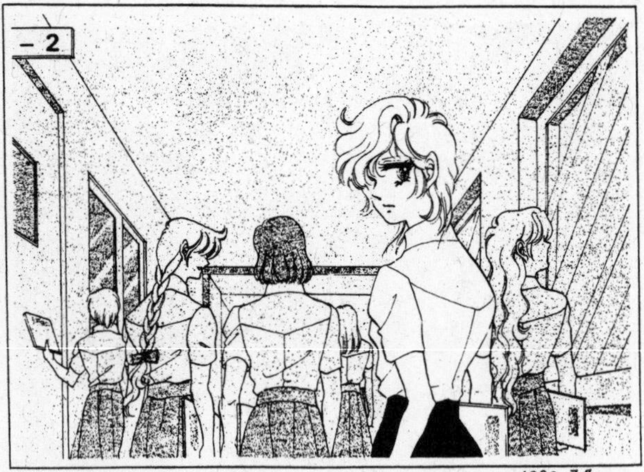
– 2

1990. ZA

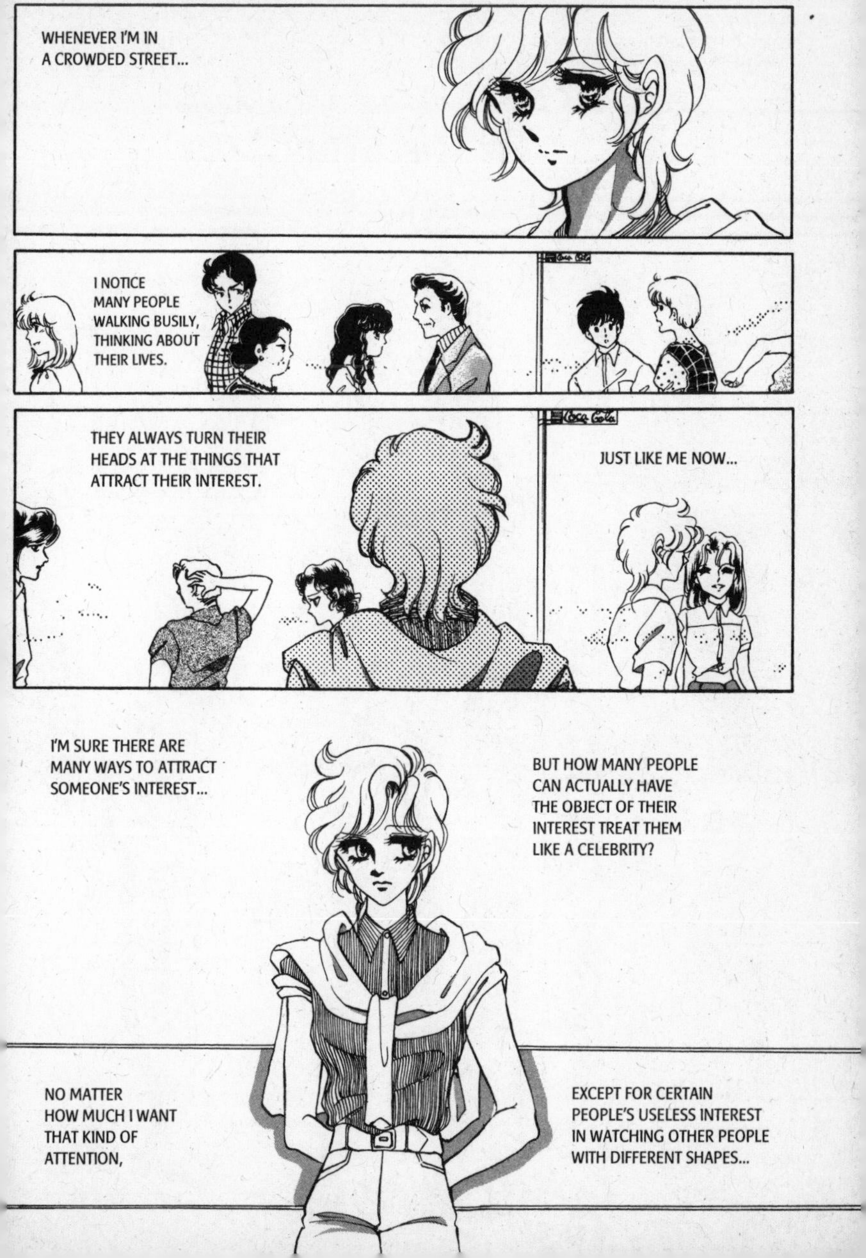
WHENEVER I'M IN
A CROWDED STREET...
I NOTICE
MANY PEOPLE
WALKING BUSILY,
THINKING ABOUT
THEIR LIVES.
THEY ALWAYS TURN THEIR
HEADS AT THE THINGS THAT
ATTRACT THEIR INTEREST.
JUST LIKE ME NOW...
I'M SURE THERE ARE
MANY WAYS TO ATTRACT
SOMEONE'S INTEREST...
BUT HOW MANY PEOPLE
CAN ACTUALLY HAVE
THE OBJECT OF THEIR
INTEREST TREAT THEM
LIKE A CELEBRITY?
NO MATTER
HOW MUCH I WANT
THAT KIND OF
ATTENTION,
EXCEPT FOR CERTAIN
PEOPLE'S USELESS INTEREST
IN WATCHING OTHER PEOPLE
WITH DIFFERENT SHAPES...

WHO WILL DISTINGUISH ME
FROM THIS CROWD OF ORDINARY PEOPLE?...

SECOND STORY

ON THE STREET

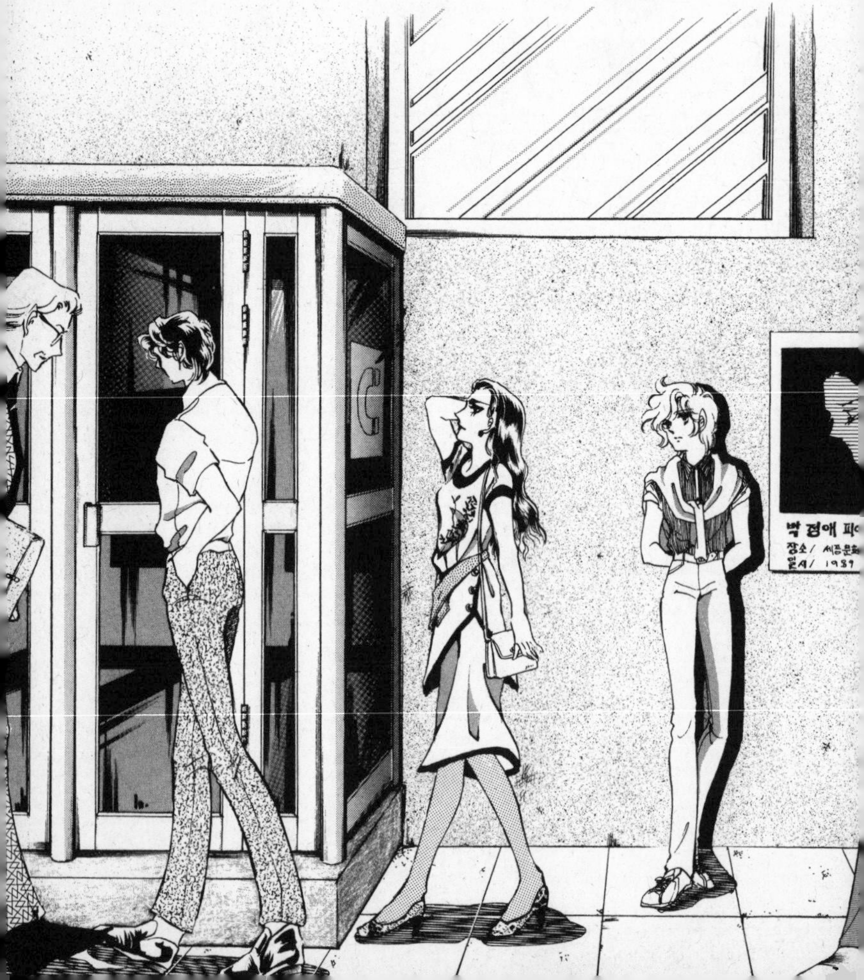
박정애
장소/
일시/ 1989

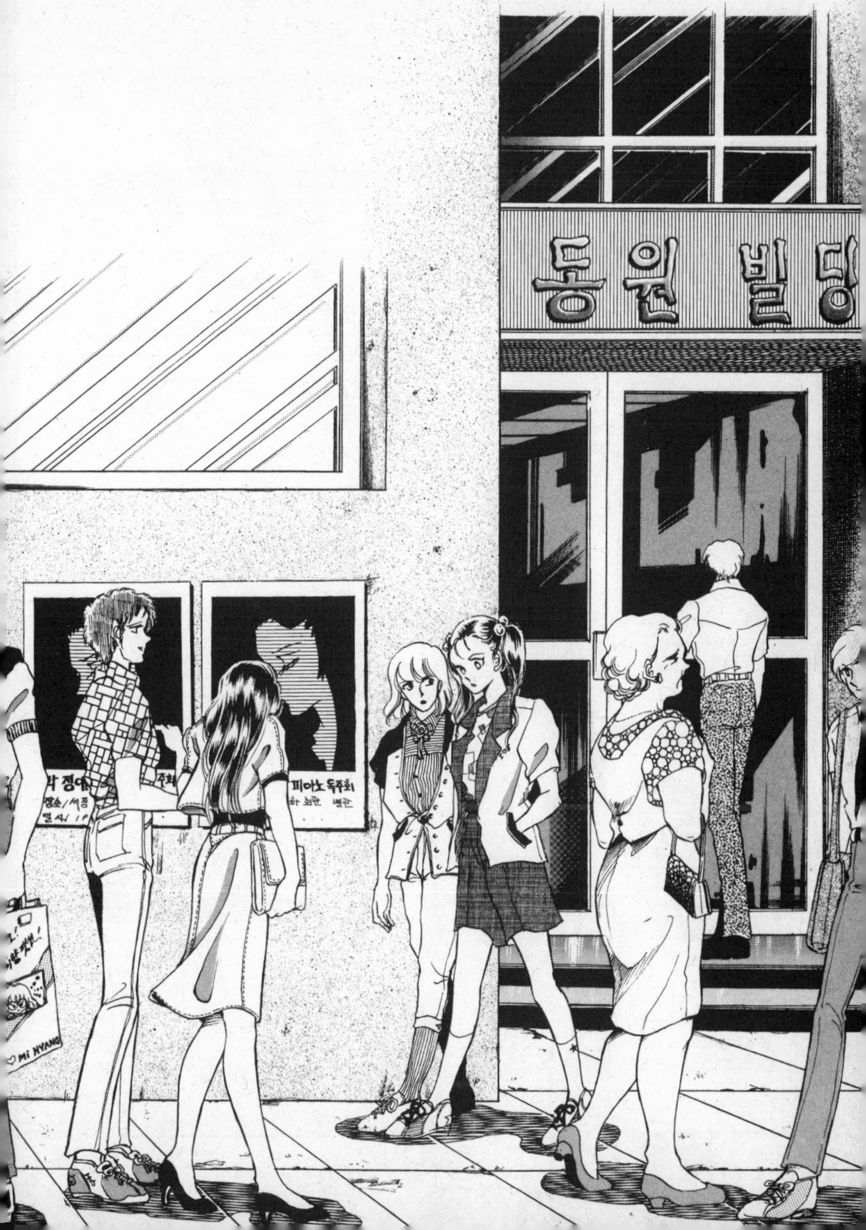

동원 빌딩
장소/세종
피아노 독주회
회관 별관
MI HYANG

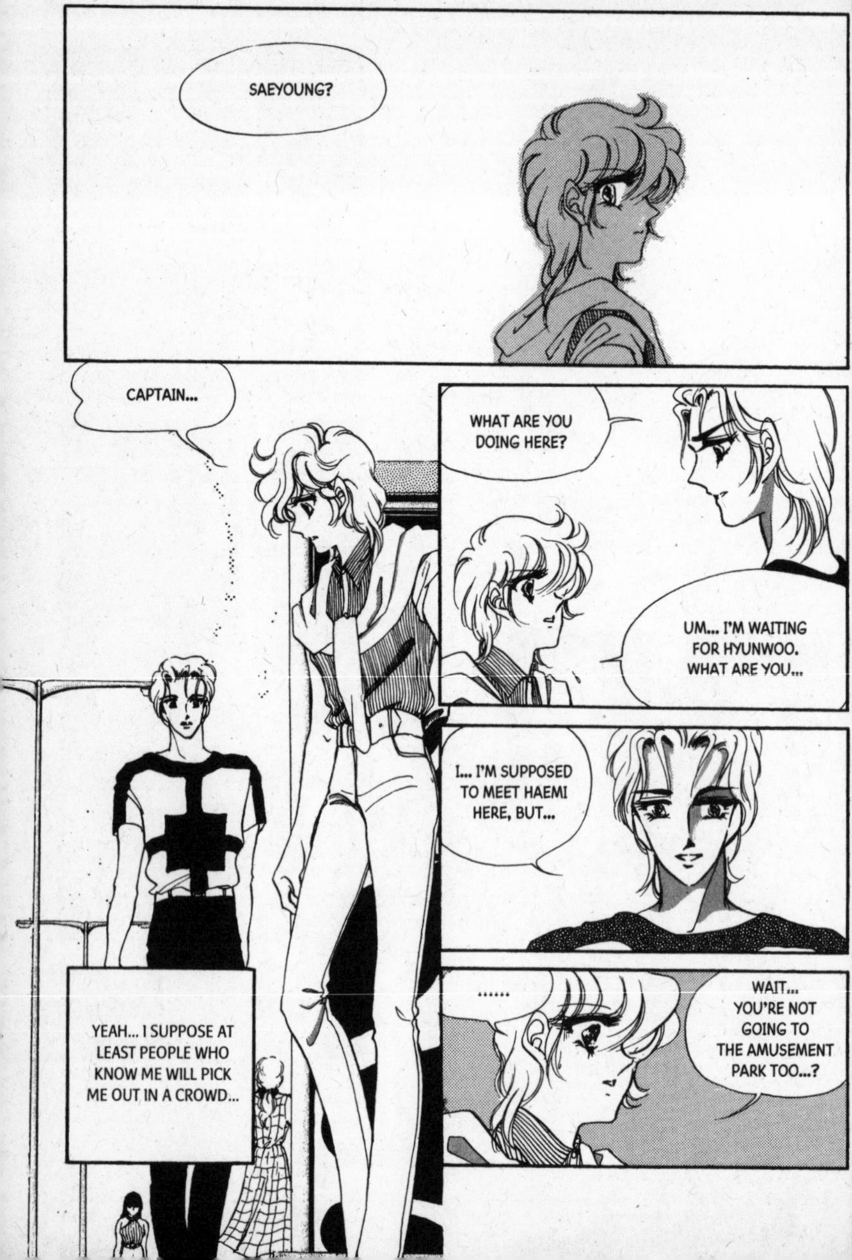
SAEYOUNG?
CAPTAIN...
YEAH... I SUPPOSE AT LEAST PEOPLE WHO KNOW ME WILL PICK ME OUT IN A CROWD...
WHAT ARE YOU DOING HERE?
UM... I'M WAITING FOR HYUNWOO. WHAT ARE YOU...
I... I'M SUPPOSED TO MEET HAEMI HERE, BUT...
......
WAIT... YOU'RE NOT GOING TO THE AMUSEMENT PARK TOO...?

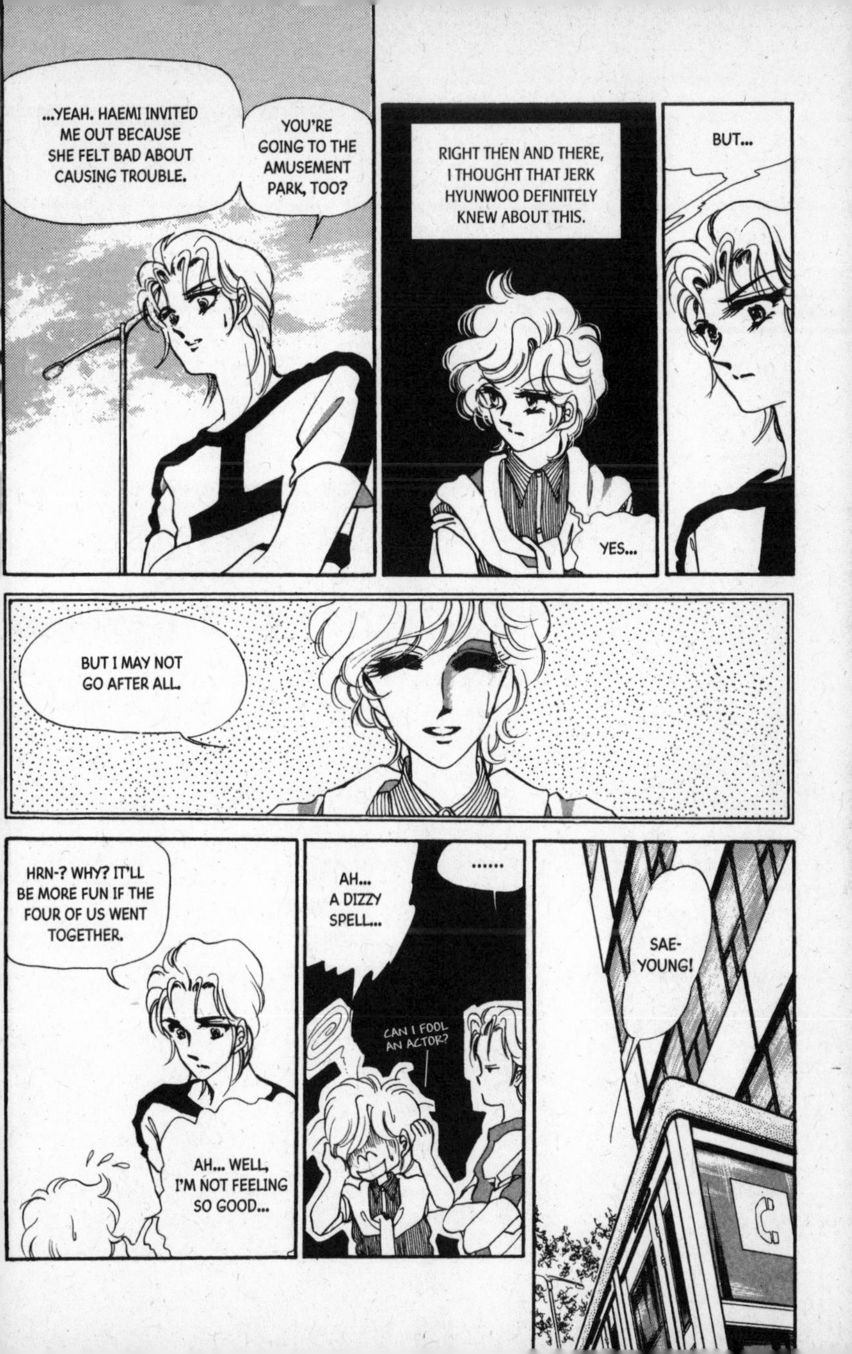
...YEAH. HAEMI INVITED ME OUT BECAUSE SHE FELT BAD ABOUT CAUSING TROUBLE.
YOU'RE GOING TO THE AMUSEMENT PARK, TOO?
RIGHT THEN AND THERE, I THOUGHT THAT JERK HYUNWOO DEFINITELY KNEW ABOUT THIS.
YES...
BUT...
BUT I MAY NOT GO AFTER ALL.
HRN-? WHY? IT'LL BE MORE FUN IF THE FOUR OF US WENT TOGETHER.
AH... WELL, I'M NOT FEELING SO GOOD...
......
AH... A DIZZY SPELL...
CAN I FOOL AN ACTOR?
SAE-YOUNG!

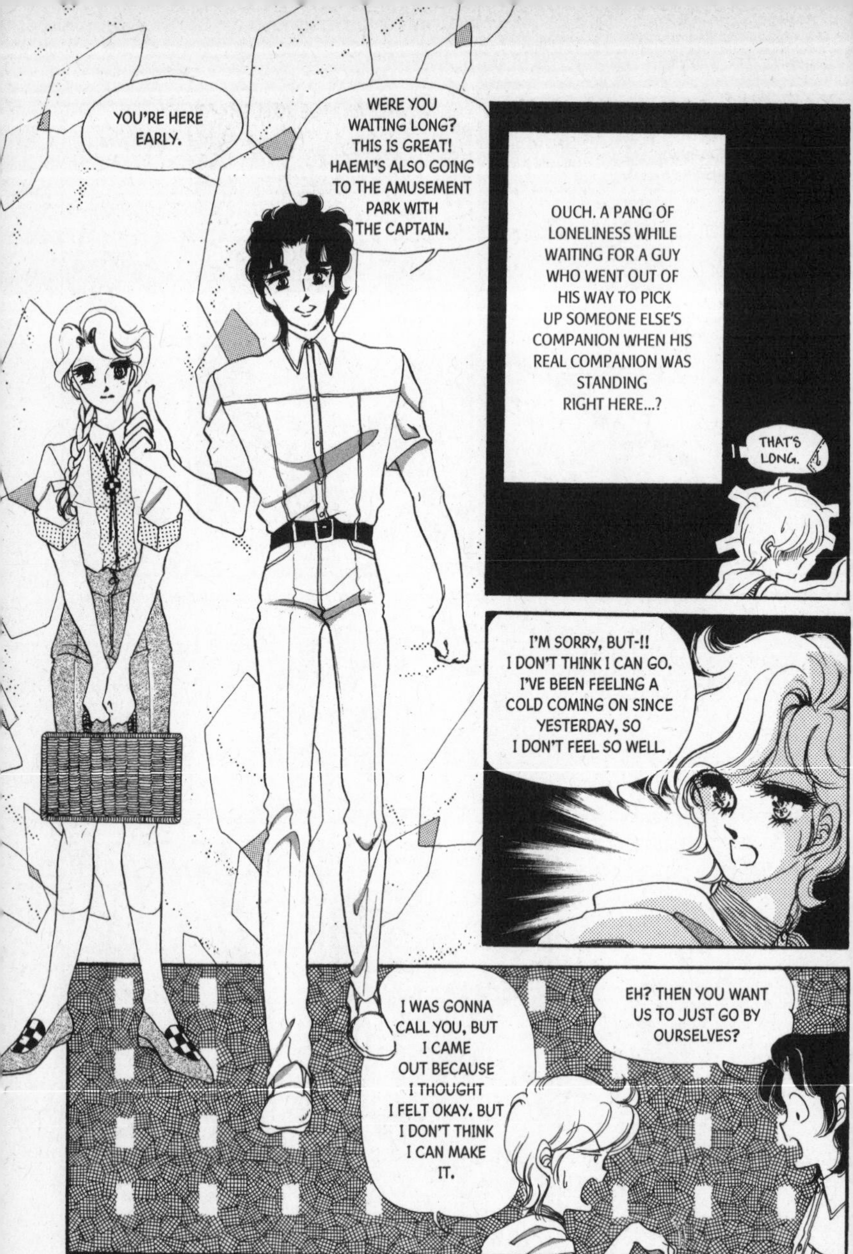
YOU'RE HERE EARLY.
WERE YOU WAITING LONG? THIS IS GREAT! HAEMI'S ALSO GOING TO THE AMUSEMENT PARK WITH THE CAPTAIN.
OUCH. A PANG OF LONELINESS WHILE WAITING FOR A GUY WHO WENT OUT OF HIS WAY TO PICK UP SOMEONE ELSE'S COMPANION WHEN HIS REAL COMPANION WAS STANDING RIGHT HERE...?
THAT'S LONG.
I'M SORRY, BUT-!! I DON'T THINK I CAN GO. I'VE BEEN FEELING A COLD COMING ON SINCE YESTERDAY, SO I DON'T FEEL SO WELL.
I WAS GONNA CALL YOU, BUT I CAME OUT BECAUSE I THOUGHT I FELT OKAY. BUT I DON'T THINK I CAN MAKE IT.
EH? THEN YOU WANT US TO JUST GO BY OURSELVES?

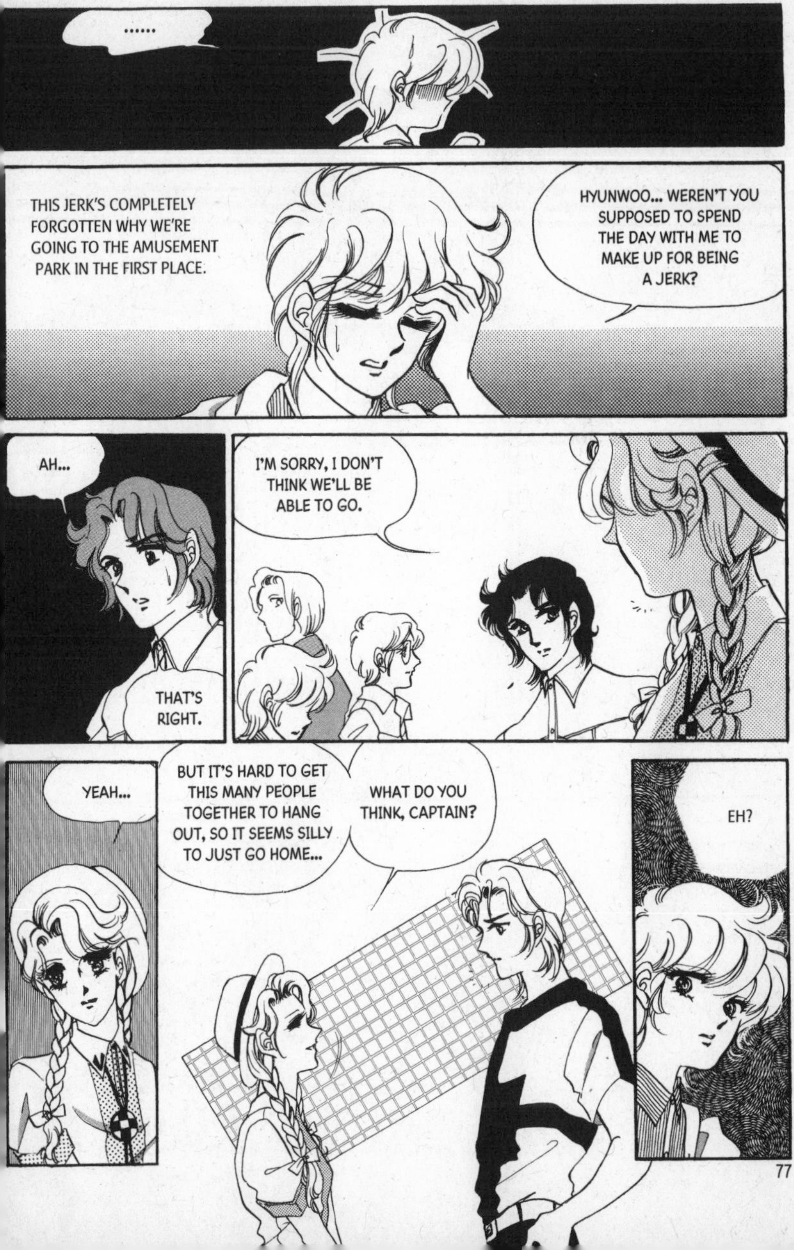
......
THIS JERK'S COMPLETELY FORGOTTEN WHY WE'RE GOING TO THE AMUSEMENT PARK IN THE FIRST PLACE.
HYUNWOO... WEREN'T YOU SUPPOSED TO SPEND THE DAY WITH ME TO MAKE UP FOR BEING A JERK?
AH...
THAT'S RIGHT.
I'M SORRY, I DON'T THINK WE'LL BE ABLE TO GO.
YEAH...
BUT IT'S HARD TO GET THIS MANY PEOPLE TOGETHER TO HANG OUT, SO IT SEEMS SILLY TO JUST GO HOME...
WHAT DO YOU THINK, CAPTAIN?
EH?

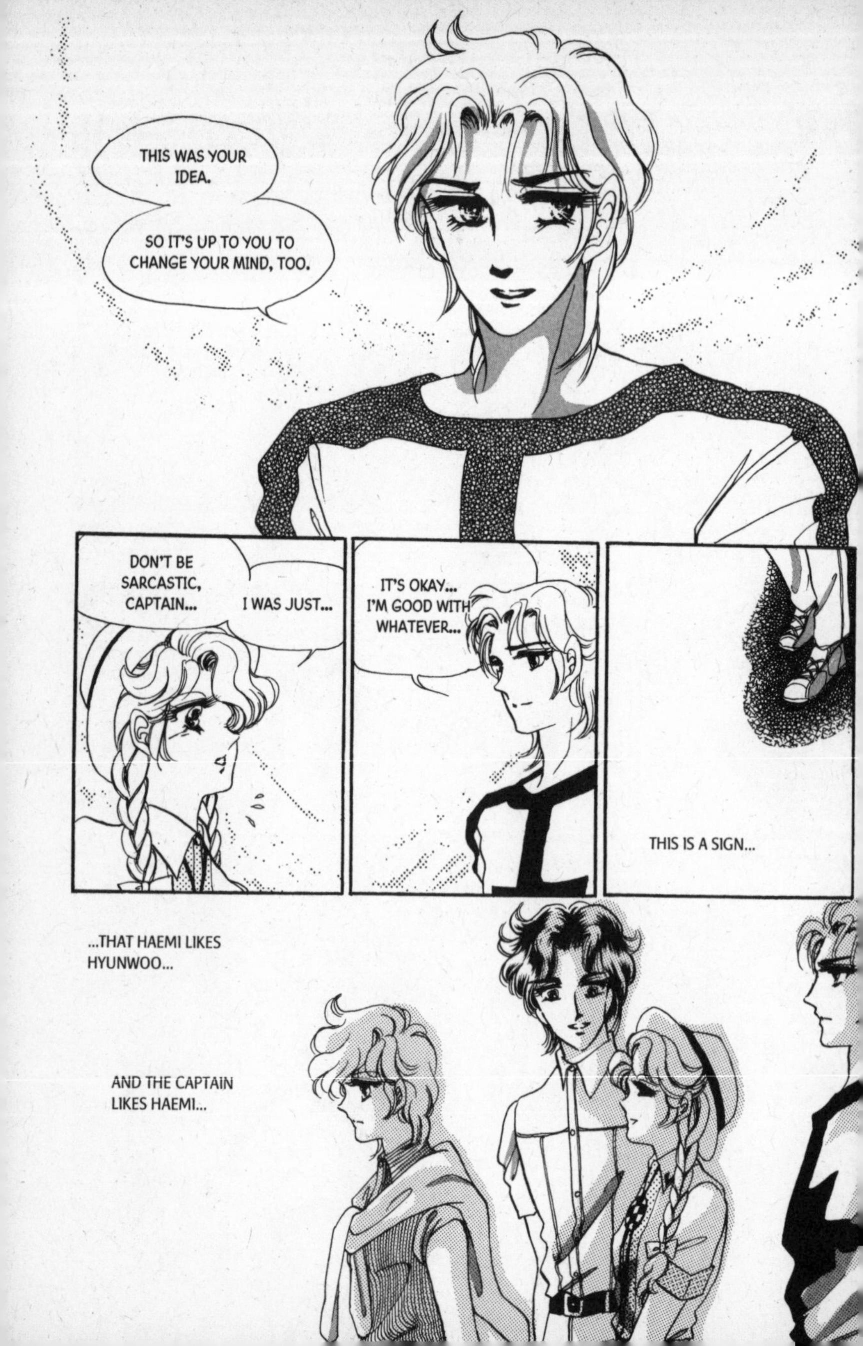
THIS WAS YOUR IDEA.
SO IT'S UP TO YOU TO CHANGE YOUR MIND, TOO.
DON'T BE SARCASTIC, CAPTAIN...
I WAS JUST...
IT'S OKAY... I'M GOOD WITH WHATEVER...
THIS IS A SIGN...
...THAT HAEMI LIKES HYUNWOO...
AND THE CAPTAIN LIKES HAEMI...

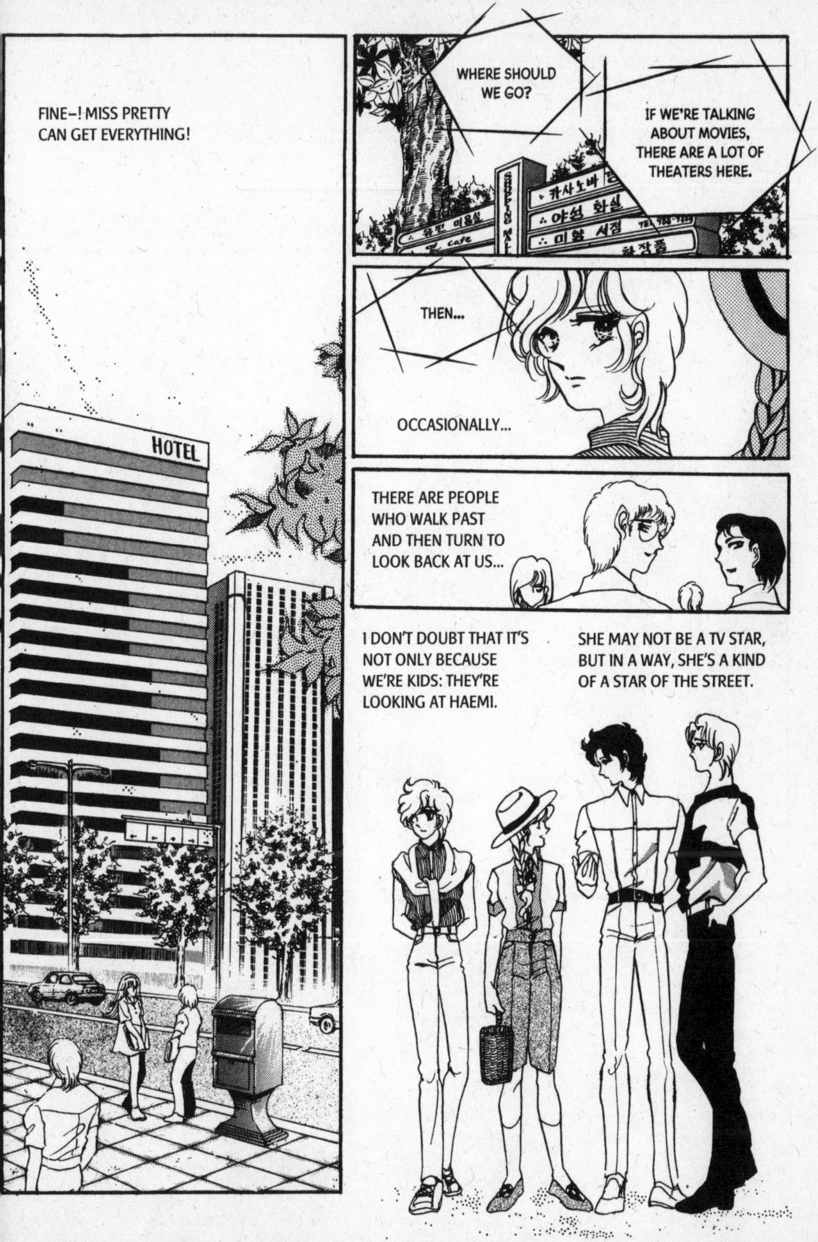
FINE–! MISS PRETTY CAN GET EVERYTHING!
HOTEL
WHERE SHOULD WE GO?
IF WE'RE TALKING ABOUT MOVIES, THERE ARE A LOT OF THEATERS HERE.
THEN...
OCCASIONALLY...
THERE ARE PEOPLE WHO WALK PAST AND THEN TURN TO LOOK BACK AT US...
I DON'T DOUBT THAT IT'S NOT ONLY BECAUSE WE'RE KIDS: THEY'RE LOOKING AT HAEMI.
SHE MAY NOT BE A TV STAR, BUT IN A WAY, SHE'S A KIND OF A STAR OF THE STREET.

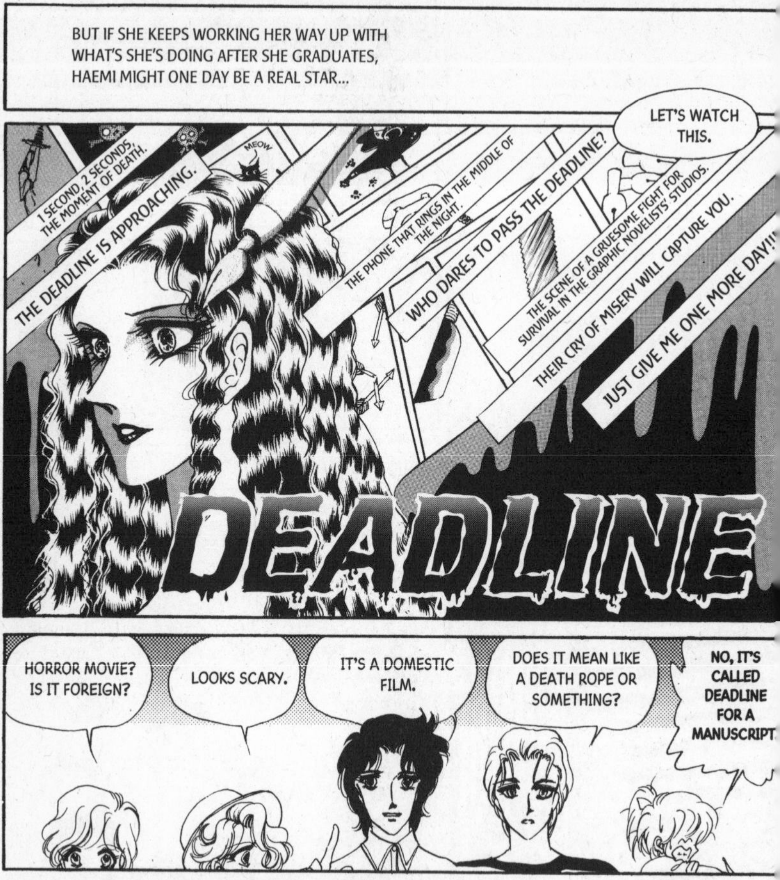
BUT IF SHE KEEPS WORKING HER WAY UP WITH WHAT'S SHE'S DOING AFTER SHE GRADUATES, HAEMI MIGHT ONE DAY BE A REAL STAR...
LET'S WATCH THIS.
1 SECOND, 2 SECONDS, THE MOMENT OF DEATH.
THE DEADLINE IS APPROACHING.
MEOW
THE PHONE THAT RINGS IN THE MIDDLE OF THE NIGHT.
WHO DARES TO PASS THE DEADLINE?
THE SCENE OF A GRUESOME FIGHT FOR SURVIVAL IN THE GRAPHIC NOVELISTS' STUDIOS.
THEIR CRY OF MISERY WILL CAPTURE YOU.
JUST GIVE ME ONE MORE DAY!!!
DEADLINE
HORROR MOVIE? IS IT FOREIGN?
LOOKS SCARY.
IT'S A DOMESTIC FILM.
DOES IT MEAN LIKE A DEATH ROPE OR SOMETHING?
NO, IT'S CALLED DEADLINE FOR A MANUSCRIPT

*DEAD LINE: A SET TIME WHEN MANUSCRIPTS ARE DUE.

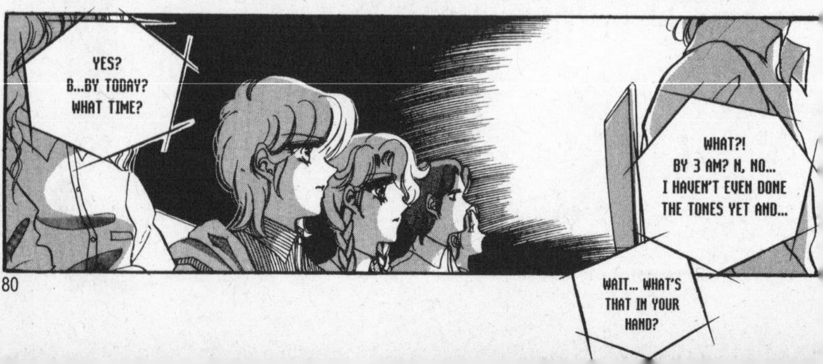
YES? B...BY TODAY? WHAT TIME?
WHAT?! BY 3 AM? N, NO... I HAVEN'T EVEN DONE THE TONES YET AND...
WAIT... WHAT'S THAT IN YOUR HAND?

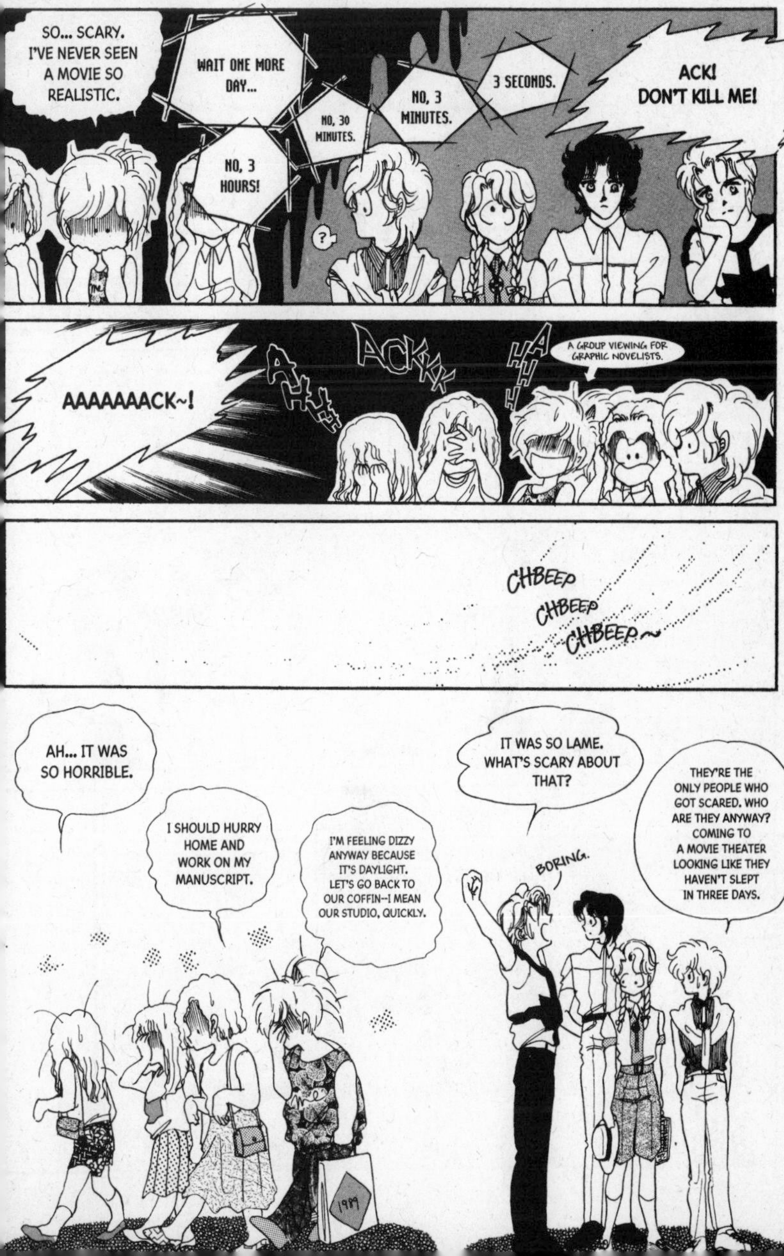
SO... SCARY. I'VE NEVER SEEN A MOVIE SO REALISTIC.
WAIT ONE MORE DAY...
NO, 3 HOURS!
NO, 30 MINUTES.
NO, 3 MINUTES.
3 SECONDS.
ACK! DON'T KILL ME!
?
AAAAAAACK~!
AHH
ACKKK
AHHHH
A GROUP VIEWING FOR GRAPHIC NOVELISTS.
CHBEEP
CHBEEP
CHBEEP~
AH... IT WAS SO HORRIBLE.
I SHOULD HURRY HOME AND WORK ON MY MANUSCRIPT.
I'M FEELING DIZZY ANYWAY BECAUSE IT'S DAYLIGHT. LET'S GO BACK TO OUR COFFIN--I MEAN OUR STUDIO, QUICKLY.
IT WAS SO LAME. WHAT'S SCARY ABOUT THAT?
BORING.
THEY'RE THE ONLY PEOPLE WHO GOT SCARED. WHO ARE THEY ANYWAY? COMING TO A MOVIE THEATER LOOKING LIKE THEY HAVEN'T SLEPT IN THREE DAYS.
1989

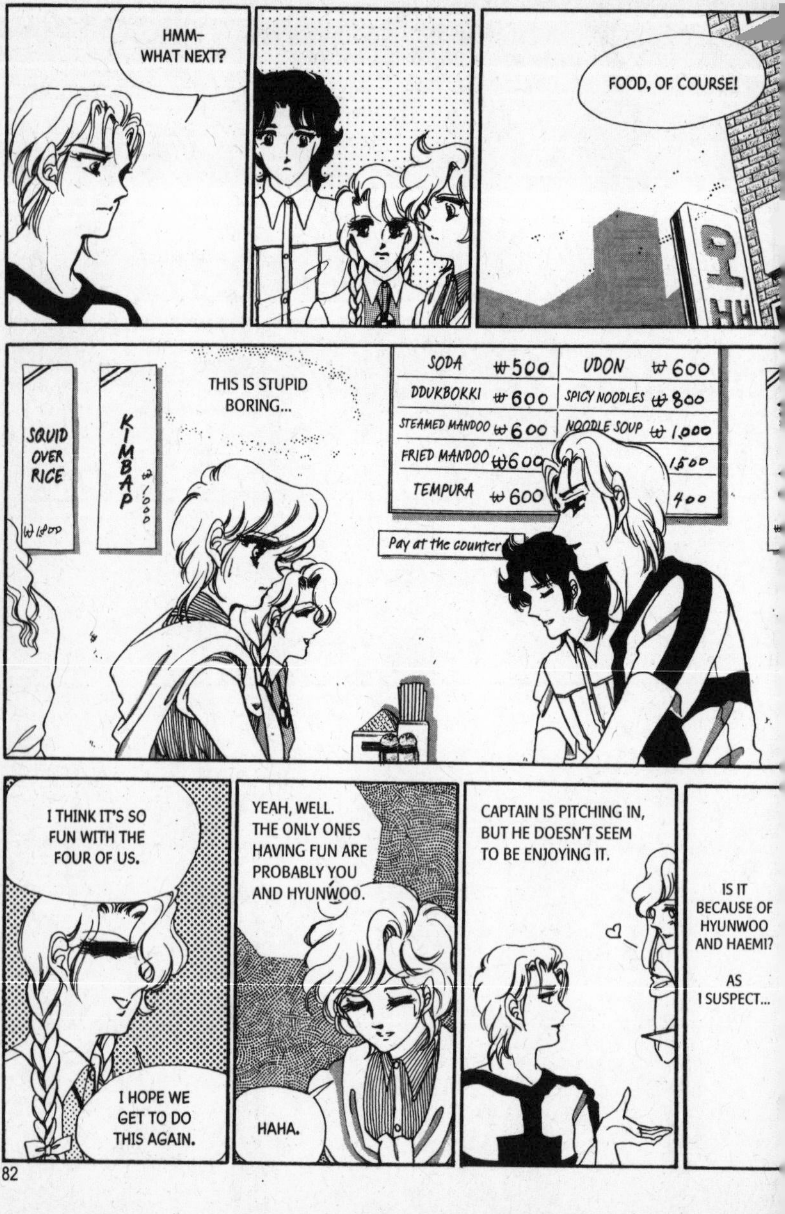

HMM–
WHAT NEXT?
FOOD, OF COURSE!
SQUID OVER RICE
₩1800
KIMBAP ₩1000
THIS IS STUPID
BORING...
SODA ₩500
UDON ₩600
DDUKBOKKI ₩600
SPICY NOODLES ₩800
STEAMED MANDOO ₩600
NOODLE SOUP ₩1,000
FRIED MANDOO ₩600
1500
TEMPURA ₩600
400
Pay at the counter
I THINK IT'S SO FUN WITH THE FOUR OF US.
I HOPE WE GET TO DO THIS AGAIN.
YEAH, WELL. THE ONLY ONES HAVING FUN ARE PROBABLY YOU AND HYUNWOO.
HAHA.
CAPTAIN IS PITCHING IN, BUT HE DOESN'T SEEM TO BE ENJOYING IT.
IS IT BECAUSE OF HYUNWOO AND HAEMI?
AS I SUSPECT...

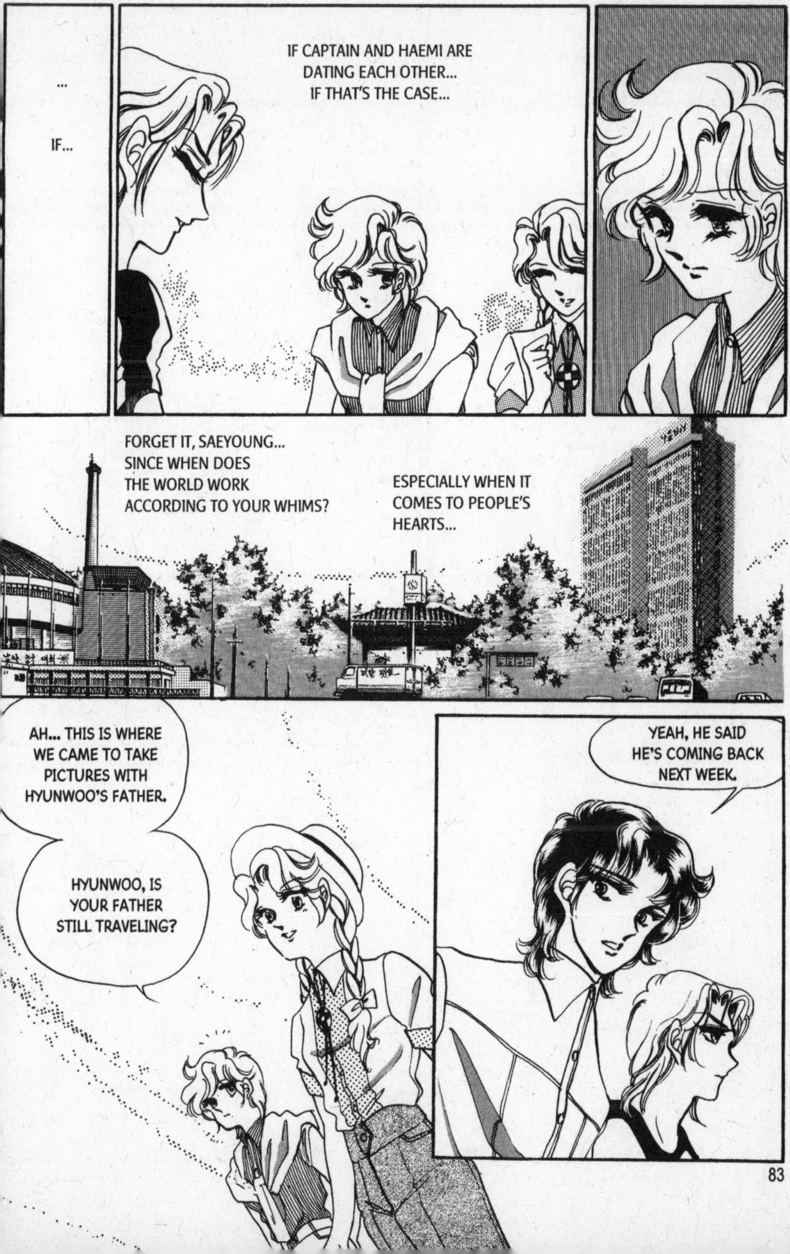
...
IF...
IF CAPTAIN AND HAEMI ARE DATING EACH OTHER... IF THAT'S THE CASE...
FORGET IT, SAEYOUNG... SINCE WHEN DOES THE WORLD WORK ACCORDING TO YOUR WHIMS?
ESPECIALLY WHEN IT COMES TO PEOPLE'S HEARTS...
AH... THIS IS WHERE WE CAME TO TAKE PICTURES WITH HYUNWOO'S FATHER.
HYUNWOO, IS YOUR FATHER STILL TRAVELING?
YEAH, HE SAID HE'S COMING BACK NEXT WEEK.

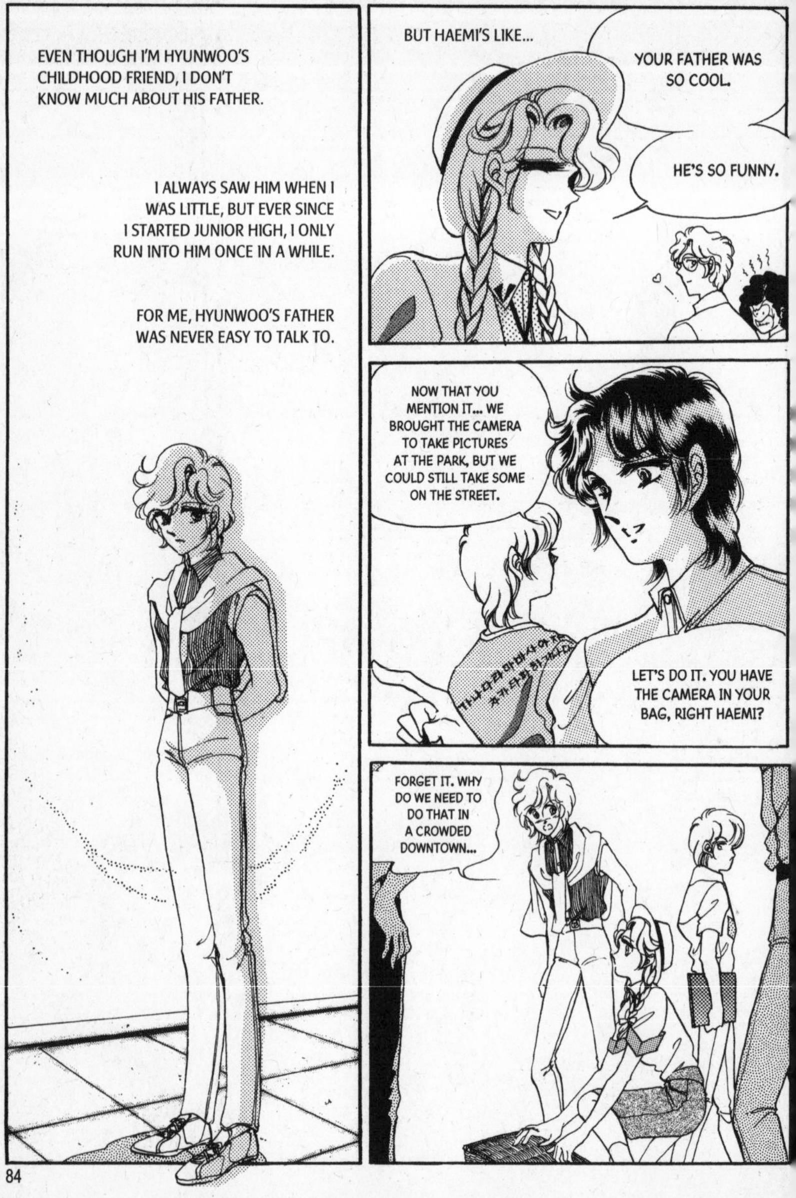
EVEN THOUGH I'M HYUNWOO'S CHILDHOOD FRIEND, I DON'T KNOW MUCH ABOUT HIS FATHER.
I ALWAYS SAW HIM WHEN I WAS LITTLE, BUT EVER SINCE I STARTED JUNIOR HIGH, I ONLY RUN INTO HIM ONCE IN A WHILE.
FOR ME, HYUNWOO'S FATHER WAS NEVER EASY TO TALK TO.
BUT HAEMI'S LIKE...
YOUR FATHER WAS SO COOL.
HE'S SO FUNNY.
NOW THAT YOU MENTION IT... WE BROUGHT THE CAMERA TO TAKE PICTURES AT THE PARK, BUT WE COULD STILL TAKE SOME ON THE STREET.
LET'S DO IT. YOU HAVE THE CAMERA IN YOUR BAG, RIGHT HAEMI?
FORGET IT. WHY DO WE NEED TO DO THAT IN A CROWDED DOWNTOWN...

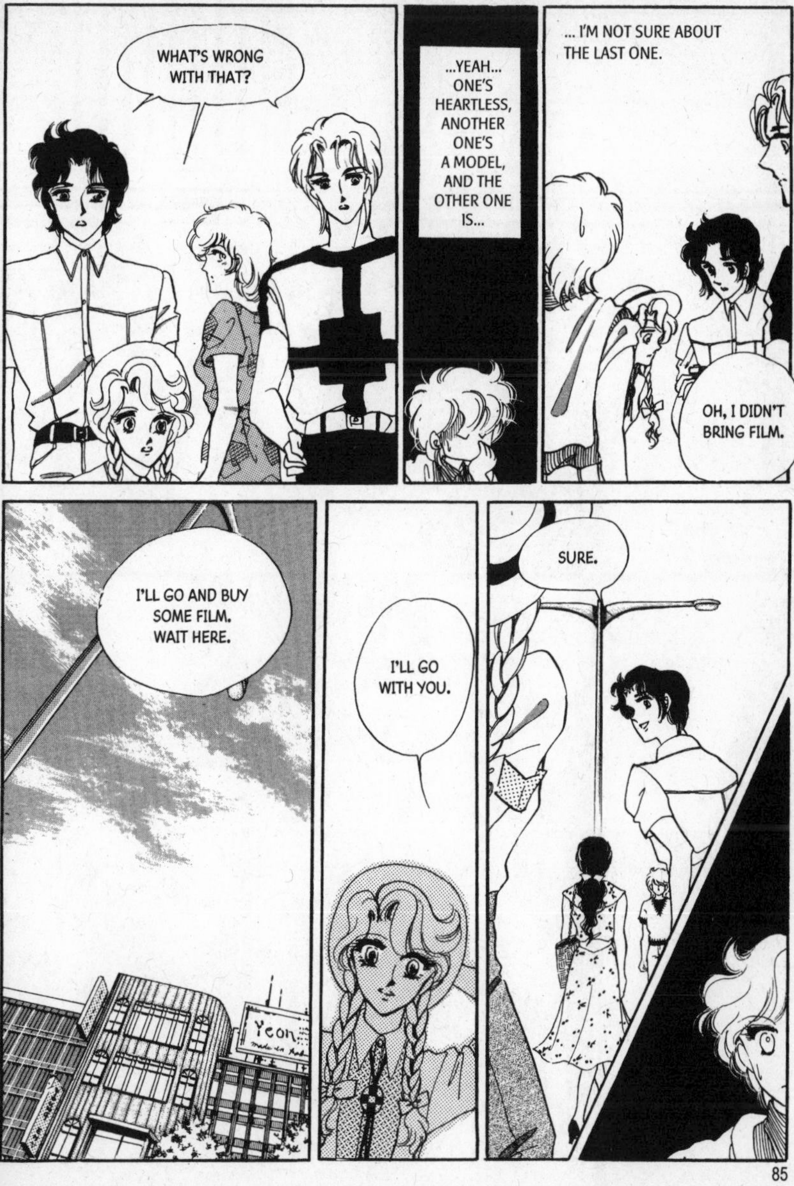
WHAT'S WRONG WITH THAT?
...YEAH... ONE'S HEARTLESS, ANOTHER ONE'S A MODEL, AND THE OTHER ONE IS...
... I'M NOT SURE ABOUT THE LAST ONE.
OH, I DIDN'T BRING FILM.
I'LL GO AND BUY SOME FILM. WAIT HERE.
I'LL GO WITH YOU.
SURE.

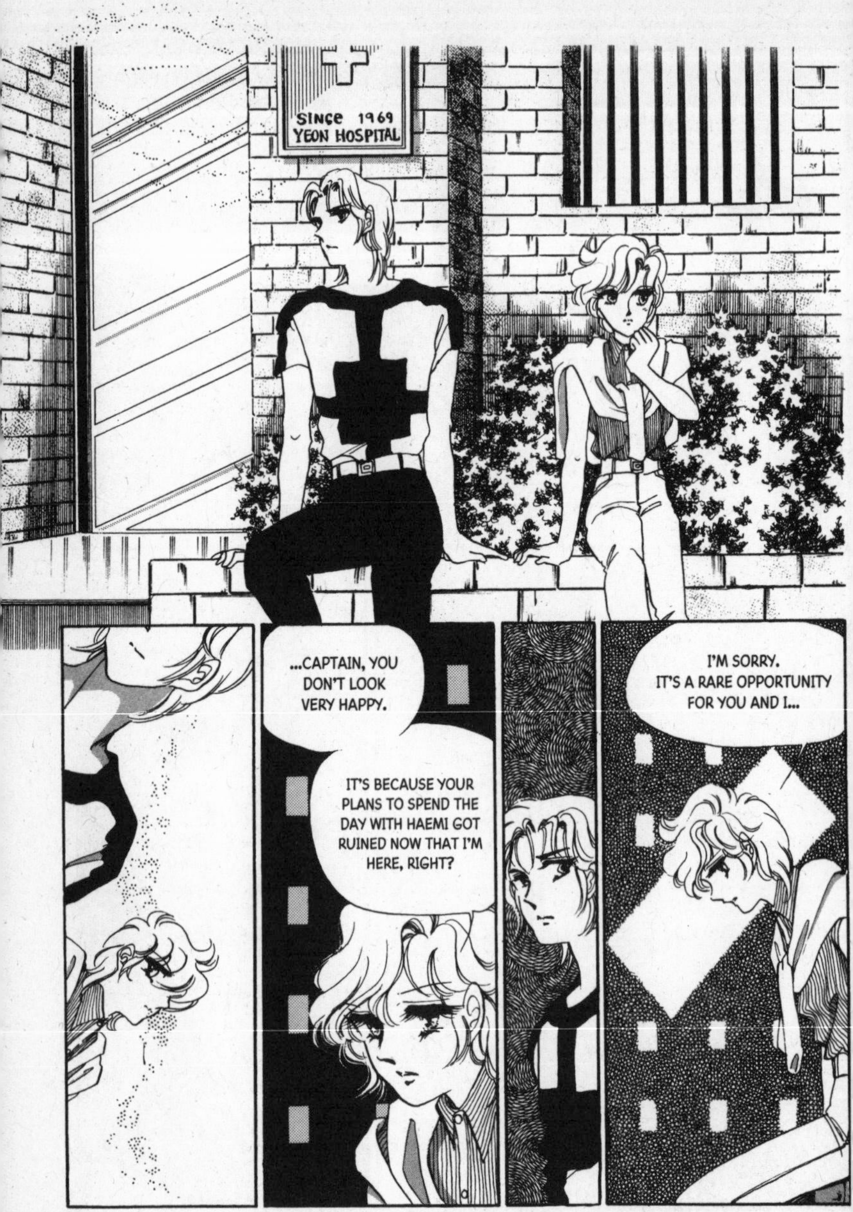
SINCE 1969
YEON HOSPITAL
...CAPTAIN, YOU DON'T LOOK VERY HAPPY.
IT'S BECAUSE YOUR PLANS TO SPEND THE DAY WITH HAEMI GOT RUINED NOW THAT I'M HERE, RIGHT?
I'M SORRY. IT'S A RARE OPPORTUNITY FOR YOU AND I...

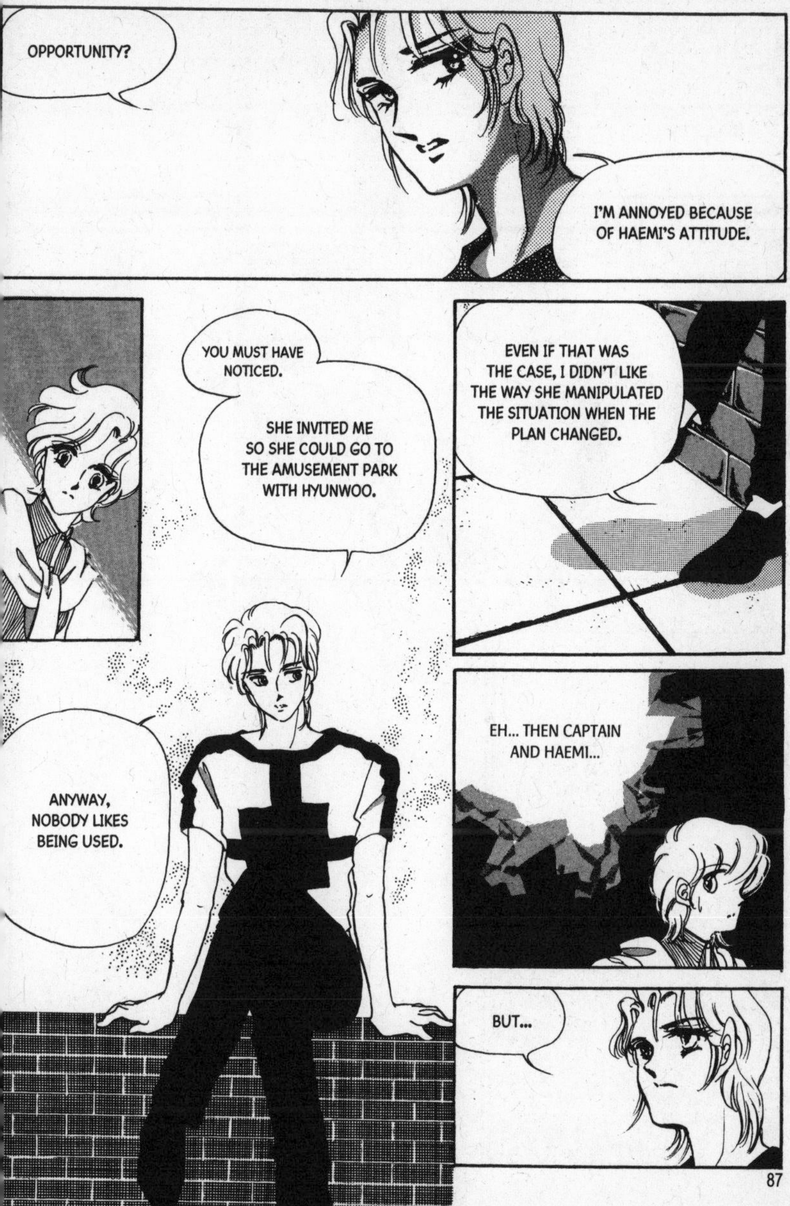
OPPORTUNITY?
I'M ANNOYED BECAUSE OF HAEMI'S ATTITUDE.
YOU MUST HAVE NOTICED.
SHE INVITED ME SO SHE COULD GO TO THE AMUSEMENT PARK WITH HYUNWOO.
ANYWAY, NOBODY LIKES BEING USED.
EVEN IF THAT WAS THE CASE, I DIDN'T LIKE THE WAY SHE MANIPULATED THE SITUATION WHEN THE PLAN CHANGED.
EH... THEN CAPTAIN AND HAEMI...
BUT...

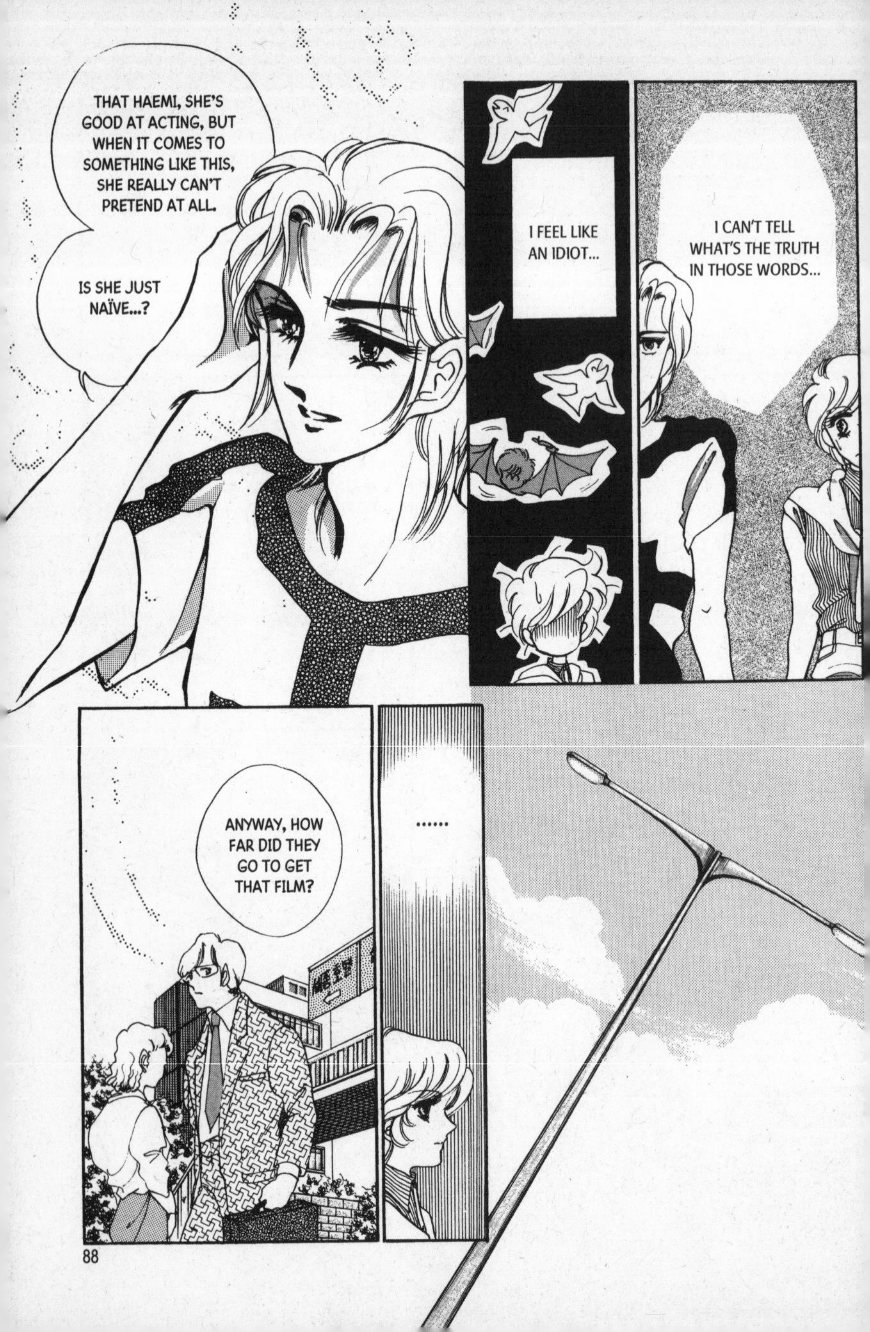
THAT HAEMI, SHE'S GOOD AT ACTING, BUT WHEN IT COMES TO SOMETHING LIKE THIS, SHE REALLY CAN'T PRETEND AT ALL.
IS SHE JUST NAÏVE...?
I FEEL LIKE AN IDIOT...
I CAN'T TELL WHAT'S THE TRUTH IN THOSE WORDS...
ANYWAY, HOW FAR DID THEY GO TO GET THAT FILM?
......

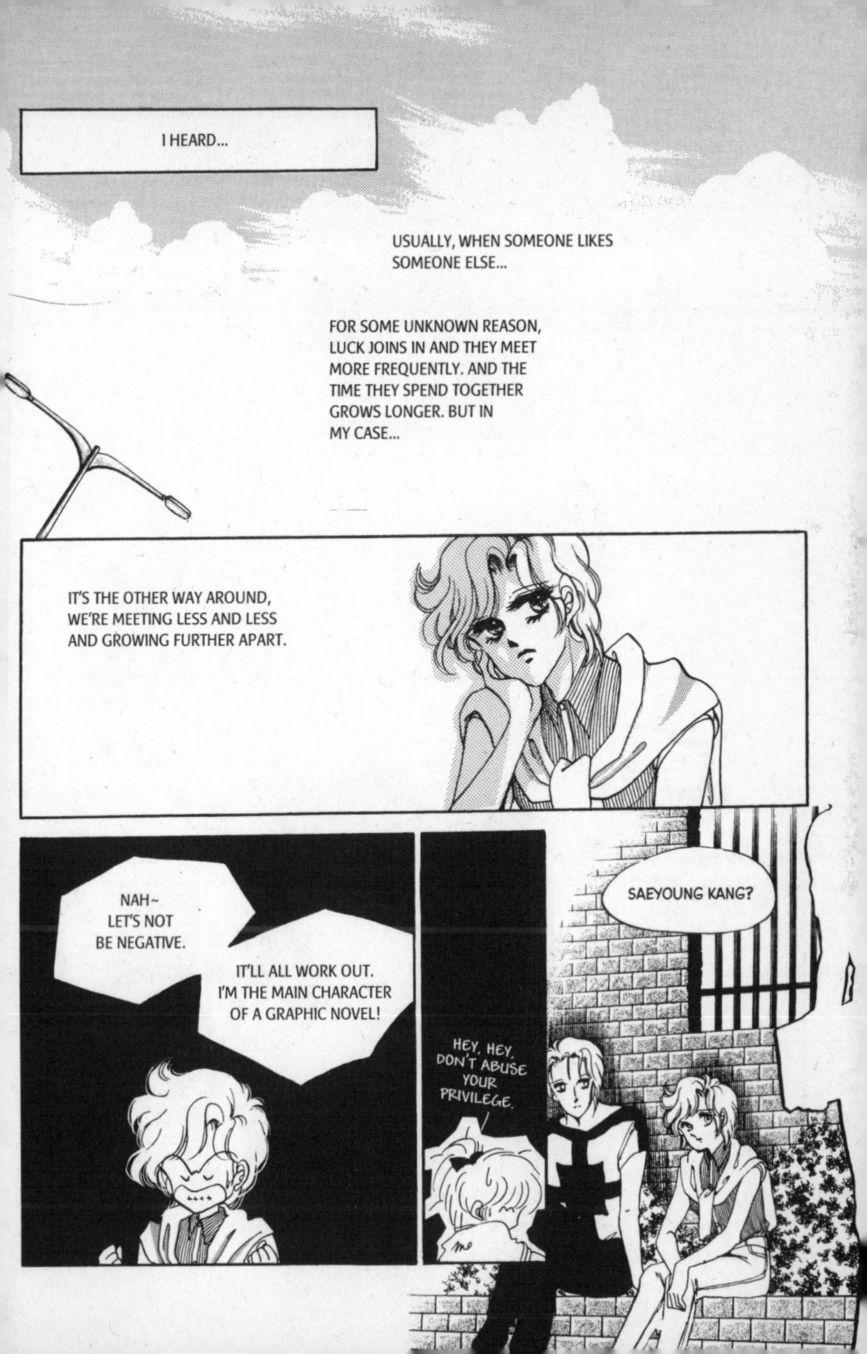
I HEARD...
USUALLY, WHEN SOMEONE LIKES SOMEONE ELSE...
FOR SOME UNKNOWN REASON, LUCK JOINS IN AND THEY MEET MORE FREQUENTLY. AND THE TIME THEY SPEND TOGETHER GROWS LONGER. BUT IN MY CASE...
IT'S THE OTHER WAY AROUND, WE'RE MEETING LESS AND LESS AND GROWING FURTHER APART.
NAH~ LET'S NOT BE NEGATIVE.
IT'LL ALL WORK OUT. I'M THE MAIN CHARACTER OF A GRAPHIC NOVEL!
SAEYOUNG KANG?
HEY, HEY, DON'T ABUSE YOUR PRIVILEGE.

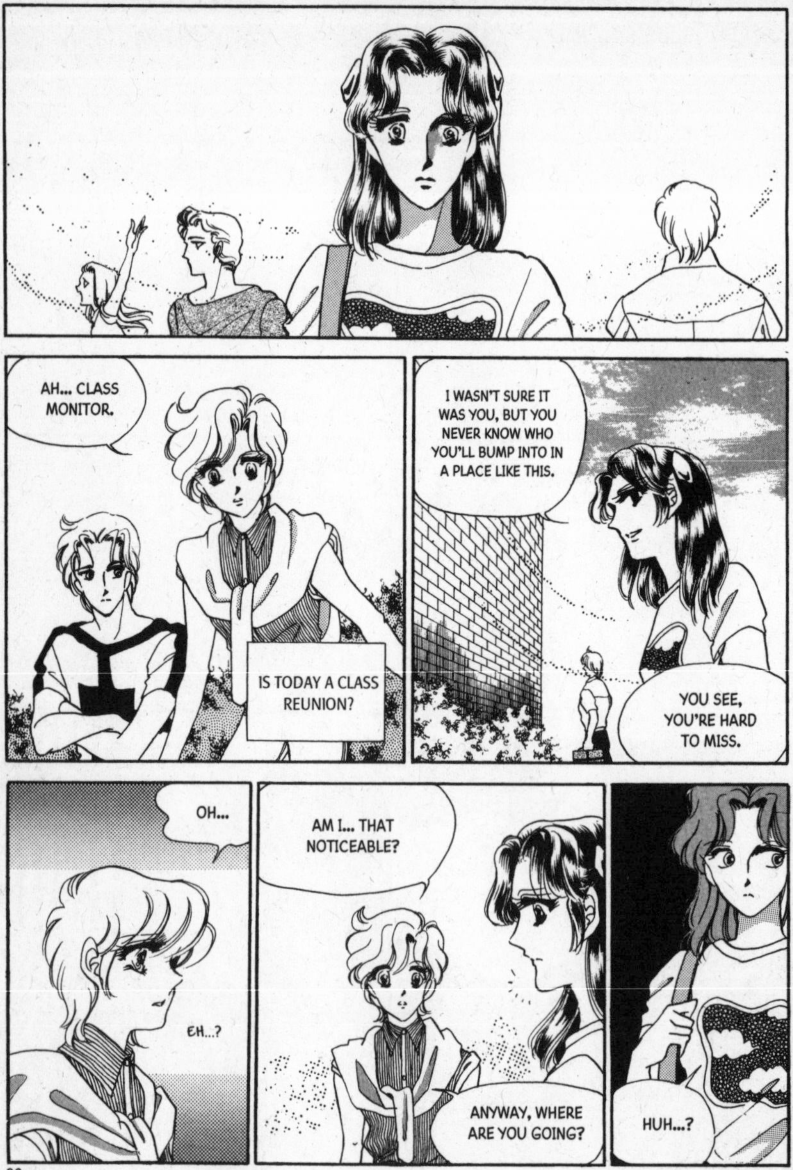
AH... CLASS MONITOR.
IS TODAY A CLASS REUNION?
I WASN'T SURE IT WAS YOU, BUT YOU NEVER KNOW WHO YOU'LL BUMP INTO IN A PLACE LIKE THIS.
YOU SEE, YOU'RE HARD TO MISS.
OH...
EH...?
AM I... THAT NOTICEABLE?
ANYWAY, WHERE ARE YOU GOING?
HUH...?

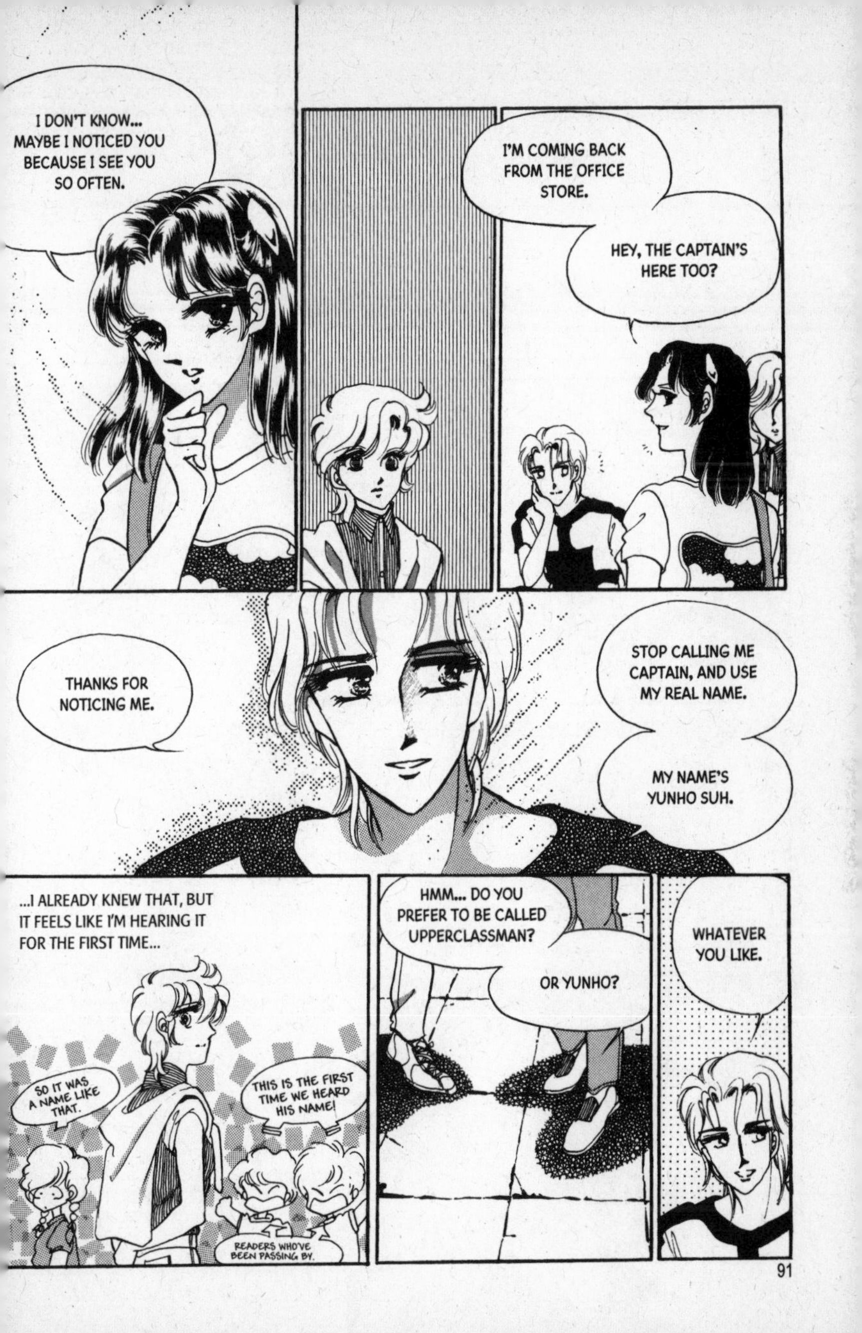
I DON'T KNOW... MAYBE I NOTICED YOU BECAUSE I SEE YOU SO OFTEN.
I'M COMING BACK FROM THE OFFICE STORE.
HEY, THE CAPTAIN'S HERE TOO?
THANKS FOR NOTICING ME.
STOP CALLING ME CAPTAIN, AND USE MY REAL NAME.
MY NAME'S YUNHO SUH.
...I ALREADY KNEW THAT, BUT IT FEELS LIKE I'M HEARING IT FOR THE FIRST TIME...
SO IT WAS A NAME LIKE THAT.
THIS IS THE FIRST TIME WE HEARD HIS NAME!
READERS WHO'VE BEEN PASSING BY.
HMM... DO YOU PREFER TO BE CALLED UPPERCLASSMAN?
OR YUNHO?
WHATEVER YOU LIKE.

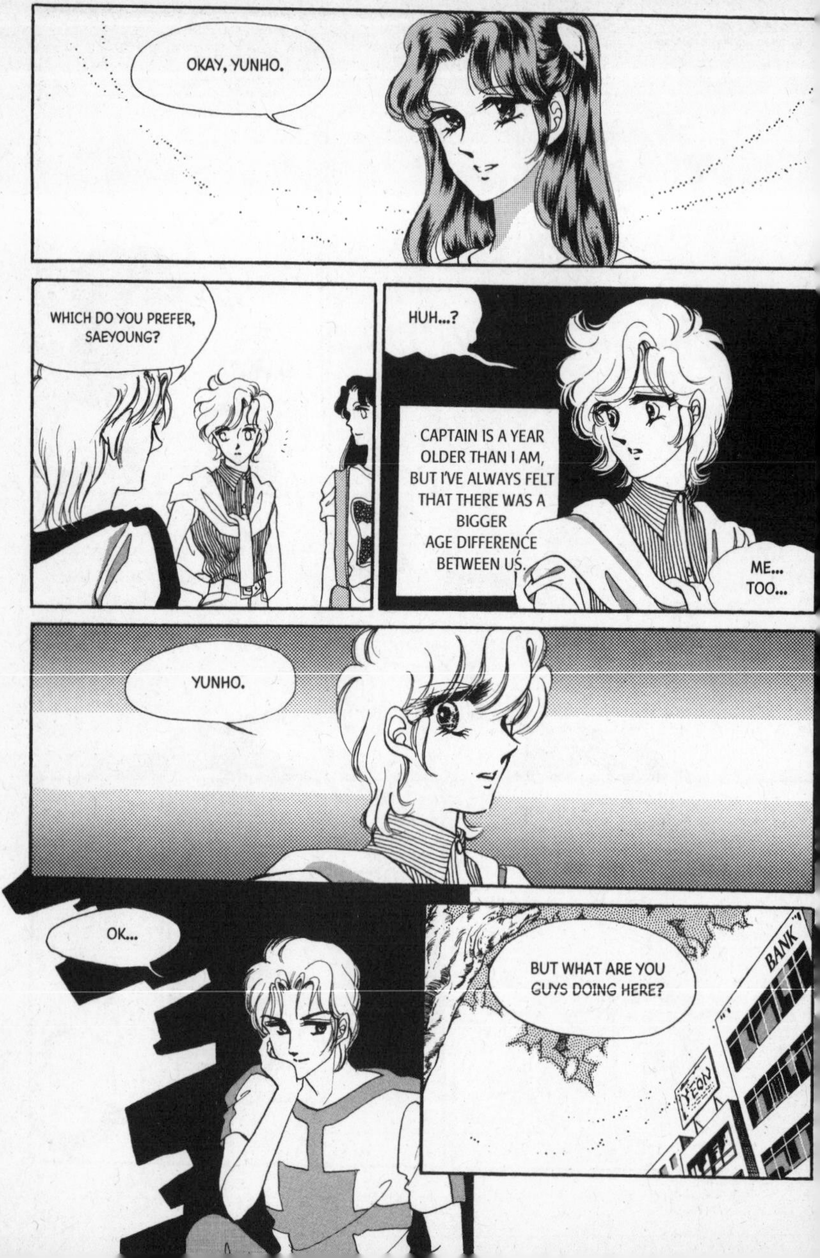
OKAY, YUNHO.
WHICH DO YOU PREFER, SAEYOUNG?
HUH...?
CAPTAIN IS A YEAR OLDER THAN I AM, BUT I'VE ALWAYS FELT THAT THERE WAS A BIGGER AGE DIFFERENCE BETWEEN US.
ME... TOO...
YUNHO.
OK...
BUT WHAT ARE YOU GUYS DOING HERE?
BANK
YEON

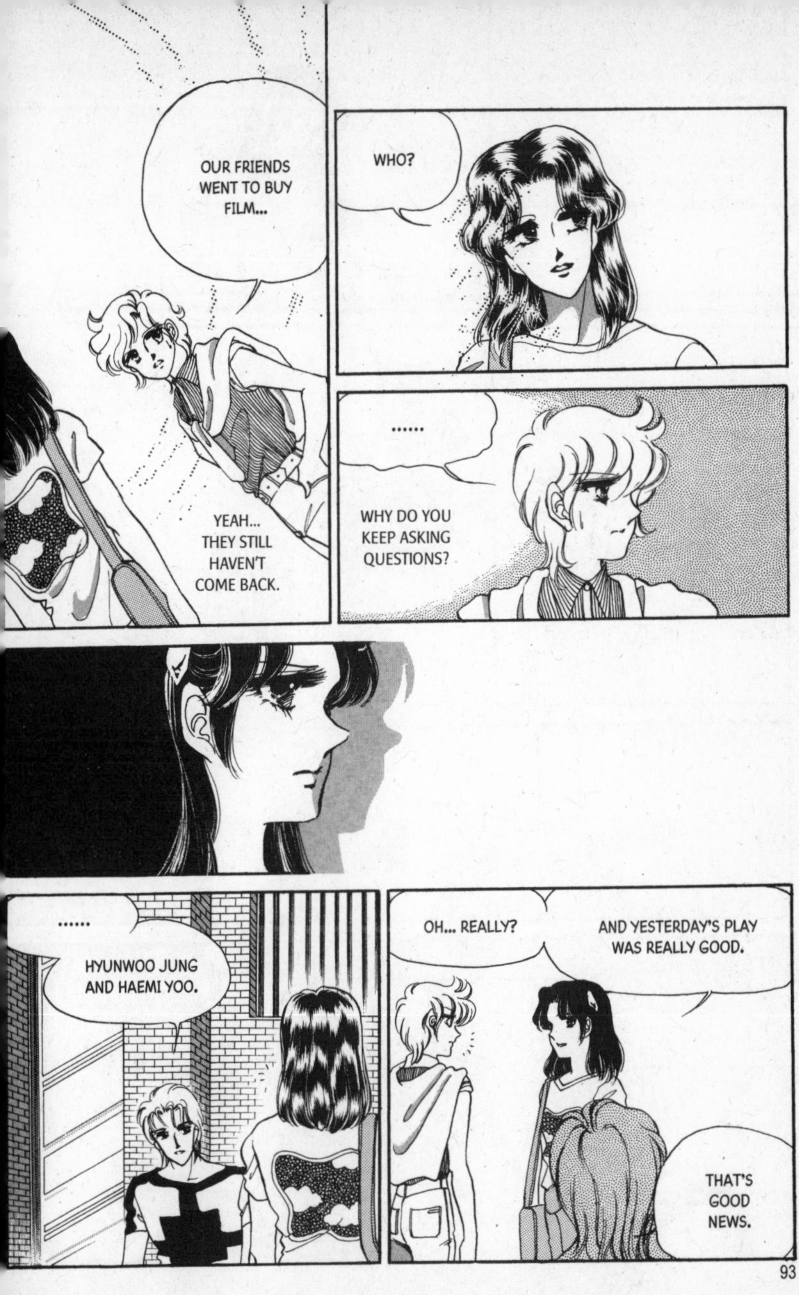
OUR FRIENDS WENT TO BUY FILM...
YEAH... THEY STILL HAVEN'T COME BACK.
WHO?
......
WHY DO YOU KEEP ASKING QUESTIONS?
......
HYUNWOO JUNG AND HAEMI YOO.
OH... REALLY?
AND YESTERDAY'S PLAY WAS REALLY GOOD.
THAT'S GOOD NEWS.

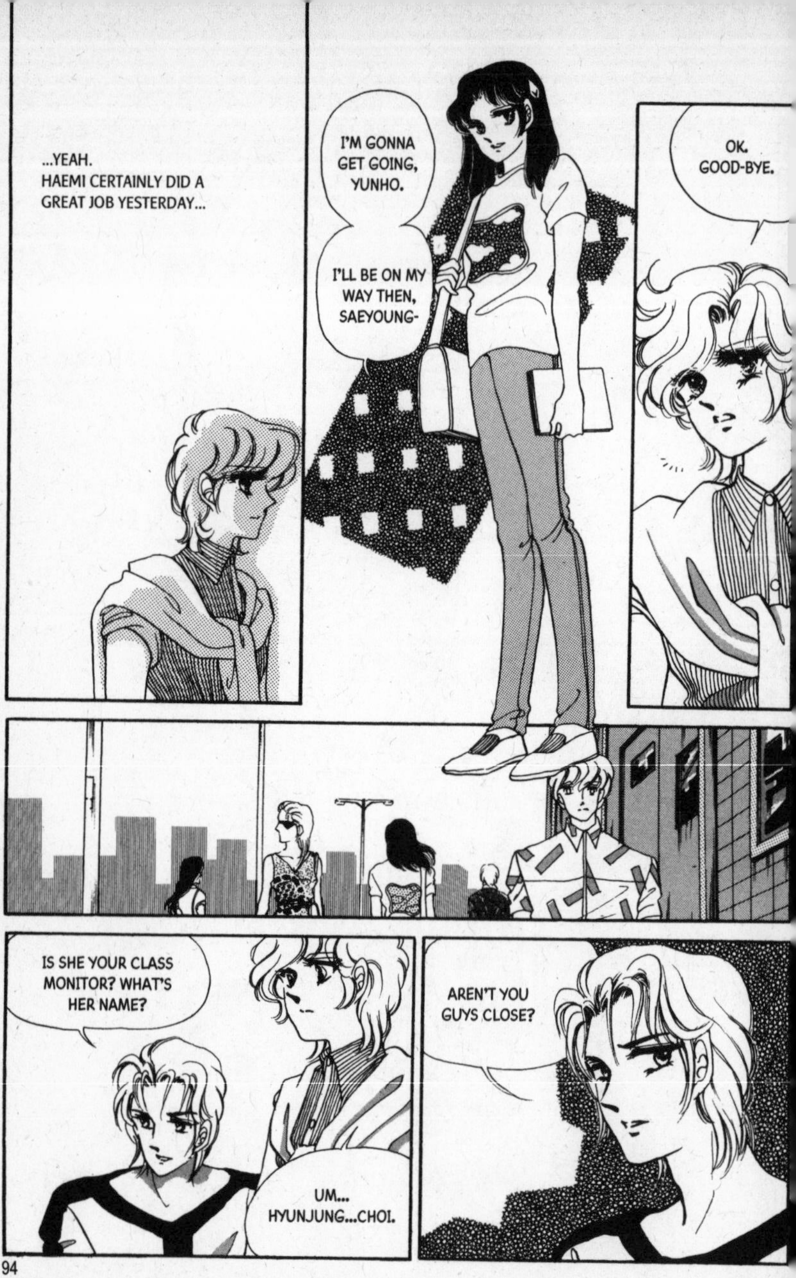
...YEAH.
HAEMI CERTAINLY DID A GREAT JOB YESTERDAY...
I'M GONNA GET GOING, YUNHO.
I'LL BE ON MY WAY THEN, SAEYOUNG-
OK. GOOD-BYE.
IS SHE YOUR CLASS MONITOR? WHAT'S HER NAME?
UM... HYUNJUNG...CHOI.
AREN'T YOU GUYS CLOSE?

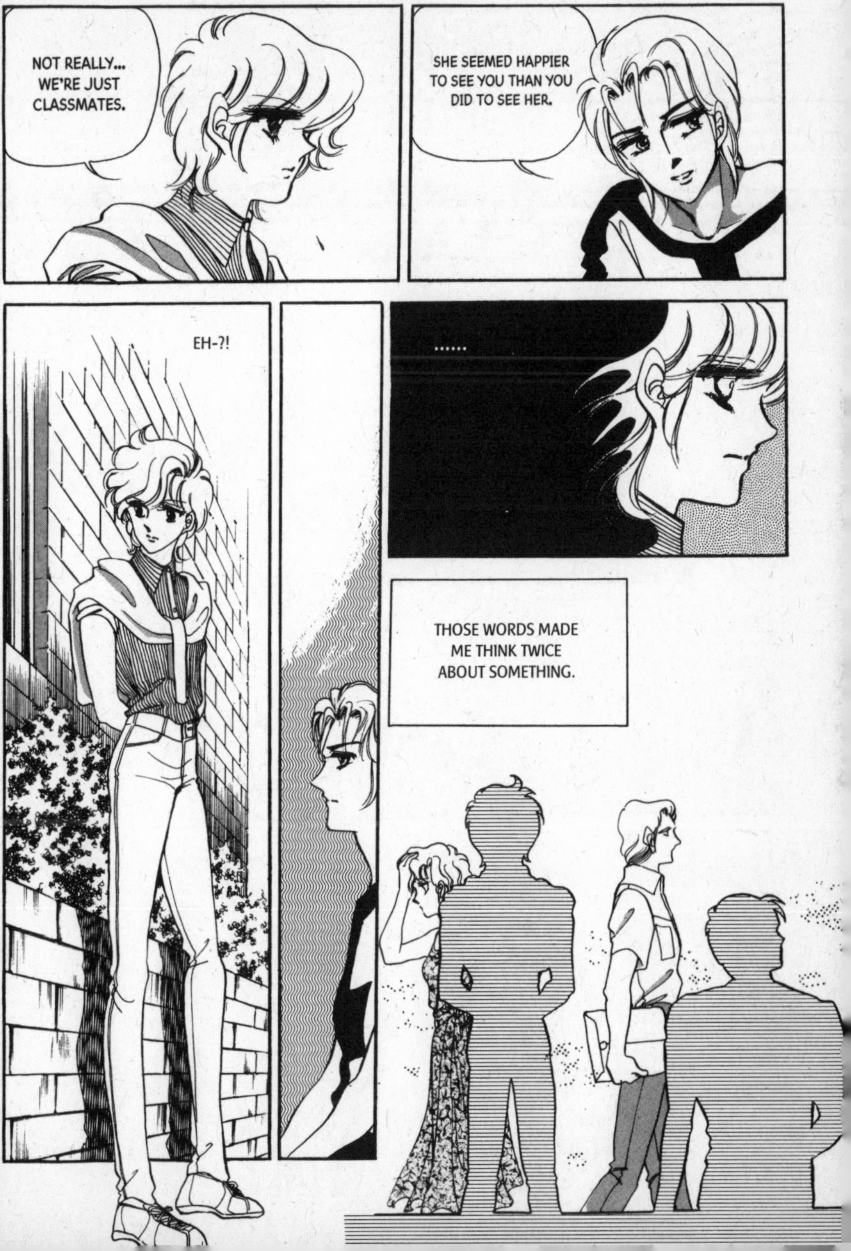
NOT REALLY... WE'RE JUST CLASSMATES.
SHE SEEMED HAPPIER TO SEE YOU THAN YOU DID TO SEE HER.
EH-?!
......
THOSE WORDS MADE ME THINK TWICE ABOUT SOMETHING.

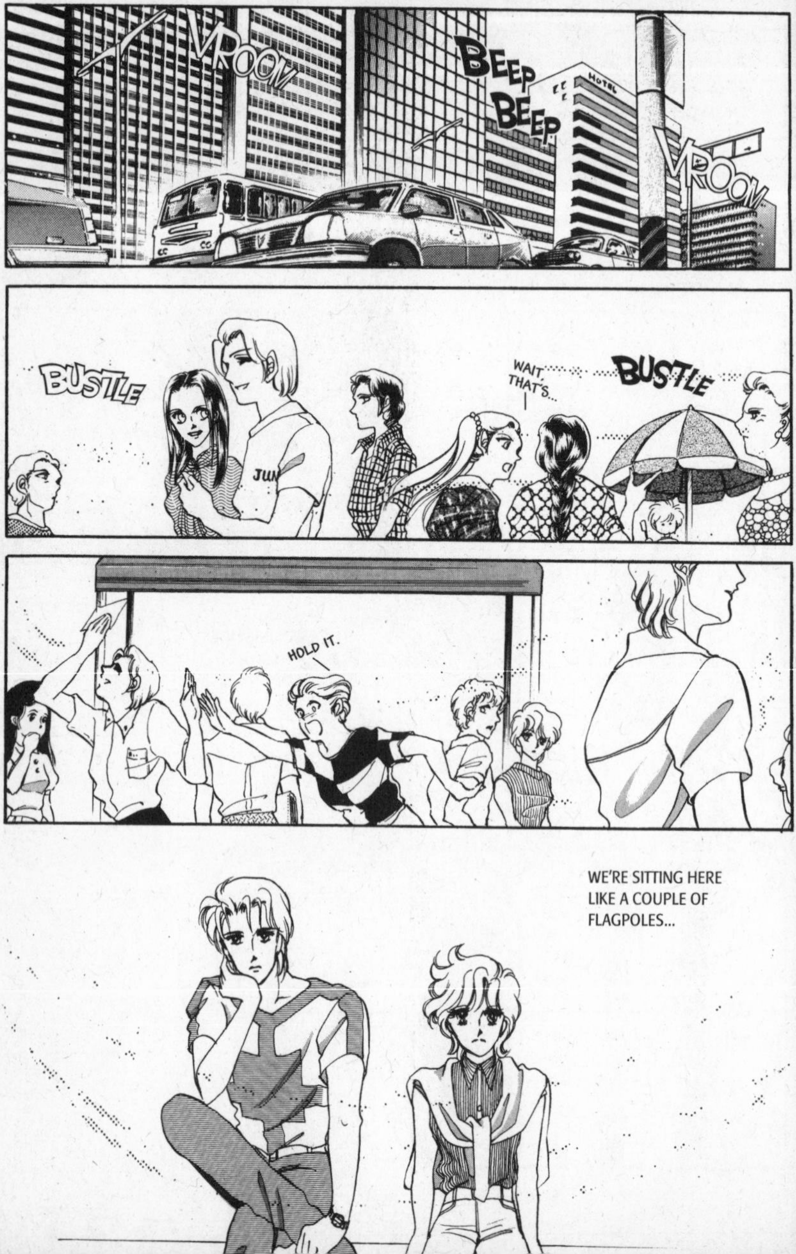
VROOM
BEEP
BEEP
VROOM
BUSTLE
WAIT, THAT'S...
BUSTLE
HOLD IT.
WE'RE SITTING HERE LIKE A COUPLE OF FLAGPOLES...

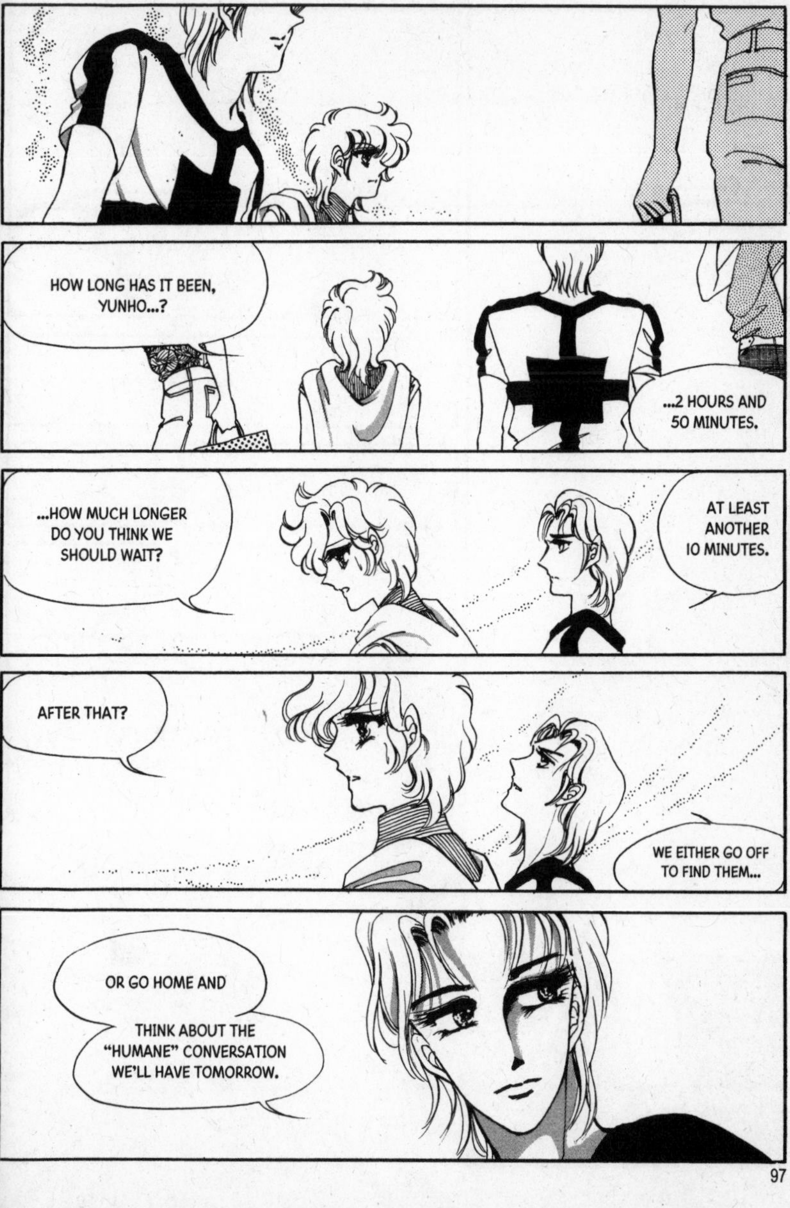
HOW LONG HAS IT BEEN, YUNHO...?
...2 HOURS AND 50 MINUTES.
...HOW MUCH LONGER DO YOU THINK WE SHOULD WAIT?
AT LEAST ANOTHER 10 MINUTES.
AFTER THAT?
WE EITHER GO OFF TO FIND THEM...
OR GO HOME AND
THINK ABOUT THE "HUMANE" CONVERSATION WE'LL HAVE TOMORROW.

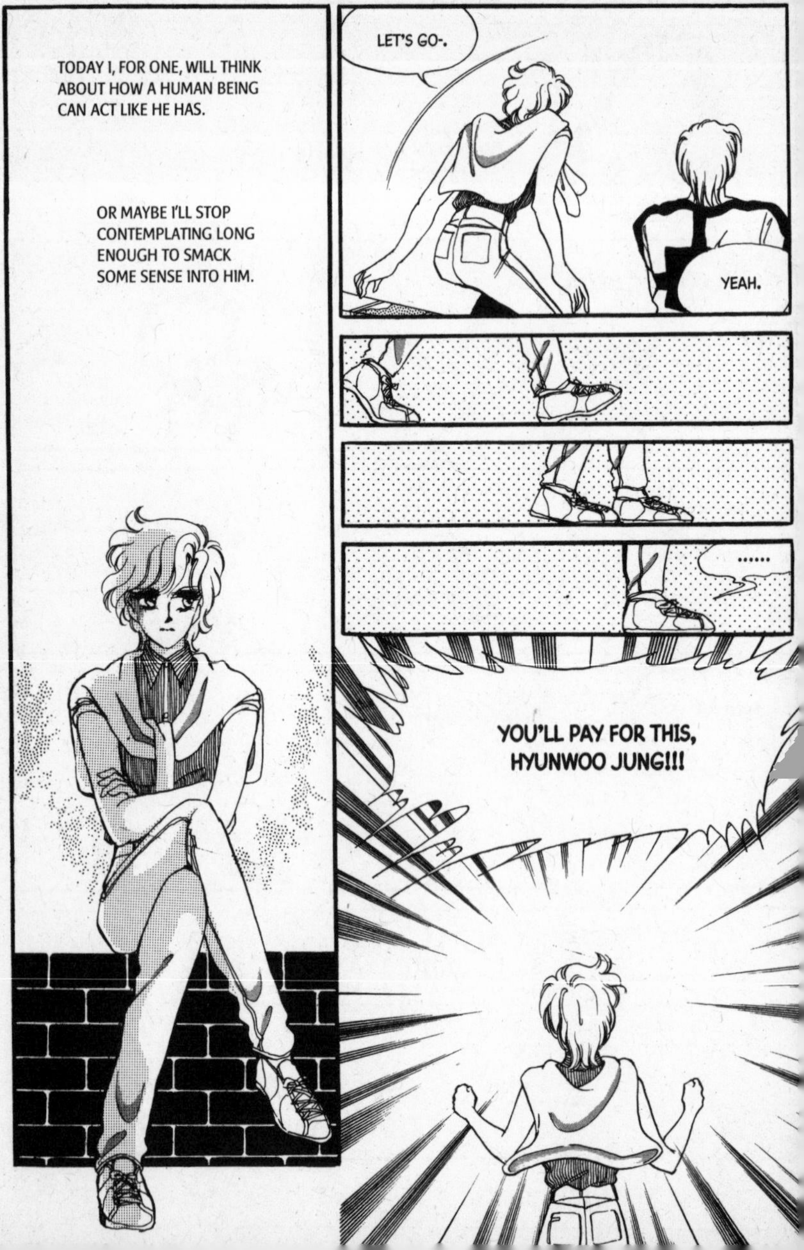
TODAY I, FOR ONE, WILL THINK ABOUT HOW A HUMAN BEING CAN ACT LIKE HE HAS.
OR MAYBE I'LL STOP CONTEMPLATING LONG ENOUGH TO SMACK SOME SENSE INTO HIM.
LET'S GO-.
YEAH.
......
YOU'LL PAY FOR THIS, HYUNWOO JUNG!!!

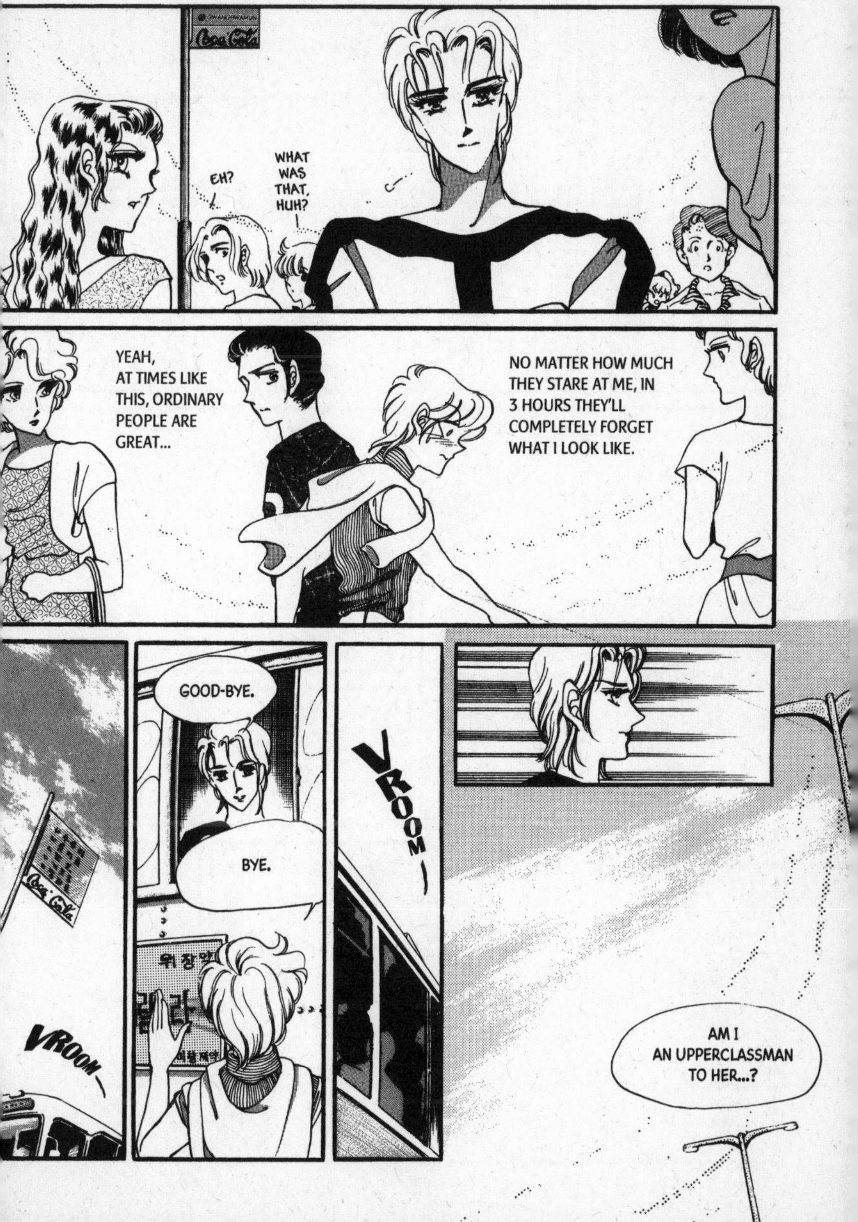
EH?
WHAT WAS THAT, HUH?
YEAH, AT TIMES LIKE THIS, ORDINARY PEOPLE ARE GREAT...
NO MATTER HOW MUCH THEY STARE AT ME, IN 3 HOURS THEY'LL COMPLETELY FORGET WHAT I LOOK LIKE.
VROOM
GOOD-BYE.
BYE.
VROOM
AM I AN UPPERCLASSMAN TO HER...?

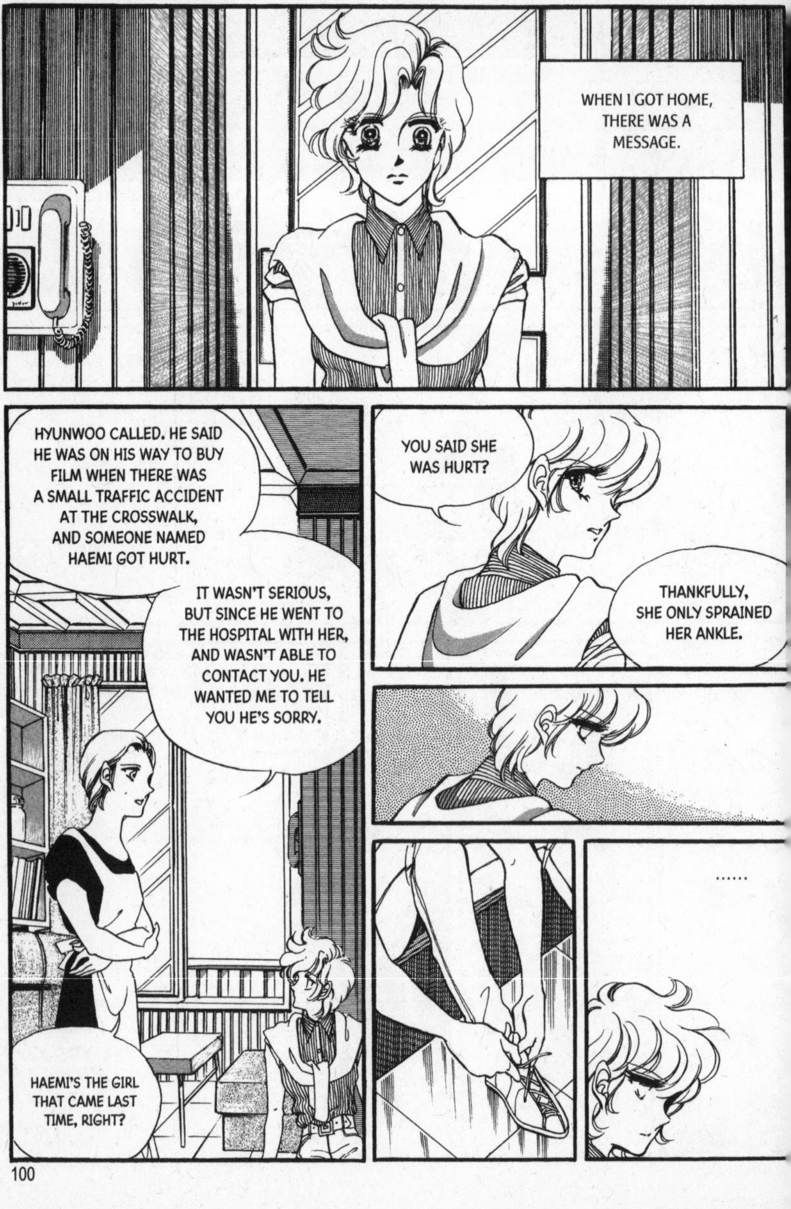
WHEN I GOT HOME, THERE WAS A MESSAGE.
HYUNWOO CALLED. HE SAID HE WAS ON HIS WAY TO BUY FILM WHEN THERE WAS A SMALL TRAFFIC ACCIDENT AT THE CROSSWALK, AND SOMEONE NAMED HAEMI GOT HURT.
IT WASN'T SERIOUS, BUT SINCE HE WENT TO THE HOSPITAL WITH HER, AND WASN'T ABLE TO CONTACT YOU. HE WANTED ME TO TELL YOU HE'S SORRY.
HAEMI'S THE GIRL THAT CAME LAST TIME, RIGHT?
YOU SAID SHE WAS HURT?
THANKFULLY, SHE ONLY SPRAINED HER ANKLE.
......

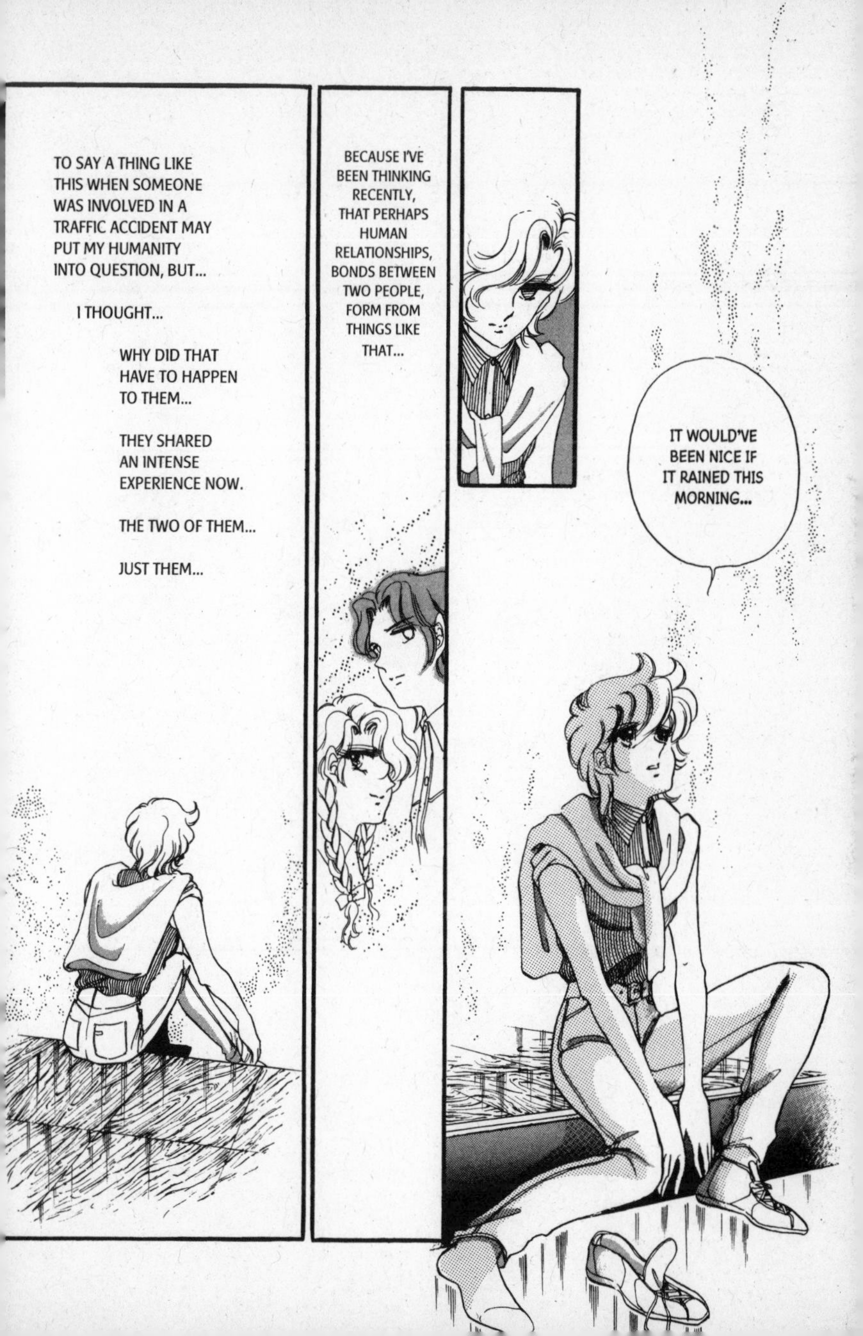
TO SAY A THING LIKE THIS WHEN SOMEONE WAS INVOLVED IN A TRAFFIC ACCIDENT MAY PUT MY HUMANITY INTO QUESTION, BUT...
I THOUGHT...
WHY DID THAT HAVE TO HAPPEN TO THEM...
THEY SHARED AN INTENSE EXPERIENCE NOW.
THE TWO OF THEM...
JUST THEM...
BECAUSE I'VE BEEN THINKING RECENTLY, THAT PERHAPS HUMAN RELATIONSHIPS, BONDS BETWEEN TWO PEOPLE, FORM FROM THINGS LIKE THAT...
IT WOULD'VE BEEN NICE IF IT RAINED THIS MORNING...

OF COURSE–NO MATTER
WHAT ANYBODY SAYS,
I AM A "PERSON."

IT'S JUST THAT I DON'T
WANT THE WORD
"ORDINARY" TO COME
IN FRONT OF "PERSON"
WHEN IT REFERS TO ME.

WHETHER THAT
FEELING COMES FROM
MY 17-YEAR-OLD WHIMSY
OR MY OWN INFERIORITY
COMPLEX-?

I DREAM
OF DISCOVERING
MY CERTAIN SPECIAL
POTENTIAL BECAUSE THERE'S
STILL THE
UNFORESEEABLE FUTURE.

EVEN THOUGH REALITY
NEVER CHANGES, AND SO
I'M INEVITABLY JUST
AN ORDINARY PERSON.

AH, AH... YES.
THIS LIFE WHERE
TODAY IS SIMPLY A NEW
YESTERDAY.

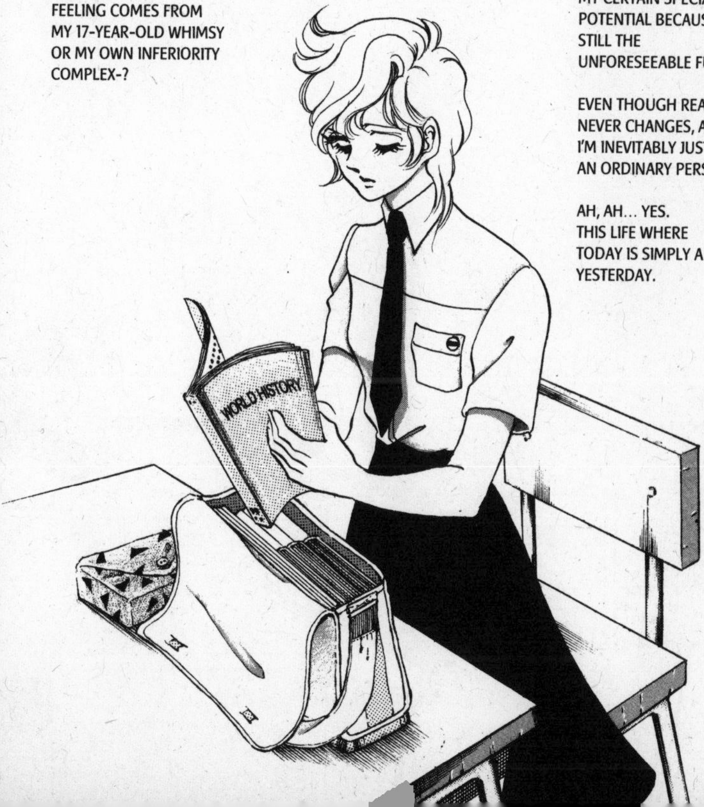
WORLD HISTORY

WHAT ARE THE SPECIAL DREAMS
THAT I WANT TO DREAM OF
IN THIS LIFE THAT IS ONLY
A CONTINUATION OF YESTERDAY...?

THIRD STORY

ORDINARY PEOPLE

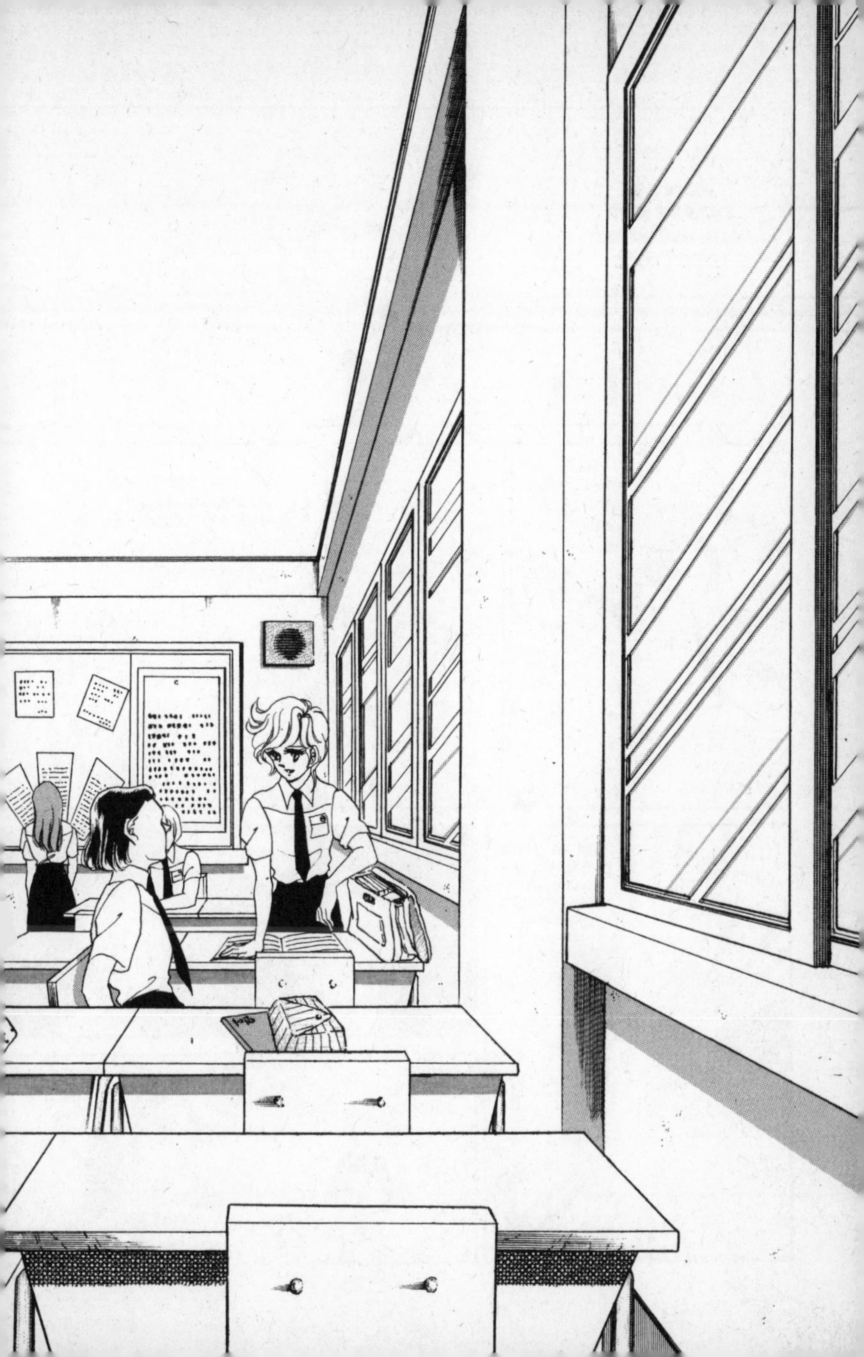

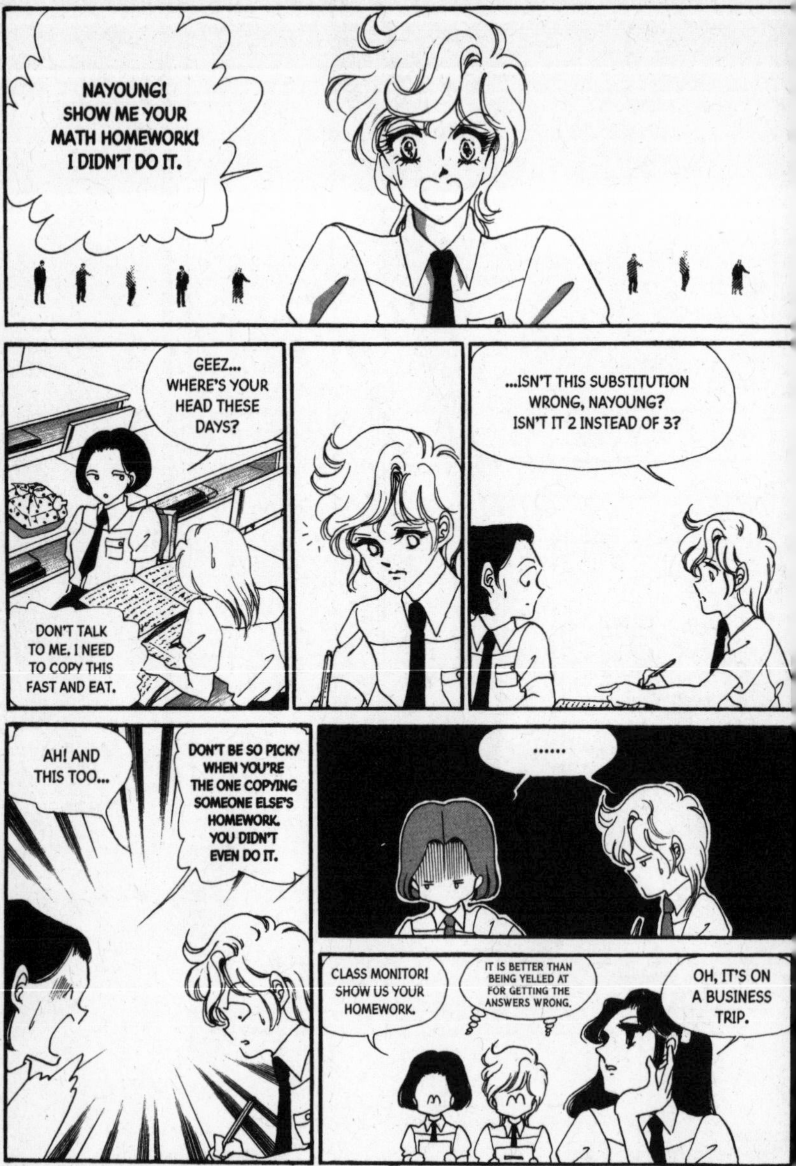
NAYOUNG! SHOW ME YOUR MATH HOMEWORK! I DIDN'T DO IT.
GEEZ... WHERE'S YOUR HEAD THESE DAYS?
DON'T TALK TO ME. I NEED TO COPY THIS FAST AND EAT.
...ISN'T THIS SUBSTITUTION WRONG, NAYOUNG? ISN'T IT 2 INSTEAD OF 3?
AH! AND THIS TOO...
DON'T BE SO PICKY WHEN YOU'RE THE ONE COPYING SOMEONE ELSE'S HOMEWORK. YOU DIDN'T EVEN DO IT.
......
CLASS MONITOR! SHOW US YOUR HOMEWORK.
IT IS BETTER THAN BEING YELLED AT FOR GETTING THE ANSWERS WRONG.
OH, IT'S ON A BUSINESS TRIP.

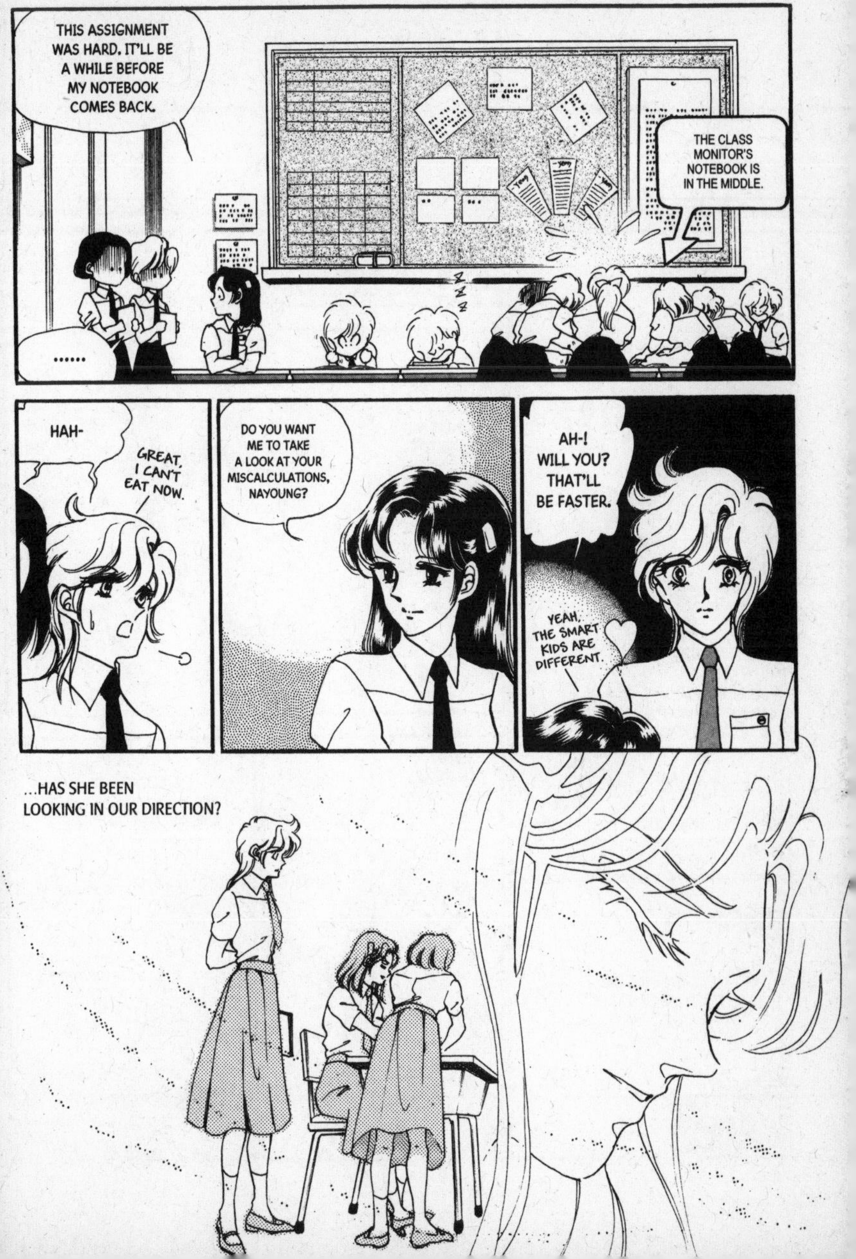

THIS ASSIGNMENT WAS HARD. IT'LL BE A WHILE BEFORE MY NOTEBOOK COMES BACK.
THE CLASS MONITOR'S NOTEBOOK IS IN THE MIDDLE.
......
HAH-
GREAT, I CAN'T EAT NOW.
DO YOU WANT ME TO TAKE A LOOK AT YOUR MISCALCULATIONS, NAYOUNG?
AH-! WILL YOU? THAT'LL BE FASTER.
YEAH, THE SMART KIDS ARE DIFFERENT.
...HAS SHE BEEN LOOKING IN OUR DIRECTION?

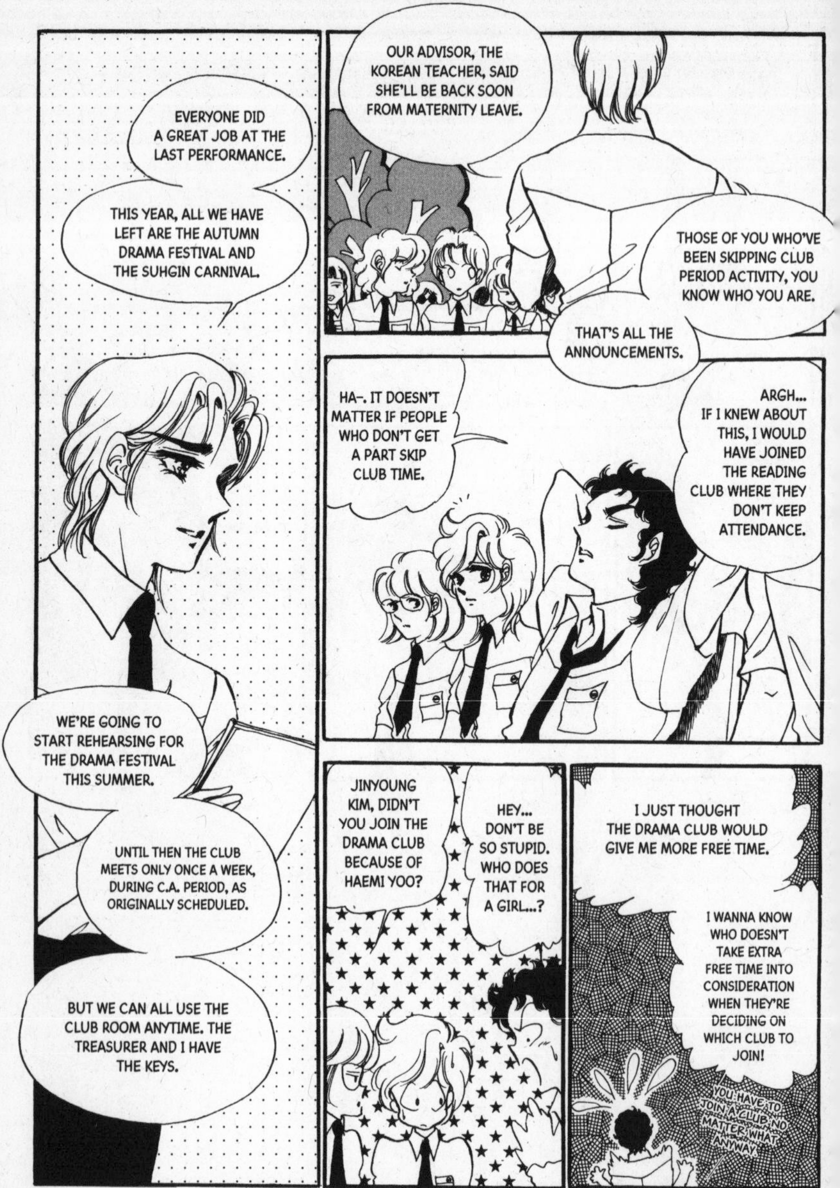
EVERYONE DID A GREAT JOB AT THE LAST PERFORMANCE.
THIS YEAR, ALL WE HAVE LEFT ARE THE AUTUMN DRAMA FESTIVAL AND THE SUHGIN CARNIVAL.
WE'RE GOING TO START REHEARSING FOR THE DRAMA FESTIVAL THIS SUMMER.
UNTIL THEN THE CLUB MEETS ONLY ONCE A WEEK, DURING C.A. PERIOD, AS ORIGINALLY SCHEDULED.
BUT WE CAN ALL USE THE CLUB ROOM ANYTIME. THE TREASURER AND I HAVE THE KEYS.
OUR ADVISOR, THE KOREAN TEACHER, SAID SHE'LL BE BACK SOON FROM MATERNITY LEAVE.
THOSE OF YOU WHO'VE BEEN SKIPPING CLUB PERIOD ACTIVITY, YOU KNOW WHO YOU ARE.
THAT'S ALL THE ANNOUNCEMENTS.
ARGH... IF I KNEW ABOUT THIS, I WOULD HAVE JOINED THE READING CLUB WHERE THEY DON'T KEEP ATTENDANCE.
HA-. IT DOESN'T MATTER IF PEOPLE WHO DON'T GET A PART SKIP CLUB TIME.
JINYOUNG KIM, DIDN'T YOU JOIN THE DRAMA CLUB BECAUSE OF HAEMI YOO?
HEY... DON'T BE SO STUPID. WHO DOES THAT FOR A GIRL...?
I JUST THOUGHT THE DRAMA CLUB WOULD GIVE ME MORE FREE TIME.
I WANNA KNOW WHO DOESN'T TAKE EXTRA FREE TIME INTO CONSIDERATION WHEN THEY'RE DECIDING ON WHICH CLUB TO JOIN!
YOU HAVE TO JOIN A CLUB NO MATTER WHAT ANYWAY.

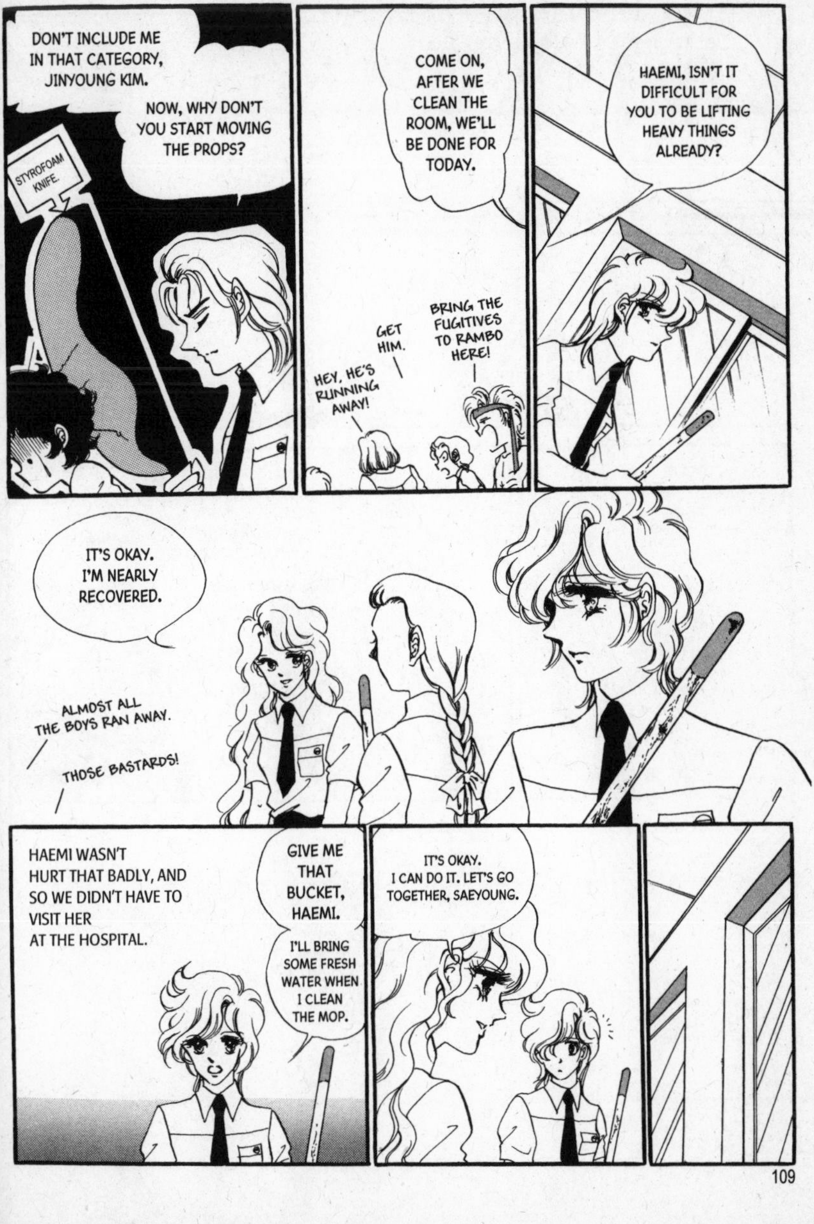
DON'T INCLUDE ME IN THAT CATEGORY, JINYOUNG KIM.
NOW, WHY DON'T YOU START MOVING THE PROPS?
STYROFOAM KNIFE.
COME ON, AFTER WE CLEAN THE ROOM, WE'LL BE DONE FOR TODAY.
HEY, HE'S RUNNING AWAY!
GET HIM.
BRING THE FUGITIVES TO RAMBO HERE!
HAEMI, ISN'T IT DIFFICULT FOR YOU TO BE LIFTING HEAVY THINGS ALREADY?
IT'S OKAY. I'M NEARLY RECOVERED.
ALMOST ALL THE BOYS RAN AWAY.
THOSE BASTARDS!
HAEMI WASN'T HURT THAT BADLY, AND SO WE DIDN'T HAVE TO VISIT HER AT THE HOSPITAL.
GIVE ME THAT BUCKET, HAEMI.
I'LL BRING SOME FRESH WATER WHEN I CLEAN THE MOP.
IT'S OKAY. I CAN DO IT. LET'S GO TOGETHER, SAEYOUNG.

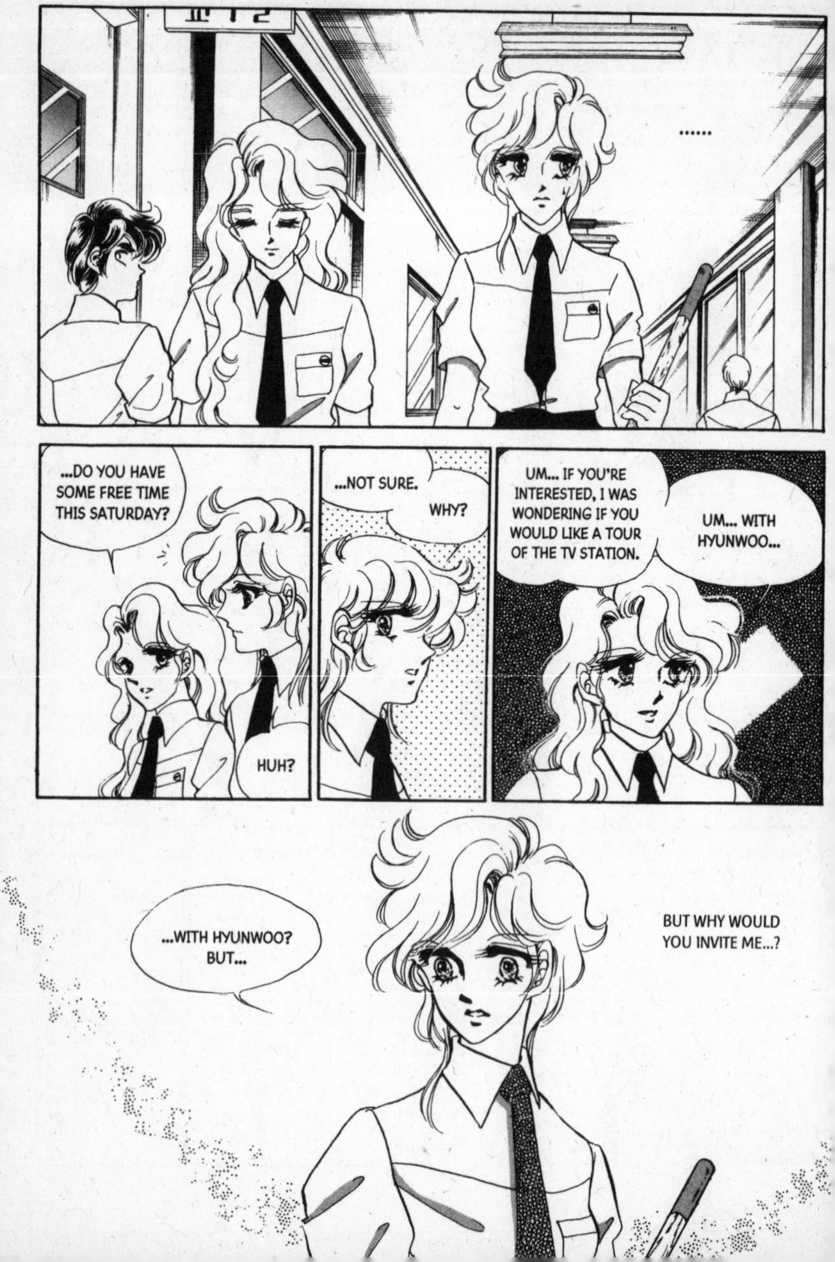
......
...DO YOU HAVE SOME FREE TIME THIS SATURDAY?
HUH?
...NOT SURE.
WHY?
UM... IF YOU'RE INTERESTED, I WAS WONDERING IF YOU WOULD LIKE A TOUR OF THE TV STATION.
UM... WITH HYUNWOO...
...WITH HYUNWOO? BUT...
BUT WHY WOULD YOU INVITE ME...?

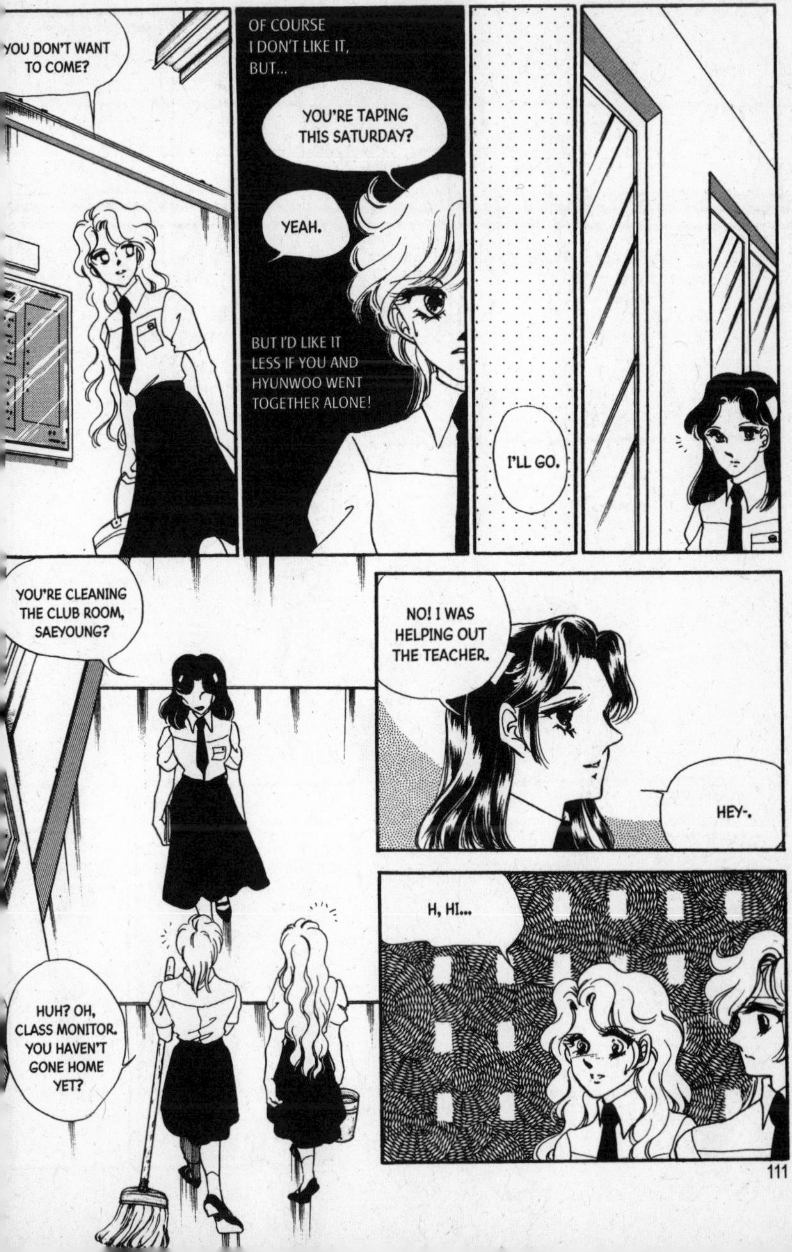
YOU DON'T WANT TO COME?
OF COURSE I DON'T LIKE IT, BUT...
YOU'RE TAPING THIS SATURDAY?
YEAH.
BUT I'D LIKE IT LESS IF YOU AND HYUNWOO WENT TOGETHER ALONE!
I'LL GO.
YOU'RE CLEANING THE CLUB ROOM, SAEYOUNG?
HUH? OH, CLASS MONITOR. YOU HAVEN'T GONE HOME YET?
NO! I WAS HELPING OUT THE TEACHER.
HEY-.
H, HI...

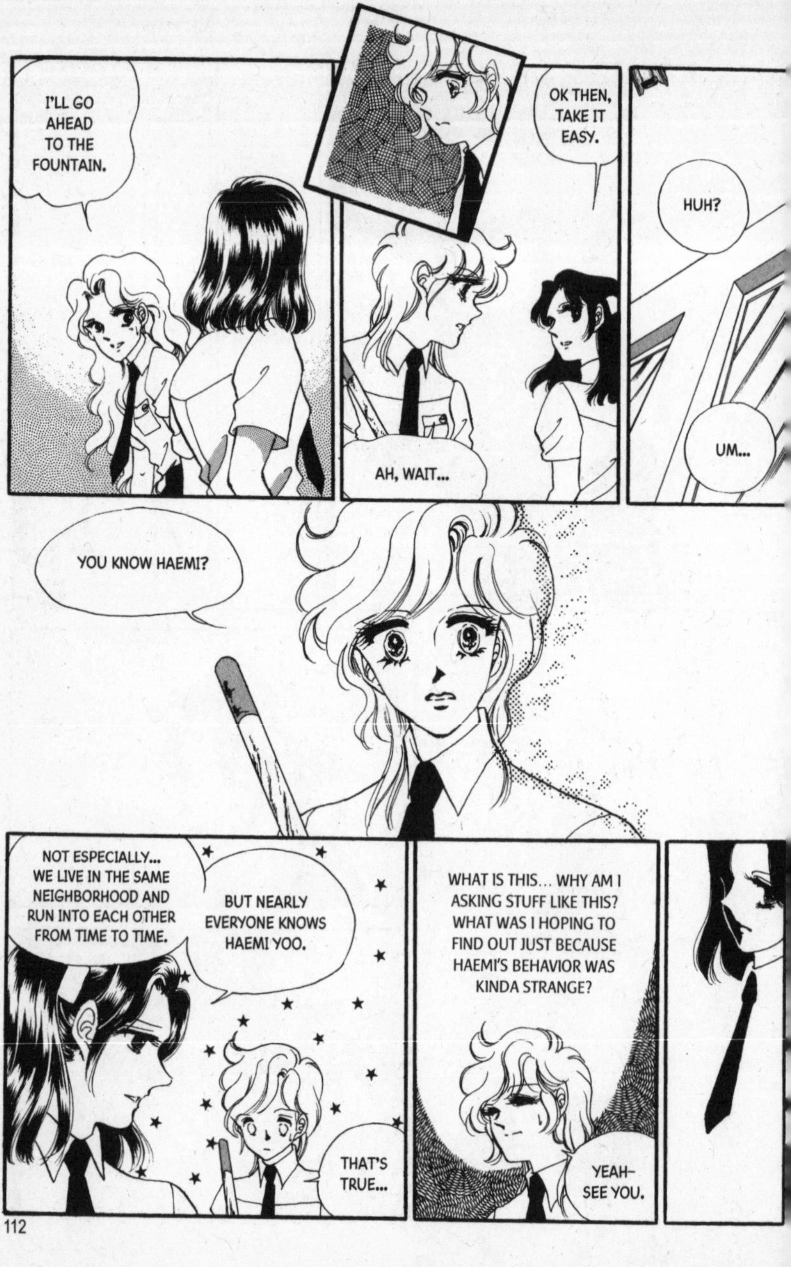
I'LL GO AHEAD TO THE FOUNTAIN.
OK THEN, TAKE IT EASY.
AH, WAIT...
HUH?
UM...
YOU KNOW HAEMI?
NOT ESPECIALLY... WE LIVE IN THE SAME NEIGHBORHOOD AND RUN INTO EACH OTHER FROM TIME TO TIME.
BUT NEARLY EVERYONE KNOWS HAEMI YOO.
THAT'S TRUE...
WHAT IS THIS... WHY AM I ASKING STUFF LIKE THIS? WHAT WAS I HOPING TO FIND OUT JUST BECAUSE HAEMI'S BEHAVIOR WAS KINDA STRANGE?
YEAH– SEE YOU.

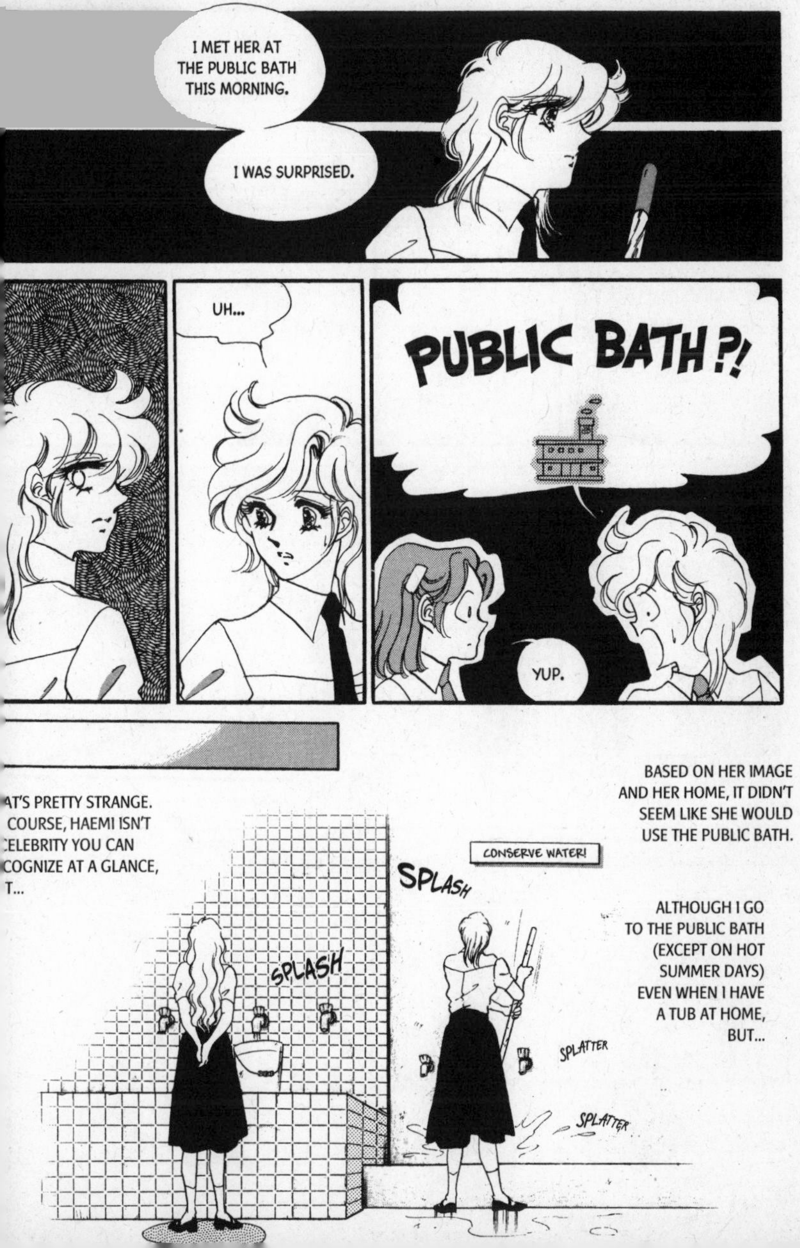

I MET HER AT THE PUBLIC BATH THIS MORNING.
I WAS SURPRISED.
UH...
PUBLIC BATH?!
YUP.
AT'S PRETTY STRANGE. COURSE, HAEMI ISN'T CELEBRITY YOU CAN COGNIZE AT A GLANCE, T...
BASED ON HER IMAGE AND HER HOME, IT DIDN'T SEEM LIKE SHE WOULD USE THE PUBLIC BATH.
CONSERVE WATER!
SPLASH
SPLASH
ALTHOUGH I GO TO THE PUBLIC BATH (EXCEPT ON HOT SUMMER DAYS) EVEN WHEN I HAVE A TUB AT HOME, BUT...
SPLATTER
SPLATTER

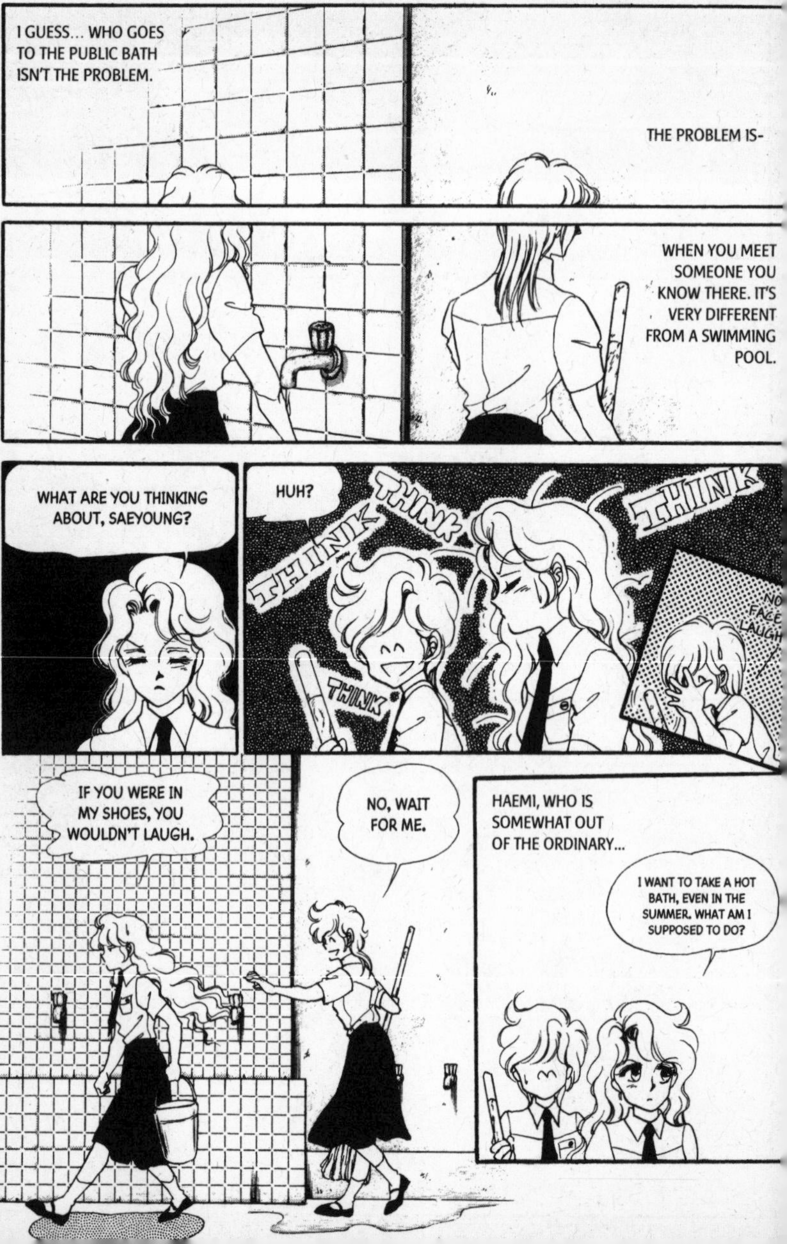
I GUESS... WHO GOES TO THE PUBLIC BATH ISN'T THE PROBLEM.
THE PROBLEM IS-
WHEN YOU MEET SOMEONE YOU KNOW THERE. IT'S VERY DIFFERENT FROM A SWIMMING POOL.
WHAT ARE YOU THINKING ABOUT, SAEYOUNG?
HUH?
THINK
THINK
THINK
THINK
NO FACE LAUGH
IF YOU WERE IN MY SHOES, YOU WOULDN'T LAUGH.
NO, WAIT FOR ME.
HAEMI, WHO IS SOMEWHAT OUT OF THE ORDINARY...
I WANT TO TAKE A HOT BATH, EVEN IN THE SUMMER. WHAT AM I SUPPOSED TO DO?

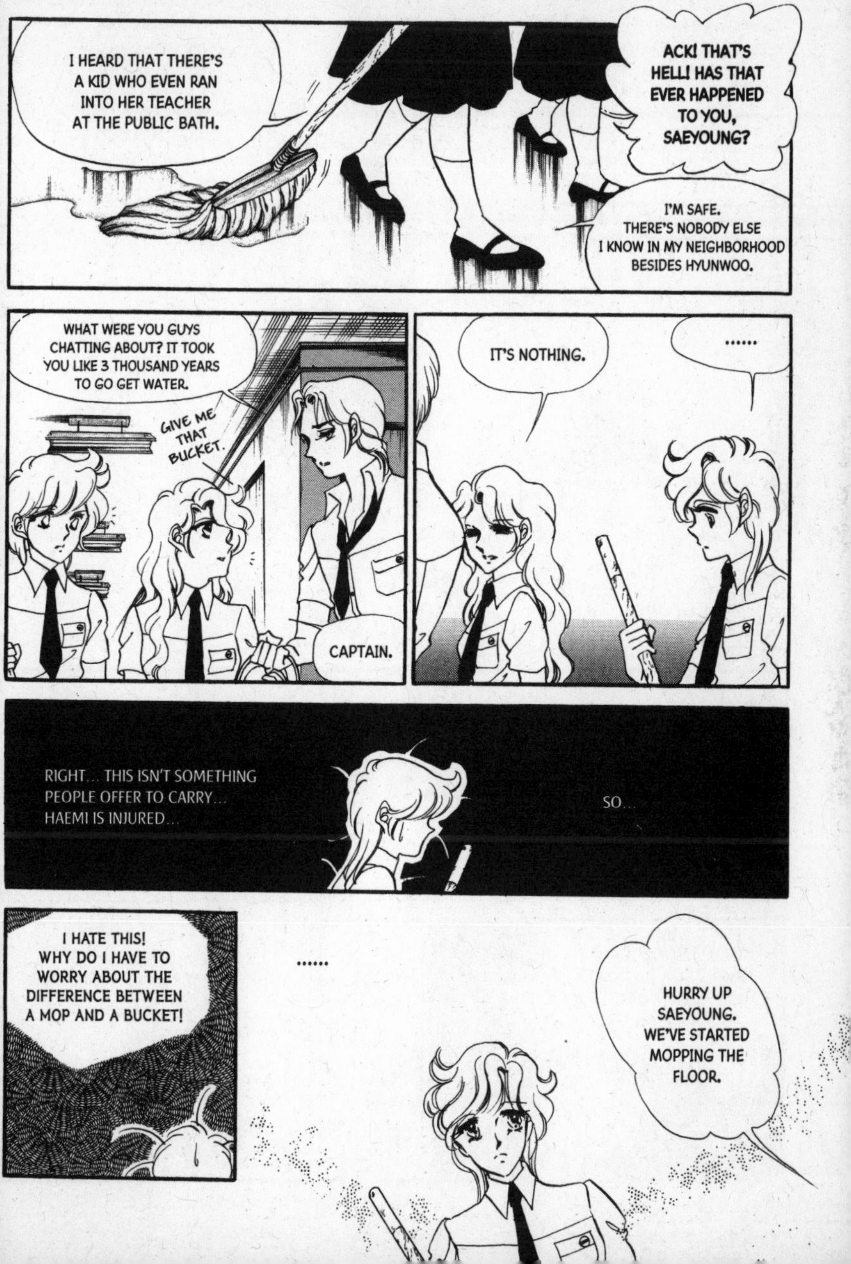
I HEARD THAT THERE'S A KID WHO EVEN RAN INTO HER TEACHER AT THE PUBLIC BATH.
ACK! THAT'S HELL! HAS THAT EVER HAPPENED TO YOU, SAEYOUNG?
I'M SAFE. THERE'S NOBODY ELSE I KNOW IN MY NEIGHBORHOOD BESIDES HYUNWOO.
WHAT WERE YOU GUYS CHATTING ABOUT? IT TOOK YOU LIKE 3 THOUSAND YEARS TO GO GET WATER.
GIVE ME THAT BUCKET.
CAPTAIN.
IT'S NOTHING.
......
RIGHT... THIS ISN'T SOMETHING PEOPLE OFFER TO CARRY... HAEMI IS INJURED...
SO...
I HATE THIS! WHY DO I HAVE TO WORRY ABOUT THE DIFFERENCE BETWEEN A MOP AND A BUCKET!
......
HURRY UP SAEYOUNG. WE'VE STARTED MOPPING THE FLOOR.

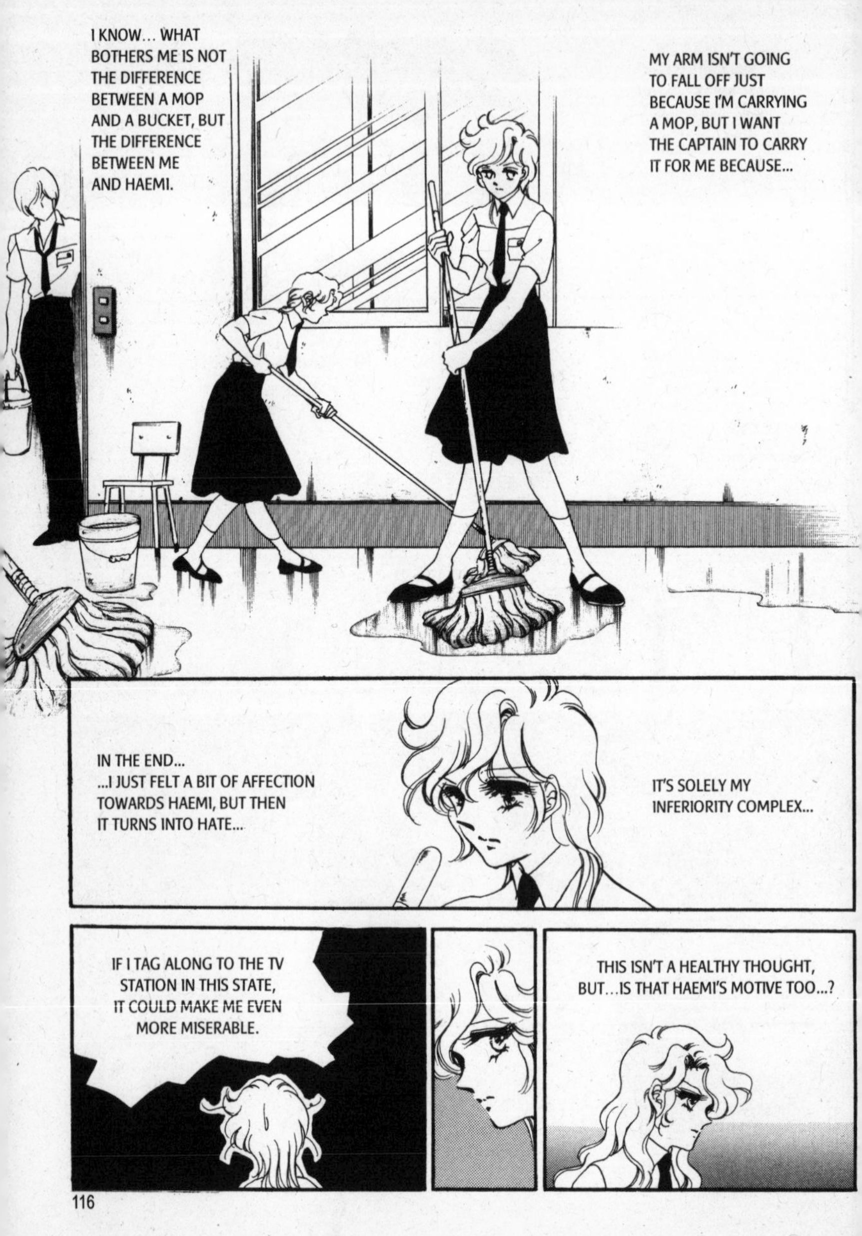
I KNOW… WHAT BOTHERS ME IS NOT THE DIFFERENCE BETWEEN A MOP AND A BUCKET, BUT THE DIFFERENCE BETWEEN ME AND HAEMI.
MY ARM ISN'T GOING TO FALL OFF JUST BECAUSE I'M CARRYING A MOP, BUT I WANT THE CAPTAIN TO CARRY IT FOR ME BECAUSE...
IN THE END... ...I JUST FELT A BIT OF AFFECTION TOWARDS HAEMI, BUT THEN IT TURNS INTO HATE...
IT'S SOLELY MY INFERIORITY COMPLEX...
IF I TAG ALONG TO THE TV STATION IN THIS STATE, IT COULD MAKE ME EVEN MORE MISERABLE.
THIS ISN'T A HEALTHY THOUGHT, BUT…IS THAT HAEMI'S MOTIVE TOO...?

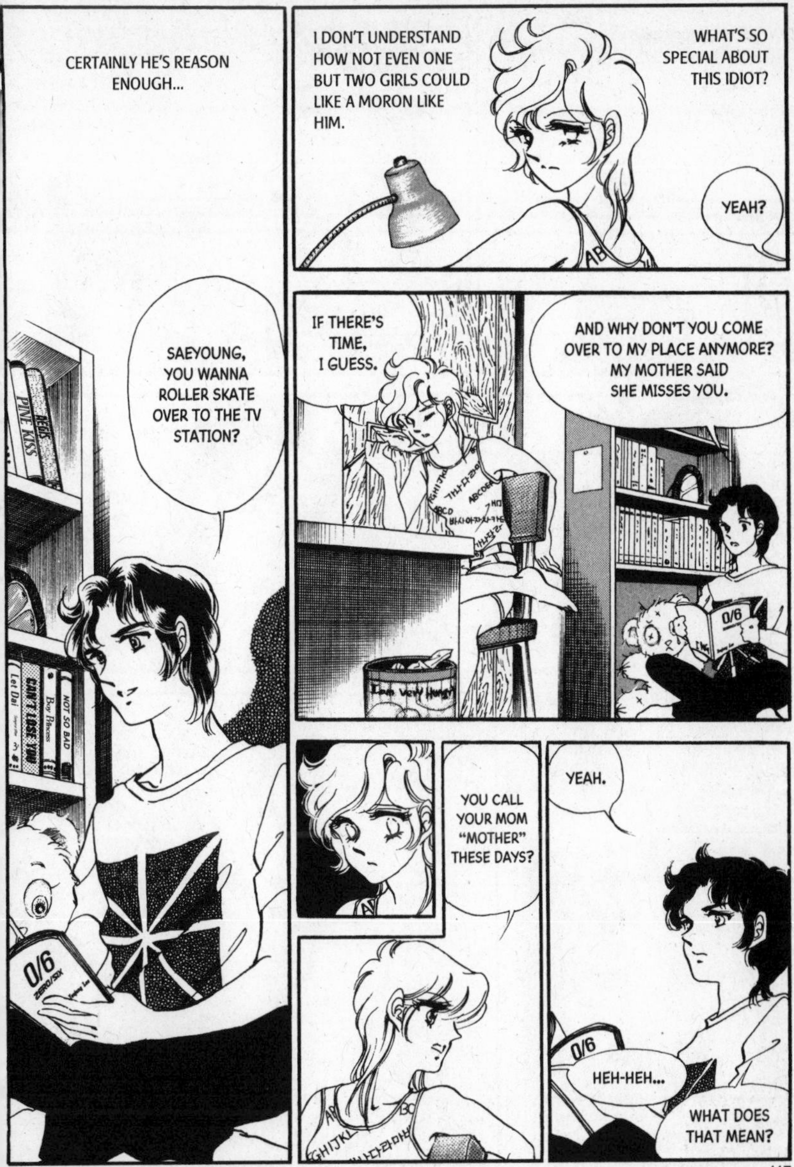
CERTAINLY HE'S REASON ENOUGH...
PINE KISS
REGIS
SAEYOUNG, YOU WANNA ROLLER SKATE OVER TO THE TV STATION?
Let Dai
CAN'T LOSE YOU
Boy Princess
NOT SO BAD
0/6 ZERO/SIX
I DON'T UNDERSTAND HOW NOT EVEN ONE BUT TWO GIRLS COULD LIKE A MORON LIKE HIM.
WHAT'S SO SPECIAL ABOUT THIS IDIOT?
YEAH?
IF THERE'S TIME, I GUESS.
AND WHY DON'T YOU COME OVER TO MY PLACE ANYMORE? MY MOTHER SAID SHE MISSES YOU.
0/6
YOU CALL YOUR MOM "MOTHER" THESE DAYS?
YEAH.
0/6
HEH-HEH...
WHAT DOES THAT MEAN?

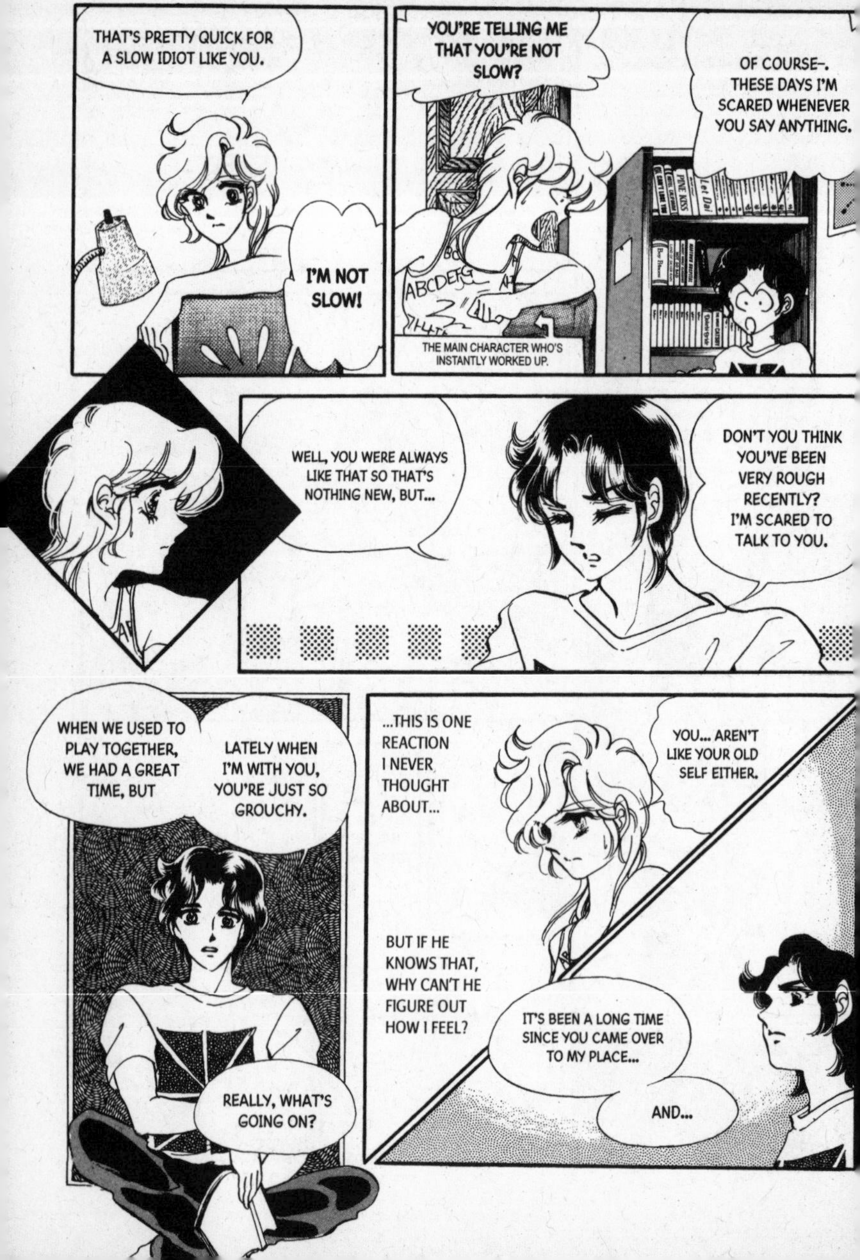
THAT'S PRETTY QUICK FOR A SLOW IDIOT LIKE YOU.
I'M NOT SLOW!
YOU'RE TELLING ME THAT YOU'RE NOT SLOW?
THE MAIN CHARACTER WHO'S INSTANTLY WORKED UP.
OF COURSE–. THESE DAYS I'M SCARED WHENEVER YOU SAY ANYTHING.
WELL, YOU WERE ALWAYS LIKE THAT SO THAT'S NOTHING NEW, BUT...
DON'T YOU THINK YOU'VE BEEN VERY ROUGH RECENTLY? I'M SCARED TO TALK TO YOU.
WHEN WE USED TO PLAY TOGETHER, WE HAD A GREAT TIME, BUT
LATELY WHEN I'M WITH YOU, YOU'RE JUST SO GROUCHY.
REALLY, WHAT'S GOING ON?
...THIS IS ONE REACTION I NEVER THOUGHT ABOUT...
YOU... AREN'T LIKE YOUR OLD SELF EITHER.
BUT IF HE KNOWS THAT, WHY CAN'T HE FIGURE OUT HOW I FEEL?
IT'S BEEN A LONG TIME SINCE YOU CAME OVER TO MY PLACE...
AND...

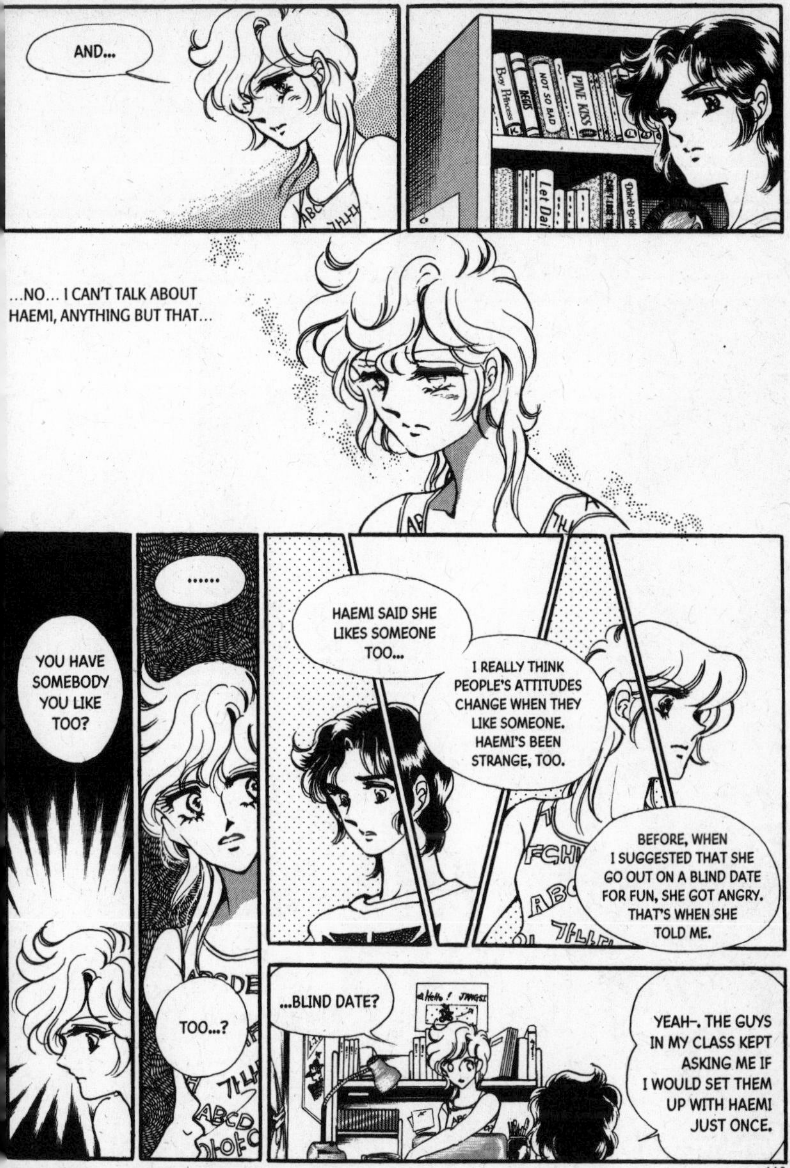
AND...
Boy Princess
NOT SO BAD
PINE KISS
...NO... I CAN'T TALK ABOUT HAEMI, ANYTHING BUT THAT...
YOU HAVE SOMEBODY YOU LIKE TOO?
......
TOO...?
HAEMI SAID SHE LIKES SOMEONE TOO...
I REALLY THINK PEOPLE'S ATTITUDES CHANGE WHEN THEY LIKE SOMEONE. HAEMI'S BEEN STRANGE, TOO.
BEFORE, WHEN I SUGGESTED THAT SHE GO OUT ON A BLIND DATE FOR FUN, SHE GOT ANGRY. THAT'S WHEN SHE TOLD ME.
...BLIND DATE?
YEAH-. THE GUYS IN MY CLASS KEPT ASKING ME IF I WOULD SET THEM UP WITH HAEMI JUST ONCE.

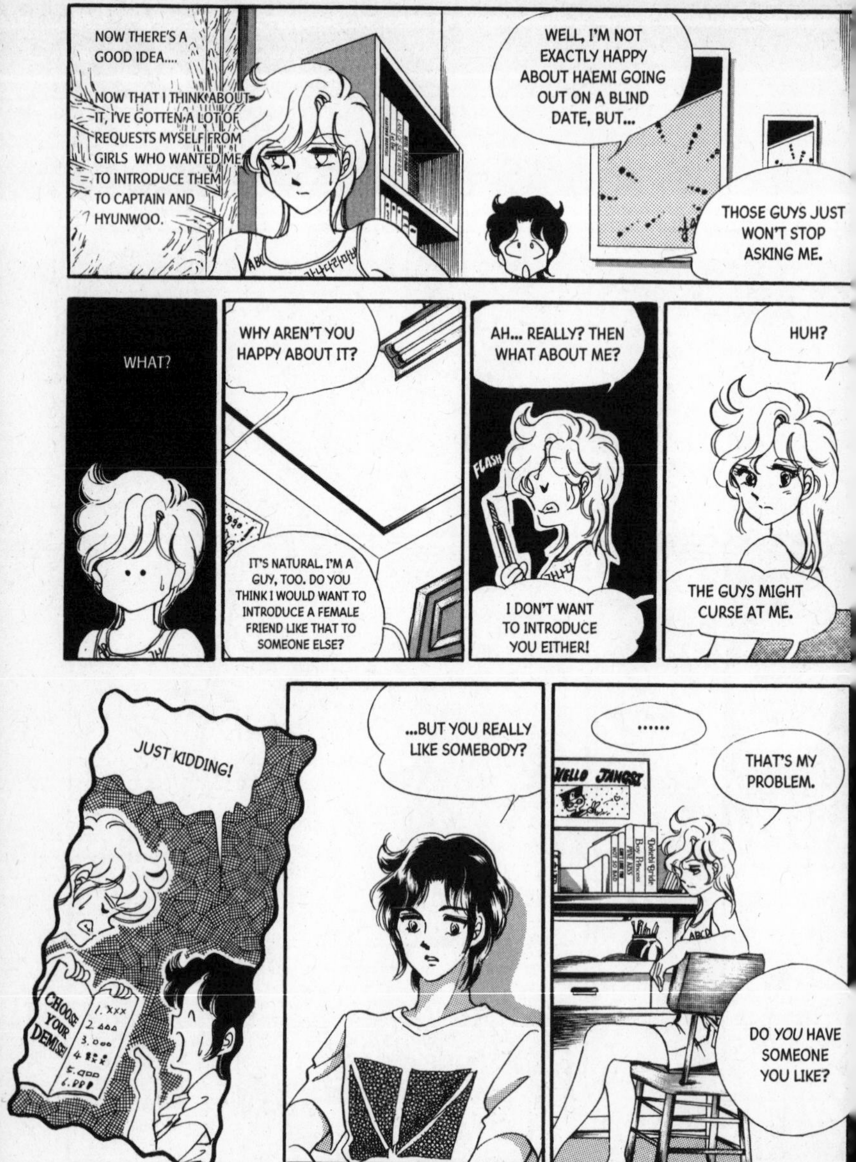
NOW THERE'S A GOOD IDEA....
NOW THAT I THINK ABOUT IT, I'VE GOTTEN A LOT OF REQUESTS MYSELF FROM GIRLS WHO WANTED ME TO INTRODUCE THEM TO CAPTAIN AND HYUNWOO.
WELL, I'M NOT EXACTLY HAPPY ABOUT HAEMI GOING OUT ON A BLIND DATE, BUT...
THOSE GUYS JUST WON'T STOP ASKING ME.
WHAT?
WHY AREN'T YOU HAPPY ABOUT IT?
IT'S NATURAL. I'M A GUY, TOO. DO YOU THINK I WOULD WANT TO INTRODUCE A FEMALE FRIEND LIKE THAT TO SOMEONE ELSE?
AH... REALLY? THEN WHAT ABOUT ME?
FLASH
I DON'T WANT TO INTRODUCE YOU EITHER!
HUH?
THE GUYS MIGHT CURSE AT ME.
JUST KIDDING!
CHOOSE YOUR DEMISE!
...BUT YOU REALLY LIKE SOMEBODY?
......
THAT'S MY PROBLEM.
DO *YOU* HAVE SOMEONE YOU LIKE?

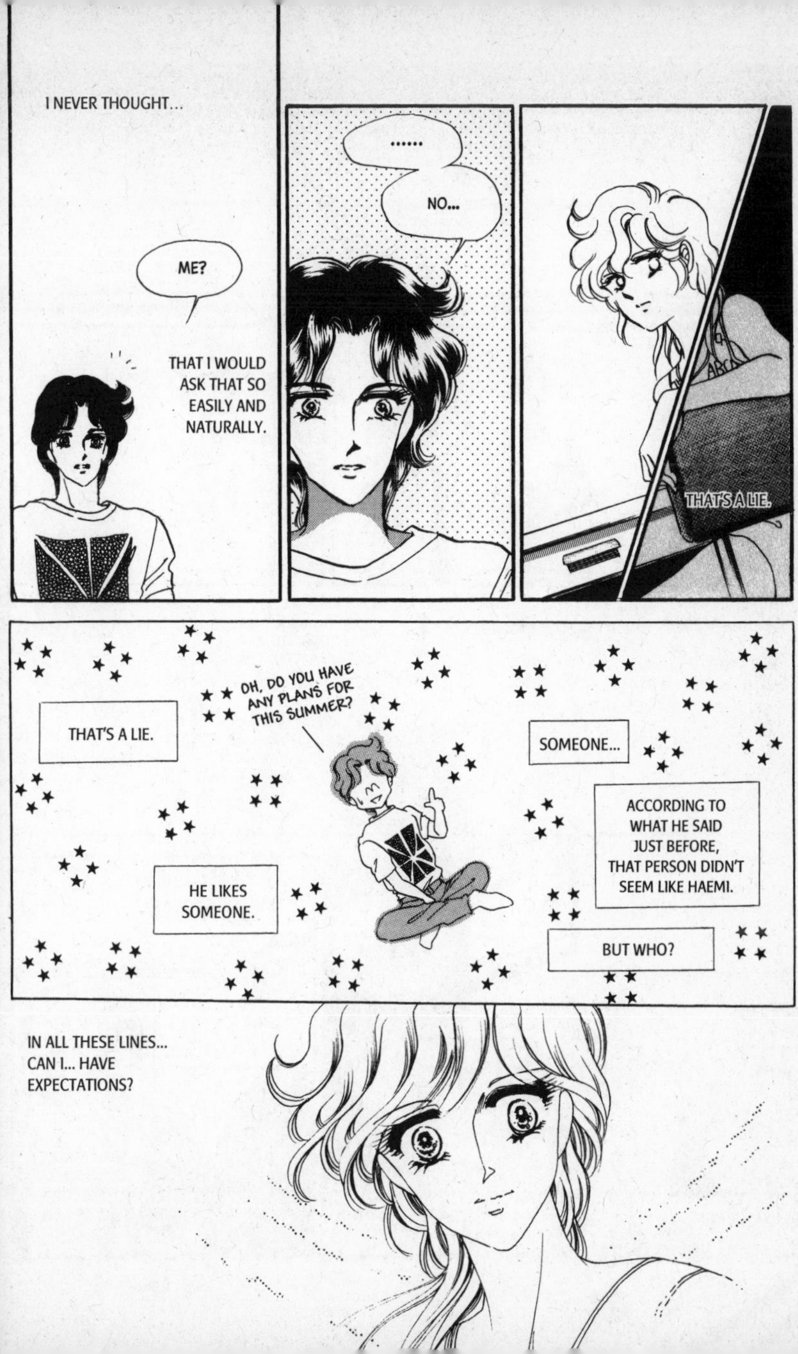

I NEVER THOUGHT…
ME?
THAT I WOULD ASK THAT SO EASILY AND NATURALLY.
......
NO...
THAT'S A LIE.
THAT'S A LIE.
OH, DO YOU HAVE ANY PLANS FOR THIS SUMMER?
HE LIKES SOMEONE.
SOMEONE...
ACCORDING TO WHAT HE SAID JUST BEFORE, THAT PERSON DIDN'T SEEM LIKE HAEMI.
BUT WHO?
IN ALL THESE LINES... CAN I... HAVE EXPECTATIONS?

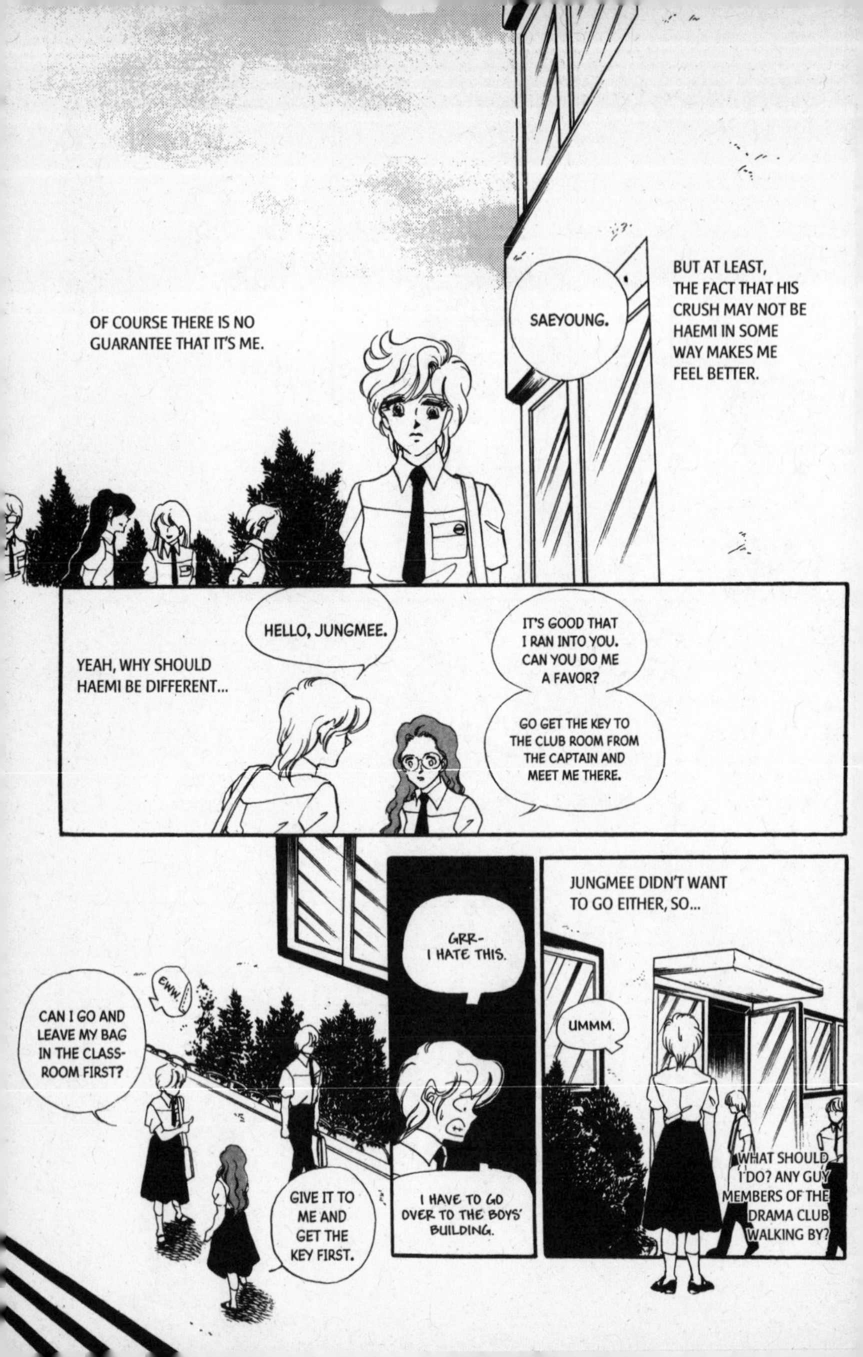
OF COURSE THERE IS NO GUARANTEE THAT IT'S ME.
BUT AT LEAST, THE FACT THAT HIS CRUSH MAY NOT BE HAEMI IN SOME WAY MAKES ME FEEL BETTER.
SAEYOUNG.
YEAH, WHY SHOULD HAEMI BE DIFFERENT...
HELLO, JUNGMEE.
IT'S GOOD THAT I RAN INTO YOU. CAN YOU DO ME A FAVOR?
GO GET THE KEY TO THE CLUB ROOM FROM THE CAPTAIN AND MEET ME THERE.
CAN I GO AND LEAVE MY BAG IN THE CLASS-ROOM FIRST?
EWW.
GIVE IT TO ME AND GET THE KEY FIRST.
GRR- I HATE THIS.
I HAVE TO GO OVER TO THE BOYS' BUILDING.
JUNGMEE DIDN'T WANT TO GO EITHER, SO...
UMMM.
WHAT SHOULD I DO? ANY GUY MEMBERS OF THE DRAMA CLUB WALKING BY?

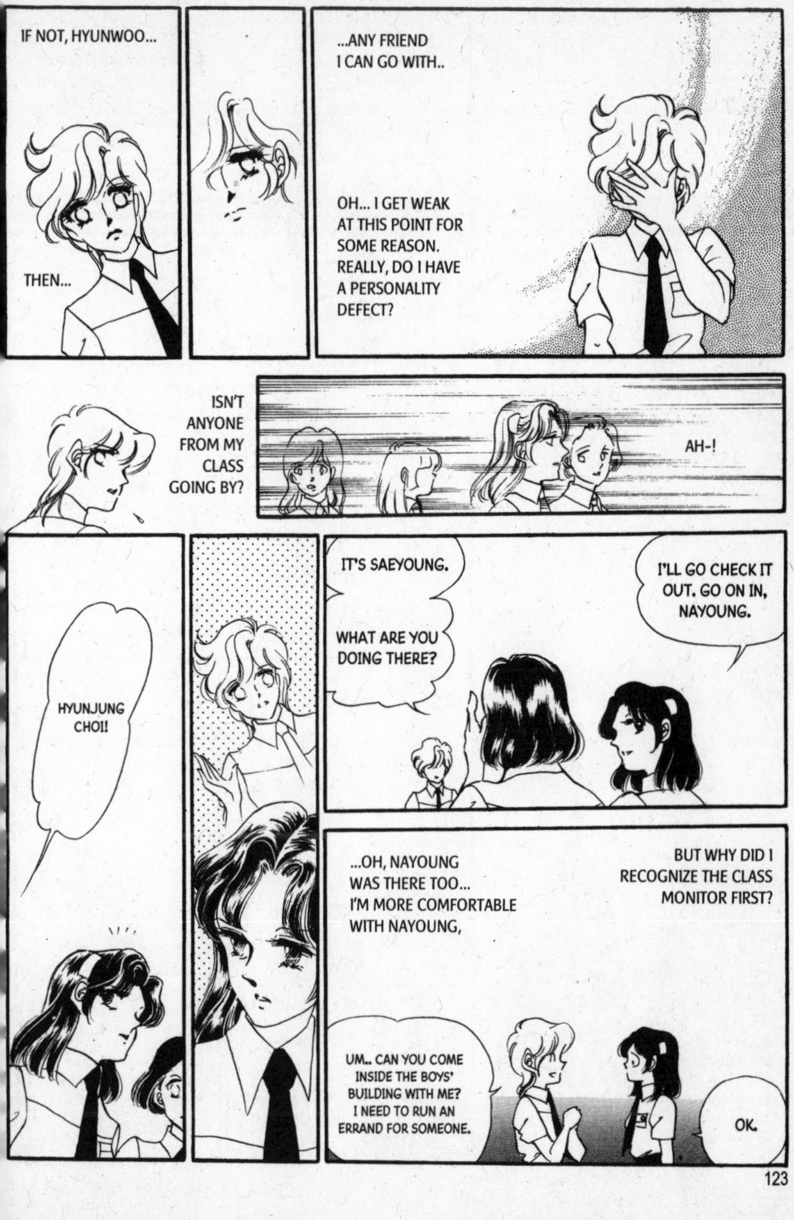
IF NOT, HYUNWOO...
THEN...
...ANY FRIEND I CAN GO WITH..
OH... I GET WEAK AT THIS POINT FOR SOME REASON. REALLY, DO I HAVE A PERSONALITY DEFECT?
ISN'T ANYONE FROM MY CLASS GOING BY?
AH-!
HYUNJUNG CHOI!
IT'S SAEYOUNG.
WHAT ARE YOU DOING THERE?
I'LL GO CHECK IT OUT. GO ON IN, NAYOUNG.
...OH, NAYOUNG WAS THERE TOO... I'M MORE COMFORTABLE WITH NAYOUNG,
BUT WHY DID I RECOGNIZE THE CLASS MONITOR FIRST?
UM.. CAN YOU COME INSIDE THE BOYS' BUILDING WITH ME? I NEED TO RUN AN ERRAND FOR SOMEONE.
OK.

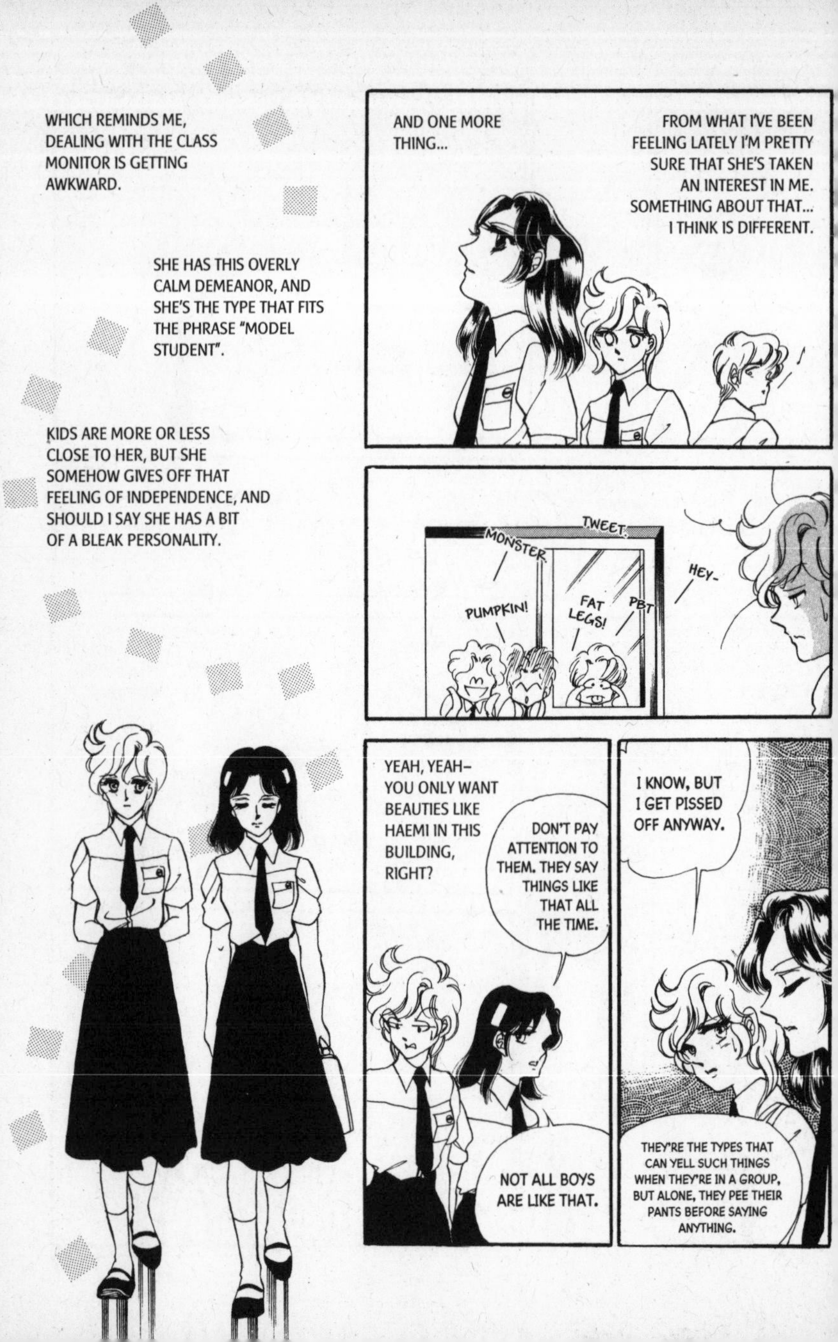
WHICH REMINDS ME, DEALING WITH THE CLASS MONITOR IS GETTING AWKWARD.
SHE HAS THIS OVERLY CALM DEMEANOR, AND SHE'S THE TYPE THAT FITS THE PHRASE "MODEL STUDENT".
KIDS ARE MORE OR LESS CLOSE TO HER, BUT SHE SOMEHOW GIVES OFF THAT FEELING OF INDEPENDENCE, AND SHOULD I SAY SHE HAS A BIT OF A BLEAK PERSONALITY.
AND ONE MORE THING...
FROM WHAT I'VE BEEN FEELING LATELY I'M PRETTY SURE THAT SHE'S TAKEN AN INTEREST IN ME. SOMETHING ABOUT THAT... I THINK IS DIFFERENT.
MONSTER.
TWEET.
PUMPKIN!
FAT LEGS!
PBT
HEY-
YEAH, YEAH- YOU ONLY WANT BEAUTIES LIKE HAEMI IN THIS BUILDING, RIGHT?
DON'T PAY ATTENTION TO THEM. THEY SAY THINGS LIKE THAT ALL THE TIME.
NOT ALL BOYS ARE LIKE THAT.
I KNOW, BUT I GET PISSED OFF ANYWAY.
THEY'RE THE TYPES THAT CAN YELL SUCH THINGS WHEN THEY'RE IN A GROUP, BUT ALONE, THEY PEE THEIR PANTS BEFORE SAYING ANYTHING.

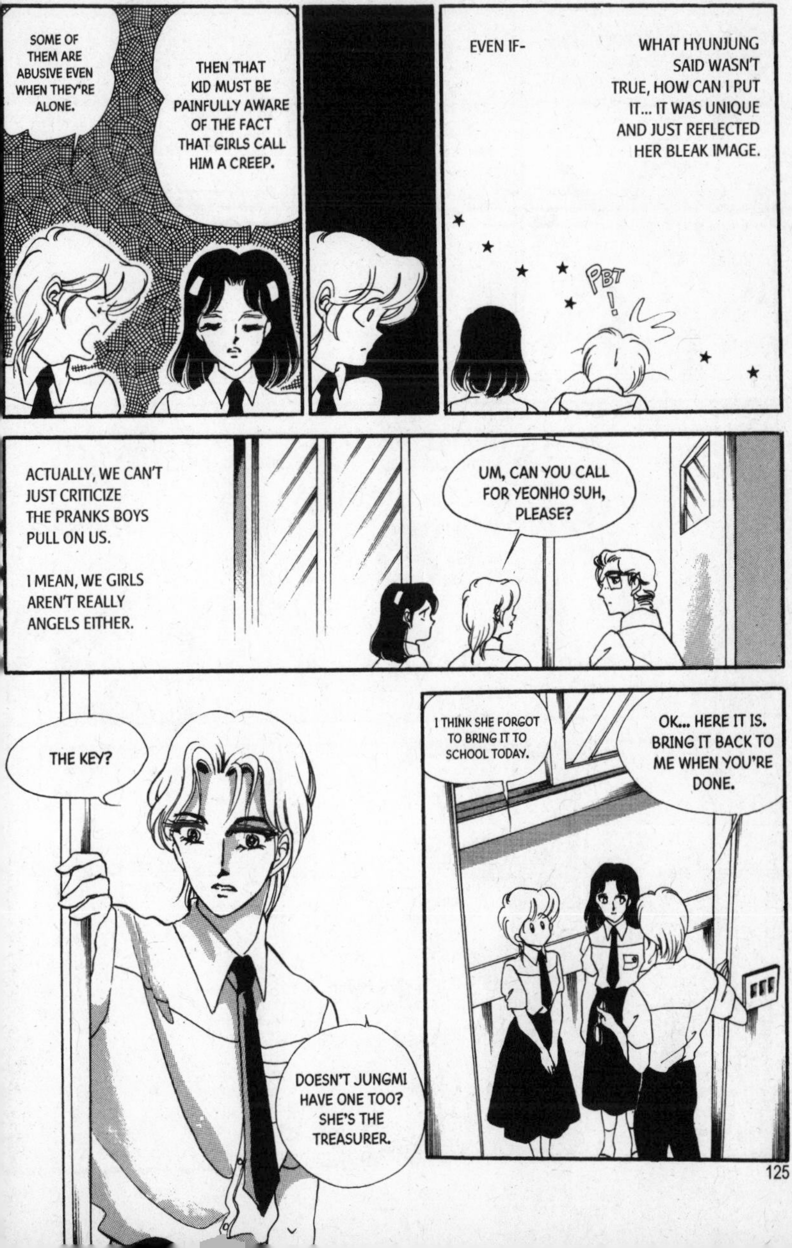
SOME OF THEM ARE ABUSIVE EVEN WHEN THEY'RE ALONE.
THEN THAT KID MUST BE PAINFULLY AWARE OF THE FACT THAT GIRLS CALL HIM A CREEP.
EVEN IF-
WHAT HYUNJUNG SAID WASN'T TRUE, HOW CAN I PUT IT... IT WAS UNIQUE AND JUST REFLECTED HER BLEAK IMAGE.
PBT
!
ACTUALLY, WE CAN'T JUST CRITICIZE THE PRANKS BOYS PULL ON US.
I MEAN, WE GIRLS AREN'T REALLY ANGELS EITHER.
UM, CAN YOU CALL FOR YEONHO SUH, PLEASE?
THE KEY?
DOESN'T JUNGMI HAVE ONE TOO? SHE'S THE TREASURER.
I THINK SHE FORGOT TO BRING IT TO SCHOOL TODAY.
OK... HERE IT IS. BRING IT BACK TO ME WHEN YOU'RE DONE.

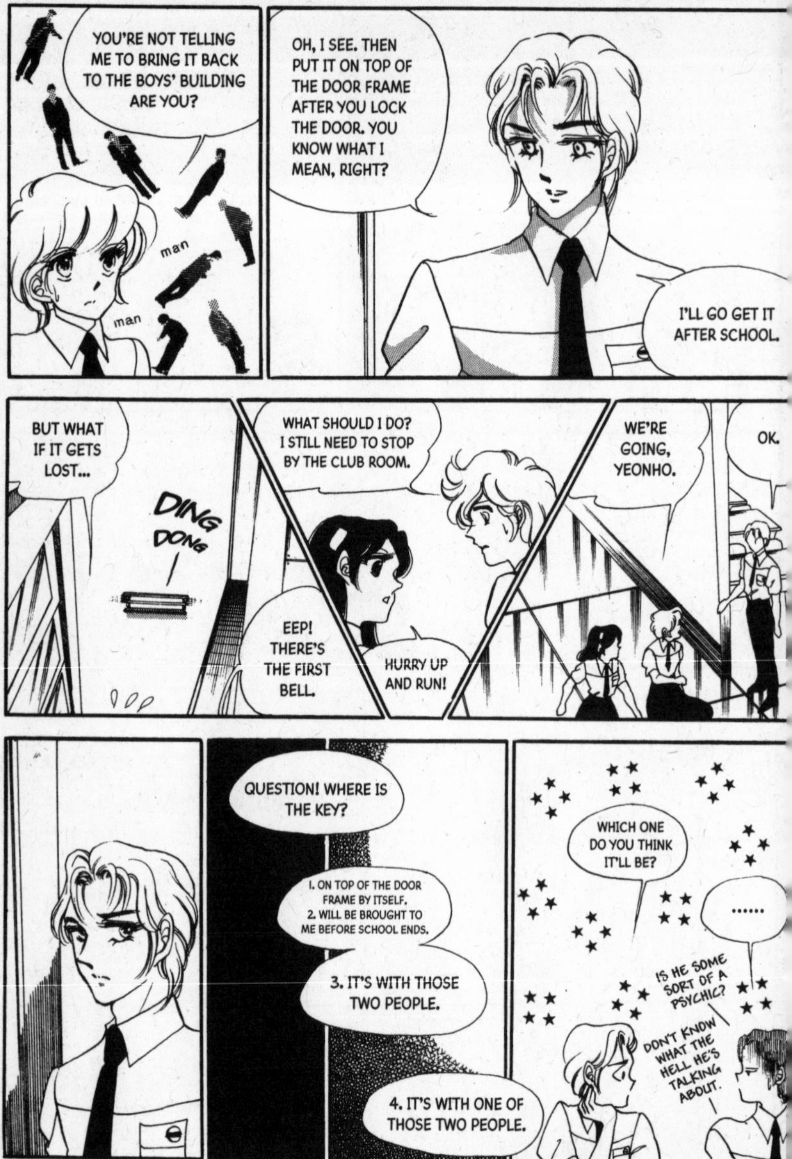
YOU'RE NOT TELLING ME TO BRING IT BACK TO THE BOYS' BUILDING ARE YOU?
man
man
OH, I SEE. THEN PUT IT ON TOP OF THE DOOR FRAME AFTER YOU LOCK THE DOOR. YOU KNOW WHAT I MEAN, RIGHT?
I'LL GO GET IT AFTER SCHOOL.
BUT WHAT IF IT GETS LOST...
DING DONG
WHAT SHOULD I DO? I STILL NEED TO STOP BY THE CLUB ROOM.
EEP! THERE'S THE FIRST BELL.
HURRY UP AND RUN!
WE'RE GOING, YEONHO.
OK.
QUESTION! WHERE IS THE KEY?
1. ON TOP OF THE DOOR FRAME BY ITSELF.
2. WILL BE BROUGHT TO ME BEFORE SCHOOL ENDS.
3. IT'S WITH THOSE TWO PEOPLE.
4. IT'S WITH ONE OF THOSE TWO PEOPLE.
WHICH ONE DO YOU THINK IT'LL BE?
......
IS HE SOME SORT OF A PSYCHIC?
DON'T KNOW WHAT THE HELL HE'S TALKING ABOUT.

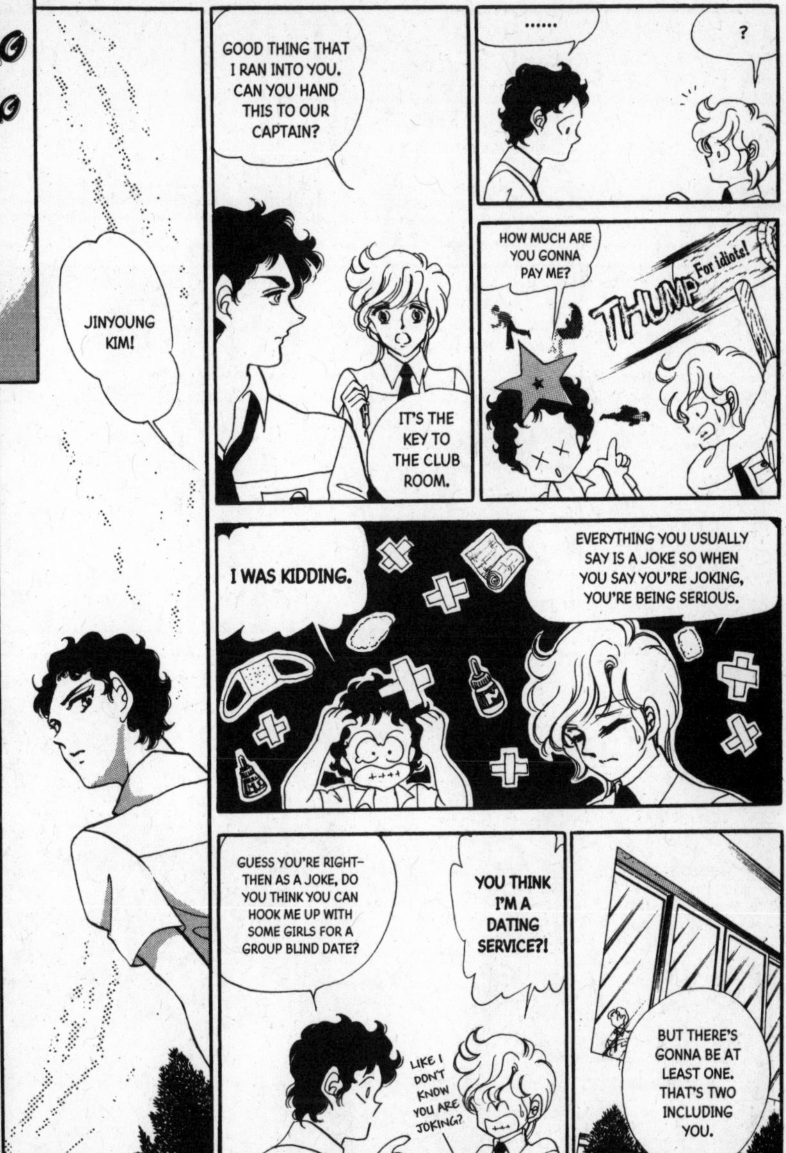
JINYOUNG KIM!
GOOD THING THAT I RAN INTO YOU. CAN YOU HAND THIS TO OUR CAPTAIN?
IT'S THE KEY TO THE CLUB ROOM.
......
?
HOW MUCH ARE YOU GONNA PAY ME?
THUMP
For idiots!
I WAS KIDDING.
EVERYTHING YOU USUALLY SAY IS A JOKE SO WHEN YOU SAY YOU'RE JOKING, YOU'RE BEING SERIOUS.
GUESS YOU'RE RIGHT– THEN AS A JOKE, DO YOU THINK YOU CAN HOOK ME UP WITH SOME GIRLS FOR A GROUP BLIND DATE?
YOU THINK I'M A DATING SERVICE?!
LIKE I DON'T KNOW YOU ARE JOKING?
BUT THERE'S GONNA BE AT LEAST ONE. THAT'S TWO INCLUDING YOU.

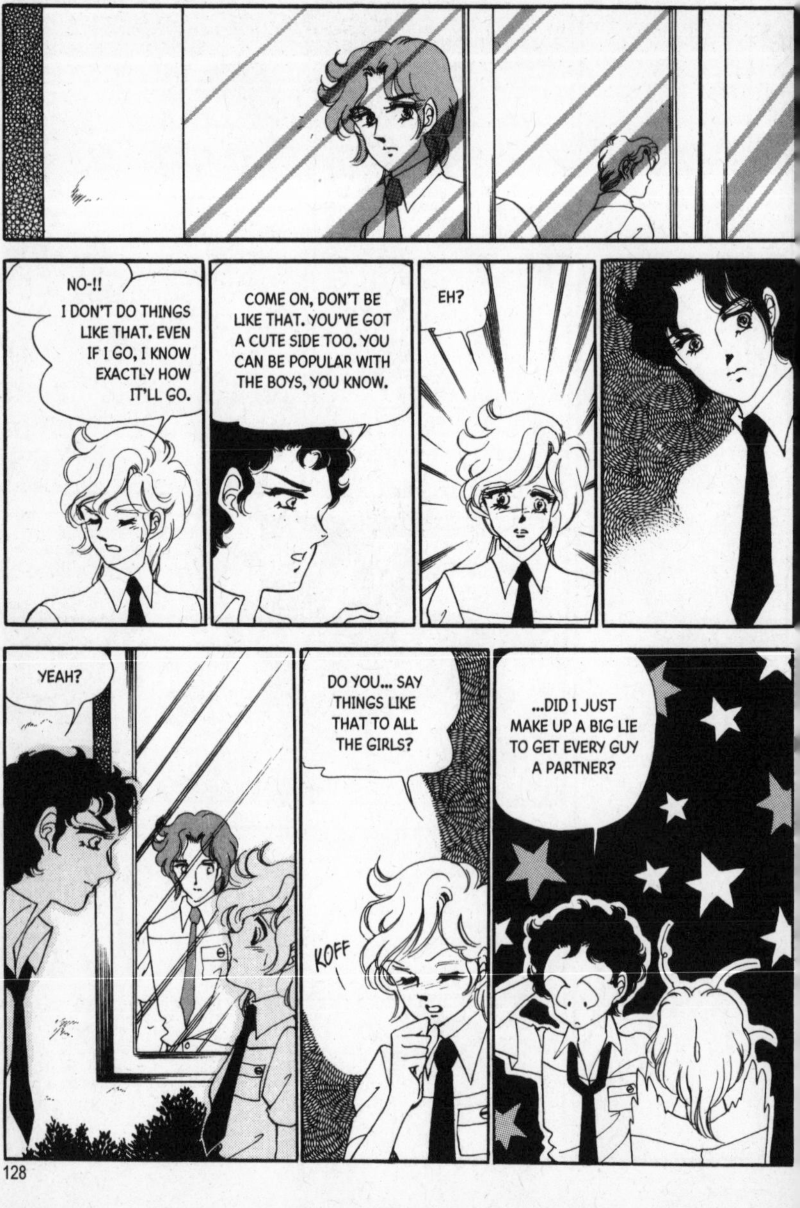
NO-!! I DON'T DO THINGS LIKE THAT. EVEN IF I GO, I KNOW EXACTLY HOW IT'LL GO.
COME ON, DON'T BE LIKE THAT. YOU'VE GOT A CUTE SIDE TOO. YOU CAN BE POPULAR WITH THE BOYS, YOU KNOW.
EH?
YEAH?
DO YOU... SAY THINGS LIKE THAT TO ALL THE GIRLS?
KOFF
...DID I JUST MAKE UP A BIG LIE TO GET EVERY GUY A PARTNER?

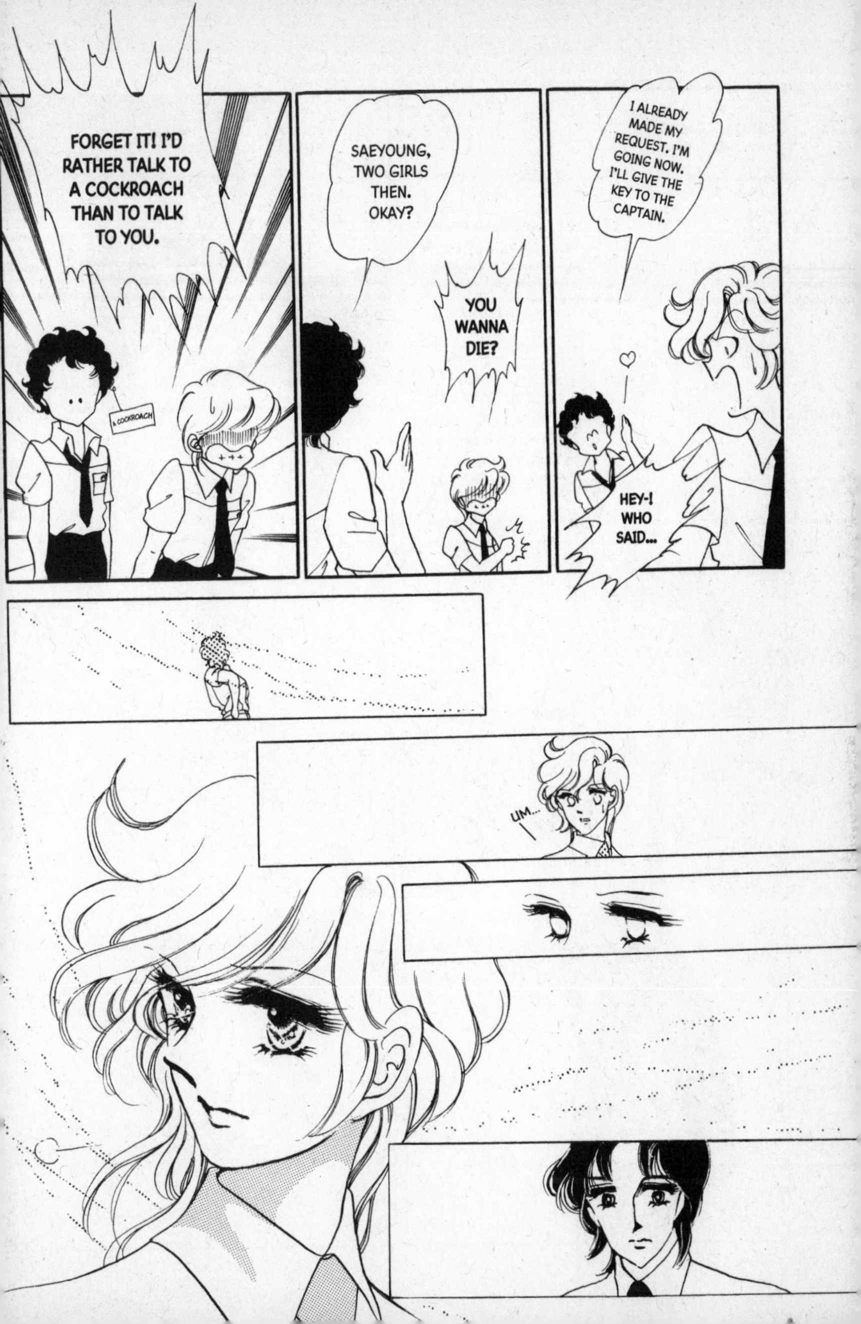
FORGET IT! I'D RATHER TALK TO A COCKROACH THAN TO TALK TO YOU.
A COCKROACH
SAEYOUNG, TWO GIRLS THEN. OKAY?
YOU WANNA DIE?
I ALREADY MADE MY REQUEST. I'M GOING NOW. I'LL GIVE THE KEY TO THE CAPTAIN.
HEY-! WHO SAID...
UM...

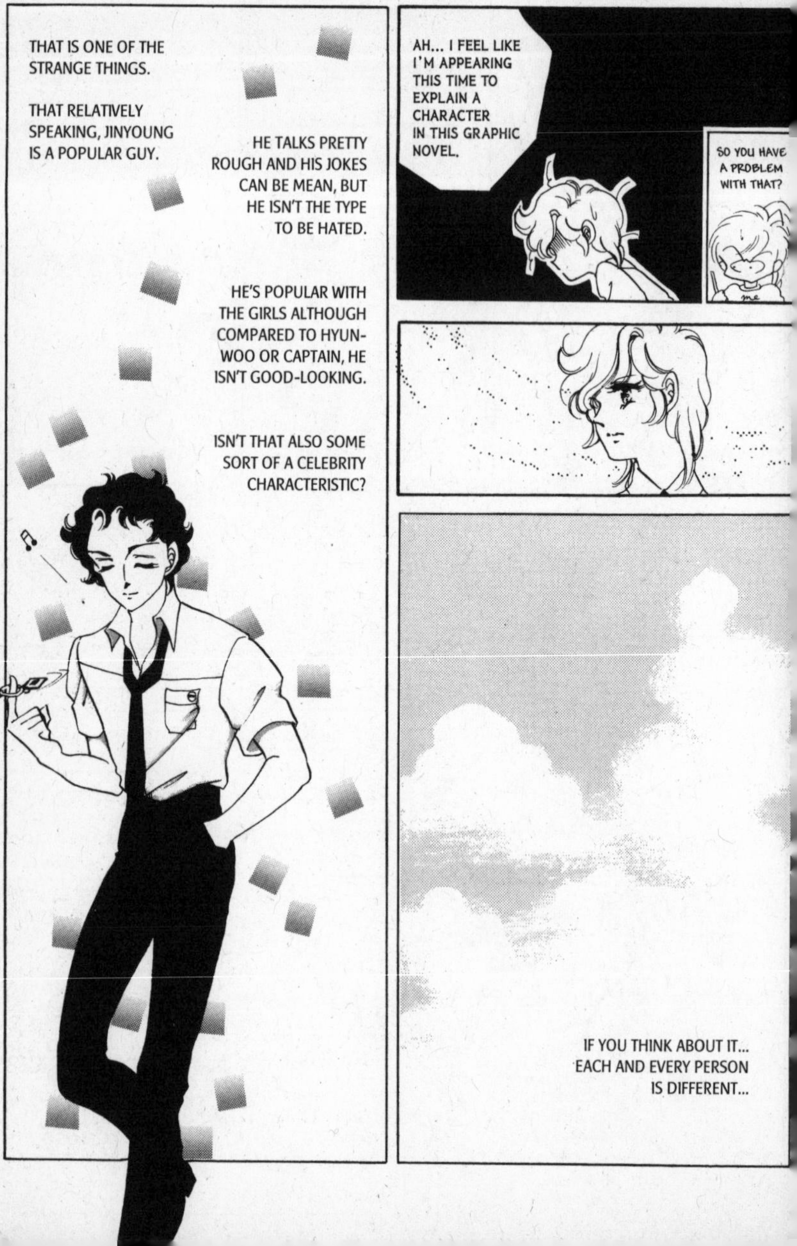
THAT IS ONE OF THE STRANGE THINGS.
THAT RELATIVELY SPEAKING, JINYOUNG IS A POPULAR GUY.
HE TALKS PRETTY ROUGH AND HIS JOKES CAN BE MEAN, BUT HE ISN'T THE TYPE TO BE HATED.
HE'S POPULAR WITH THE GIRLS ALTHOUGH COMPARED TO HYUN-WOO OR CAPTAIN, HE ISN'T GOOD-LOOKING.
ISN'T THAT ALSO SOME SORT OF A CELEBRITY CHARACTERISTIC?
AH... I FEEL LIKE I'M APPEARING THIS TIME TO EXPLAIN A CHARACTER IN THIS GRAPHIC NOVEL.
SO YOU HAVE A PROBLEM WITH THAT?
me
IF YOU THINK ABOUT IT... EACH AND EVERY PERSON IS DIFFERENT...

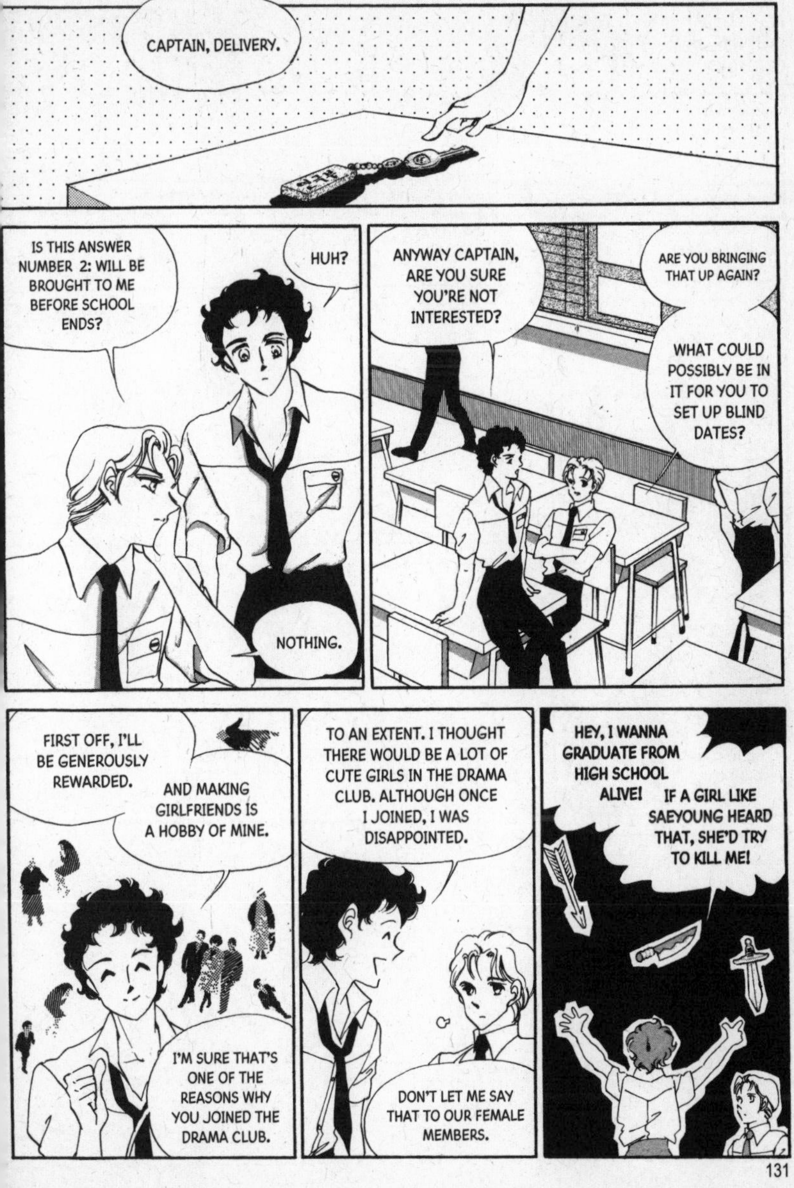
CAPTAIN, DELIVERY.
IS THIS ANSWER NUMBER 2: WILL BE BROUGHT TO ME BEFORE SCHOOL ENDS?
HUH?
NOTHING.
ANYWAY CAPTAIN, ARE YOU SURE YOU'RE NOT INTERESTED?
ARE YOU BRINGING THAT UP AGAIN?
WHAT COULD POSSIBLY BE IN IT FOR YOU TO SET UP BLIND DATES?
FIRST OFF, I'LL BE GENEROUSLY REWARDED.
AND MAKING GIRLFRIENDS IS A HOBBY OF MINE.
I'M SURE THAT'S ONE OF THE REASONS WHY YOU JOINED THE DRAMA CLUB.
TO AN EXTENT. I THOUGHT THERE WOULD BE A LOT OF CUTE GIRLS IN THE DRAMA CLUB. ALTHOUGH ONCE I JOINED, I WAS DISAPPOINTED.
DON'T LET ME SAY THAT TO OUR FEMALE MEMBERS.
HEY, I WANNA GRADUATE FROM HIGH SCHOOL ALIVE!
IF A GIRL LIKE SAEYOUNG HEARD THAT, SHE'D TRY TO KILL ME!

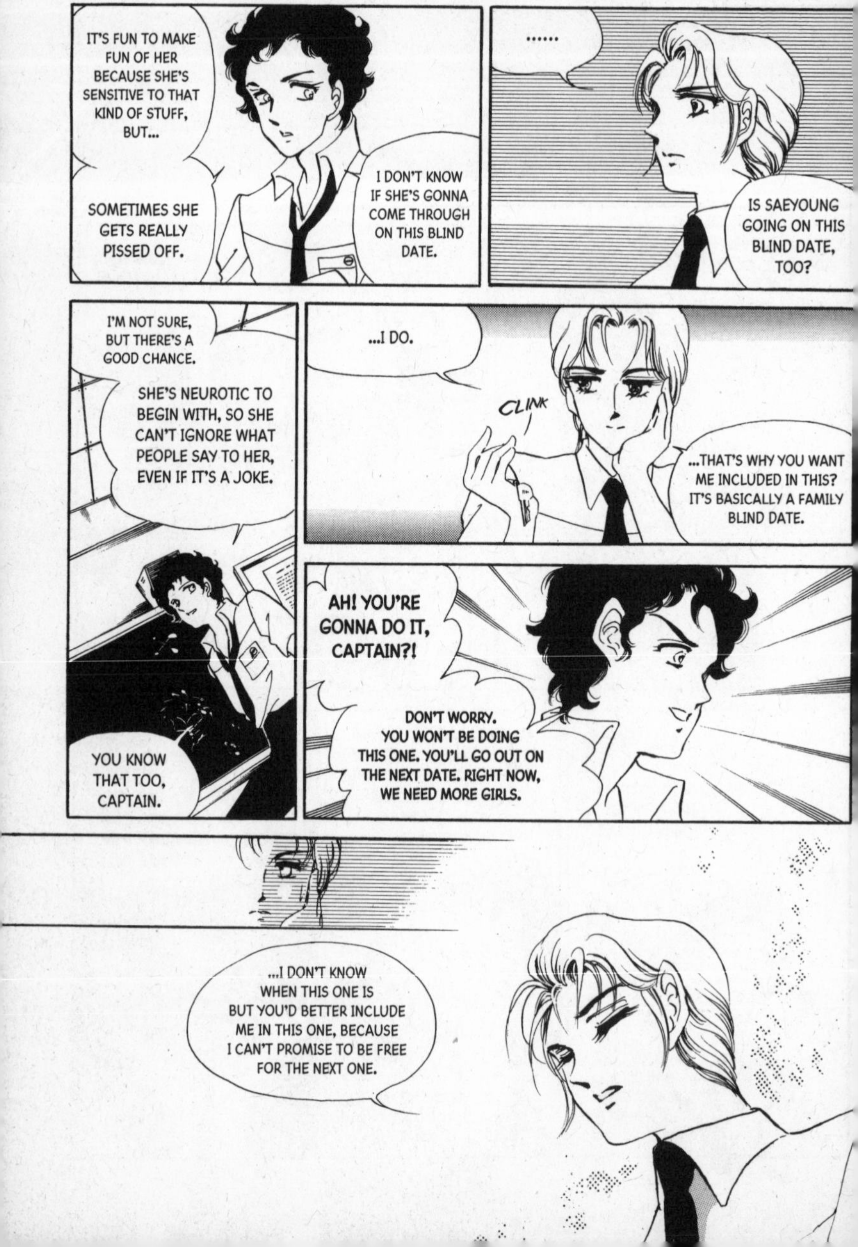
IT'S FUN TO MAKE FUN OF HER BECAUSE SHE'S SENSITIVE TO THAT KIND OF STUFF, BUT...
SOMETIMES SHE GETS REALLY PISSED OFF.
I DON'T KNOW IF SHE'S GONNA COME THROUGH ON THIS BLIND DATE.
......
IS SAEYOUNG GOING ON THIS BLIND DATE, TOO?
I'M NOT SURE, BUT THERE'S A GOOD CHANCE.
SHE'S NEUROTIC TO BEGIN WITH, SO SHE CAN'T IGNORE WHAT PEOPLE SAY TO HER, EVEN IF IT'S A JOKE.
YOU KNOW THAT TOO, CAPTAIN.
...I DO.
CLINK
...THAT'S WHY YOU WANT ME INCLUDED IN THIS? IT'S BASICALLY A FAMILY BLIND DATE.
AH! YOU'RE GONNA DO IT, CAPTAIN?!
DON'T WORRY. YOU WON'T BE DOING THIS ONE. YOU'LL GO OUT ON THE NEXT DATE. RIGHT NOW, WE NEED MORE GIRLS.
...I DON'T KNOW WHEN THIS ONE IS BUT YOU'D BETTER INCLUDE ME IN THIS ONE, BECAUSE I CAN'T PROMISE TO BE FREE FOR THE NEXT ONE.

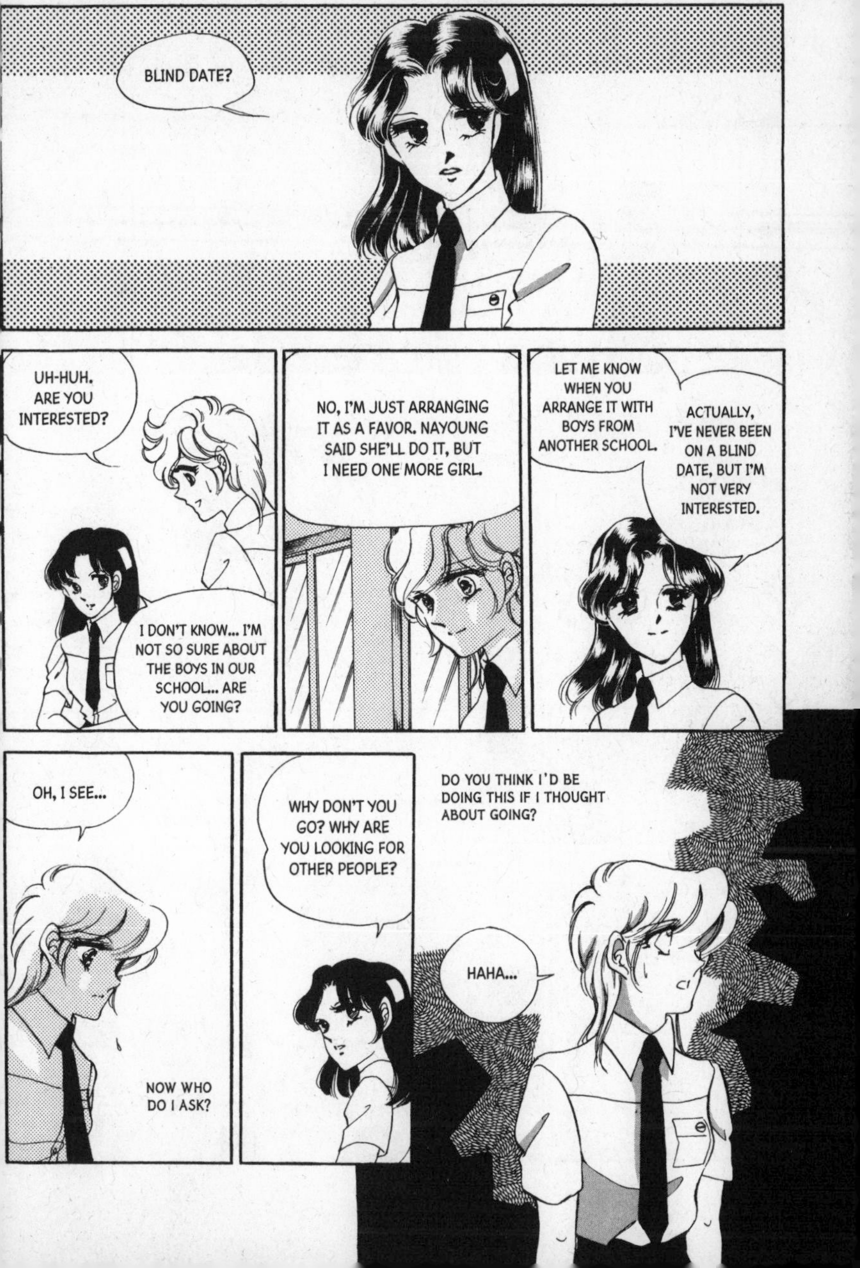
BLIND DATE?
UH-HUH. ARE YOU INTERESTED?
I DON'T KNOW... I'M NOT SO SURE ABOUT THE BOYS IN OUR SCHOOL... ARE YOU GOING?
NO, I'M JUST ARRANGING IT AS A FAVOR. NAYOUNG SAID SHE'LL DO IT, BUT I NEED ONE MORE GIRL.
LET ME KNOW WHEN YOU ARRANGE IT WITH BOYS FROM ANOTHER SCHOOL.
ACTUALLY, I'VE NEVER BEEN ON A BLIND DATE, BUT I'M NOT VERY INTERESTED.
OH, I SEE...
NOW WHO DO I ASK?
WHY DON'T YOU GO? WHY ARE YOU LOOKING FOR OTHER PEOPLE?
DO YOU THINK I'D BE DOING THIS IF I THOUGHT ABOUT GOING?
HAHA...

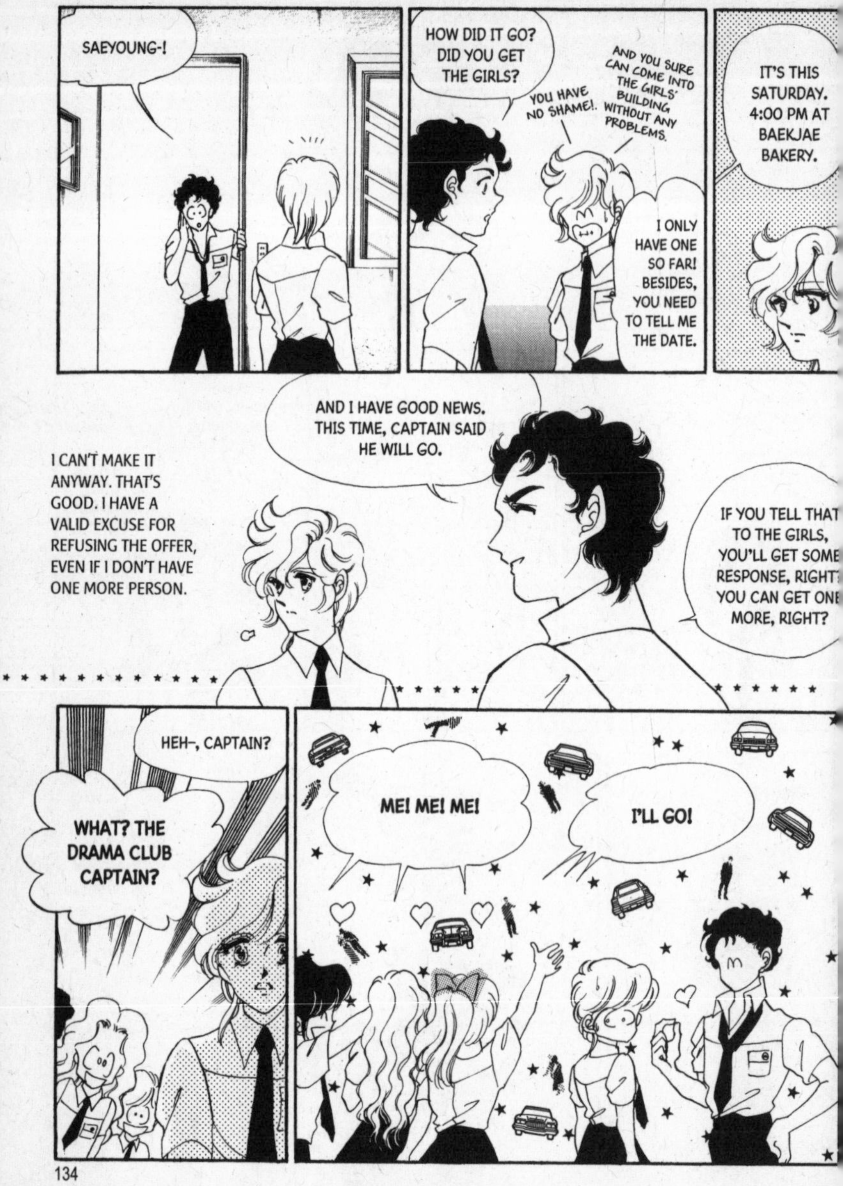
SAEYOUNG-!
HOW DID IT GO? DID YOU GET THE GIRLS?
YOU HAVE NO SHAME!.
AND YOU SURE CAN COME INTO THE GIRLS' BUILDING WITHOUT ANY PROBLEMS.
I ONLY HAVE ONE SO FAR! BESIDES, YOU NEED TO TELL ME THE DATE.
IT'S THIS SATURDAY. 4:00 PM AT BAEKJAE BAKERY.
AND I HAVE GOOD NEWS. THIS TIME, CAPTAIN SAID HE WILL GO.
I CAN'T MAKE IT ANYWAY. THAT'S GOOD. I HAVE A VALID EXCUSE FOR REFUSING THE OFFER, EVEN IF I DON'T HAVE ONE MORE PERSON.
IF YOU TELL THAT TO THE GIRLS, YOU'LL GET SOME RESPONSE, RIGHT? YOU CAN GET ONE MORE, RIGHT?
HEH-, CAPTAIN?
WHAT? THE DRAMA CLUB CAPTAIN?
ME! ME! ME!
I'LL GO!

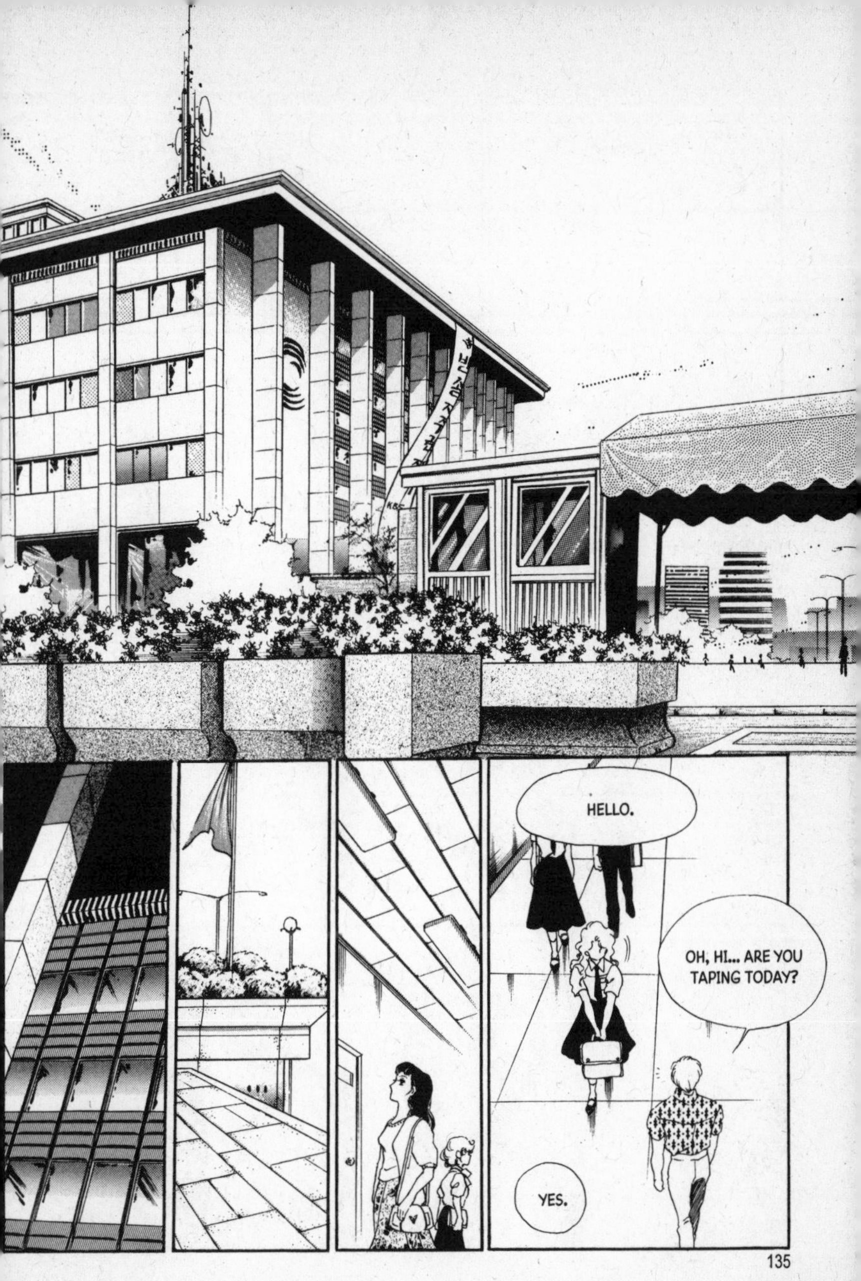
HELLO.
OH, HI... ARE YOU TAPING TODAY?
YES.

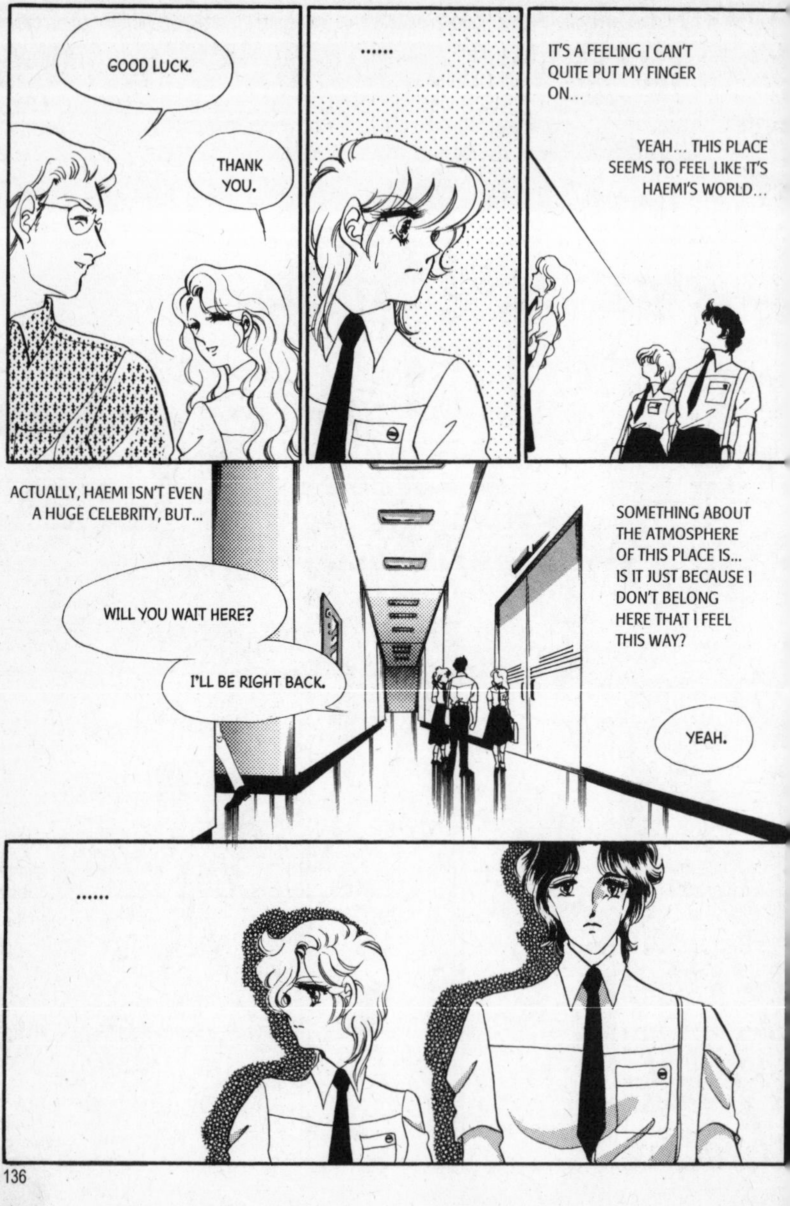
GOOD LUCK.
THANK YOU.
......
IT'S A FEELING I CAN'T QUITE PUT MY FINGER ON...
YEAH... THIS PLACE SEEMS TO FEEL LIKE IT'S HAEMI'S WORLD...
ACTUALLY, HAEMI ISN'T EVEN A HUGE CELEBRITY, BUT...
WILL YOU WAIT HERE?
I'LL BE RIGHT BACK.
SOMETHING ABOUT THE ATMOSPHERE OF THIS PLACE IS... IS IT JUST BECAUSE I DON'T BELONG HERE THAT I FEEL THIS WAY?
YEAH.
......

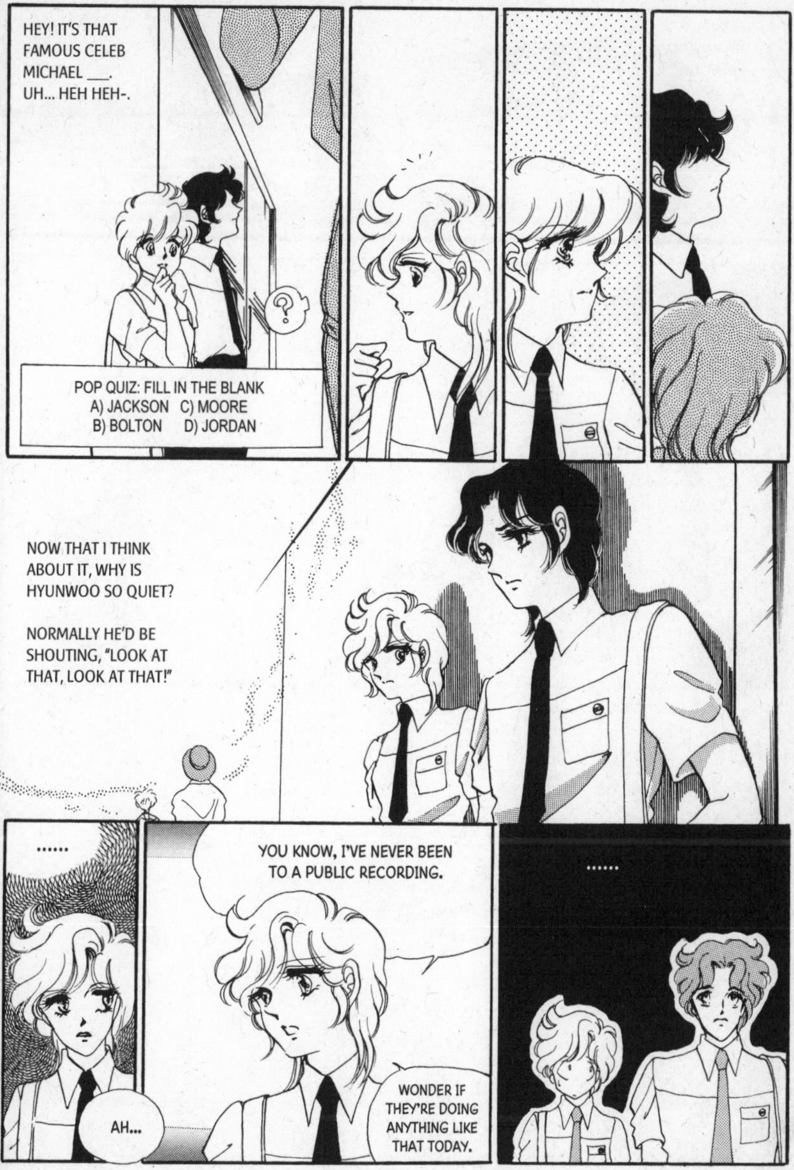
HEY! IT'S THAT FAMOUS CELEB MICHAEL ___. UH... HEH HEH-.
POP QUIZ: FILL IN THE BLANK
A) JACKSON C) MOORE
B) BOLTON D) JORDAN
?
NOW THAT I THINK ABOUT IT, WHY IS HYUNWOO SO QUIET?
NORMALLY HE'D BE SHOUTING, "LOOK AT THAT, LOOK AT THAT!"
......
AH...
YOU KNOW, I'VE NEVER BEEN TO A PUBLIC RECORDING.
WONDER IF THEY'RE DOING ANYTHING LIKE THAT TODAY.
......

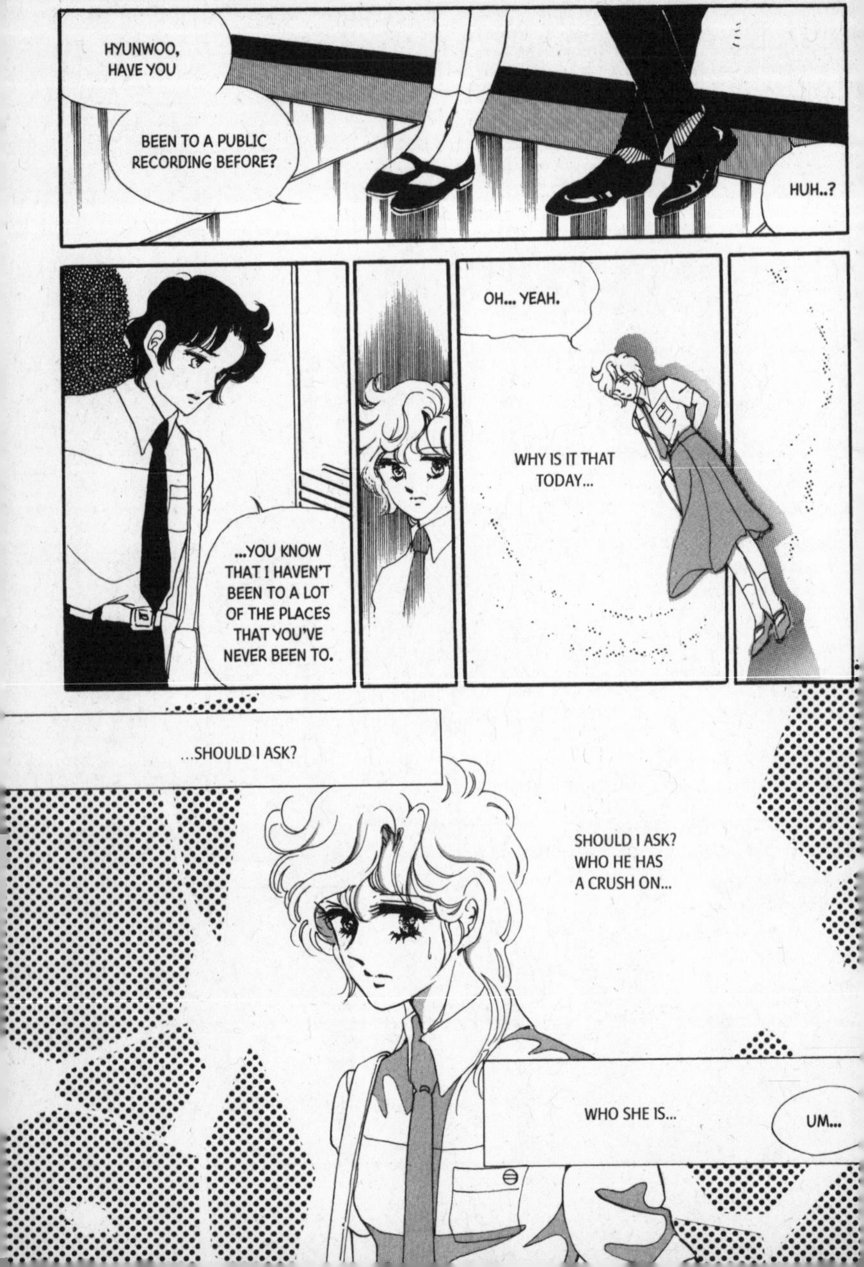
HYUNWOO, HAVE YOU
BEEN TO A PUBLIC RECORDING BEFORE?
HUH..?
...YOU KNOW THAT I HAVEN'T BEEN TO A LOT OF THE PLACES THAT YOU'VE NEVER BEEN TO.
OH... YEAH.
WHY IS IT THAT TODAY...
...SHOULD I ASK?
SHOULD I ASK? WHO HE HAS A CRUSH ON...
WHO SHE IS...
UM...

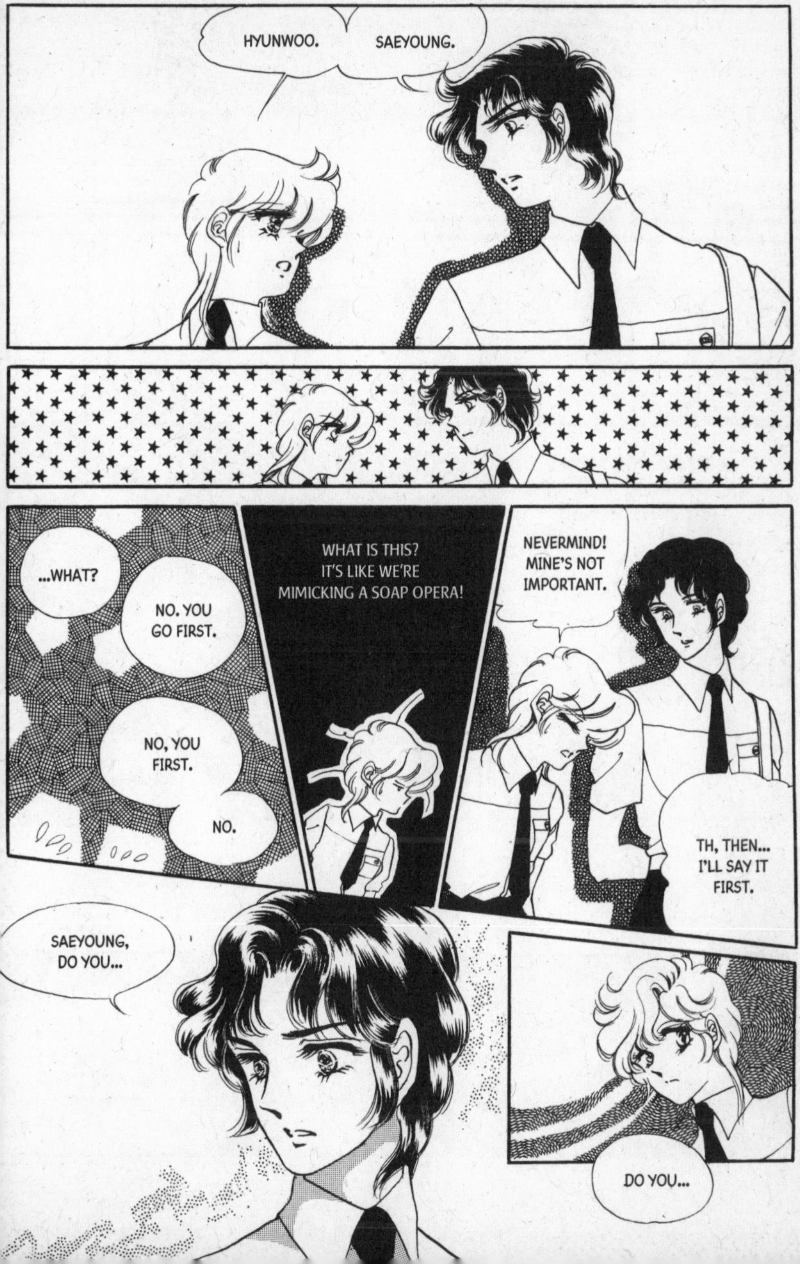
HYUNWOO.
SAEYOUNG.
...WHAT?
NO. YOU GO FIRST.
NO, YOU FIRST.
NO.
WHAT IS THIS? IT'S LIKE WE'RE MIMICKING A SOAP OPERA!
NEVERMIND! MINE'S NOT IMPORTANT.
TH, THEN... I'LL SAY IT FIRST.
SAEYOUNG, DO YOU...
DO YOU...

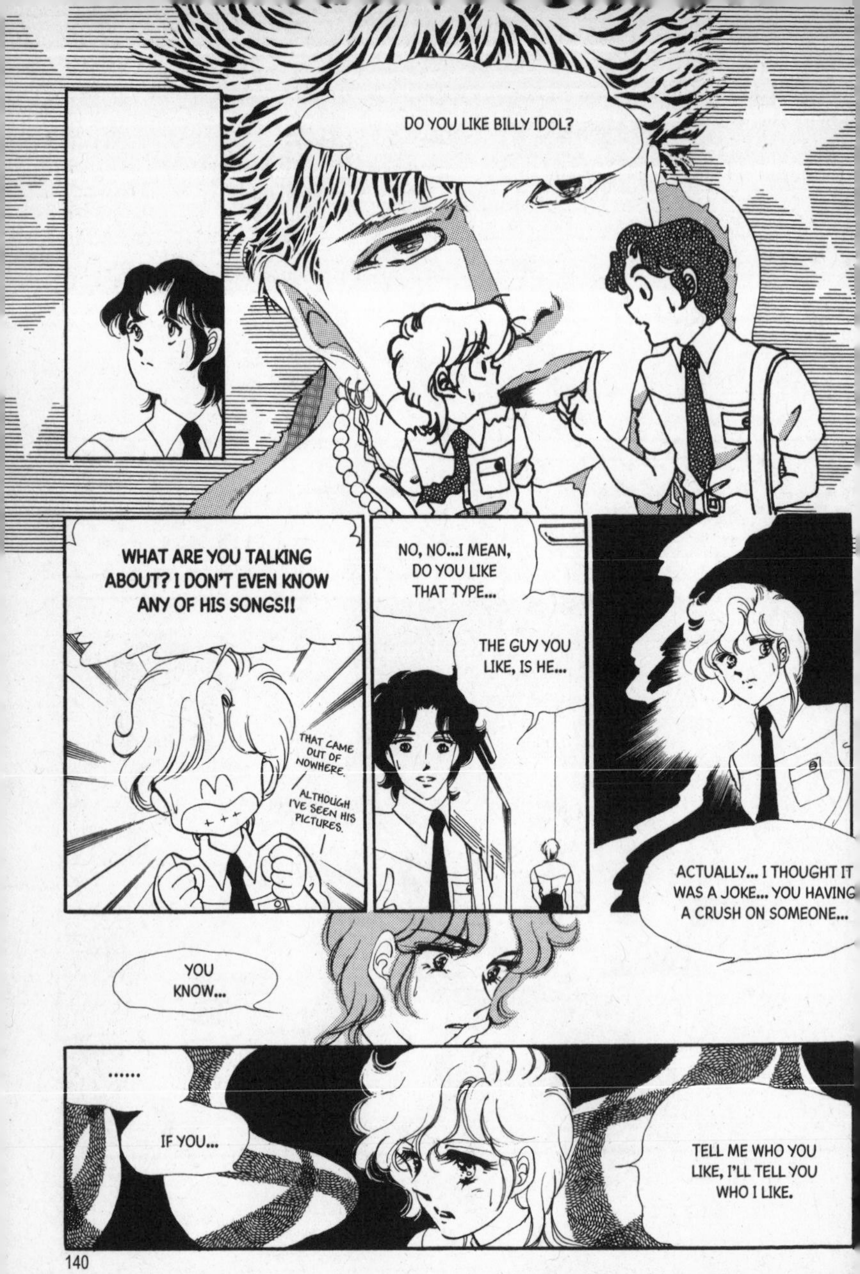
DO YOU LIKE BILLY IDOL?
WHAT ARE YOU TALKING ABOUT? I DON'T EVEN KNOW ANY OF HIS SONGS!!
THAT CAME OUT OF NOWHERE.
ALTHOUGH I'VE SEEN HIS PICTURES.
NO, NO...I MEAN, DO YOU LIKE THAT TYPE...
THE GUY YOU LIKE, IS HE...
ACTUALLY... I THOUGHT IT WAS A JOKE... YOU HAVING A CRUSH ON SOMEONE...
YOU KNOW...
......
IF YOU...
TELL ME WHO YOU LIKE, I'LL TELL YOU WHO I LIKE.

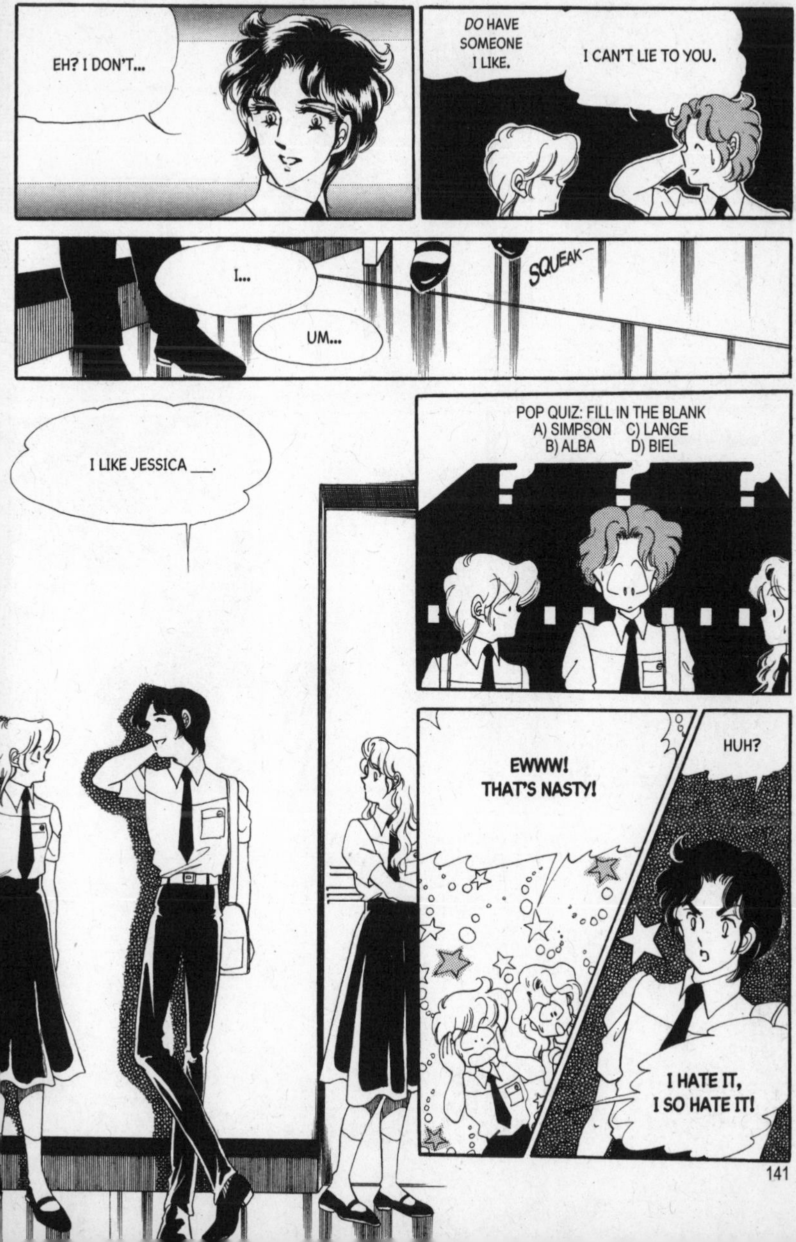
EH? I DON'T...
DO HAVE SOMEONE I LIKE.
I CAN'T LIE TO YOU.
I...
UM...
SQUEAK—
I LIKE JESSICA ___.
POP QUIZ: FILL IN THE BLANK
A) SIMPSON C) LANGE
B) ALBA D) BIEL
EWWW! THAT'S NASTY!
HUH?
I HATE IT, I SO HATE IT!

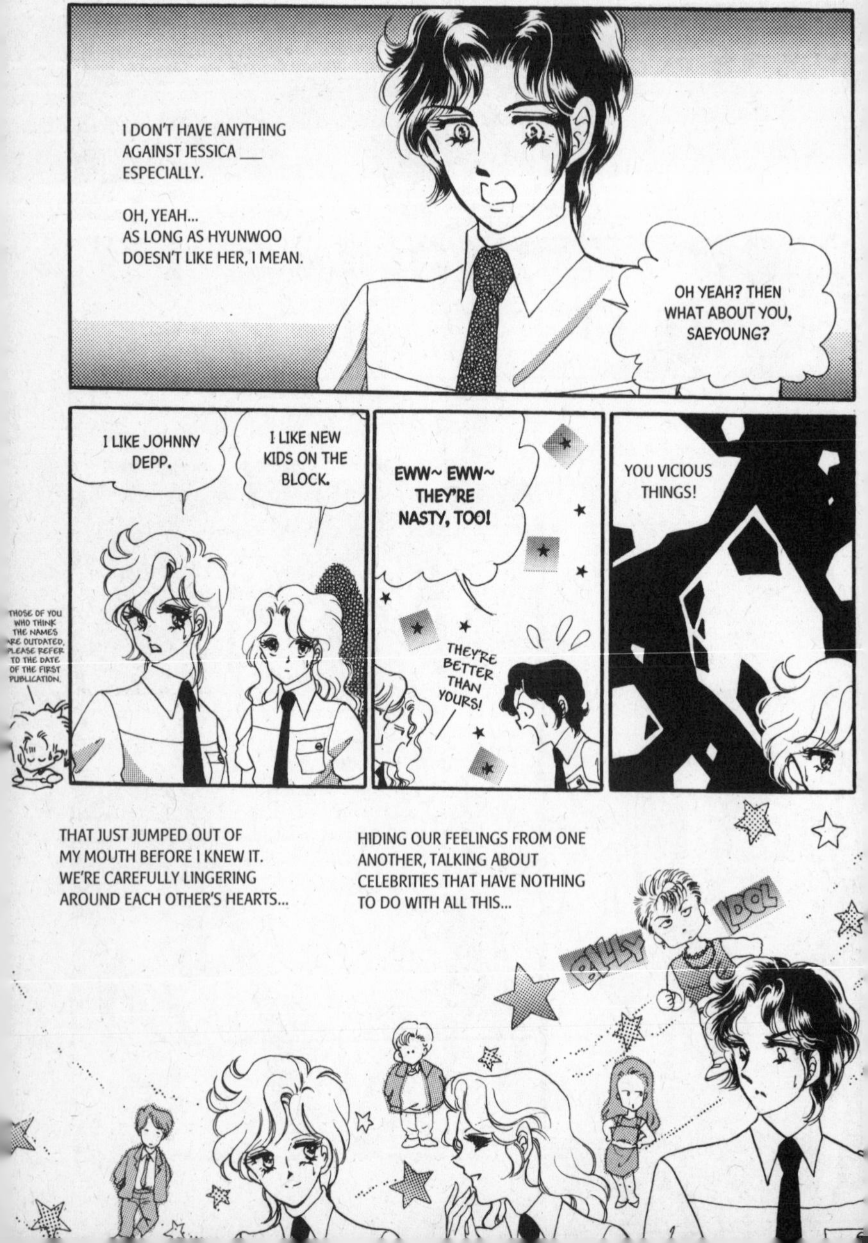
I DON'T HAVE ANYTHING AGAINST JESSICA ___ ESPECIALLY.
OH, YEAH... AS LONG AS HYUNWOO DOESN'T LIKE HER, I MEAN.
OH YEAH? THEN WHAT ABOUT YOU, SAEYOUNG?
THOSE OF YOU WHO THINK THE NAMES RE OUTDATED, PLEASE REFER TO THE DATE OF THE FIRST PUBLICATION.
I LIKE JOHNNY DEPP.
I LIKE NEW KIDS ON THE BLOCK.
EWW~ EWW~ THEY'RE NASTY, TOO!
THEY'RE BETTER THAN YOURS!
YOU VICIOUS THINGS!
THAT JUST JUMPED OUT OF MY MOUTH BEFORE I KNEW IT. WE'RE CAREFULLY LINGERING AROUND EACH OTHER'S HEARTS...
HIDING OUR FEELINGS FROM ONE ANOTHER, TALKING ABOUT CELEBRITIES THAT HAVE NOTHING TO DO WITH ALL THIS...
BILLY IDOL

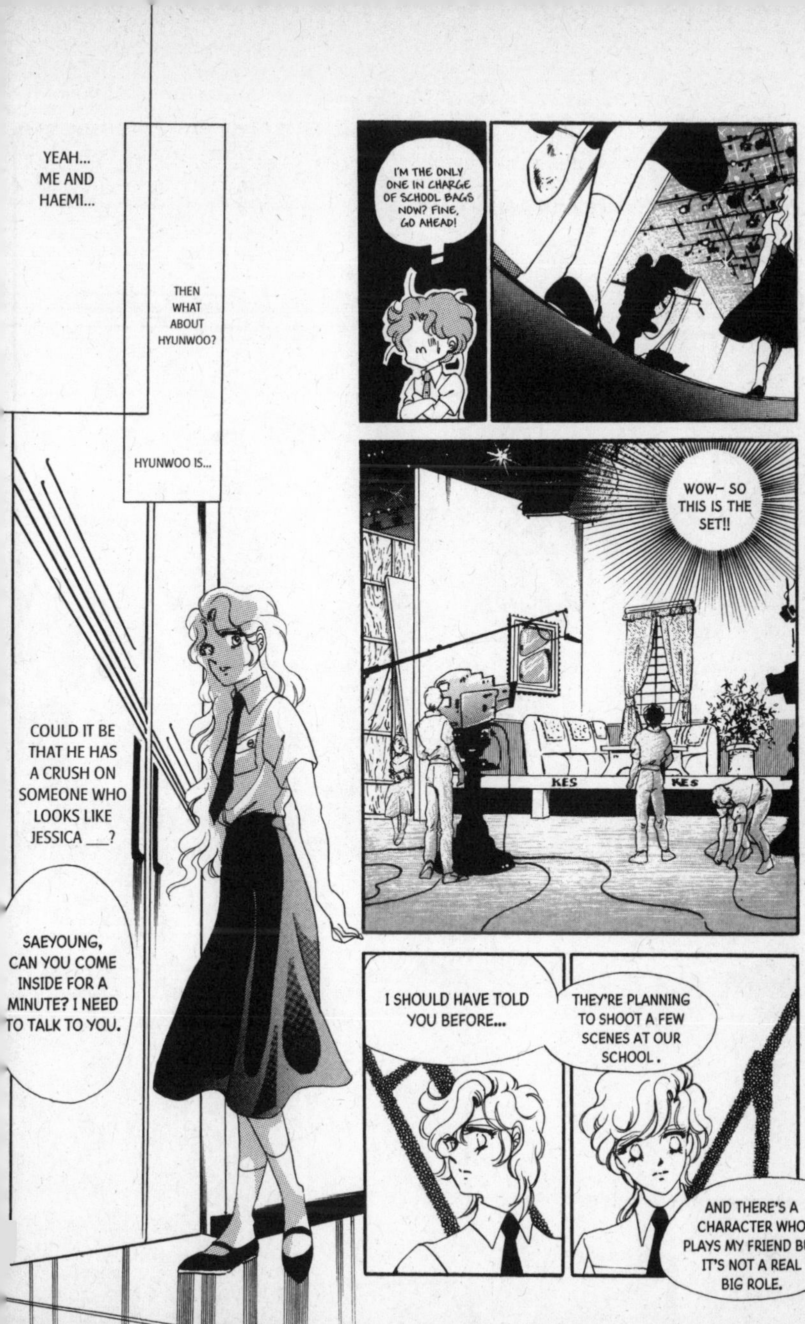
YEAH... ME AND HAEMI...
THEN WHAT ABOUT HYUNWOO?
HYUNWOO IS...
COULD IT BE THAT HE HAS A CRUSH ON SOMEONE WHO LOOKS LIKE JESSICA ___?
SAEYOUNG, CAN YOU COME INSIDE FOR A MINUTE? I NEED TO TALK TO YOU.
I'M THE ONLY ONE IN CHARGE OF SCHOOL BAGS NOW? FINE, GO AHEAD!
WOW- SO THIS IS THE SET!!
KES
KES
I SHOULD HAVE TOLD YOU BEFORE...
THEY'RE PLANNING TO SHOOT A FEW SCENES AT OUR SCHOOL.
AND THERE'S A CHARACTER WHO PLAYS MY FRIEND BUT IT'S NOT A REAL BIG ROLE.

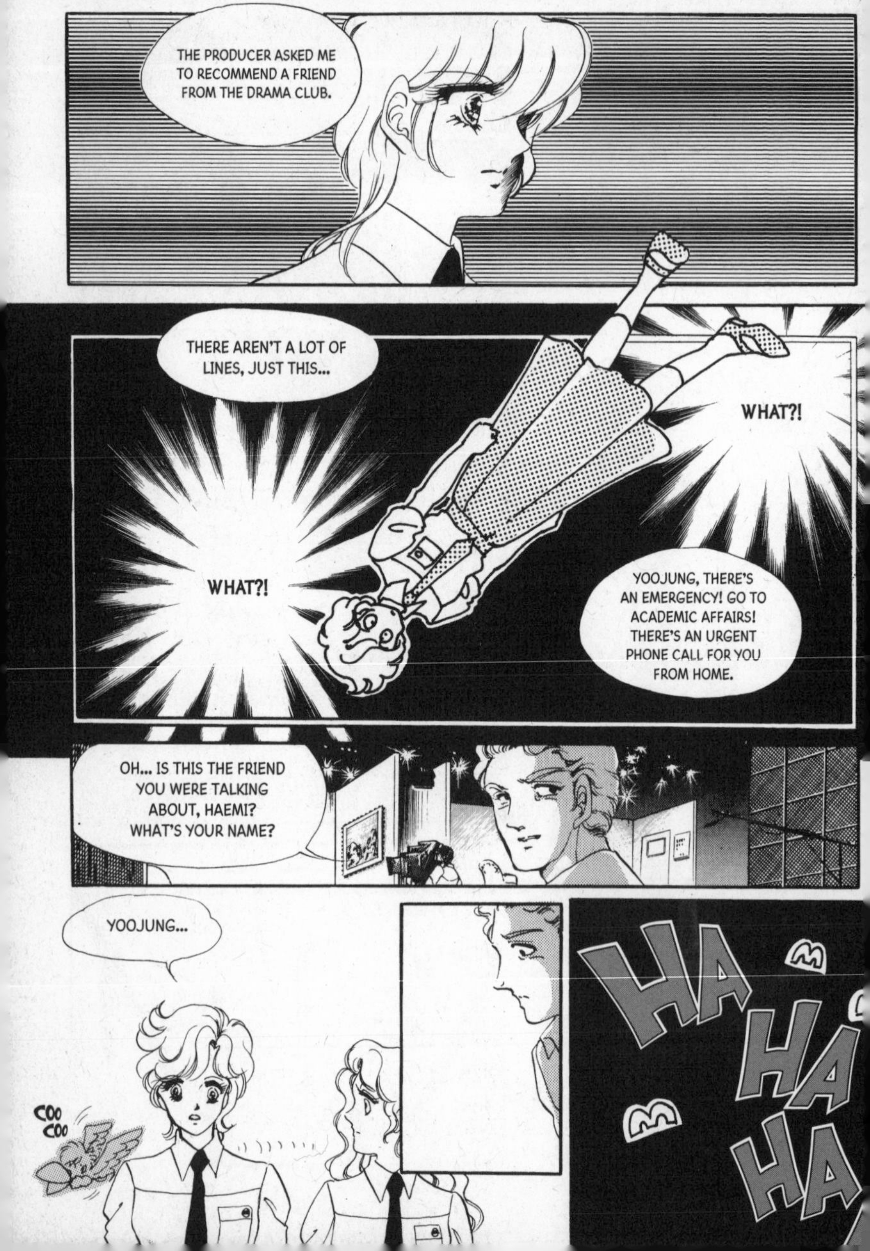
THE PRODUCER ASKED ME TO RECOMMEND A FRIEND FROM THE DRAMA CLUB.
THERE AREN'T A LOT OF LINES, JUST THIS...
WHAT?!
WHAT?!
YOOJUNG, THERE'S AN EMERGENCY! GO TO ACADEMIC AFFAIRS! THERE'S AN URGENT PHONE CALL FOR YOU FROM HOME.
OH... IS THIS THE FRIEND YOU WERE TALKING ABOUT, HAEMI? WHAT'S YOUR NAME?
YOOJUNG...
COO COO
HA HA HA HA

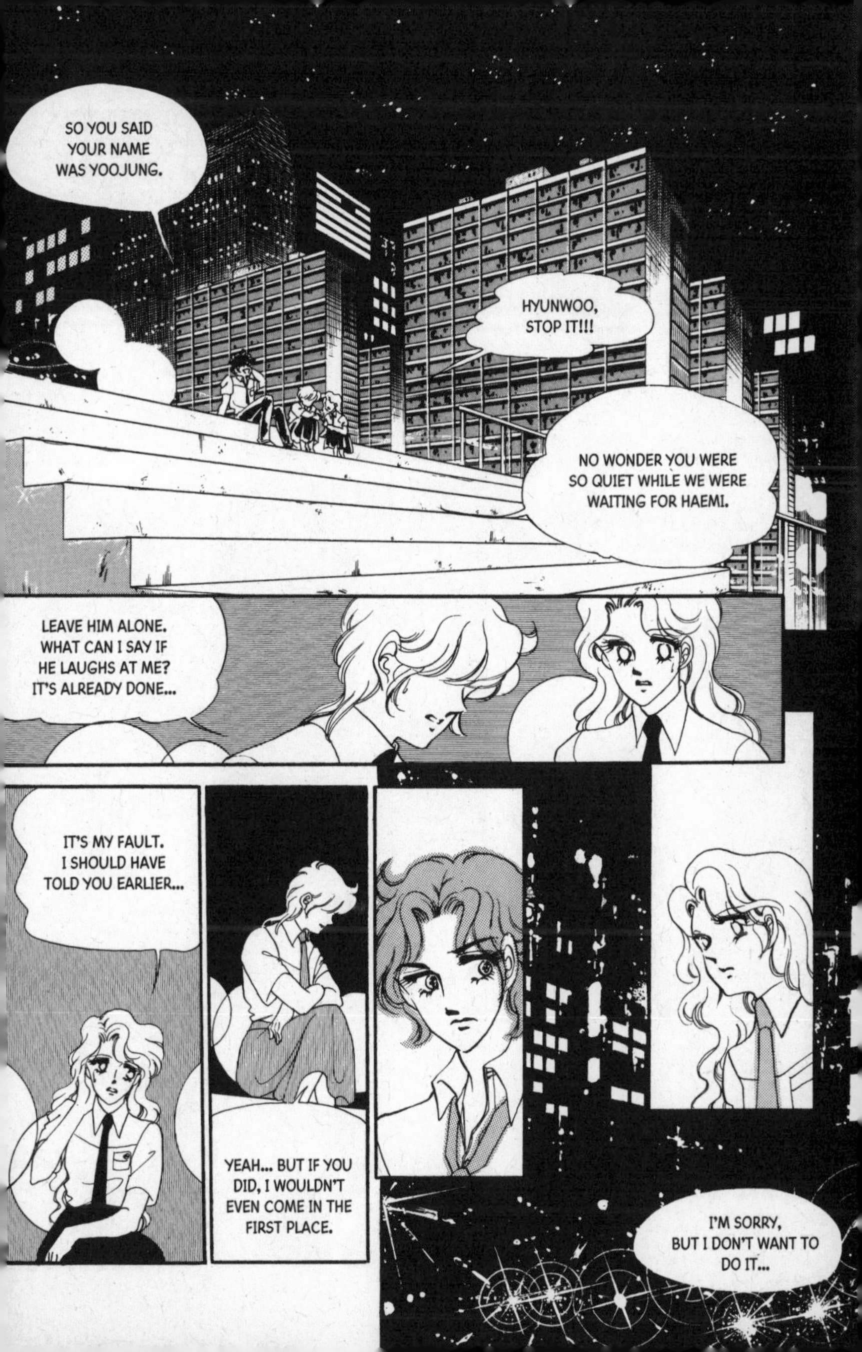
SO YOU SAID YOUR NAME WAS YOOJUNG.
HYUNWOO, STOP IT!!!
NO WONDER YOU WERE SO QUIET WHILE WE WERE WAITING FOR HAEMI.
LEAVE HIM ALONE. WHAT CAN I SAY IF HE LAUGHS AT ME? IT'S ALREADY DONE...
IT'S MY FAULT. I SHOULD HAVE TOLD YOU EARLIER...
YEAH... BUT IF YOU DID, I WOULDN'T EVEN COME IN THE FIRST PLACE.
I'M SORRY, BUT I DON'T WANT TO DO IT...

SAEYOUNG... I SHOULD'VE ASKED YOU BEFORE, BUT...

WHY?

UM... I FELT BAD FOR TAKING THE LEADING ROLE BACK FROM YOU, SO...

THAT WAS RIGHTFULLY YOUR PART... THERE'S NO REASON FOR YOU TO FEEL SORRY ABOUT IT.

I ACCEPTED IT THAT WAY AND HANDED IT OVER TO YOU.

YEAH... REALLY...

I HATE THIS... THE FEELING OF MYSELF BECOMING MISERABLE...

YOU MIGHT NOT HAVE MEANT HARM HAEMI, BUT THAT'S NOT HOW I'M TAKING IT.

AND NOW IT FEELS LIKE YOU'RE THROWING ME A BONE WHEN I DIDN'T BEG FOR ANYTHING.

I FEEL AS IF I'VE BEEN MADE FUN OF...

...I'M SOR

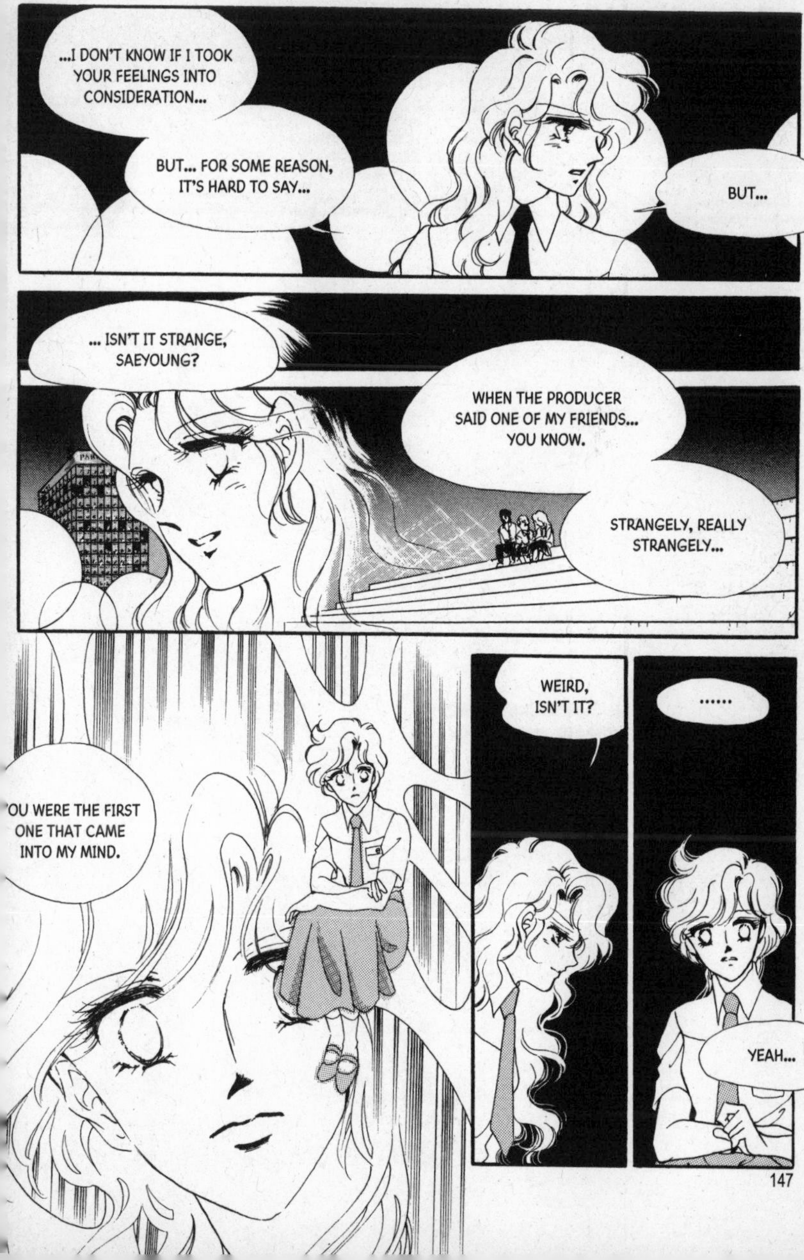

...I DON'T KNOW IF I TOOK YOUR FEELINGS INTO CONSIDERATION...
BUT... FOR SOME REASON, IT'S HARD TO SAY...
BUT...
... ISN'T IT STRANGE, SAEYOUNG?
WHEN THE PRODUCER SAID ONE OF MY FRIENDS... YOU KNOW.
STRANGELY, REALLY STRANGELY...
'OU WERE THE FIRST ONE THAT CAME INTO MY MIND.
WEIRD, ISN'T IT?
......
YEAH...

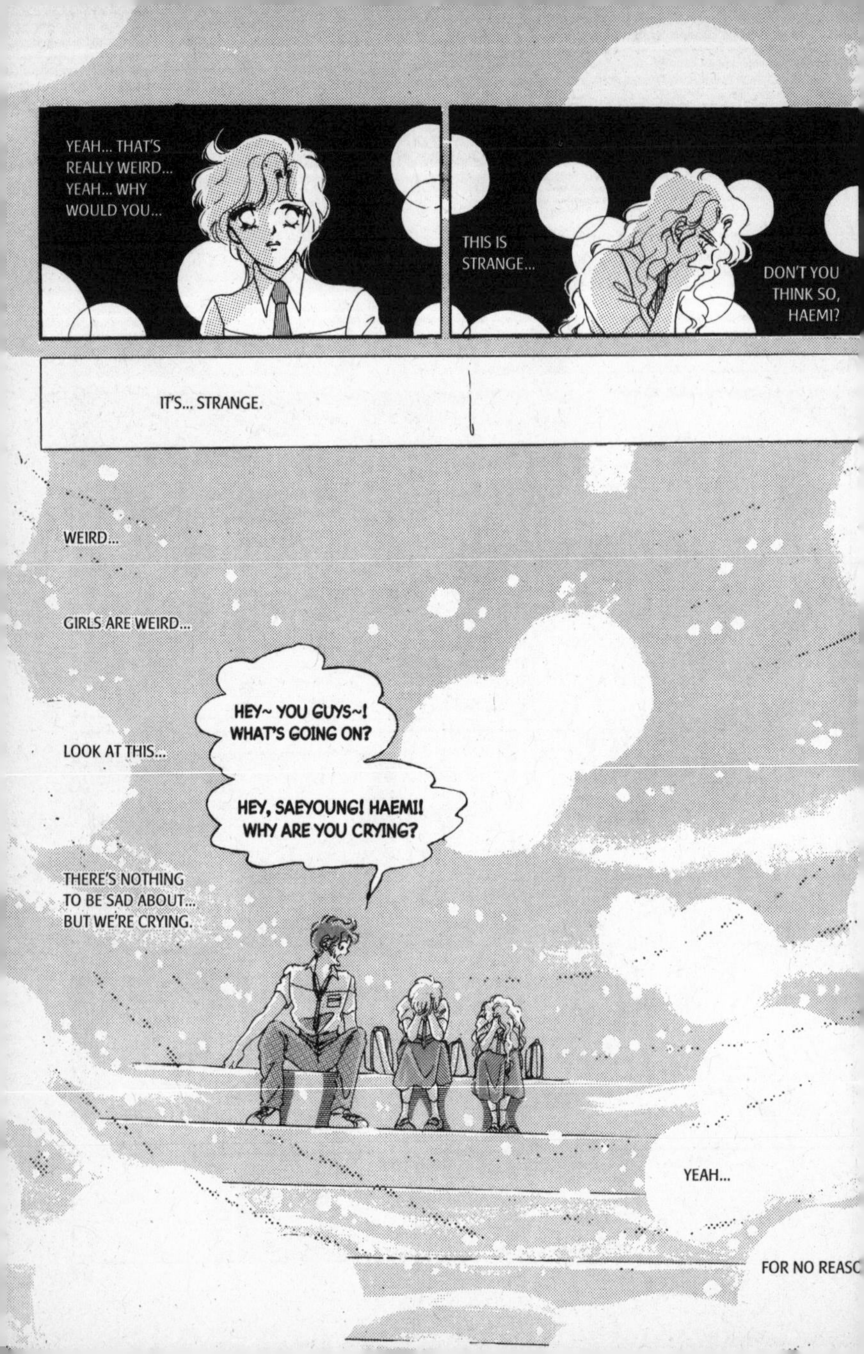
YEAH... THAT'S
REALLY WEIRD...
YEAH... WHY
WOULD YOU...
THIS IS
STRANGE...
DON'T YOU
THINK SO,
HAEMI?
IT'S... STRANGE.
WEIRD...
GIRLS ARE WEIRD...
LOOK AT THIS...
HEY~ YOU GUYS~!
WHAT'S GOING ON?
HEY, SAEYOUNG! HAEMI!
WHY ARE YOU CRYING?
THERE'S NOTHING
TO BE SAD ABOUT...
BUT WE'RE CRYING.
YEAH...
FOR NO REAS

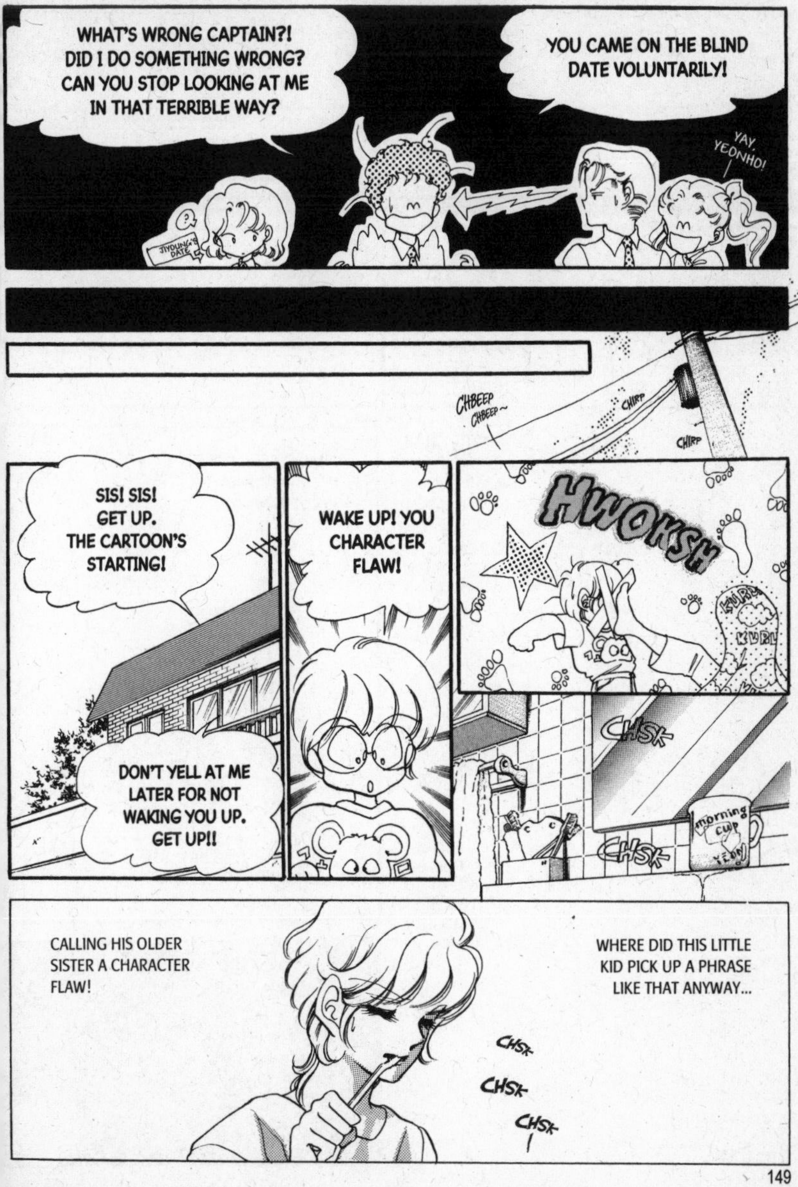
WHAT'S WRONG CAPTAIN?! DID I DO SOMETHING WRONG? CAN YOU STOP LOOKING AT ME IN THAT TERRIBLE WAY?
YOU CAME ON THE BLIND DATE VOLUNTARILY!
?
JIYOUNG'S DATE
YAY, YEONHO!
CHBEEP CHBEEP~
CHIRP
CHIRP
SIS! SIS! GET UP. THE CARTOON'S STARTING!
DON'T YELL AT ME LATER FOR NOT WAKING YOU UP. GET UP!!
WAKE UP! YOU CHARACTER FLAW!
HWOKSH
KURL
KURL
CHSK
CHSK
morning cup
CALLING HIS OLDER SISTER A CHARACTER FLAW!
WHERE DID THIS LITTLE KID PICK UP A PHRASE LIKE THAT ANYWAY...
CHSK
CHSK
CHSK

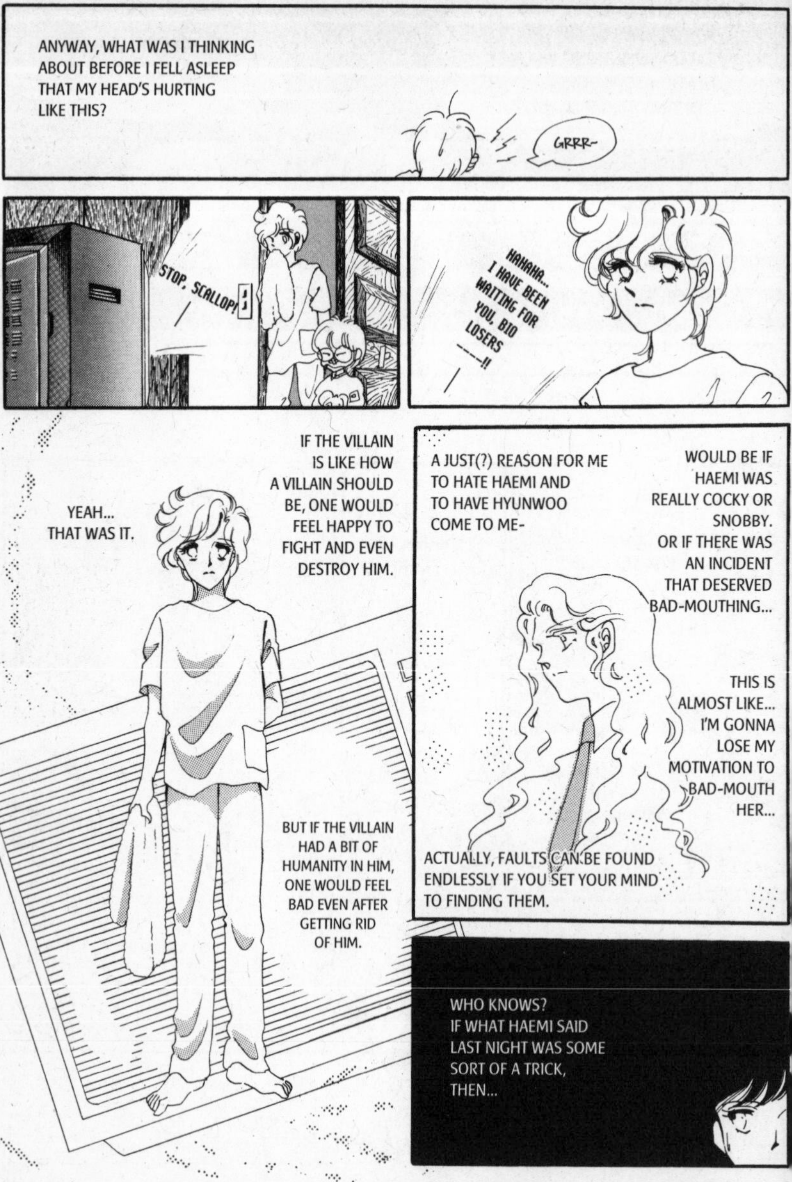

ANYWAY, WHAT WAS I THINKING ABOUT BEFORE I FELL ASLEEP THAT MY HEAD'S HURTING LIKE THIS?
GRRR-
STOP, SCALLOP!
HAHAHA... I HAVE BEEN WAITING FOR YOU, BIO LOSERS ----!!
YEAH... THAT WAS IT.
IF THE VILLAIN IS LIKE HOW A VILLAIN SHOULD BE, ONE WOULD FEEL HAPPY TO FIGHT AND EVEN DESTROY HIM.
BUT IF THE VILLAIN HAD A BIT OF HUMANITY IN HIM, ONE WOULD FEEL BAD EVEN AFTER GETTING RID OF HIM.
A JUST(?) REASON FOR ME TO HATE HAEMI AND TO HAVE HYUNWOO COME TO ME-
WOULD BE IF HAEMI WAS REALLY COCKY OR SNOBBY. OR IF THERE WAS AN INCIDENT THAT DESERVED BAD-MOUTHING...
THIS IS ALMOST LIKE... I'M GONNA LOSE MY MOTIVATION TO BAD-MOUTH HER...
ACTUALLY, FAULTS CAN BE FOUND ENDLESSLY IF YOU SET YOUR MIND TO FINDING THEM.
WHO KNOWS? IF WHAT HAEMI SAID LAST NIGHT WAS SOME SORT OF A TRICK, THEN...

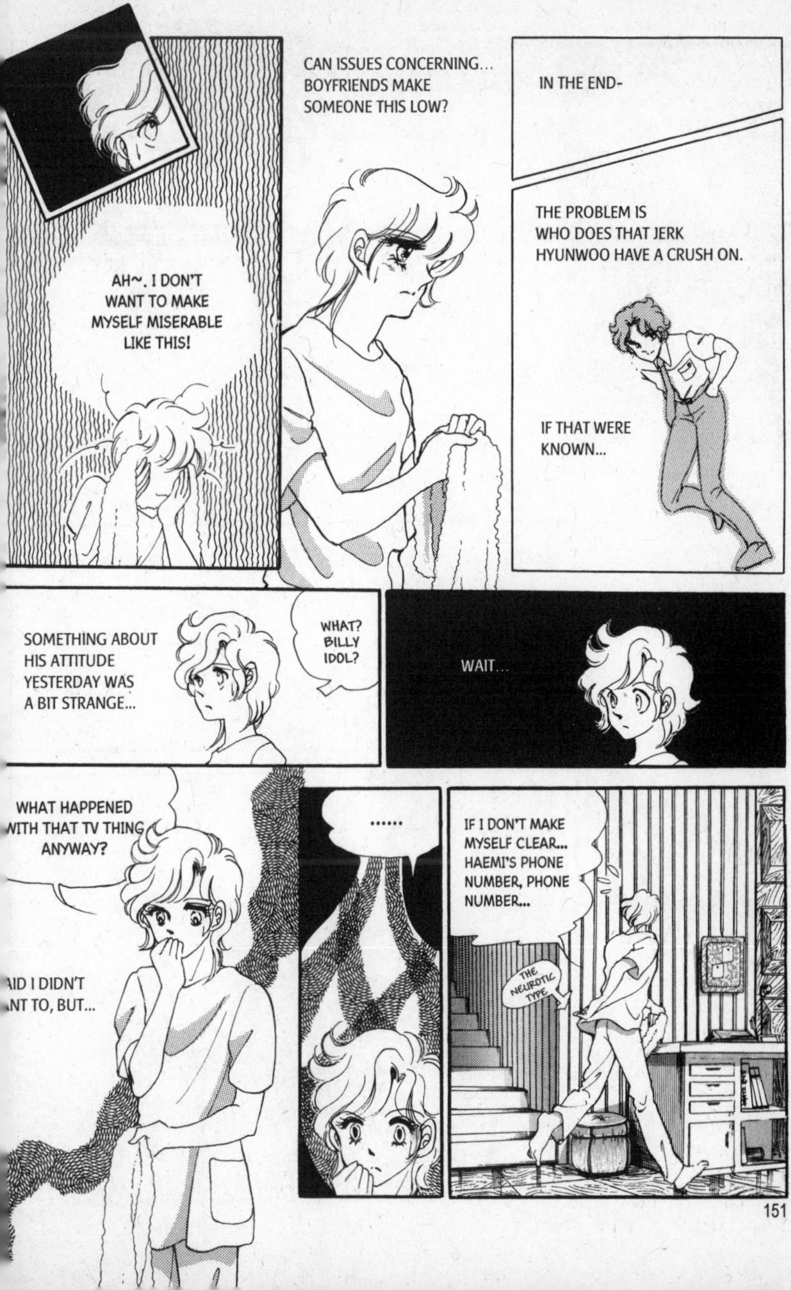
CAN ISSUES CONCERNING... BOYFRIENDS MAKE SOMEONE THIS LOW?
AH~. I DON'T WANT TO MAKE MYSELF MISERABLE LIKE THIS!
IN THE END-
THE PROBLEM IS WHO DOES THAT JERK HYUNWOO HAVE A CRUSH ON.
IF THAT WERE KNOWN...
SOMETHING ABOUT HIS ATTITUDE YESTERDAY WAS A BIT STRANGE...
WHAT? BILLY IDOL?
WAIT...
WHAT HAPPENED WITH THAT TV THING ANYWAY?
AID I DIDN'T ANT TO, BUT...
......
IF I DON'T MAKE MYSELF CLEAR... HAEMI'S PHONE NUMBER, PHONE NUMBER...
THE NEUROTIC TYPE

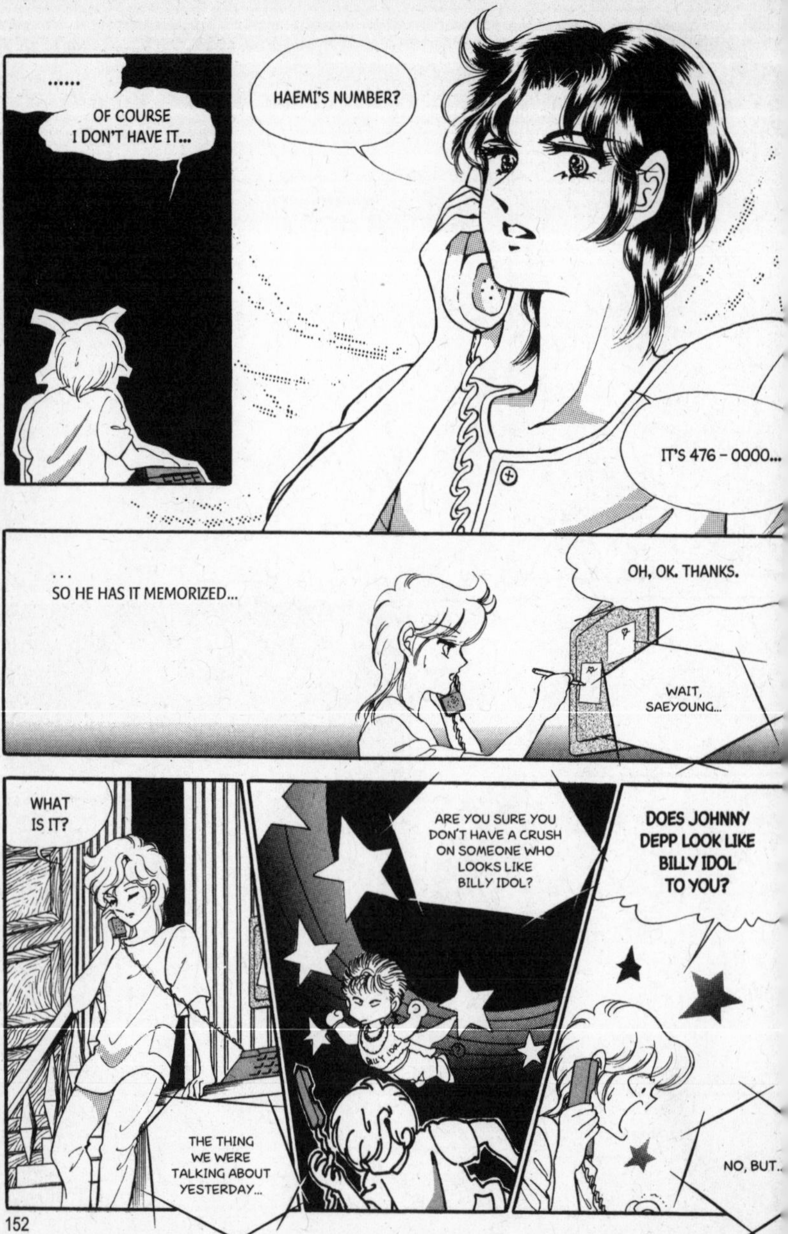

......
OF COURSE I DON'T HAVE IT...
HAEMI'S NUMBER?
IT'S 476 - 0000...
. . .
SO HE HAS IT MEMORIZED...
OH, OK. THANKS.
WAIT, SAEYOUNG...
WHAT IS IT?
THE THING WE WERE TALKING ABOUT YESTERDAY...
ARE YOU SURE YOU DON'T HAVE A CRUSH ON SOMEONE WHO LOOKS LIKE BILLY IDOL?
BILLY IDOL
DOES JOHNNY DEPP LOOK LIKE BILLY IDOL TO YOU?
NO, BUT...

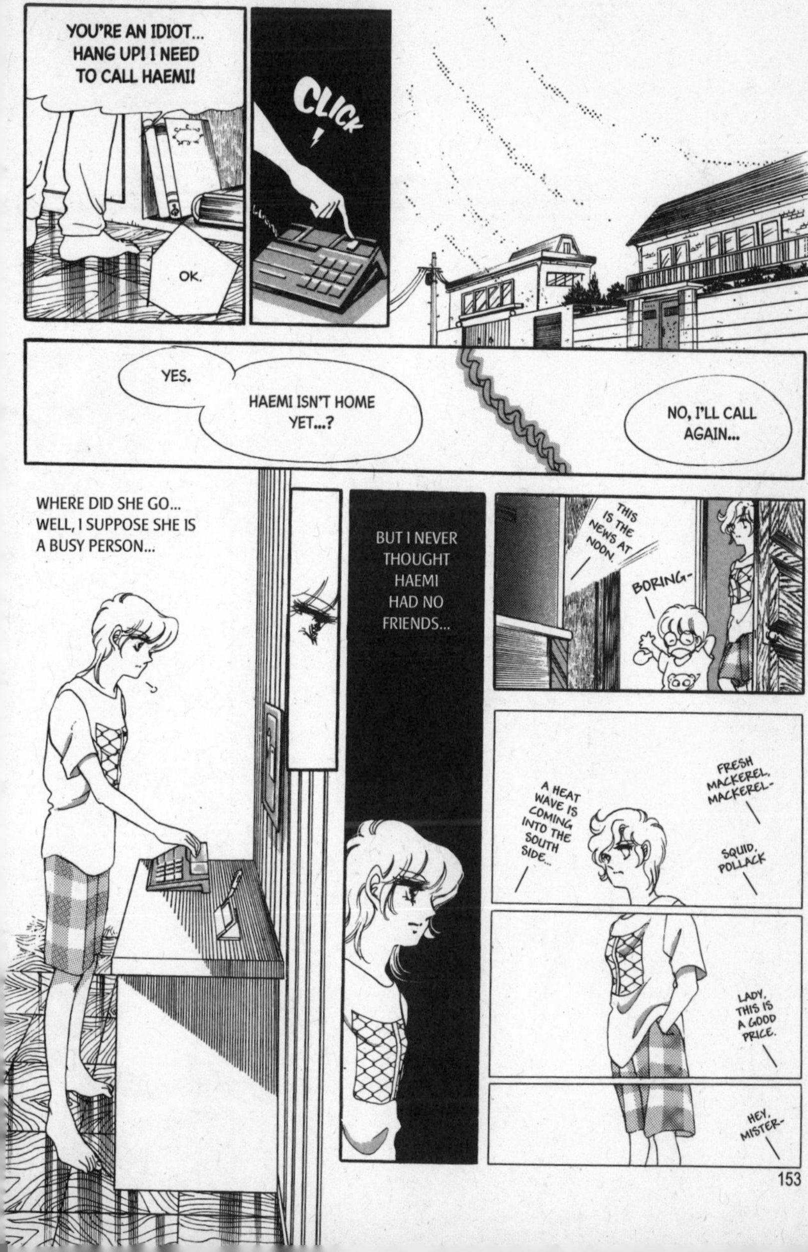

YOU'RE AN IDIOT... HANG UP! I NEED TO CALL HAEMI!
OK.
CLICK
YES.
HAEMI ISN'T HOME YET...?
NO, I'LL CALL AGAIN...
WHERE DID SHE GO... WELL, I SUPPOSE SHE IS A BUSY PERSON...
BUT I NEVER THOUGHT HAEMI HAD NO FRIENDS...
THIS IS THE NEWS AT NOON.
BORING-
A HEAT WAVE IS COMING INTO THE SOUTH SIDE...
FRESH MACKEREL, MACKEREL-
SQUID, POLLACK
LADY, THIS IS A GOOD PRICE.
HEY, MISTER-

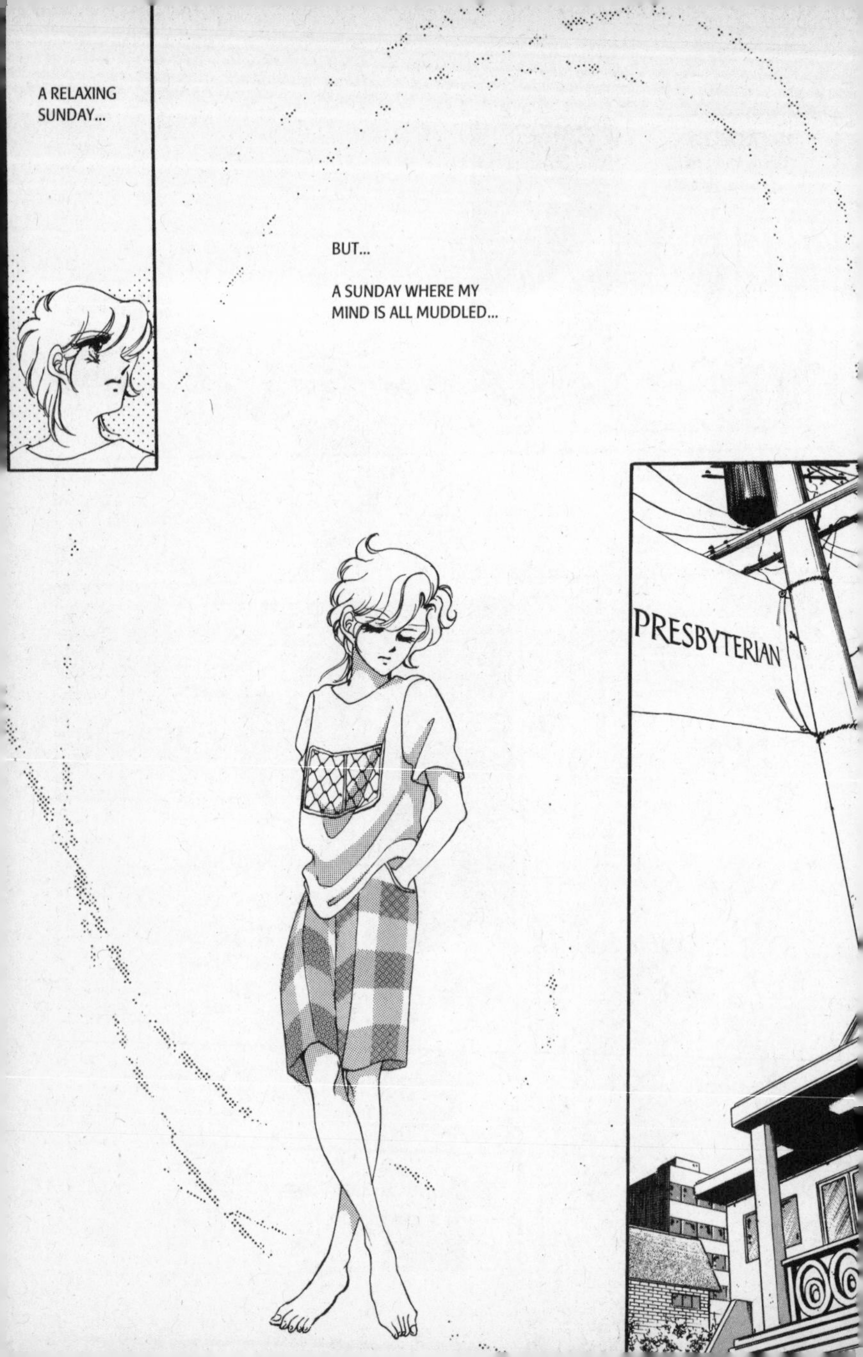
A RELAXING SUNDAY...
BUT...
A SUNDAY WHERE MY MIND IS ALL MUDDLED...
PRESBYTERIAN

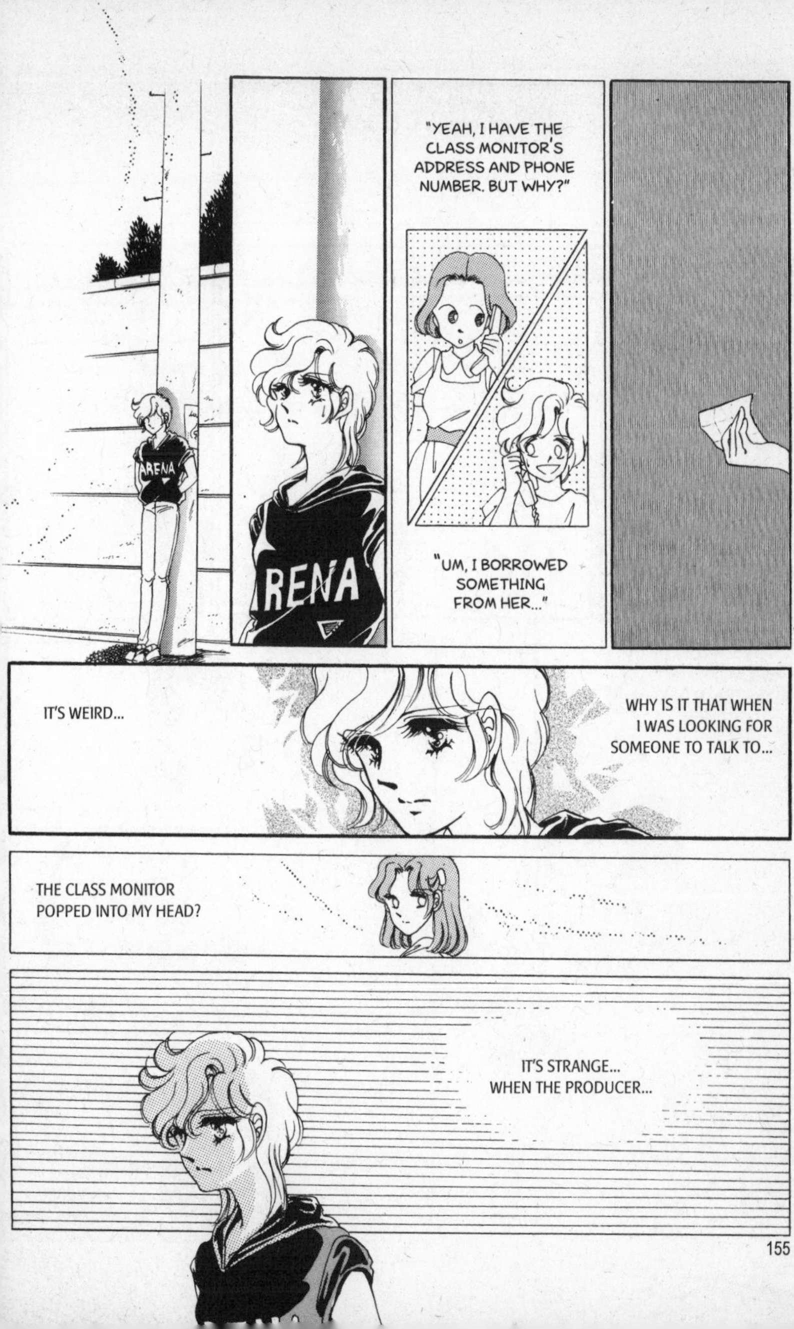
"YEAH, I HAVE THE CLASS MONITOR'S ADDRESS AND PHONE NUMBER. BUT WHY?"
"UM, I BORROWED SOMETHING FROM HER..."
IT'S WEIRD...
WHY IS IT THAT WHEN I WAS LOOKING FOR SOMEONE TO TALK TO...
THE CLASS MONITOR POPPED INTO MY HEAD?
IT'S STRANGE... WHEN THE PRODUCER...

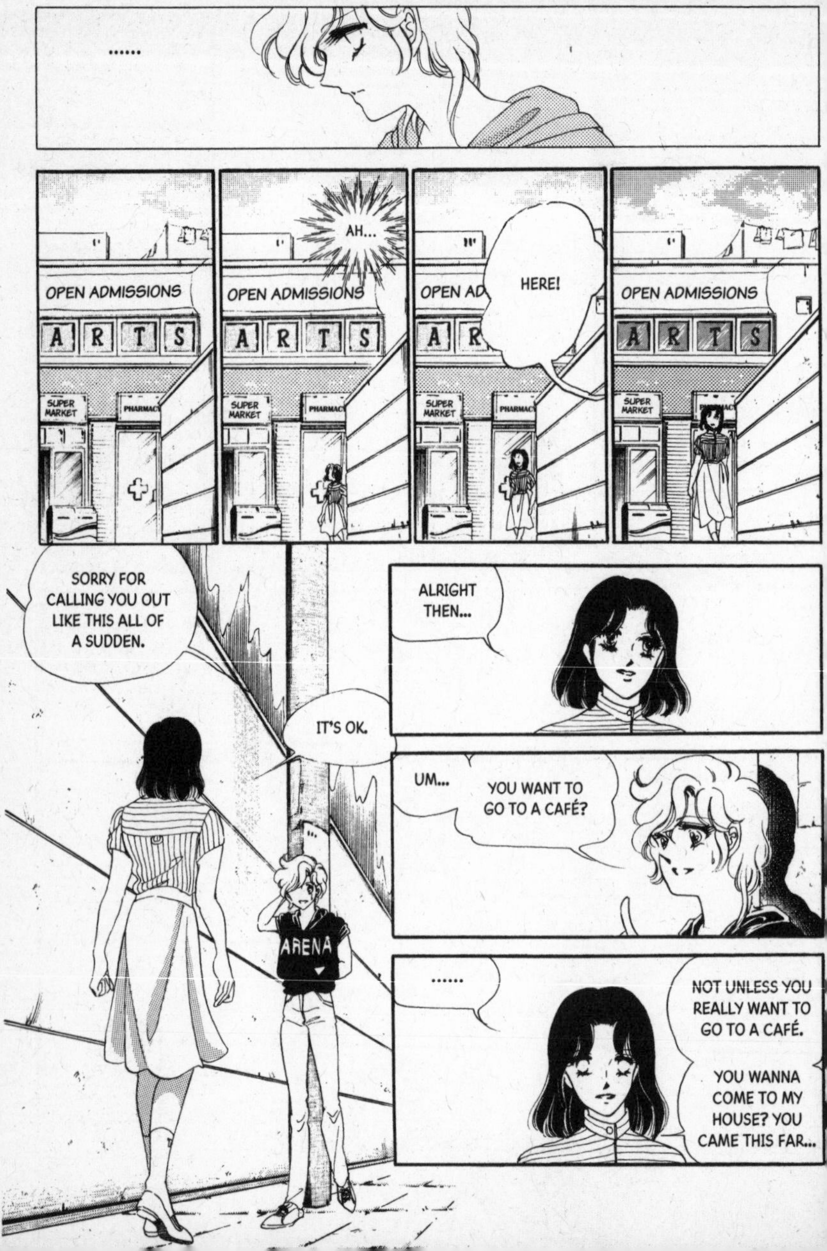
......
OPEN ADMISSIONS
ARTS
SUPER MARKET
PHARMACY
AH...
HERE!
SORRY FOR CALLING YOU OUT LIKE THIS ALL OF A SUDDEN.
IT'S OK.
ARENA
ALRIGHT THEN...
UM...
YOU WANT TO GO TO A CAFÉ?
......
NOT UNLESS YOU REALLY WANT TO GO TO A CAFÉ.
YOU WANNA COME TO MY HOUSE? YOU CAME THIS FAR...

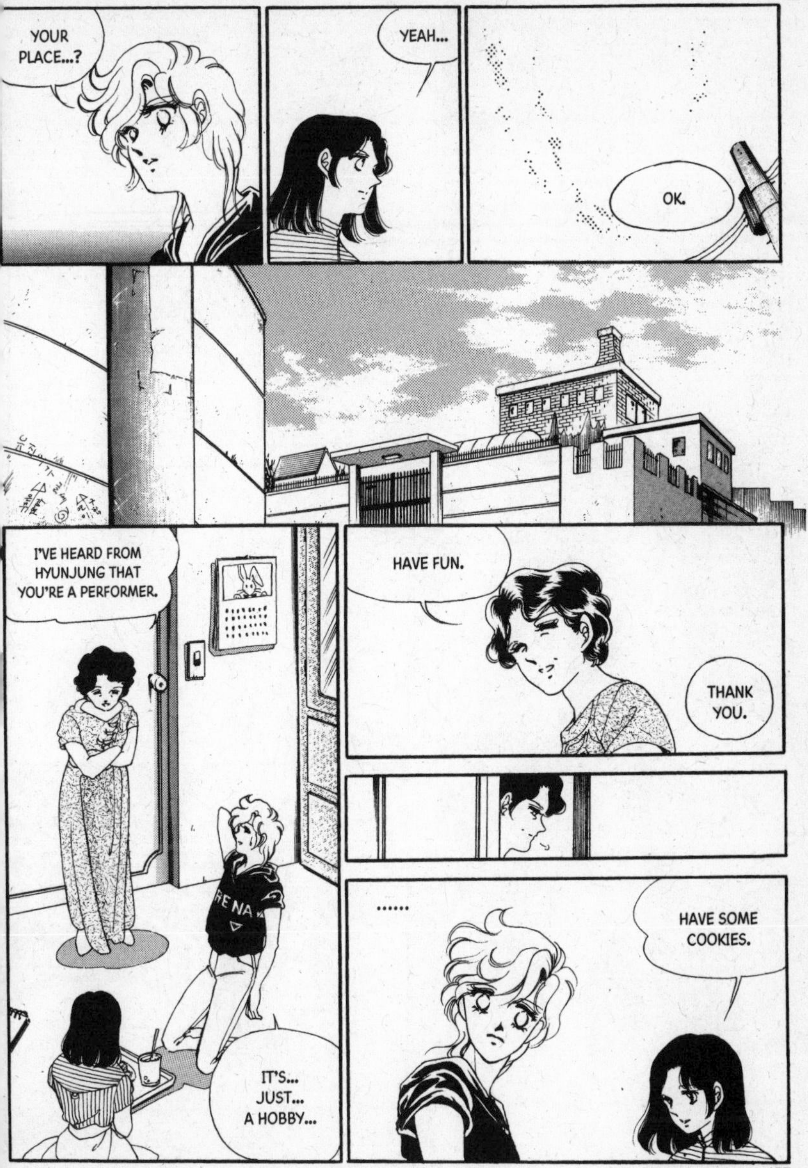
YOUR PLACE...?
YEAH...
OK.
I'VE HEARD FROM HYUNJUNG THAT YOU'RE A PERFORMER.
IT'S... JUST... A HOBBY...
HAVE FUN.
THANK YOU.
......
HAVE SOME COOKIES.

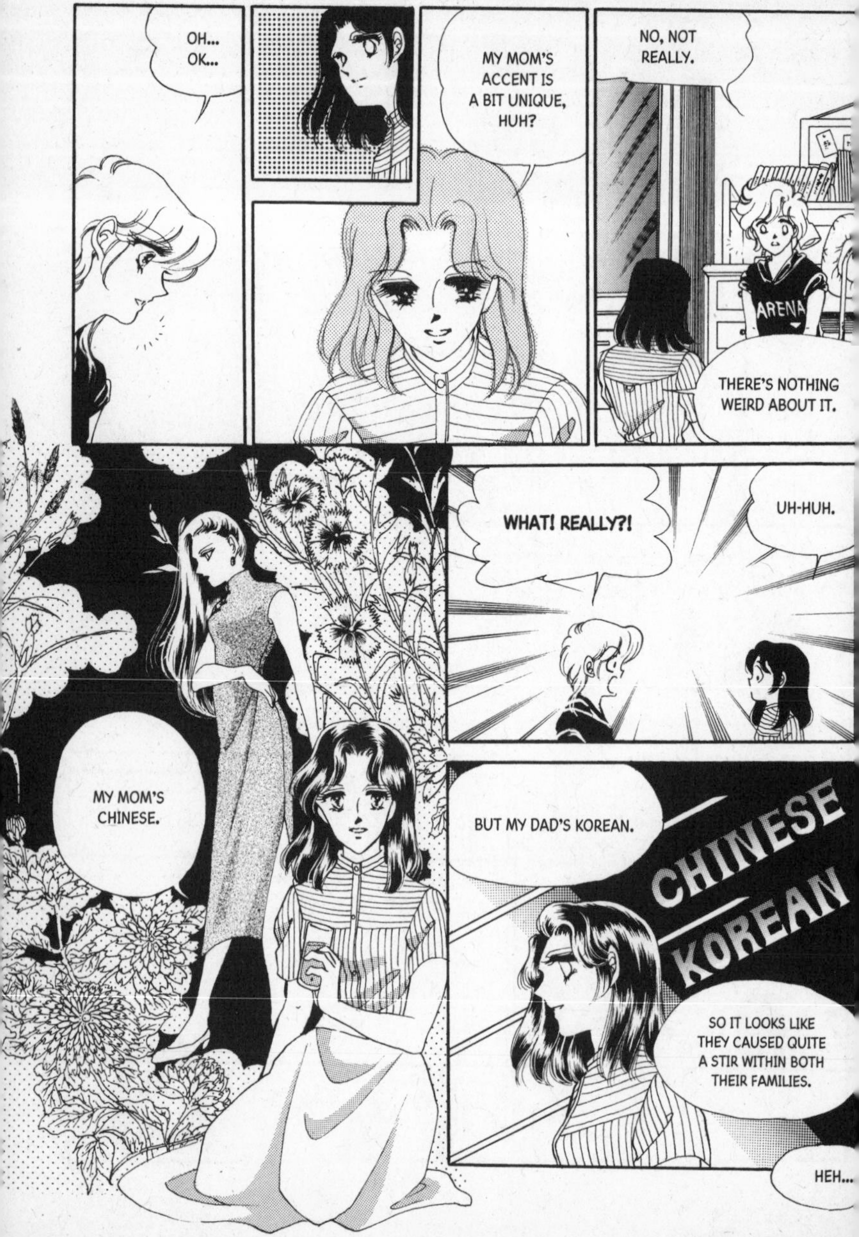
OH... OK...
MY MOM'S ACCENT IS A BIT UNIQUE, HUH?
NO, NOT REALLY.
ARENA
THERE'S NOTHING WEIRD ABOUT IT.
MY MOM'S CHINESE.
WHAT! REALLY?!
UH-HUH.
BUT MY DAD'S KOREAN.
CHINESE
KOREAN
SO IT LOOKS LIKE THEY CAUSED QUITE A STIR WITHIN BOTH THEIR FAMILIES.
HEH...

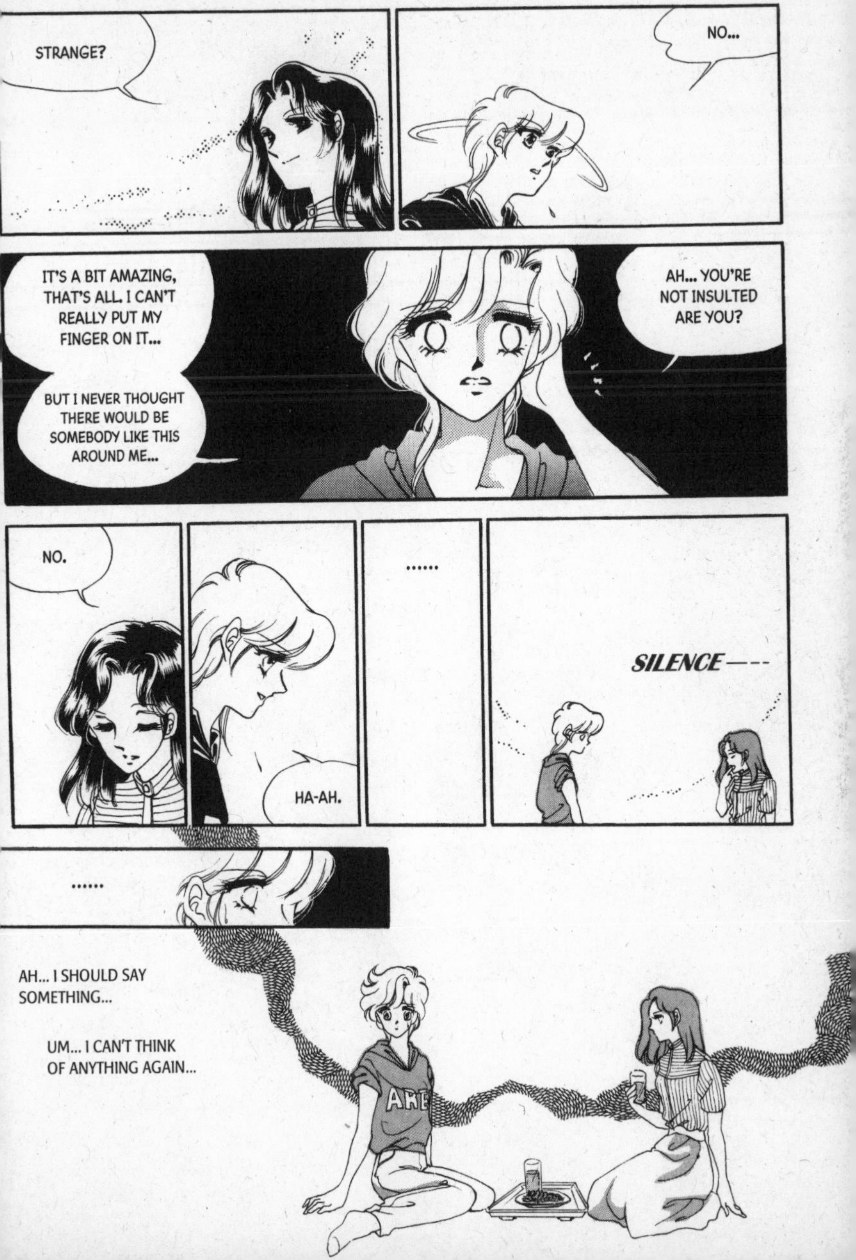
STRANGE?
NO...
IT'S A BIT AMAZING, THAT'S ALL. I CAN'T REALLY PUT MY FINGER ON IT...
BUT I NEVER THOUGHT THERE WOULD BE SOMEBODY LIKE THIS AROUND ME...
AH... YOU'RE NOT INSULTED ARE YOU?
NO.
HA-AH.
......
SILENCE---
......
AH... I SHOULD SAY SOMETHING...
UM... I CAN'T THINK OF ANYTHING AGAIN...
ARE

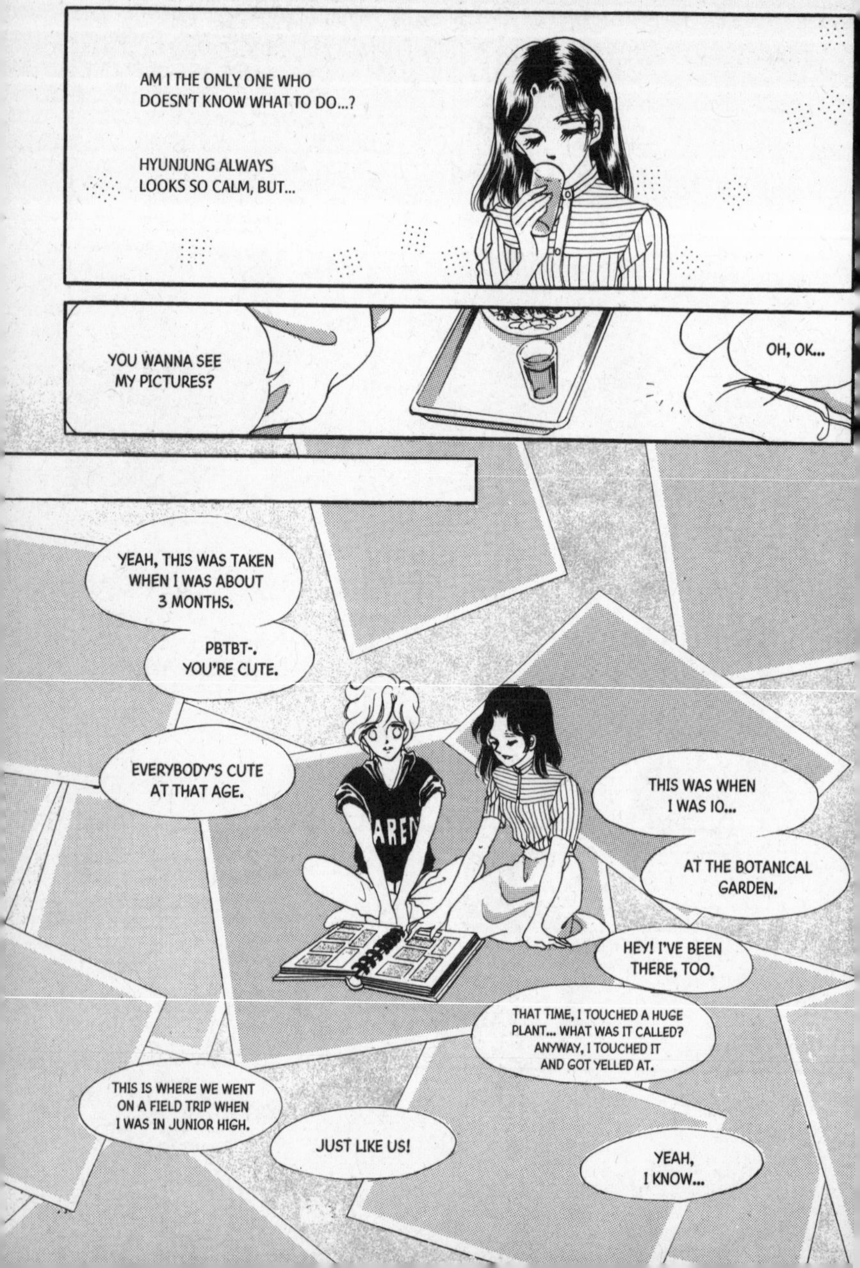
AM I THE ONLY ONE WHO DOESN'T KNOW WHAT TO DO...?
HYUNJUNG ALWAYS LOOKS SO CALM, BUT...
YOU WANNA SEE MY PICTURES?
OH, OK...
YEAH, THIS WAS TAKEN WHEN I WAS ABOUT 3 MONTHS.
PBTBT-. YOU'RE CUTE.
EVERYBODY'S CUTE AT THAT AGE.
THIS WAS WHEN I WAS 10...
AT THE BOTANICAL GARDEN.
HEY! I'VE BEEN THERE, TOO.
THAT TIME, I TOUCHED A HUGE PLANT... WHAT WAS IT CALLED? ANYWAY, I TOUCHED IT AND GOT YELLED AT.
THIS IS WHERE WE WENT ON A FIELD TRIP WHEN I WAS IN JUNIOR HIGH.
JUST LIKE US!
YEAH, I KNOW...

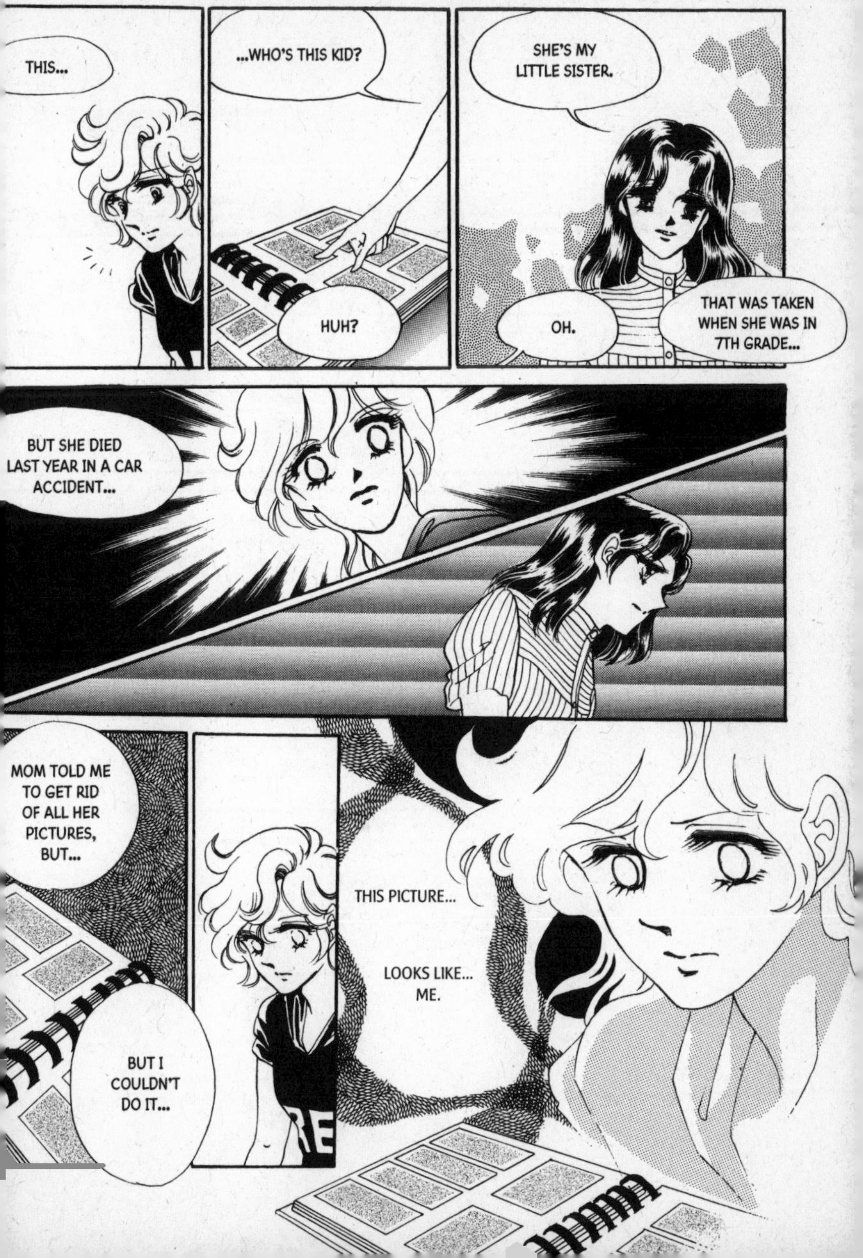
THIS...
...WHO'S THIS KID?
HUH?
SHE'S MY LITTLE SISTER.
OH.
THAT WAS TAKEN WHEN SHE WAS IN 7TH GRADE...
BUT SHE DIED LAST YEAR IN A CAR ACCIDENT...
MOM TOLD ME TO GET RID OF ALL HER PICTURES, BUT...
BUT I COULDN'T DO IT...
THIS PICTURE...
LOOKS LIKE... ME.
RE

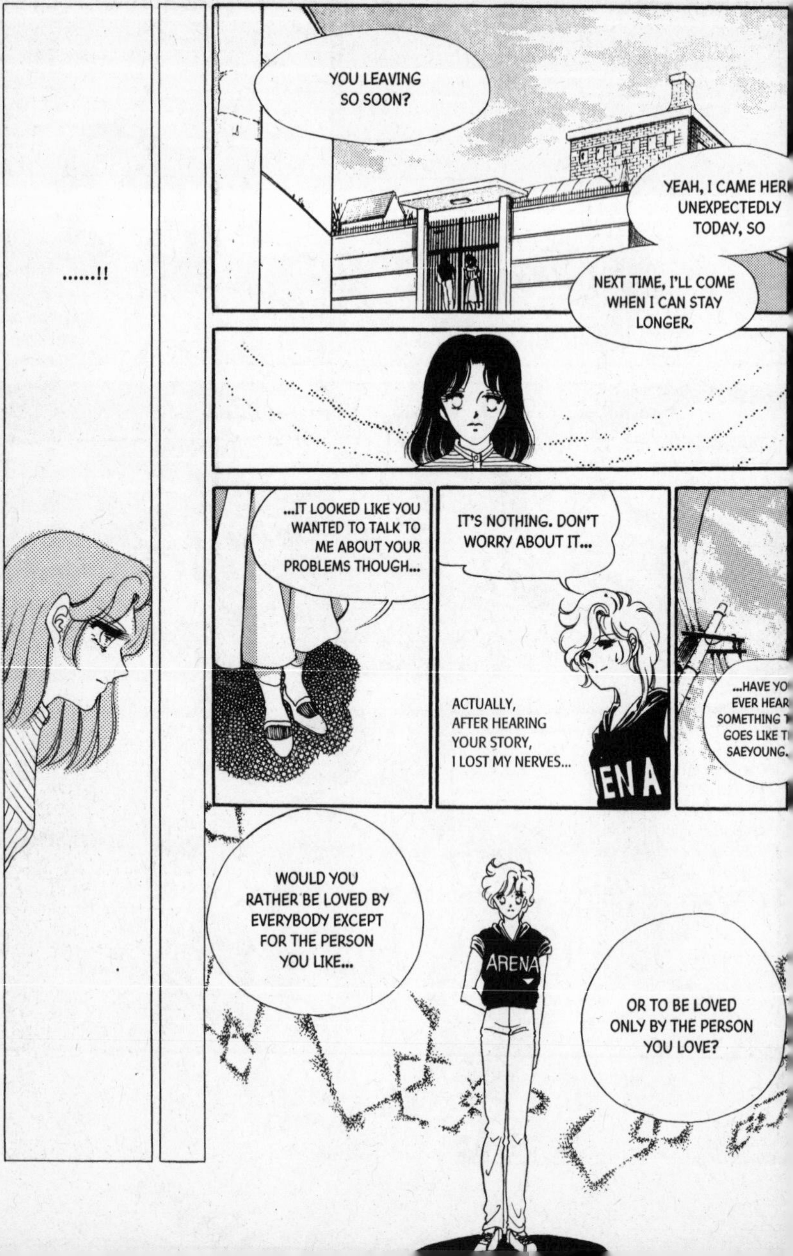
......!!
YOU LEAVING SO SOON?
YEAH, I CAME HER UNEXPECTEDLY TODAY, SO
NEXT TIME, I'LL COME WHEN I CAN STAY LONGER.
...IT LOOKED LIKE YOU WANTED TO TALK TO ME ABOUT YOUR PROBLEMS THOUGH...
IT'S NOTHING. DON'T WORRY ABOUT IT...
ACTUALLY, AFTER HEARING YOUR STORY, I LOST MY NERVES...
EN A
...HAVE YO EVER HEAR SOMETHING T GOES LIKE T SAEYOUNG.
WOULD YOU RATHER BE LOVED BY EVERYBODY EXCEPT FOR THE PERSON YOU LIKE...
ARENA
OR TO BE LOVED ONLY BY THE PERSON YOU LOVE?

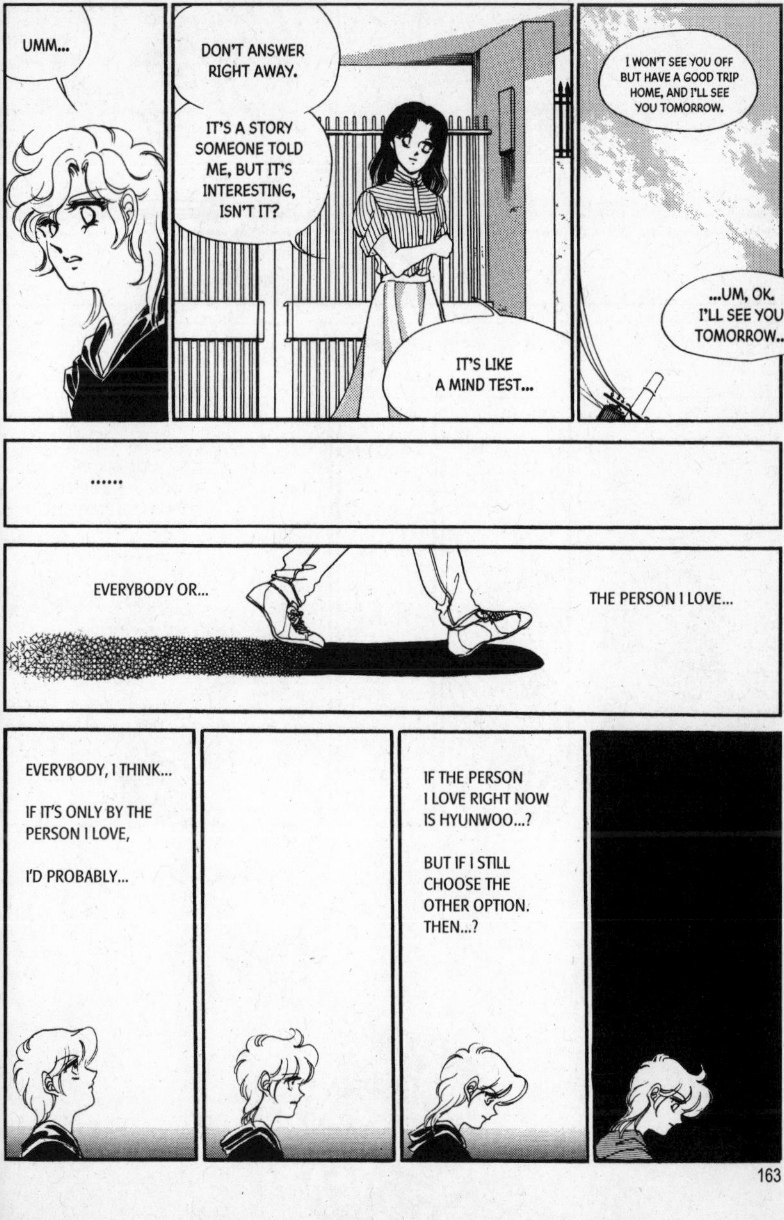
UMM...
DON'T ANSWER RIGHT AWAY.
IT'S A STORY SOMEONE TOLD ME, BUT IT'S INTERESTING, ISN'T IT?
IT'S LIKE A MIND TEST...
I WON'T SEE YOU OFF BUT HAVE A GOOD TRIP HOME, AND I'LL SEE YOU TOMORROW.
...UM, OK. I'LL SEE YOU TOMORROW...
......
EVERYBODY OR...
THE PERSON I LOVE...
EVERYBODY, I THINK...
IF IT'S ONLY BY THE PERSON I LOVE,
I'D PROBABLY...
IF THE PERSON I LOVE RIGHT NOW IS HYUNWOO...?
BUT IF I STILL CHOOSE THE OTHER OPTION. THEN...?

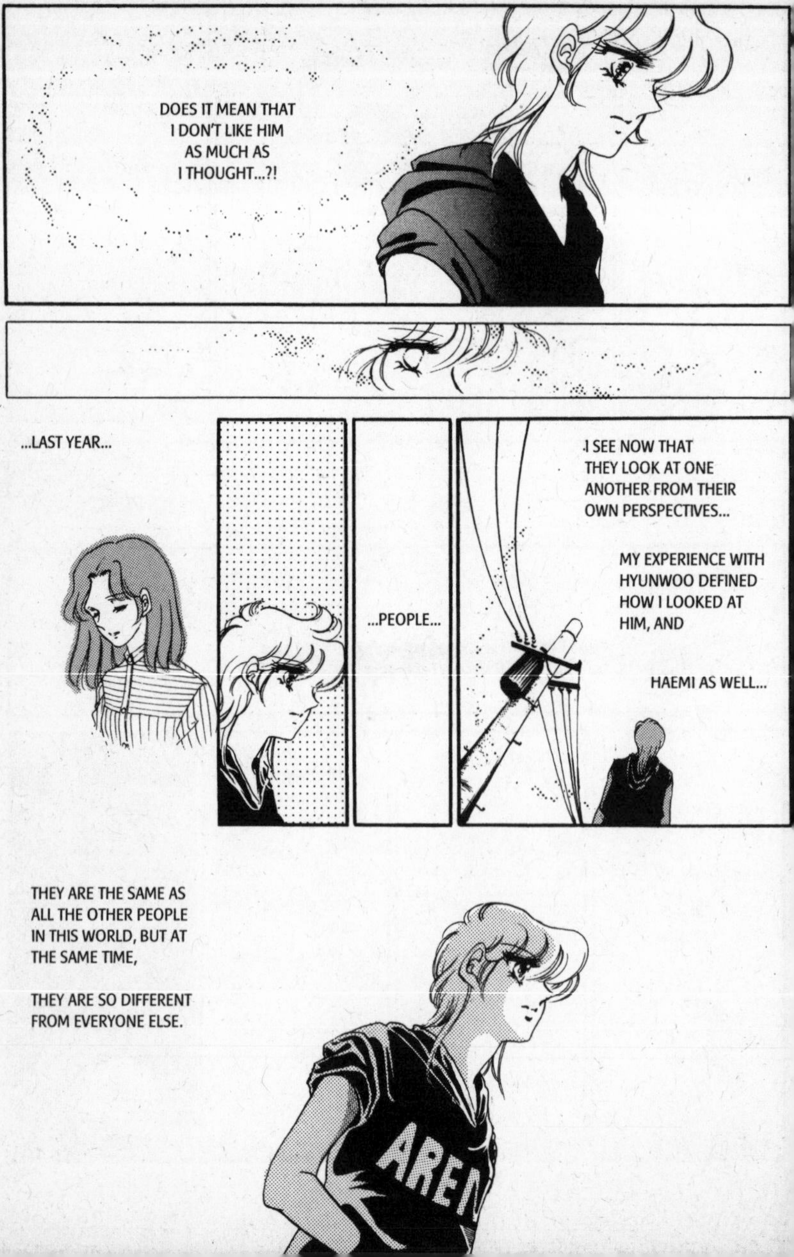
DOES IT MEAN THAT I DON'T LIKE HIM AS MUCH AS I THOUGHT...?!
...LAST YEAR...
...PEOPLE...
I SEE NOW THAT THEY LOOK AT ONE ANOTHER FROM THEIR OWN PERSPECTIVES...
MY EXPERIENCE WITH HYUNWOO DEFINED HOW I LOOKED AT HIM, AND
HAEMI AS WELL...
THEY ARE THE SAME AS ALL THE OTHER PEOPLE IN THIS WORLD, BUT AT THE SAME TIME,
THEY ARE SO DIFFERENT FROM EVERYONE ELSE.

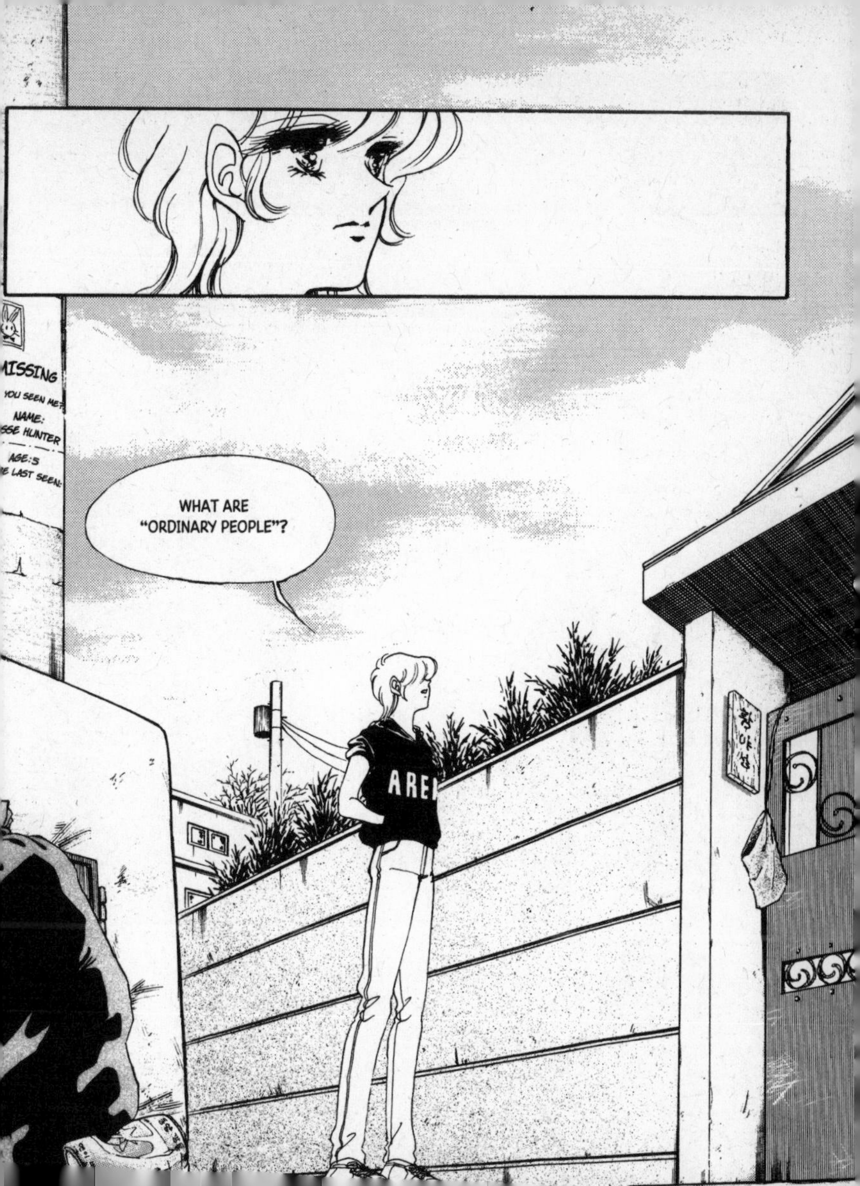
MISSING
NAME:
AGE:5
WHAT ARE "ORDINARY PEOPLE"?

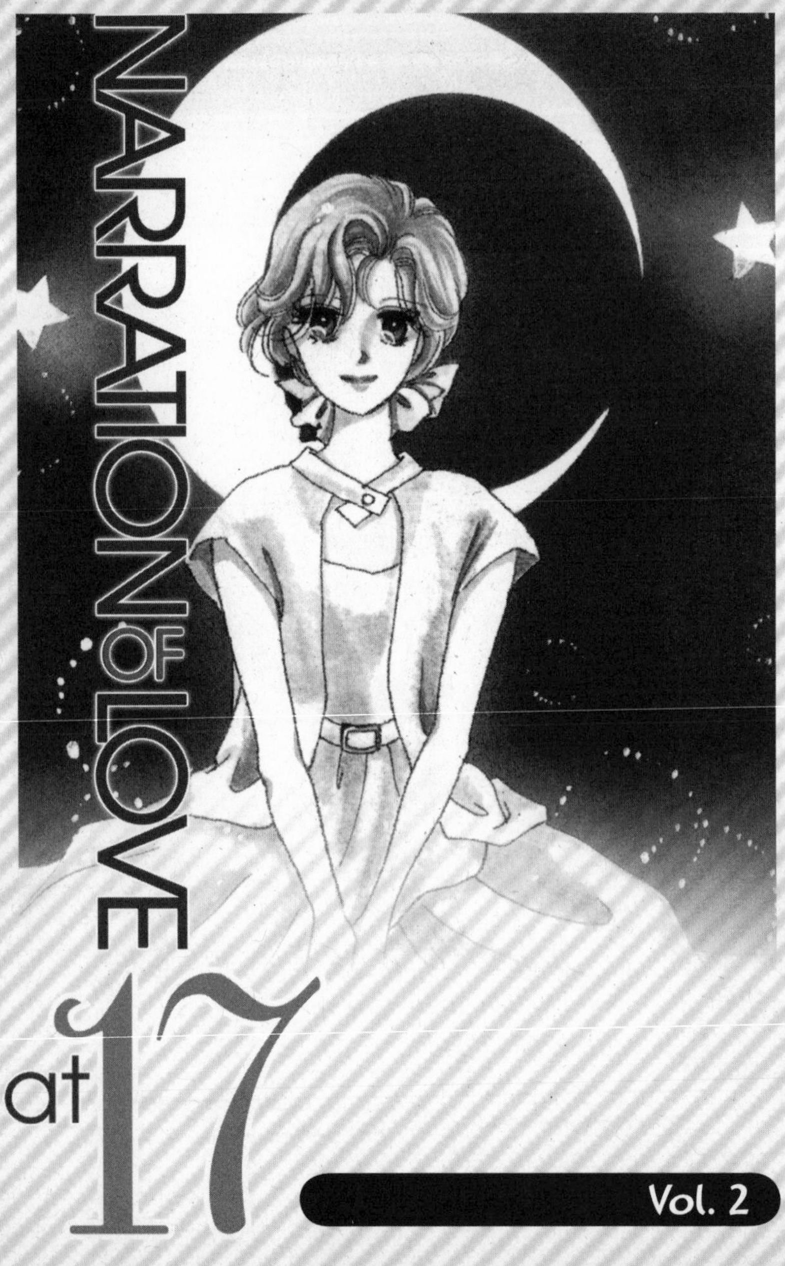
NARRATION OF LOVE
at 17
Vol. 2

In Volume 2 of *Narration of Love at 17*, Seyoung lands a minor part in a TV drama where her archrival Hyemi stars in the leading role.

One evening, she finds herself at the door of Hyunwoo's house for no apparent reason, only to discover him returning home with Hyemi. Seyoung overhears their conversation and discovers that Hyemi has feelings for Hyunwoo and that he has had feelings for Seyoung, too, but chose to give up on them because he considered her to be his family. No matter how much she despairs over her feelings for him, the aloof Hyunwoo has no idea of what is amiss and can't seem to understand why Seyoung always bursts into anger whenever they talk. Meanwhile, the captain of the drama club, Yunho, harbors secret feelings for Seyoung, though it is only a matter of time before they bubble to the surface.

Narration of Love at 17 vividly recounts the sensitivities of a pubescent girl who is as impressionable as she is reactive--and who is ever true to the shifting affectability of youth.

NETCOMICS July 2006 Release

Youjung Lee

0/6

ZERO/SIX

VOL. 3

Unseen dangers creep ever closer to Moolchi. Jong-E suspects Kanghee is the threat, but can't tell Moolchi the truth about his situation or who he really is. She challenges Kanghee, but discovers that the parasitic presence inside Moolchi's girlfriend is much more than she bargained for. The mysterious creature inside of Kanghee manipulates Moolchi's love for her to deadly advantage in the lethal game between itself and Jong-E. Who sent the creature after Moolchi? More importantly, who will survive? The answer won't be known before the powerful student Narutbae makes his play. Meanwhile, seriously injured and restrained in a hospital far from Korea, a father dreams of returning home...

Available now at your favorite bookstores.
Read it online at www.NETCOMICS.com!

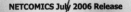
NETCOMICS July 2006 Release

Boy Princess

Vol. 3
Seyoung Kim

Bewildered Nicole aches to discern his feelings for Jed, risky as they may be, and feels compelled to be close to him once more. He wanders lost in the forest until he practically stumbles upon Jed. But his surprise and delight are quickly surpassed by the dismay at Jed's cold reaction. Perhaps they never had the spark that fuels his conflicting feelings for Jed after all? Suspicious eyes and ears loom everywhere, especially with jealous Princess Reiny always on her brother's heels, waiting to influence his next move. Jed feels the pressures of his position in his kingdom coming down hard, but he stands firm until Princess Elena arrives and...

Available now at your favorite bookstores.
Read it online at www.NETCOMICS.com!

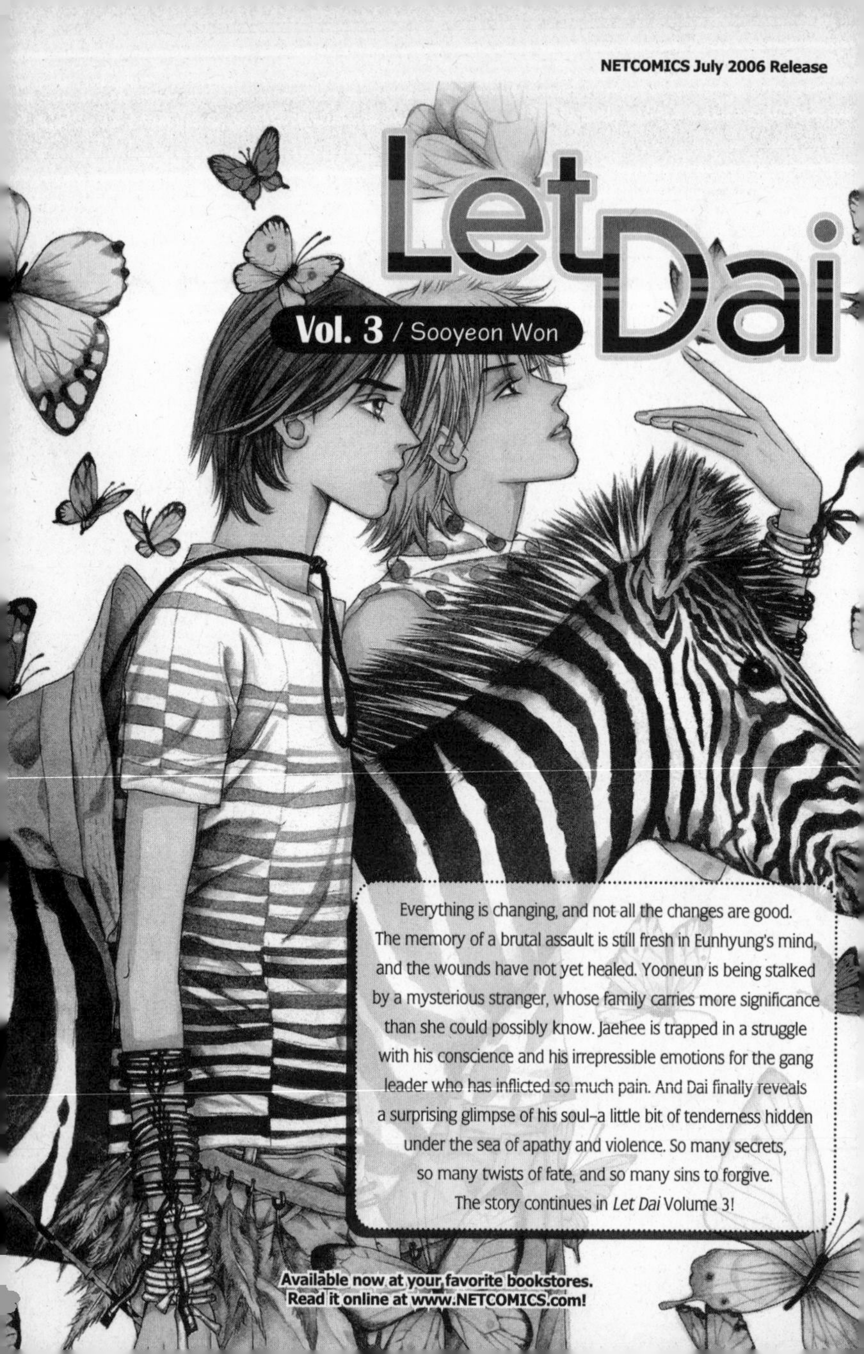
NETCOMICS July 2006 Release
Let Dai
Vol. 3 / Sooyeon Won
Everything is changing, and not all the changes are good. The memory of a brutal assault is still fresh in Eunhyung's mind, and the wounds have not yet healed. Yooneun is being stalked by a mysterious stranger, whose family carries more significance than she could possibly know. Jaehee is trapped in a struggle with his conscience and his irrepressible emotions for the gang leader who has inflicted so much pain. And Dai finally reveals a surprising glimpse of his soul–a little bit of tenderness hidden under the sea of apathy and violence. So many secrets, so many twists of fate, and so many sins to forgive. The story continues in Let Dai Volume 3!
Available now at your favorite bookstores.
Read it online at www.NETCOMICS.com!

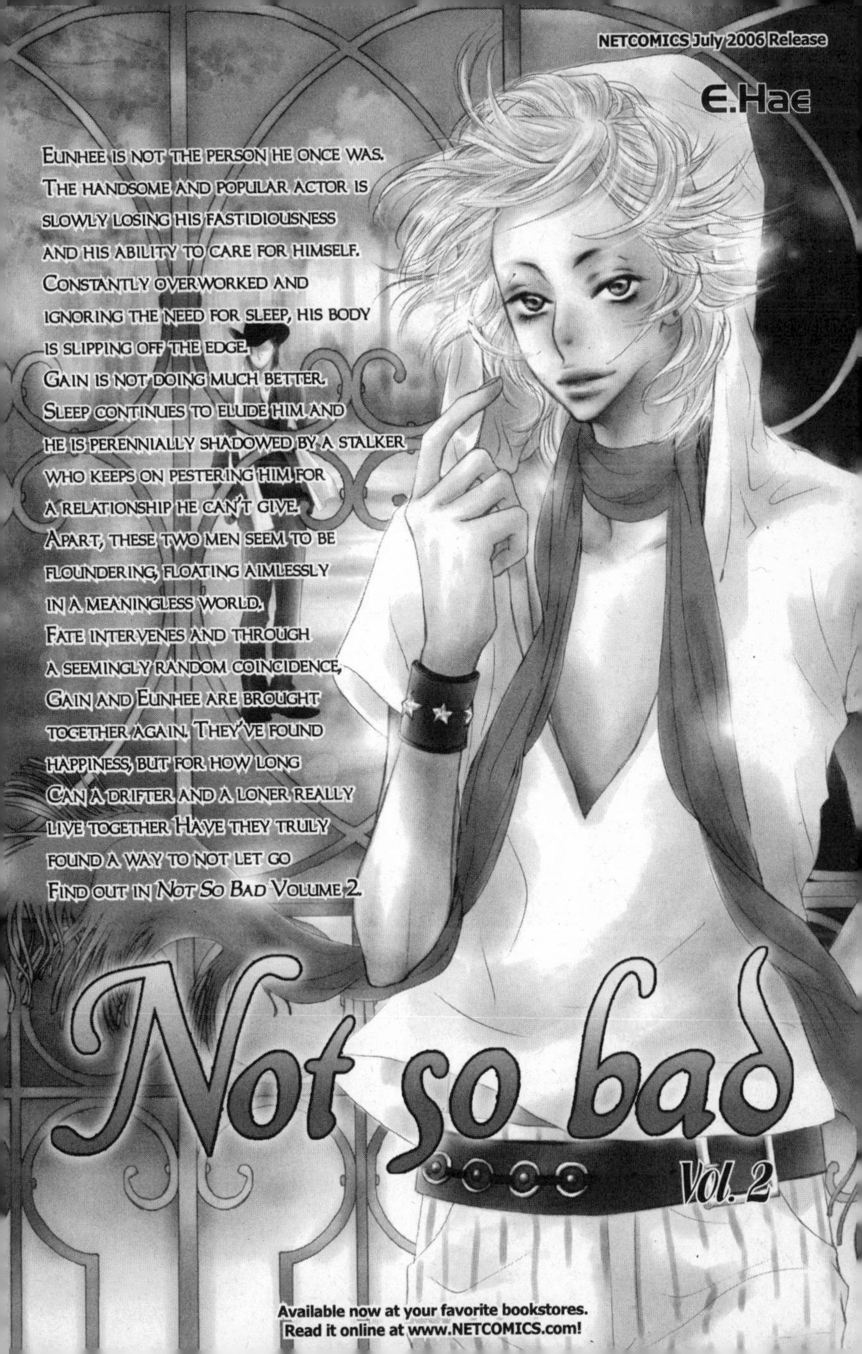
NETCOMICS July 2006 Release
E.Hae
Eunhee is not the person he once was.
The handsome and popular actor is slowly losing his fastidiousness and his ability to care for himself.
Constantly overworked and ignoring the need for sleep, his body is slipping off the edge.
Gain is not doing much better.
Sleep continues to elude him and he is perennially shadowed by a stalker who keeps on pestering him for a relationship he can't give.
Apart, these two men seem to be floundering, floating aimlessly in a meaningless world.
Fate intervenes and through a seemingly random coincidence, Gain and Eunhee are brought together again. They've found happiness, but for how long
Can a drifter and a loner really live together Have they truly found a way to not let go
Find out in Not So Bad Volume 2.
Not so bad
Vol. 2
Available now at your favorite bookstores.
Read it online at www.NETCOMICS.com!

Hot gangster action, Emperor's Castle Vol. 1

by Sungmo Kim

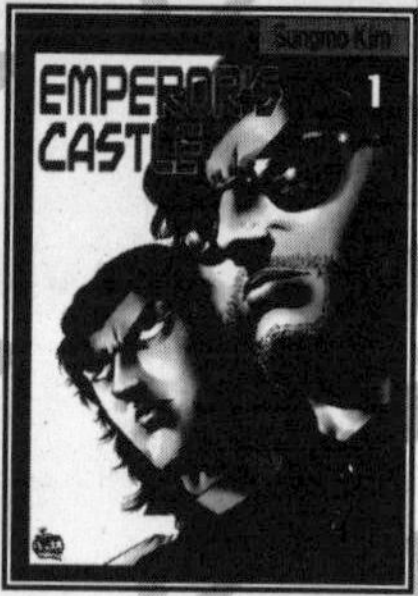
Sungmo Kim
EMPEROR'S CASTLE
1

Chunhoo Kang lives in a world of crime, sex and intrigue. He's the Nihon Saikono Warrior, Japan's greatest fighter in the yakuza underworld. However, he's also Korean. Haunted by past sins, Chunhoo abandons his crime life to search for the young woman and son he abandoned decades ago. But his yakuza bosses are unforgiving. They want his honor and title back. Who is the Emperor that Chunhoo seeks to become? Will he be for good or evil?

Sweetest love fantasy, Land of Silver Rain Vol. 3

by Mira Lee

Sirius' nanny is thunderstruck when she finds out that the young prince has made a contract with the 10th sea witch to stay in the human world, so he can be with his beloved Misty-Rain. Meanwhile, Misty-Rain recovers the memories of her past and Sirius risks his life to protect her from the dangers that are sure to come. Amid the confusion, the schemes, and all the magic twists, will their love ever have a chance to bloom? Let the story unravel in *Land of Silver Rain* V3.

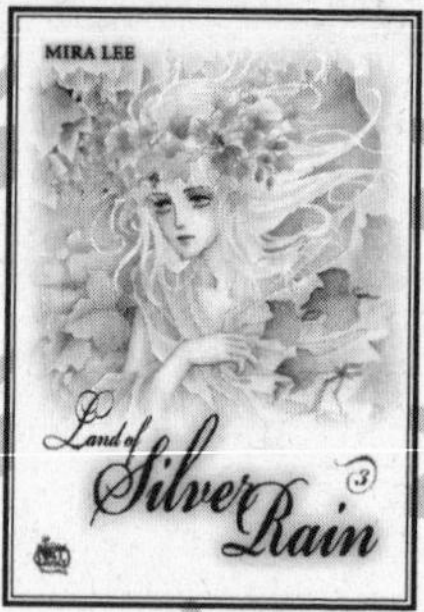
MIRA LEE
Land of Silver Rain
3

Gut-busting black comedy, Madtown Hospital Vol. 3

by JTK

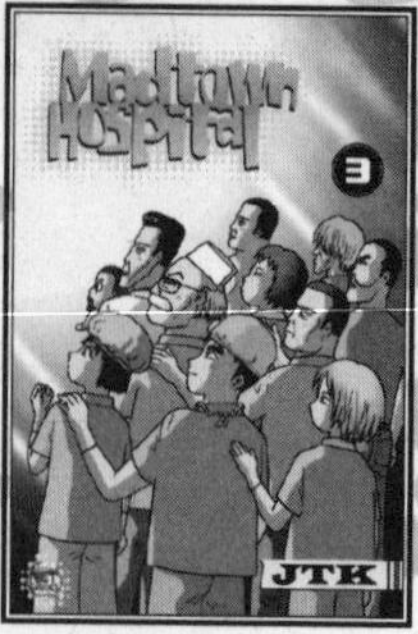
Madtown Hospital
3
JTK

Madtown's staff must transplant someone else's head on to Dr. Woong-Dam's body to prevent the further spread of the dangerous Cuba Gooding Jr. disease. Madtown Hospital's Sex Education Class takes a wild ride when the doctors start discussing love motels and performing free vasectomies! Buckle up for another episode of hilarious chaos, crazy antics, and a lot of medical mayhem!
The insanity continues in *Madtown Hospital* Volume 3!

Read them ahead at www.NETCOMICS.com!

First-ever, Manhwa Novella Collection Vol. 1

by Youngran Lee

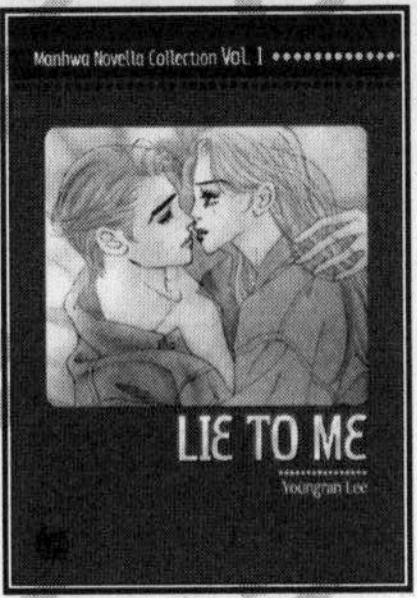
Manhwa Novella Collection Vol. 1
LIE TO ME
Youngran Lee

Lie to Me –Youngran Lee

Presenting the very first series of NETCOMICS' Manhwa Novella Collections—an anthology of the most prominent Korean authors and their works in which every page demonstrates their uniqueness and originality! Volume 1 of this sensational, groundbreaking new monthly series contains three of the most popular shorter works by one of the most famous shojo writers in Korea.

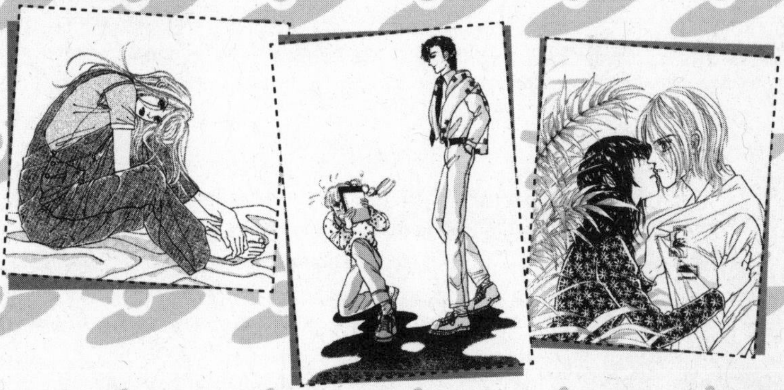

Contemporary high school drama, Pine Kiss Vol. 3

by Eunhye Lee

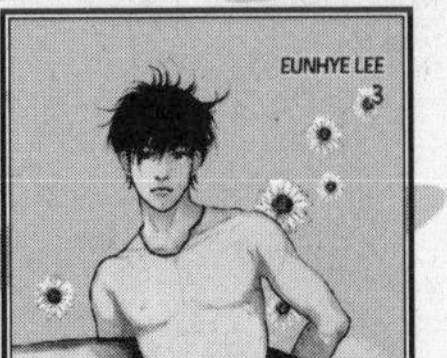
EUNHYE LEE
3
Pine Kiss

Dali and Sanghyung are in love with two different people, but they feel a strange chemistry between them. Meanwhile, Sebin's most vulnerable secret is revealed to the world. This revelation has Orion's co-worker urging him to leave the country. What is she afraid of?
What is the connection between White Snake and Orion? And what other secrets are waiting to be cast into the light? Find out as the love search of young, wandering souls continues in *Pine Kiss* Volume 3.

Read them ahead at www.NETCOMICS.com!

DOKEBI BRIDE VOLUMES 1 & 2

MARLEY

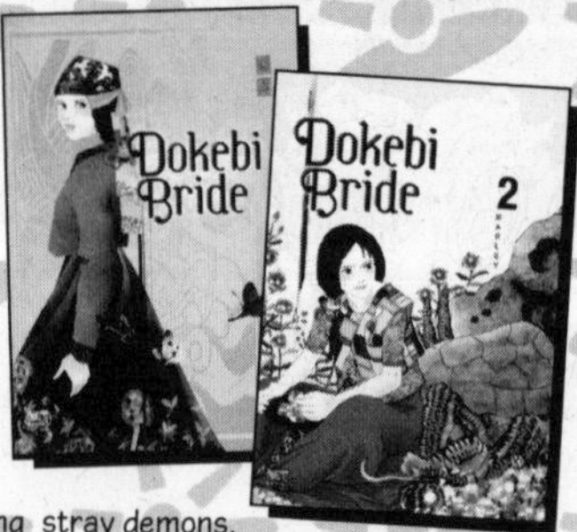
Dokebi Bride
Dokebi Bride
2

Born into a shaman family, Sunbi has inherited the power to see and communicate with spirits just like hergrandmother, a notable shaman and savior of their little fishing village in the South Sea. Her powers make her the amorous target of hedonistic demons even as a child. But with her grandmother gone, Sunbi experiences the twin pains of loss and loneliness. Through frightening and unceasing attacks by the wandering stray demons, Sunbi discovers just how dangerous this hidden world is. To survive, she must confront her greatest fear and traverse its terrible depths. Watch Sunbi as she bravely fights against the sinister dokebis in this mind-boggling psychological chiller!

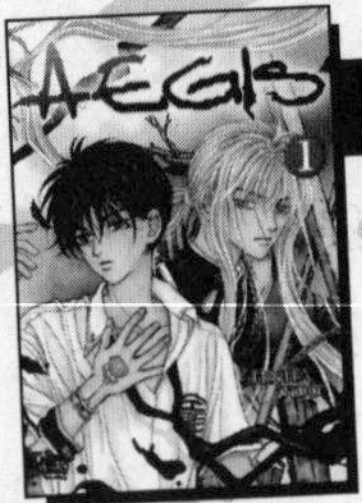
AEGIS
1

AEGIS VOL. 1

Jinha Yoo

A grand-scale masterpiece of life in a dystopian future, *AEGIS* paints a picture of the love and friendship between orphans Jino and Izare. Having gained independence from Revro, the Earth secretly trains an army of boys. Jino and Izare are abandoned to the camp, but Jino escapes the soul-killing cruelty of the camp. For Earth, can peace and utopia be won?

HOTEL CALIFORNIA

JTK

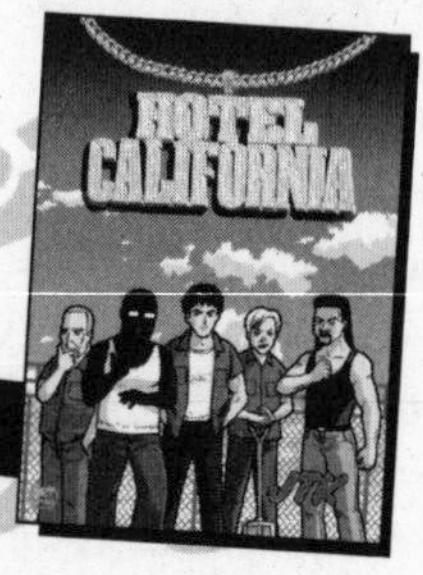
HOTEL CALIFORNIA

Dallas Westcoast took revenge for his father's murder. But he killed the wrong man. Now he's sucked into the twilight zone's demented sister--Collin Prison: Hotel California. Joy, the prison's only woman is actually a transsexual martial arts master.

The warden is a country music fanatic who brainwashes his prisoners with relentless music broadcast.

Welcome to the Hotel California!

Available now at your favorite bookstores.
Read them online at www.NETCOMICS.com!

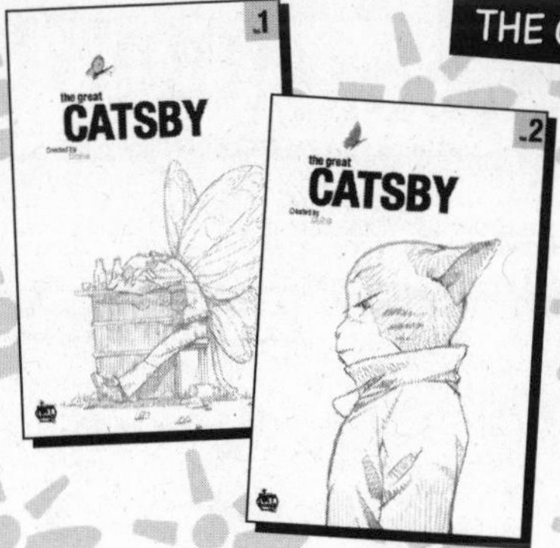
1
the great
CATSBY
2
the great
CATSBY

THE GREAT CATSBY VOLUMES 1 & 2

Doha

Catsby, twenty-something nobody, loses his girl-friend to another man. A richer man. His pal Houndu treats him to wine, women and song, but there's no forgetting the lost Persu. The thousand humiliations of youth are poured upon Catsby, whose prospects go from bad to worse. Now he's petrified by his father, now drunk on the floor, now freaking over a blind-date, now convinced it's all for nothing. Meanwhile a new woman arrives on the scene with some very interesting ideas about what couples can get up to when there's no one else around. No detail however vulgar or delicate is left out as the angst of youth is beautifully dissected.

CAN'T LOSE YOU VOLUMES 1 & 2

WANN

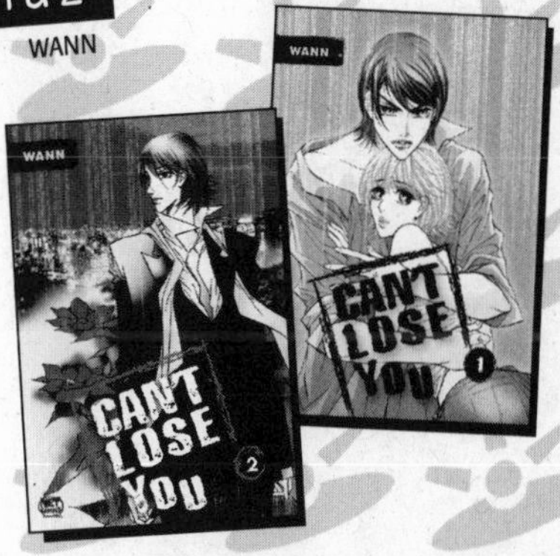
WANN
CAN'T
LOSE
YOU
2
WANN
CAN'T
LOSE
YOU
1

In a whirlwind narrative of vanity and conceit, *Can't Lose You* is the story of two characters who come from opposite worlds: Yooi is a desperate girl working day and night to earn pennies in hopes of one day paying off her father's debts. Lida comes from privilege and excess, the heiress to an unbelievable fortune. But as Yooi accepts the irresistible offer of becoming Lida's double, she finds herself in over her head, being chased by assassins and falling head over heels for Lida's fiancé. A revelation of social boundaries and emotional limitlessness, this story will have your heart beating faster with every turn of the page!

Available now at your favorite bookstores.
Read them online at www.NETCOMICS.com!

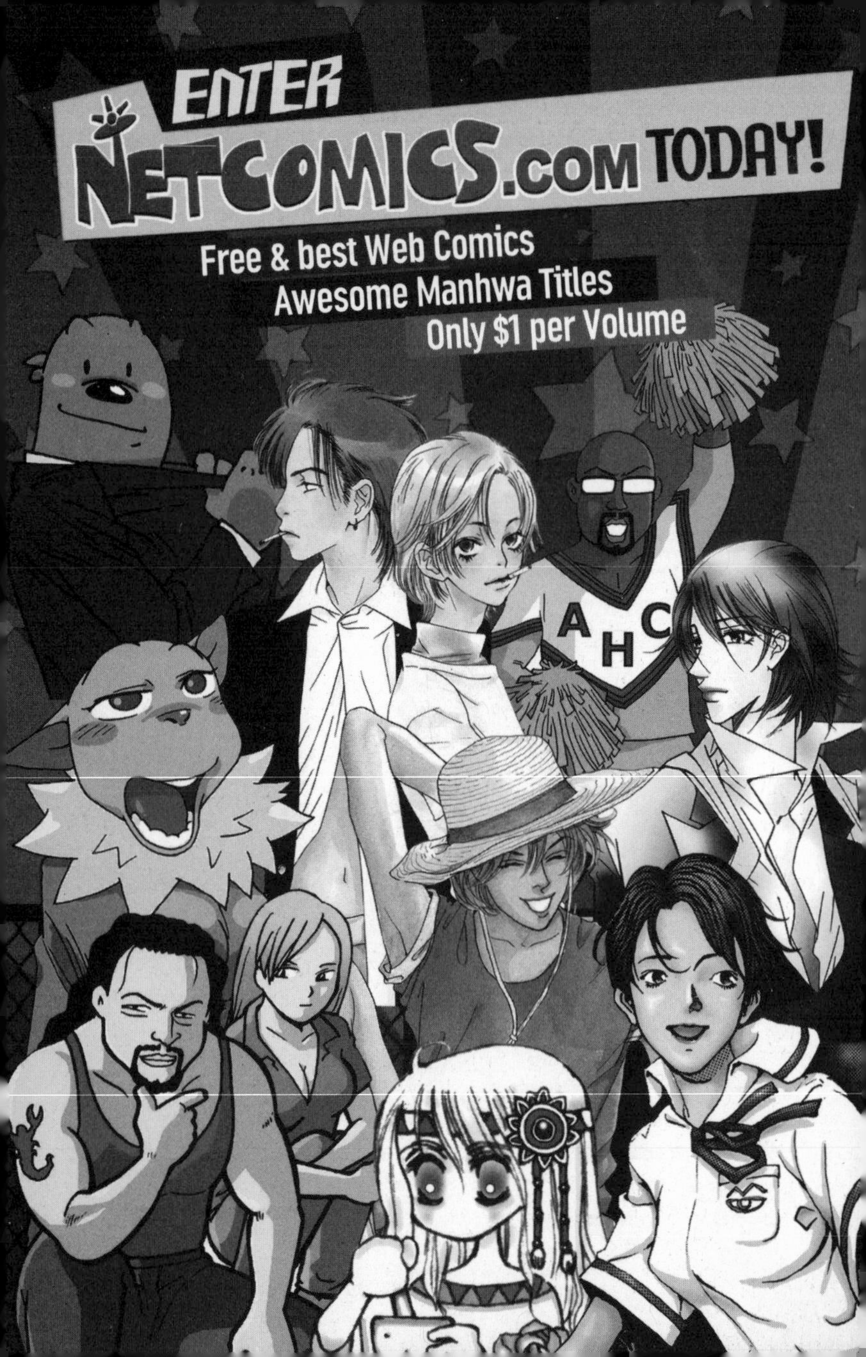
ENTER
NETCOMICS.COM TODAY!
Free & best Web Comics
Awesome Manhwa Titles
Only $1 per Volume
A H C